7 HOURS TO SOFIA

CHALLENGES AND DISCOVERIES OF A PEACE CORPS VOLUNTEER

LOUISE MAE HOFFMANN

BURNING DAYLIGHT
COLORADO

Cover design: Paperwork

Burning Daylight is an imprint of
Pearn and Associates, Inc., Book Publishing
4500 Parkview Drive, Suite 211
Cheyenne, WY 82001
Publishing Books People Love Reading

For manuscript submission query by mail,
or email victorpearn@ymail.com

Library of Congress Control Number: 2017931713

Hoffmann, Louise Mae
7 Hours to Sofia, by Louise Mae Hoffmann
ISBN 978-0-9897242-7-2

Printed in the United States of America

1st edition.

Ten percent of publishing profits from this book are given to
Denver Rescue Mission.

Title page: The "slow train" from Septemvri to Dobriniste, Bulgaria.

For My Grandchildren
Who I Hope Someday Will Have
the Honor of Serving
in the U.S. Peace Corps

CONTENTS

AUTHOR'S NOTE

"Peace Corps volunteers don't carry our culture; they carry our universal values and principles that are so incredibly important for all mankind." —G.W. Bush

To have had the opportunity to serve in the United States Peace Corps has indeed been an honor. "Life is calling, how far will you go?" is a Peace Corps recruiting tool that they have often used. It was for me, and continues to be the calling card of what I see as service to my country. It was an honor and a privilege to serve in the Peace Corps, but also a challenge that at times felt overwhelming. Could I learn the language? Could I manage to live overseas for twenty-seven months? Am I too old? How much will my experience help me?

And, day by day, I managed. I learned. I found myself looking forward to seeing my students, appreciating the beautiful countryside and admiring the resiliency of the people. Learning about Bulgaria's rich history was an unexpected added bonus. All of the above made everything else seem totally worth the effort. It was hard work, but I would not change it for a day. Thank you Bulgaria. Thank you Peace Corps.

I want to also especially thank my children for their support while I pursued my dream. I want to thank my extended family for their help. And I want to thank my friends all over the United States who supported me. My family and friends took the time to write to me, to mail me care packages and to send books to Topolitsa for the English school library. I also want to thank my wonderful new friends in Bulgaria: the students, teachers, administrators, Peace Corps staff, village folks from Banitsa and Topolitsa who gave me encouragement. They welcomed me into their home and shared stories of their life. They were proud and happy to share with me their beautiful country and its amazing history. I want to give a special thank you to the Peace Corps staff in Bulgaria, especially the language teachers who helped me as an older volunteer learn the language, even though many times she doubted herself. Thank you.

Moving to a new country on the dawn of your 65th birthday is a big step. I faltered many times. But with the aid and encouragement of family and friends I was able to pursue my dream and serve my country and hopefully helped the children and adults in Bulgaria learn more about the United States, its people, its history and its hope for peace, health and education as it extends the hand of friendship through Peace Corps workers throughout the world.

The Goals of Peace Corps: To help the people of interested countries meet the needs for trained men and women. To help promote better understanding of American people on the part of people served.To help promote better understanding of other people on the part of the American people.

I kept a journal while in Bulgaria and hand wrote many letters to friends and family as well as emails. Following are some of these entries and a portion of the letters I sent as well as received. I hope by sharing the journals, letters and special report projects that I was involved in, you the reader, will get a better understanding of what it is like to be a Peace Corps Volunteer, the frustrations we may encounter, but also the joys of adapting to a new culture and making many new friends in the process.

LOUISE HOFFMANN
PCV B-25 / December 2016

MAP OF BULGARIA

Peace Corps came to Bulgaria in 1991 after the fall of Communism in the fall of 1989. It had been ravaged by years with corrupt political government having an agricultural society forced to export most of their food stuff to supply other Soviet Bloc nations. Many families were forced to work in factories and live in ugly block housing leaving their village homes behind.

It is a country filled with rich traditions going back to the Thracian times about 5000 BC. For a country about the land size of Tennessee, it has an amazing variety of natural resources and biologic diversity, with over 29,000 animal species having been confirmed. It is filled with a variety of mountains, rivers and agricultural lands. It has four distinct regions: the Danube Plain, the Balkan Mountains, the Transitional Mountain-Plateau Region and the Rila-Rhodope Region. The highest mountain peak is Musaia in the Rilas, 9,500 feet.

In the West it is bordered by Macedonia and Serbia. Belogradchik provides a wonderful mountain trek in the Northwest region. Romania lies to the North, just across the Danube River. The Black Sea coast provides the Eastern boundary with its beautiful beaches and port cities of Varna and Burgas. Nesebar and Sozopol, UNESCO sites are both a short drive from Burgas.

The Strandzha Nature Reverse south of Burgas is filled with wildlife, especially birds as they migrate through the area each year. Turkey forms the Southeast border and Greece the Southwest. Forests cover a third of the country.

LIFE IS CALLING

Depending on the seed, it can take years for a plant to germinate. The same is true with ideas and dreams. And so it was with me and the Peace Corps.

I grew up in rural Wisconsin. It was a German farming community in the Fox River Valley, about fifty miles southwest of Green Bay. I walked the short distance up the road to the Lutheran grade school passing fields of farm animals, barns and a few houses along the way.

My father was both the principal of the school and the teacher. My family moved there from the town of Kaukauna in 1944 when I was an infant. My father had thirty-five to forty-five students a school year encompassing all eight grades. Besides religion, he taught reading, grammar, American and world history, science, mathematics, music and physical education. I recount many of the experiences in my earlier book *Goulash and Picking Pickles: An almost Boomer growing up in rural Wisconsin with recipes from Grandma and other relatives*. My father was also the choir director, church organist and church secretary. Many nights he was at a church or school meeting. My father served Zion Church for twenty-one years.

One of the lasting legacies I received from my father was a love of learning. He especially loved history and religion. He always had a stack of books to read on his desk in those subjects, as well as, a stash of magazines which included *Time, The National Geographic, Reader's Digest* and various church and education journals. Even when money was very scarce back in the 1930s he joined *Book of the Month Club* as a young teacher with a young family and bought many of their selections.

One of the Christmas gifts I remember receiving was a set of classic books. I had asked my dad for either Cherry Ames or Nancy Drew, but instead he gave me a box of books that included *The Prince and the Pauper, Huckleberry Finn,* and *Tom Sawyer*. I remember being very disappointed, not realizing at the time what a treasure trove he had given to me.

After the eighth grade I rode a sixty-four yellow passenger school bus into New London until I graduated from high school. New London is a town of around five thousand people located twelve miles from my house. The bus stopped at numerous homes and went on many back roads. Via the back roads the distance traveled was probably closer to forty miles. The bus route zigzagged country roads so it took over an hour before we arrived at the high school. The bus stopped in front of my house around 7 AM each morning and it was usually 5 PM before I was dropped off at my home again.

On the way to high school I used the travel time to study or finish an assignment. On the way home I saw it as a social time to catch up on the day's news with my friends. Washington High offered many new experiences to me. It was both a thrilling yet scary experience. How would I fit in? Would I know what to say to the city kids?

I felt like a country bumpkin. For the first time I had a variety of teachers. I went from having four students in my class to 132 classmates. There were around five hundred students in the high school. By the end of my freshmen year I knew most of them by name.

My father had prepared me well for the class work. I was an avid reader. I could easily handle the algebra class, the science class and history. I wanted to join the band, but the only instruments I knew how to play were the piano and the organ. My mother was a piano teacher and I had taken lessons from her for several years. My sister had been in the band, so the band director was willing to give me a try out. He wanted me to play the French Horn, the same instrument as she had played. I wanted a different instrument but I accepted his decision and started to practice. I could rent a horn from the school for four dollars a month and take it home each night to practice.

Besides the regular band concerts and playing for the school sports events and musicals, the band was invited to march in New York City, representing Wisconsin for the Rotary Club. We also toured Washington, D.C., and played on the Capitol steps and stopped in Gettysburg on the bus ride back to Wisconsin. It was my first trip to see this area of the United States and it opened up a whole new world of possibilities to me.

In my sophomore year of high school I had World History with Jerry Madison, a new teacher. He was a recent graduate from the University of Wisconsin at Madison. He loved history and taught it with a passion. Mr. Madison was also involved in the Young Democrats of Wisconsin and was interested to help his students learn more about how government worked. My father also liked politics. He had taught us the basic Civic Government procedures: "How bills become laws," "How to get elected," and now Mr. Madison brought it down to our level where we understood more about how it affected us on a daily basis.

And he was a Democrat. I knew my father was a Republican as were many of the folks around this rural area of Wisconsin. I didn't understand why, or what the difference was between the two political parties. It became an opportunity to look at politics through different eyes.

This was the year that television played a bigger role in politics. Wisconsin has an Open Primary. Your political party didn't matter when you voted in the primary. The Primary in Wisconsin was held like a general election. Dwight Eisenhower had been an extremely popular President and his vice president Richard Nixon was running now for President. He was very popular in this area of Wisconsin. Mr. Madison, as President of the Young Democrats of Wisconsin, was able to arrange for John Kennedy, to visit Washington High and speak to the students. He was coming to the visit the state as he had very little name recognition in the Midwest. Mr. Madison got his sophomore history students very excited and interested in hearing a current Senator from Massachusetts speak who now was an actual United States candidate for President.

Most of his students had very little opportunity to meet a person running for President. While Eisenhower seemed like a nice man he was old. We didn't know much about Nixon, except that he had a young family. When John Kennedy walked on the stage of our auditorium it was like magic. Here was a young handsome man who smiled at all of us and appeared like a movie star.

Senator Kennedy talked with a beautiful New England accent. He spoke about his family, serving your country, what it was like being an U.S. senator and how happy he was to visit Wisconsin. Wow

We were invited to ask him questions. I was sitting up in the balcony and was frantically thinking of what I could ask him. Time flew by. This was a special assembly for all the high school students in mid-afternoon. Regular classes had been shortened to give time for the assembly. An announcement was heard over the loud speaker system that the students riding the bus needed to leave. Oh no. I didn't want to miss a minute of this fascinating question and answer session. I would figure out another way on how to get home. I was not going to rush out and catch the bus.

Senator Kennedy was surprised by the announcement but quickly recovered and said that he would take one more question. Could the students stay five more minutes? That was allowed.

It was a Friday and our school newspaper, the *School Daze* had been given out in the last class of the day. I had it in my hand and realized it would be the perfect paper to get his signature. I hurried down the back steps to get near the stage. Students were scrambling all around Senator Kennedy. He reached out for my hand and shook it. Then I asked him to please sign my *School Daze*. He obliged.

It was an unforgettable experience.

From that moment on I followed his career. I was too young to vote for him but I followed the election. The rest of my family were Nixon fans, but I didn't care. I was the only person in my family who had a chance to meet Senator Kennedy and I felt that he really cared about our country and would make a wonderful President.

The Inauguration was broadcast on television. It was a school day, but again Mr. Madison arranged that we could watch this important event in the high school auditorium.

It was very thrilling and inspiring for many of us students at Washington High to see John Kennedy, the person who had visited our school earlier in the spring, be sworn in as President of the United States.

His speech was so inspiring. I heard him say the words, "Ask not what your country can do for you, but what you can do for your country." This was not that long after the end of World War II. He was not talking to just the military but to all Americans on how they too could serve their country. What inspiring words. I did not forget them, but for many years the opportunity for me to serve took a different path.

After high school I went to Concordia University in River Forest, Illinois to become a teacher. It was ten miles west of downtown Chicago. Many of the professors saw this as a wonderful opportunity to expand horizons and incorporated many of the museums, concerts and neighborhoods in their lectures and assignments.

I loved college life. I made many new friends and enjoyed my classes. In addition to the regular required classes of history, geography, education, art, chemistry, physical education I was also able to have private piano lessons and in my third semester organ lessons.

To support myself at this time and cover my room and board, and tuition I worked a variety of jobs. I had a regular job on campus in the Duplicating Department. Now it would be called the Copy and Print Shop. I had several housecleaning jobs and numerous baby sitting jobs. The university was located in an affluent suburb so there were always a variety of jobs posted.

I met Paul when I was a sophomore. He was waiting for me one day as I left the Duplicating Office. He asked to walk me back to the dorm. I knew who he was, but hadn't paid any attention to him. While I noticed different guys on campus, I really had little time for dating.

Paul was a senior when we met and six years older. He had started college in Pittsburgh and worked a few years before transferring to Concordia. Before long we were dating regularly and he was going to graduate. Before his graduation he asked me if I would become his wife. I wanted to finish college. I left the option open. I agreed to get married after my junior year at Concordia. That allowed me to finish the Student Teaching requirements of the Education program. I could finish my Bachelor's degree over the next several summers on campus and take a few courses through their Correspondence program.

Paul got an assignment to teach in an elementary school in southern Indiana. It was falling on hard times and losing students to the area public school. It was a modern school house, with a small library, kitchen, gymnasium and two big classrooms. St. John's, the church who oversaw the building and paid the bills had recently built a new house for the principal. In order to meet all their expenses with the declining enrollment, they cut back to one teacher and went down to six grades instead of the full eight grades.

Paul was to teach all six grades. He was overwhelmed. He did not have a musical background so did not need to play the organ or direct the choir, but was expected to take an active role in church activities. At the same time, the minister of the church had recently left so a nearby vacancy pastor was filling in on Sunday mornings.

Paul came up with the idea that when we got married, the school could go back to two teachers. The public school did not have a kindergarten. Paul was hoping that we could recruit enough students to start a kindergarten for the region and thus help cover the added expense of my salary.

The parents would be asked to pay tuition to send their child to kindergarten. This was before the day of *Sesame Street* and pre-school programs. Many of the families in this rural area of Indiana did not think of sending their five year old child to school.

Paul sold the idea to the voting members of the congregation. As we would be married they felt I did not need the same salary as a regular teacher. Nor would they cover Social Security or pay into the church retirement program for me. Married women teachers were accepted in church supported schools, but women's salaries were not commonly equal to a man's salary.

That spring Paul started advertising the idea of a kindergarten. I came down during spring break and became acquainted with the church and school programs. We got married the week after I finished Student Teaching in my junior year at Concordia. The following week I was in summer school at Concordia. Paul also enrolled as he decided to take a couple of classes to start work on a Master's program. During this time also, we went down to southern Indiana several times and sold the idea of kindergarten to 13 families.

In addition to the thirteen kindergarten students I would have seven students in the first grade plus three students in the second grade, 23 students in all. I was young and energetic but by Friday night I was exhausted. I asked around and found a few mothers who would come in for an hour or two on a rotating basis to help out with the Kindergarten students. They could help them with learning colors, paste activities and cutting. During this time I worked with the first and second graders on their studies. School was also very new for the first graders as they did not have the benefit of going to kindergarten.

I developed the kindergarten program as I went along. I arranged field trips to nearby Cincinnati for all the primary students. I combined as many of the topics as I could with the five and six year old children. We played games outdoors. We did a music program for the parents. All in all it was a very successful program.

The summer of 1966 we again lived in the dorm on campus. Taking four full semester courses in twelve weeks is intense. I was a history minor. I had many pages of required reading to do. Thankfully, we ate most of our meals in the cafeteria on campus so we didn't have to worry about fixing meals and grocery shopping. I only had our dorm room to clean, so that gave me more time to devote to studying. I would be starting my second year of teaching. I started off with high hopes feeling much more experienced.

I liked teaching. But it was still a very busy schedule having the combination of kindergarten, first and second grade together. Paul wasn't enjoying teaching much at all. He found it hard to relate to the younger children. He was frustrated by the rural farming and the culture that was thrust upon him. He wanted to move to the city.

I was starting to get acquainted with some of the women in the various church groups. They welcomed me to their quilting bees. The region had a big fall festival called the Turkey Shoot. It brought people in from all over Indiana, Kentucky, Ohio and further parts of the country. There were lots of contests with different types of rifles. I didn't know anything about guns. But it was fun having that big festival in the area and meeting folks from all walks of life.

As a newcomer to the area it takes awhile to appreciate all the different aspects of a region. As a new teacher I had ideas about teaching, and had read many educational psychology books. The women of the area however, had a lot to teach me about life. I knew if we moved I would miss them.

In the three summers since our wedding I finished my Bachelor's Degree. I was now a fully certified licensed teacher for elementary school, licensed both in Indiana and Illinois. Paul was not happy living in the country. He had grown up in Pittsburgh and missed the city. He wanted to get back to Chicago and finish his Master's program. After two years of teaching this combination of grades I agreed. I found a first grade teaching position in a suburban Lutheran grade school and assisted with their music program, played church services for a nearby church and in that way supported us while Paul went back to school at Concordia.

After Paul earned his Master's Degree we moved to Philadelphia where I found another position to teach. I again taught first grade. I also organized the school library, assisted in the music program, joined several of the church service clubs and started my Master's in Library Science at Drexel University.

Our first two children were born in Philadelphia. Nancy, a new friend and teacher at the high school where Paul taught introduced me to the Lamaze Method of Child Birth. Elizabeth Bing was just introducing this natural child birth method in the United States. It was an amazing experience and thankfully I was able to successfully use this method with all three of my children's birth.

After my daughter was born, I worked part-time at Redeemer and continued to manage the school library. I also started giving music lessons in our home. I sold cosmetics door to door. I joined the Historic Bicentennial Committee in Philadelphia and I became a docent at the Deshler Morris House, part of the National Park Service. I joined the League of Women Voters and became an active member. I started a book discussion group and joined the co-op with parents for sharing parenting ideas and child care. Philadelphia was an amazing rich experience for me. They were busy and satisfying years. Then Paul suggested that we move. The Lutheran High School where he was at was not doing well and he did not like teaching at the high school level. He wanted to buy and manage a General Store and be his own boss. I was totally surprised.

MOVE TO NEW ENGLAND

In the beginning it seemed an overwhelming transition to move from the metropolitan area of Philadelphia to very rural northern Vermont. Commuting was easy; we lived in an apartment above the store. The idea was that we would work together in the store and could keep hired help to the minimum.

It wasn't long though before reality hit. In order to buy supplies, heat the store, cover insurance and other regular expenses more income was needed. I was getting acquainted in the community and helping out at the Kinder School. This is where we had enrolled both children. However, in order to keep the store afloat we realized that I would need to get an outside job to earn the extra needed money.

Fortunately the following year a music position became available at a nearby school. It was only part-time but it put my foot in the door. I would teach music to the students at the Jay Country School each morning. At this time too I found out that I was pregnant.

Our third child was born in March. Within a week I was back teaching and brought him along to school with me. The children were delighted. We had been practicing for the spring program, *The Wizard of Oz*. I had done a small Christmas program with the children, but this would be a much bigger production with lots of props, costumes to make and many new songs to teach them.

Around this time I also started a book discussion group and met some other residents who were interested in starting a local historical society. The closed Anglican Church was available as a site. I had learned to use the jig saw cutting out new letters for our General Store and a life size nativity set to place on the flat front roof of the store. Now I was asked to cut out the letters for the Missisquoi Valley Historical Society. I became the secretary of the group and then Vice-President.

The library in town closed shortly before we moved to Troy. The book shelves were being given away to interested parties. Maybe I could set up a few book cases in the store and allow customers to check them out rather than having to drive the twelve miles into Newport. I arranged through the Regional District Center in St. Johnsbury to borrow several hundred books. If I would be willing to come down to pick up books on a regular basis they would allow me to have as many books as I had room for the shelves.

The following year the North Country Regional School District received an Arts Grant and I was hired by them to teach music to three area elementary schools making it a full time position. My days and nights were very full.

We had pets, the children were happy living in the country and after my year of being a traveling music teacher, I was hired to teach first grade in North Troy. The next year I was offered the music position at the new school where our children attended. In addition, they asked me if I could also develop a regular school library program for the 200 plus students, grades kindergarten through eighth grade. It would be a challenge to do both programs, but I agreed with the understanding that in a year or two they would search for another music teacher and I could concentrate on the library program full-time.

In the summers I worked on a Master's Degree in Education through the University of Vermont. The University had no Master's in Library Science program, but the Vermont state librarian taught a course on developing school libraries in the Education track. Running a General Store was not as expected and like rural Indiana, country life lost its appeal to Paul. It took several years to find a buyer, but again we packed up and moved. This time we moved to Pittsburgh where Paul had grown up. I applied to the University of Pittsburgh so that I could continue my graduate studies and worked at an inner-city parish developing their outreach and education program.

Teaching overseas was considered, but dismissed. Selling insurance seemed worthwhile and so things continued on an even keel for a while, but Paul could not find his footing. After over nineteen years of marriage, we mutually agreed to a divorce.

While I was finishing up my Master's Degree I applied for the job to develop a public library out in the suburban area where we were living. I was hired. The library was located in a public school that had recently closed. Many renovations needed to be done. Thankfully, the children were all in school now and their schools were close to the library where I worked. In 1984 I finished the course work and was granted a Master's Degree in Library Science from the University of Pittsburgh. It was exciting and challenging to develop a new public library. It was the time when new technologies were being developed and a community library could be seen as the anchor of an area. With many volunteers, an active board and grant writing for funding the library took off. I developed programs to bring in extra revenue and a concerted effort was made to the local government councils to fund this new enterprise on a regular basis. I helped form regional based library fund drives and collaboration. I enjoyed the challenge. The library grew. They were very busy intense years.

The children were growing up and Gretchen would soon be off to college. I had housed several foreign exchange students and suggested the idea to Gretchen and Marcus for them to consider a year abroad. Marcus was especially interested so I researched various programs.

It was arranged that Marcus would spend his 16th year, as a junior in high school in Belgium. My youngest son, David was starting junior high. Gretchen was at her first year of college. Would this be the time now for me to think of getting a job overseas?

I felt that Peace Corps would not work at this time as David was still in junior high but perhaps I could get a teaching job through an American abroad teaching program. I knew several people who had done this. I got the necessary forms. With Gretchen off to college, and Marcus in Belgium maybe now was the time to try for an overseas position. But then reality set in. I realized I still had too many family responsibilities to give it real consideration. Maybe I should just "be".

During this time period I joined a local singles network with a friend. We went to a few of their outings, one being a hike in the beautiful Pennsylvania fall woods. It was there I met Jeff. We had a great time together and I realized I missed male companionship. I had been very busy with my career, my degree, developing a new library, serving on boards, and raising three children. I had little time for myself.

Jeff and I continued to date and within two years we decided to get married. He had a steady job with the government and I thought my life was now set until retirement.

As things turned out I found out that he was not happy with his job. He wanted to leave Pennsylvania. David had graduated from high school and was now in college.

Could I undergo another move? My mother and oldest brother lived out West. I decided to consider the possibility. I have learned that a person makes the best decision one can at the time with the facts you know at the time. We moved to New Mexico.

NEW MEXICO

When Jeffrey and I moved to New Mexico I took a job with a large book company to head their Western development as book seller. As these plans were being developed I also took a temporary job working for a large independent book store. The following spring I attended the New Mexico Library Association's annual conference in Albuquerque and set up a vendor booth. Talking to attendees I was approached and asked to apply for a school librarian position up in the Four Corners area of the state.

David was still in college and I did not want to jeopardize his schooling. I felt I needed a job with a more steady income than book selling offered. I decided to drive up the 180 miles two-lane road to northern New Mexico for the interview.

I liked Albuquerque and the amenities that a larger city had to offer. If I took the library position, it would mean another move and lose the deposit on the house that we had hoped to buy. But, at the same time I felt it was the right thing to do at this time as Jeffrey hadn't found a regular full-time job. In July we packed up once more and I took a job as a junior high school librarian in the northern part of the state.

In August I drove to Arizona and picked up my mother so that we could spend more time together. Mesa was very warm in August and Farmington while warm, was definitely cooler than southern Arizona. Even though I had to work at the school library to get everything set up for the coming year we had a wonderful three-week visit.

It was fun being back in a school setting. I always enjoyed managing a school library and working with the students and faculty. It would be a good year I felt. I worked on the idea of a book fair and set up the new bulletin boards to interest the students in new titles to read.

The next Sunday I received a call from my oldest brother. He had to take our mom to the hospital. He wasn't sure what was going on, but the doctor wanted her to be admitted. He would stay in touch with me. I hadn't expected this. And although she had assorted health concerns she was basically healthy for her age of 87. I was looking forward to having her being in my life a few more years. Monday morning Lyle called me and told me that the doctor was uncertain about her prognosis.

He suggested I should come and see her if I could get permission to leave from my school. Right away I went down the hall to find my principal and told her the situation. She agreed that it would be only right for me to drive to Arizona and be with my mom. I called Jeff to let him know the news and hurried home. We were renting a house about two miles from the school.

I packed up a quick suitcase and headed out. Jeff would stay home as we had animals to attend and he was hoping to go on some job interviews. It seemed a very long drive through the northern desert area of New Mexico and Arizona.

Finally I arrived at the hospital about 6 PM She was weak, but was happy to see me. It was so good to see her. I didn't want to lose her. She had always been there for me and now finally I was going to be able to spend more time with her. But it was not to be.

Looking back I realize how fortunate I was to have been relatively close by and had the last few days with her, but at the time it was a big shock to my system. I had so many more questions to ask her, I wanted to hear more stories about her life, and above all I just wanted her to know that she was an amazing mother.

The same week that my mother died Jeff saw an advertisement in the paper for Director of Library Services at San Juan College. I knew I was qualified but did I again want to take the responsibility for heading a major library?

After some soul searching, I decided to apply and give it due consideration. After a round of interviews that lasted until Christmas, I was asked to take the position. They were planning to build a new library and with my experience at development back in Pittsburgh I would be a perfect fit. However, as it was still mid school year, both the college and I agreed that I would fulfill my contract as junior high librarian and start at San Juan College in the following June.

I became Director of Library Services. In my ten plus years there, I supervised their technological advancements, oversaw a new library building, organized the plans to move the entire collection into a new facility and became involved in various committees on and off campus.

I enjoyed my work in the broader library world and was glad to help build bridges between the different types of libraries. I became involved in the New Mexico legislative process for funding libraries.

I saw the correlation between funding and public relations in the communities that libraries strove to serve. In addition to other positions, I was elected President of the New Mexico Library Association and also served as Secretary/Treasurer of the Academic Library Consortium.

In my personal life things fell apart again. Jeff had gone back to school to earn an education degree but teaching jobs were scarce. After much soul searching and counseling we agreed to a divorce. Jeff decided to move back to Pittsburgh and once again I was on my own.

LIFE MOVED ON

I continued to follow politics and continued to read and learn more about history, both of the United States and other cultures. I never could quite see how I could work overseas, but the idea of serving in the Peace Corps which Kennedy brought to fruition always stayed in back of my mind

I started to do research on the possibility of entering the Peace Corps upon my retirement at San Juan College. As I was getting closer to retirement I realized that perhaps that long ago dream of serving my country as a Peace Corps Volunteer could still be. Years ago, I had read Lillian Carter's book, *Away from Home Letters to my Family* about her service in India as an older volunteer. She was 67 years old when she joined the Peace Corps. Maybe I could follow in her footsteps.

Peace Corps has a rather daunting selection procedure but through it all I could see that I qualified. I had two college degrees, I was in good health and my children were now graduated from college and all had post graduate degrees. I was on my own.

The main hindrance seemed to be my house. I had bought it ten years ago. I liked New Mexico but I had been thinking that after I retired I would either move to Albuquerque or maybe somewhere else closer to my children. However, my children lived in three different states, scattered throughout the lower forty-eight so I found it hard to make a decision as to where this move should be.

It was time to move on. I decided to put my house on the market as a first step in the Peace Corps process.

The housing market in Farmington was doing fairly well at this time. It is an oil and gas region so the housing market fluctuates. Currently we were still on an up swing, or so it appeared. I hired a realtor and he didn't think I would have any trouble selling my house. I gave myself a year to sell which seemed like plenty of time. I had a good friend at the college who offered me a place to stay if my house sold quickly and would need a place to live before I retired. But as I had a fully furnished three-bedroom house and several cats and she had a dog, I thought renting a place short-term would save us and our animals the trauma of all living under the same roof.

I received an offer on the house in mid-summer. Closing on the house was arranged for early September. I found a nearby place to rent and proceeded to have a huge garage sale. I sold off many of the tools I had accumulated over the years, garden equipment and supplies and some of my extra furniture.

My son David lived the closest and he offered to drive down from Colorado and help me with the final moving arrangements. I moved out the weekend before the closing. On that Saturday I received a call from my realtor. He told me that there was going to be a slight delay with the closing, but it should happen within the week.

Changing the closing date was very unusual especially this close to the appointed day. This was the fifth house I was selling in my lifetime and it had never happened to me before. On Monday the news did not sound good from my realtor. He was not sure what had happened. He had listed my house, but was not the actual realtor who sold the house, nor was it through the company that I had listed the house with earlier in the spring.

Reading and hearing the news about the real estate market now had me worried. What had happened? Betty, the woman who co-owned the realty company with her brother came and visited me at the rental place. She owned this property. She was not sure what had happened, but appeared worried. She asked if I wanted to move back into my house. I had paid a moving company to move the heavier pieces of my furniture, which included a piano and several large bookcases. My house was now standing empty.

I did not know what to do. There still was a chance that the original deal could still go through. The buyers were going to another lender to try and get the funds. In the meantime, my house was off the market so any other potential buyers were not looking at my place.

By the end of September the deal was canceled. My house sale had fallen through. What was I to do?

In the meantime I received my acceptance from the Peace Corps. I was officially accepted and I would be hearing from them soon as to where I would be sent. The date of departure would be sometime later in the spring. Before Christmas I heard from the Peace Corps office in Washington D.C. that my appointment would be Bulgaria.

The realtor thought my house could still sell in the next six months. I decided to leave it on the market. In addition to my moving expenses, I had both my mortgage payment and the rent to cover each month. This was turning out to be a very expensive year.

I decided to wait until the winter months to make a decision about moving back into my house. I didn't want to pay another mover and I hoped that by leaving my house empty and spacious looking that it would still attract a buyer. I had read about the collapse of the market, the banking crisis and all the variables that make for a weak economy, but did not realize yet the extent of the housing crisis.

The realtor offered me a small discount at the apartment as she realized that they were in part to blame for the closing fiasco. There should have been closer follow up with the potential buyer and the agent who actual had sold the house. Everyone told me, "This doesn't usually happen." But it did.

In late summer thinking that my house sold, and planning on joining the Peace Corps I had made arrangements to travel over my last Christmas holiday. I had a number of vacation days saved up and realized this would be my last time with paid vacation days.

Lillian Carter's account of her serving in India in the Peace Corps had struck a cord with me. I needed to see this diverse country for myself. My two oldest children had visited India and I was charmed by their accounts. I wanted to see it for myself. I decided to join a small group tour with fourteen other individuals and visited India for nineteen days over my Christmas break.

The morning I drove down to Albuquerque to catch my flight to New York City and subsequently New Delhi, it was snowing heavily. I had no choice but to hope that the weather in Albuquerque would hold off and allow flights out. I made it, although not without some drama.

It is about a four hour drive from Farmington to the Albuquerque airport depending on traffic and the weather. It is a drive of one hundred and ninety miles and includes crossing the Continental Divide, the Bisti Badlands, and a few pueblos set back from the road. Cuba, a town of about two thousand population is the only town along the way.

In the last four years, Highway 550 was greatly improved and had been expanded into a four- lane road. There was always a lot of truck traffic as it was the main through road north to south from Farmington to Albuquerque. A few miles outside of Cuba the elevation goes over seven thousand feet as you cross the Continental Divide.

It was snowing heavily the morning I had to drive down to Albuquerque to catch my flight. I approached the Continental Divide. The few cars on the road were going slowly. The usual speed limit is 70 miles per hour. And then in front of me there was a big rig across the road nearly blocking both sides of the highway. I inched up slowly as I felt that stopping was not the smart thing to do. I would have to cross over to the oncoming side of traffic, but given the situation I saw it as my best choice. I managed to make it around the rig and then did the slow descent down into Cuba. I had another one hundred and twenty miles to go to the airport on the other side of Cuba the weather and roads improved with the slightly lower elevation. Albuquerque is 5,200 above feet sea level, about the same elevation as Farmington.

The trip to India proved as great as I could expect it to be. The group was an interested group of folks all of whom wanted to learn more about the culture and the geography of this amazing place. For three weeks we rode in assorted vehicles, including camel, elephant, train and small bus. We visited several private homes including visiting and having dinner with a Maharaja and his family. We visited a school and talked to the teachers and students.

We saw the amazing Taj Mahal and visited Jaipur, the pink city. We rode a jeep through a nature reserve and spotted a tiger in the distance. We went to a Bollywood movie and attended a midnight Christmas Eve service with singing both in Hindi and English.

The two most moving events to me were going to Varanasi and Sarnath. Varanasi is the holy city of India on the Ganges River. We listened and we watched the Hindi ceremony of burning cremations from a boat out on the River. In Sarnath we walked around the stupa where Buddha lived as a young man on his on his way to Enlightenment. A stupa is the oldest Buddhist religious monument.

All to soon the trip was over and I would be retiring from San Juan College and my career of serving over forty-four years in education. The last four months went quickly. I attended my last American Library Association mid-winter conference in Denver, prepared my last report for the New Mexico Library Association and sorted and cleared out files.

I finished all the necessary library reports and filled out numerous retirement paperwork that the college required. I visited the Social Security office and filled out the necessary paperwork to apply for Social Security. I would turn sixty-five in a few months. I had now reached the magic number of "75" where my years of working for the New Mexico Education plus my age equaled seventy-five. There was little time to worry about my house sale, or the lack of it. I moved back into my house for a brief time and arranged to have someone live in it while I would be in the Peace Corps.

I gave away many books, dishes, clothes and many mementos. Except for my bigger pieces of furniture which I left in the house I packed the rest of my things into boxes and moved those to my storage shed, which was located on my side yard. Boxes of records that I thought my son might need while I was overseas I carried and placed into my 1995 green van. This included a huge box of photo albums, including two special collections that I especially made of photographs from my life to show my colleagues and future friends in Bulgaria.

I bought two new light weight wheeler suitcases. Peace Corps only allowed us to bring 100 pounds of personal items plus a small carry on for our 27 month commitment of living overseas. I bought a light weight back pack as returned volunteers recommended a pack in lieu of a carry on for travel on the trains and buses while in Peace Corps.

In March I drove up in Denver for my youngest son's birthday. He helped me shop to find a light weight down sleeping bag. He loved camping and outdoor sports so he knew what features to consider. I wanted a bag that was not too restrictive as I sometimes got claustrophobic. I wanted a special travel purse with a zipper that fastened securely as on a prior overseas trip my Passport was stolen out of an ordinary zipped bag as I was wearing it. Just before Christmas my personal laptop computer got a virus and so I also bought a new laptop computer to take with me. I bought my first digital camera.

I looked and looked for homes for my three cats. In the prior school year I had found a new home for my dog but had kept my three cats. I hoped to find a home for each of them.

Time was running out and no luck on finding a suitable home. When I had thought my house was sold and moved into the rental property I was only allowed to keep two cats. Sadly, I took my one cat whom I had rescued years ago to a nearby Humane Society where they assured me they would find a home for her. I cried and cried when I had to leave McGaffity.

Before I left for my Peace Corps assignment I needed a home for Tasha and Pooh. I had both of these cats since they were young and both were rescued kittens. Fortunately a friend came to my rescue and offered to give them a home. It was sad leaving them, but I knew she would take good care of them.

Final paperwork, instructions for my house and forms for change of address to California all were done in my last several weeks. My last official day at the college was April 30.

Needless to say, my last week in Farmington was very hectic. The young couple who were going to stay in my house wanted to move in May 1. I was facing my retirement, packing for Peace Corps and the subsequent drive to California. Would I have all the necessary paperwork complete and be packed and ready to fly to Washington, D.C., by mid-May?

My library staff was very supportive. They gave me a wonderful send off party, inviting the entire Learning Community which included administration, faculty, professional and support staff at the college. Everyone came to wish me well.

I agreed to vacate my house April 30. It was the week before I was to leave for the thousand and one hundred mile drive to California. A friend from my church offered me her home. She was gracious and happy to let me use her spare room for a few days. Another colleague whom I had traveled with was also willing to share her home.

May 5 found me on the road to California. I was leaving my van with my oldest son and his wife in Berkeley. I was using their home address for my U.S. mailing address while I was in the Peace Corps. He would handle my finances and see that all my bills got paid. Many accounts I had put on auto pay, but I still felt I needed him to see that everything stayed in order.

The first day I drove as far as Flagstaff, Arizona. It turned out to be graduation week at Northern Arizona State. Fortunately, I had made a reservation at a motel. Finding a place to eat, which did not have a long waiting list, proved to be a little trickier. Finally, I managed to find a spot at a local pizza place where I enjoyed a beer and some pepperoni pizza.

The next day my goal was to make it to dear college friends, Ellie and Bob. They lived on the Pacific Coast outside of Los Angeles. Traffic was very heavy the last fifty miles and there was no place where I could pull over for a reprieve. Thankfully I had the directions to their place printed out, but it was still a bit tricky to follow as I plowed through the traffic patterns along the San Bernardino Highway. They were now managers of a Retirement Village. I had visited them several times in California but this would be the first time at this new locale and driving by myself. With a great sigh of relief I found their home.

That night they took me out to eat at a wonderful seafood restaurant overlooking the Pacific Ocean. What an amazing view. I could relax. I felt now I could manage the rest of the car trip. I had only four hundred miles to go up the coast to San Francisco.

Ellie rode with me the next day. The plan was for us to have some time in Morro Bay together. Then the next day we would drive to San Luis Obispo. From there she would take the Amtrak train back to Los Angeles and I would continue on to Berkeley by myself.

There was a lot of traffic. I was thankful to be on the home stretch. I arrived just in time to go to an Oakland A's baseball game with Marcus and Stacey and their friends. I really don't remember much about the game, but on a picture I have I am smiling. I imagine I was just relieved to have the road trip behind me.

I had a week in Berkeley to sort through my final selection of clothes and books for my time overseas. My brother Loren and his wife Anita were visiting their son and his family in California. We spent an afternoon together seeing some sights around the area. The Sunday before I left for Washington, D.C., Marcus and Stacey invited Loren and Anita and their son Gabe, his wife Katy and their new baby Zoe to their home. My nephew David and his wife Elaine and their sons, Daniel and Jason who lived near Sacramento were able to come and join us for this family get together. It was great having this special time together before I would be heading overseas. I had no idea if I would have a chance to see any family or friends during my time in Bulgaria.

Was I ready to join the ranks of Peace Corps Volunteers to serve? Was I ready to live in this country that had been part of the Soviet Bloc? In only two days I would be on my way to become part of the 200,000 volunteers who had followed the legacy of John Kennedy. My dream of long ago was now becoming reality.

ORIENTATION

I flew from San Francisco to Washington, D.C., Dulles airport with a stopover in Chicago. I came in a day early. This allowed me to have a day with my daughter Gretchen. She came down from Boston. We planned to explore D.C. She would be there see me and all the other Peace Corps Volunteers off on our way to Bulgaria.

With my layover in Chicago, O'Hare Airport I had a long trek to connect to the next gate. My backpack was heavy. I had not carried a backpack for many years. Years ago I had enjoyed some backpacking trips with Marcus, David and Jeff in the back woods of Pennsylvania. I liked the walking, but I never found carrying a pack all that pleasant. As I trekked through the O'Hare Airport with a pack on my back I realized it was awful. The pack felt extremely heavy and my back already hurt from carrying it.

I stopped at the restroom. First off, airport restrooms don't give a person much wiggle room. I managed somehow to turn around and shut the door. I had my purse to maneuver. The seats don't have a lid on them, so it is quite a feat to keep anything from falling into the water. I managed to get the pack off, but how in the world was I going to get it on me again? I took it outside and tried to find a chair to help me maneuver the pack back on. I figured out that I could kneel and then slip it back over my shoulders.

I began to wonder why I had decided on a pack in the first place. On the Peace Corps page of suggested items to bring a back pack was listed. And then a light bulb went off in my head. It is one thing for a twenty something young man or woman to wear a back pack and think nothing of it. It is quite another thing when an almost sixty-five-year-old wears a pack and tries to go into a restroom, a restaurant or board an airplane. I had not taken the time either in New Mexico or California to practice taking it on and off once it was completely packed.

I had one day in Washington D.C. before I needed to report to the Peace Corps Orientation program. I had hoped to have this day to go with Gretchen and explore D.C. We both had been there many times, but it had been some time since we had a chance to have a day together. However, rather than go sightseeing I decided to ask her to go shopping with me to look for a small carry-on suitcase with wheels. I was staying at a motel near the airport. The Crystal City shops in Arlington, Virginia were close by. The Orientation meeting at the Holiday Inn near the capitol building wasn't until the following day.

Gretchen arrived early the next morning from Boston. She understood my dilemma and was willing to check out the stores that were near our motel. Thankfully the Mall appeared to be within walking distance. I did not realize that this would be my last Mall shopping experience for many months. It was a very warm May Day.

I decided it would be a good time to try out my new sandals. I had left my old comfortable sandals in California. Again, another mistake I made.

While the Mall wasn't terribly far away, it was a good thirty minute walk. By the time we arrived at the Mall my toes were getting blisters. Years ago I had worn flip flops, but it was not the accepted shoe for working at a college library. My toes were used to low heels, worn with nylons.

There was not a drug store in sight. Thankfully a kind clerk at a Mall shoe store had some band-aids in her private supply that she was willing to give to me to cover my blisters. We then located the luggage store. We found several small suitcases that could work in place of the back pack. At this point I didn't care too much about the price. I wanted something small that I could easily wheel around. I knew that I would be riding buses and trains in Bulgaria. I needed a small suitcase that I could easily carry by myself.

Luggage companies were now coming up with new light weight designs and with wheels. I gravitated towards the hard pack suitcases as they made more sense for me if you have breakables. And I knew the suitcase would receive a lot of wear and tear.

The deciding factor was that the small gray carry on had a side handle so that I could either lift it with this side handle or with its top handle. It also had a lock TSA compliant embedded with the zipper closing. I felt much better. We walked back to the hotel. By now it was early afternoon and it hardly seemed that there was time or energy to do much sightseeing. Plus I needed to make sure all the things I had in my back pack fit in this small rolling suitcase.

It was great having her there. She is a terrific organizer. Gretchen suggested we look at all the items in my suitcases and see if there were any items that could be eliminated. The main things that were discarded were packaging material of new items I had purchased. Even though the weight seemed minuscule I knew every ounce counted.

By then it was dinner time. We found a small Italian restaurant nearby. There was a long wait to sit at a table so we had our dinner served to us at the bar. Tomorrow my adventure would begin. Was I ready? The next morning it was time to report to the Peace Corps Orientation Meeting. What an experience this has been so far.

The Holiday Inn offered shuttle service between the two motels. By nine the next morning we were off. Gretchen came with me, but needed to leave for an appointment. The Orientation started at 11 AM.

I was the first volunteer there. I decided to take a short walk around the area and settle my jitters. By the time I returned other Peace Corps Volunteers were in the room. They all looked very young to me. They appeared to be mostly students just out of college; 62 volunteers were in our group. The original number was 64. I was told one couple changed their mind at the last minute. Another volunteer left after we arrived at the Orientation site in Bulgaria. The group that formally started was 61 volunteers with about half of the group in education. A few other volunteers left on or around Christmas. I had read that older volunteers were signing up for the Peace Corps. Where were they?

The people that I viewed looking into the room all appeared to be barely out of their teen age years.

It was time to find a seat. The tables were rapidly filling up. And then I noticed another volunteer and while young, I could tell that she was more my daughter's age, than a twenty something just out of college. I walked over to her table and saw a empty chair.

"May I join you at this table?"

"Yes, certainly," a friendship was born.

Felicia and I shared notes. We were both excited, but scared. This was a bold new adventure for both of us. She had left a blossoming career to join the Peace Corps, a dream she had had for a number of years.

This first gathering left us with far more questions than answers. But, the fact was made that tomorrow afternoon we would be boarding a plane on our way to Sofia, Bulgaria. Peace Corps volunteers served throughout the country and were involved in many projects, community, education and youth programs. About 1300 volunteers had served in Bulgaria the last 22 years. I was thankful to be joining their ranks.

One more clothes item surfaced. I had not brought any dress shoes along, at least that I could recall. The point was made that Bulgarian teachers dress up in the classroom, even with their limited means of income. What did I have?

Were there shoe stores around this hotel? Could I buy a pair yet this evening? I was meeting Gretchen for dinner and maybe we could locate a store. While I had my laptop computer, I was not so tech savvy as to think of using it for locating a shoe store. Smart phones still weren't on the market.

By asking at the hotel lobby we were directed to a street with some shops. Most were closed. There was one nice looking shoe shop that carried several possibilities. Color and size were a problem though. I splurged and bought a pair of brown leather flats. They were a half size too small, but I was hoping that with wear they would stretch. The woman at the store even offered to stretch them for me while we went out to dinner. Truth to tell, I never did wear those shoes. They always felt tight. The streets in my village where I would teach needed me to wear comfortable shoes. Later when I was settled in my village I would find several pairs of appropriate teaching style shoes in second-hand shops. My roommate that night at the Holiday Inn was Ursula, a young woman from New Jersey.

Her suitcase was even bigger than mine. Many volunteers had to pay the extra fee for going over the 100-pound weight limit on the two allotted bags. Thankfully I did not. What a relief. I had already spent quite a bit of money in preparation. I had easily spent over two thousand dollars.

On the first leg of the flight to Sofia I slept very little. Our seats were assigned. I sat in the middle seat between Susie and Tyler. Susie was very gregarious and out going. She was in community or youth development. She sat at the window seat but was up and down seeing what everybody was doing. Tyler was more reserved and easier for me to carry on a conversation with him. He went to college at Ft. Lewis in Durango, Colorado, which gave us any number of things that we could talk about as Durango was only 45 miles from Farmington and one of my favorite Colorado towns. It was a nine hour flight to Frankfurt, Germany.

The Frankfurt airport was warm, but we were there only to switch planes. We had to go through security twice at the Frankfurt airport. It seemed to take forever as we had to take items out of our carry on suitcases, throw out water, take off shoes, belts and jackets. Some of us had to empty our purses. Finally we boarded a smaller plane which would fly directly into Sofia. My seat was in the back and once more I found myself in the middle seat. Even so, I slept as I was exhausted. After about three hours of flying we arrived in Sofia. It seemed unreal. Was this my new home?

There was a welcome by some of the Peace Corps staff and current volunteers. They would be serving in Bulgaria for another ten months. There is usually an overlap between current and new volunteers. We had to leave our two big suitcases. We would be reunited with them in several days. We were divided into two groups and went on a small bus for a drive to the service orientation located in the mountains. In was near the town of Dupnitsa on the edge of the Rila National Park. We were staying at a small resort called Panichishte. It was about two hours from Sofia. We drove up a windy narrow road that reminded me of Wolf Creek Pass in Colorado.

Seeing the Cyrillic alphabet along the road as we traveled made me soon realize that I indeed was now in a foreign country and I didn't know one word of the language

I roomed with Felicia. We had made these arrangements when we sat together in Washington, D.C. Before we could even unpack we were to report to our first meeting. It was intensive. Packets of materials were handed out including the full schedule for the next two days. Everything from learning to speaking Bulgarian, placement interview, staff introductions, and medical overview was covered.

During a break the Bulgarian staff danced the *hora* for us. We were invited to join in. The music was lively and was a nice change of pace, but I felt overwhelmed with it all.

We were given a short break before supper and told to dress up. Felicia and I went up to our room totally exhausted but there was no time to relax now. Thankfully we had a bathroom in our room and quickly found some clean clothes from our small carry on suitcases.

One of the first things we learned in Bulgaria is that you do not throw your toilet paper in the toilet bowl. A person is to put it in the garbage can that sits next to the toilet. Thankfully it had a cover. This practice held true all over the country. It was a year later when I visited the Hilton Hotel in Sofia that I saw a Western style toilet in practice.

The food at supper was labeled in Bulgarian with an English translation. It was tasty. It was my first experience with *shopska salada,* a cucumber / tomato salad with fresh white cheese sprinkled over the top. We also had *Tarator,* a cold soup made with yogurt. They also served spaghetti and meatballs that first night and fruit and cookies for dessert.

I sat with Diana, Anna and Albin. We had found out earlier in the day that we were going to be living in the same village for our ten weeks of training. Lazar, a Bulgarian literature teacher, would be our Bulgarian teacher. It was a lot to absorb and many of us were still on jet lag as this was still the day we had arrived.

After our meal, a small group of us decided to check out the mountains that were all around us. The food must have given us an exhilarating feeling, or else we were so exhausted that we knew we just couldn't relax and fall asleep. It was a lovely spot. We walked and walked and saw the lovely mountainous region. I had little idea what Bulgaria looked like, and decided on that walk that if this was where I would live the next two years, it would be an exciting, wonderful and very satisfying experience.

I have a picture of me holding up my water bottle and exclaiming, "Life is good."

The next two days were equally intensive. We had some sessions with the entire group of volunteers where we were filled in on basic Peace Corps expectations. This included everything from a dress code to our pay stipend to medical procedures. We were given several briefings on current Bulgarian politics.

Most of the time was spent in teaching us the Bulgarian alphabet and basic greetings and expressions. We had several sessions where we were expected to pronounce new words and ask questions of each other in Bulgarian

The first Bulgarian word I remember learning is *dash ter ya* – daughter. I learned to say: "I have a daughter" – *imam dashterya,* and then "I have two sons" – *imam dava sina.*

BULGARIAN: THE CYRILLIC ALPHABET

The basic greeting in the morning is *dobur den* unless it's before 9 AM, then it would be *dobur ootro*. This is the Bulgarian for "Good morning" when you wake up or come to the breakfast table. *Dobur den* is used for later in the morning and generally up to mid-afternoon.

It was very hard for me to recognize these phrases when they were spelled in the Cyrillic alphabet.

The only other foreign language that I had studied was German. My father spoke German fluently and I had heard him speak it often. German expressions were familiar to my ears. However, the German alphabet uses the Roman alphabet, not Cyrillic. At times I found myself remembering the German word that I had not heard for many years and couldn't remember the Bulgarian word for the object I had only heard a day earlier.

My brain seemed to have gone into a complete shock. It was very difficult at first to comprehend that while it had some of the same letters that we used in English, the pronunciation of many of the letters were hard on my tongue. There were actually only six letters where the style of the letter and its' sound was the same in both Cyrillic and Roman. An example would be the M sounding and written the same as in moon, or the T as in toy.

Of course in Bulgarian the words are very different: an example, moon is *luna*, луна, not moon, and toys are *igrachki*.

We were given a Pons small green dictionary. This became invaluable to me and I carried it with me wherever I went.

On Sunday we would all be leaving Panichishte and be divided into our smaller groups of four to six persons. We would now get to see each other only when we had meetings at our regional site in Vratsa or next year at our One-year in country conference. That seemed a long way off.

Our suitcases were packed. We would be driving again in two vans and reunited with our big suitcases. Once in Vratsa we were to meet our Host Family. And while we were all going to be in the same region for the next sixty-five days, we did not know the transportation system and as yet did not have phones. We would be very dependent on our language teacher and the three or four other persons in our group.

One of the more stringent and enforced rule of Peace Corps is that a PCV cannot use their own transportation. Only public transportation, e.g., buses or trains are allowed. Taxis are only found in the bigger towns and could be very expensive.

Also, during this Orientation training period of ten weeks a PCV is not allowed to sleep anywhere other than at the Host Family house. Even if a volunteer had the means, no meetings or sleepovers at another site was allowed. We were in total immersion and were expected to obey the rules.

We arrived in Vratsa mid-afternoon. The Host Families were all there eager to meet us. It was in Vratsa that I met Todora for the first time.

Dobro den (Good afternoon) *Zdravey* (Hello)

Priyatno mi e. (Nice to meet you.)

Her middle-aged son Boris was also there. Todora spoke not a word of English. Her son knew a few words. We shook hands. It was another beginning.

Our large suitcases were all lined up on the sidewalk in front of the local high school waiting for us. I pointed them out to Boris and he helped me bring them to the van. Peace Corps had arranged a Peace Corps driver and van transportation for this initial visit to my Host Family.

Did I need anything else? As it was a very warm day in May I mentioned water (pronounced *voda* spelled вода in Bulgarian) one of the few words that I knew in Bulgarian. We stopped at a small store (called magazine in Bulgaria) and Boris went in and came out with a plastic bottle of water for me. *Blagodarya,* благодоруа, Thank you.

Albin was met by his family and they had their own transportation. Anna's family also came in their family car. Diana was also on the van with me. When Diana was let off at her home, I realized again, "This is it." This is the beginning of my serving in the Peace Corps. I was on my way.

It was time to go with our host family and get settled in. We would meet at the school house in town the next morning at 8 AM.

BANITSA

Arrival: Musings from my Journal: May 31, 2009

Monday morning we were met at the village school by Lazar. The school was still in session. We would be doing some work with the regular teachers and their students. Only one of the teachers was able to speak in English with us. Teaching classes would present a challenge.

On Tuesday we would be taking the bus into Vratsa to do more paperwork. We needed to register our Passport with the local officials and register at the Police Department. And we each needed to buy a cell phone. There were a number of styles to choose from; most of us chose the very basic model and the cheapest. This had to be purchased out of our Peace Corps allotment. During our ten-week training period we were given a small allowance to cover these and any other expenses we might have, like postage stamps, laundry soap, towel, bus and train tickets, school supplies and of course any other personal items. .

We had been given a bank card that would be the means of how Peace Corps would give us our bi-weekly stipend. During our weeks of training we were given a stipend of 98 lev every two weeks. This is about fifty

U.S. dollars which didn't seem too bad. As we were not allowed to go anywhere on our own, we really had no place to spend it at this time. After the training period we would receive a monthly allotment. However, in order to get the cash, we needed to go to a bank machine. There was no bank machine in the village of Banitsa, nor was there one later on when I moved and lived in Topolitsa.

Bulgaria is very much still a cash economy so it was very important to have the money withdrawn and carefully set aside. Only in Sofia and a few of the bigger towns were credit cards accepted at some of the bigger stores, restaurants and hotels. Generally in towns with a population of five thousand or ore ATM bank machines could be found.

I have written letters to David, Gretchen, Liv and Ginny and today to Marcus and last night to Irma. I have asked them all to save the letters for me for my record/journal when I come home. I wish I had carbon paper. I may ask Albin for some of his, or ask Marcus to mail me some. There is so much to write about. Today is our first day off since registration in D.C. on May 18.

In Banitsa there really is nothing around to buy, nor do I have any place to put anything. Hopefully, when on our own I will be able to travel and see some folk jewelry, crafts, and other Bulgarian related items.

Diana has walked over to my house a few times and helped me study. I am so glad for her help.

Todora is pleasant and will help me learn to speak the language. Boris is very intense and it is very hard to study when he is around. He wants to carry on a conversation, but I don't know enough words to do that so I find it frustrating.

Today I did my laundry by hand. Todora warmed up water with an electric coil immersed in a big kettle. I used a pot that I bought along with my soap that I bought on Monday in Vratsa. Last night I had to wash my sneakers as they were very dirty from the walk back from the Banitsa festival. It had rained all day. We had taken the bus into Vrasta for the education cluster meeting. Lazar got permission for the four of us in his group to leave early to attend the festival. It was interesting. There was some folk dancing, food and craft exhibits. Lazar's wife is deputy mayor of Vratsa and she was there, along with Luben, the mayor of Banitsa.

According to an old tradition every year the village of Banitsa celebrates the village feast on June 2nd with a competition for the most delicious cheese pastry *banitsa*. It is called "To Banitsa with a *banitsa*." The housewives from the village are famous for preparing delicious Banitsa pastry and other local dishes.

On Monday, we visited the Mayor's office in Vratsa, who happened to be Lazar's wife. We were interviewed by a reporter and had our picture taken both of which made the local paper. Lazar gave me a copy that I could keep. Of course it's all in Bulgarian. We were served tea and fancy cookies in her office. His wife had spent a year in Boston so knew English well. While in the United States, she taught French in Boston.

Now it is time to get ready for bed. I've showered in the little room outside. I didn't realize they expected me to turn off the electric to heat the water. Boris was upset. It appears he can have a temper, as he was also upset with his mother earlier today. His wife has only appeared here once. Boris lives in Vratsa but has been here most of the week. They have two sons, but he doesn't talk about them. I know that they can drive and each have a car. Boris drives a motorcycle.

We'll see how this week goes . . . .

Meals are the hardest . . . and then the classes.

Diana came over again today, along with the young daughter from the home where she is staying and helped me study. She is very nice. I find it very difficult learning the sounds of the different letters, and now gender and verb usage. I just can't remember the words. Anna is busier on the weekends with her host family and their activities. Albin is also kept quite busy with his host family and has at times helped out in the fields with hauling in hay and other types of farm work. A few times after our formal lessons we have all walked over together to a small cafe that is in the village. We may buy a beer and often a small bag of pretzels all for one lev. Lazar has joined us a few times. It is nice to relax and share experiences with each other.

Generally our study days are 8 AM – 5 PM, with a 90 minute break for lunch. A few days I brought my lunch along as it was confusing on the time, plus I'm not used to such heavy food. And then when Boris is there, he is anxious to speak conversations with me, and I don't know how. Todora is a gentle person and is content it appears to say few words and use body language to communicate.

The lessons are intense and we are expected to pick up the words after one or two tries. While I generally understand the concept, remembering the different vowel sounds for each symbol I find confusing. And it is especially confusing for me on the symbols that have different sounds but are shaped like the same symbols we have in our English alphabet.

For example, H sounds like our N, P is R, C is always S and so on. The vowels either have different symbols altogether or are either long or short, and y comes in various formats. The backwards R which is very common is ya. Also then, there is feminine, masculine and neuter like in the German language which give different endings to the same word. It also depends on whether it is plural or singular. We do have similar complicated rules in English but these I have learned now for over 60 years.

In less than two weeks to pick up all these rules is very difficult for me.

The three younger volunteers in my group are patient with me which is helpful, but I must learn it. In a few weeks, Peace Corps gives a test which we are required to pass to get recommended for the full program. I don't think that teaching English will be a problem, but I must learn to do some communication.

Tonight I'm trying to figure out how to charge up my iPOD that my children gave me before I left. This wasn't discussed. It seems it must be charged through the computer. At least I hope that works. It indicated low battery yesterday and tonight I couldn't get it to play. If this doesn't work, I'll talk to my three classmates and see what they know about it. It seems to be charging so I will let it be for now and read my book, *1968* by Mark Kurlansky. I know I should study more, but I have been at it all day, and I think it is good to give my brain a rest.

Tomorrow we go by bus to Vratsa for a big meeting with the Peace Corps. Saturday was just the education group, but tomorrow the entire group will be there. Bulgarian history, PC rules and more items I am sure will be covered. I also hope to find the post office with Albin to buy more stamps to send letters to the U.S. The village post office in Banitsa doesn't have stamps for the U.S. rate. It costs 1. 60 lev for each letter. As we have had less than an hour for the Internet, letters seem the best way to write to family and friends.

There's an Internet café in Vratsa, but there will be no time tomorrow. At the school it is either down or busy. Today I had ten minutes, doesn't give much time to answer emails in any detail. I think it is difficult for folks in the U.S. to comprehend the situation here. They think it's just the matter of me taking the time, rather than realizing that no Internet is available in this village, and in many of the other villages. The Internet is mainly found in the bigger cities. First of course, you must find the Internet Cafe during your limited free time. Then you need to find the correct clerk to pay her or him directly, locate a free computer and log in, plus a few more rules. It doesn't bother me to do all these steps, but I hope friends and family will understand what's all involved and take the time to write to me.

Vratsa is a bigger town and has many shops but as volunteers we do not have cars and are not allowed in those first weeks to go into town even by bus on our own. It seemed to me we were much like young children completely dependent on their parent. Vratsa Mountain is on the outskirts of the town. The town has a lovely plaza with a big fountain and a modern day hotel is off on one side. Also on the plaza is a statue of Hristo Botev, one of the most famous Bulgarians who was instrumental in gaining their independence in the 1800's from the Ottoman Empire.

At this point I haven't had any U.S. news except seeing briefly on Yahoo the other day that Obama nominated a woman to the Supreme Court. Amazing how in the United States you feel a need to keep up with the news everyday, and here that doesn't seem to matter.

Todora does have a television which I have seen for a few minutes, but it was all in Bulgarian so that didn't really help me with learning the news or events of the day. Perhaps there is a news show, but what I've heard from Albin and Anna who have TV's that it's mainly music and lots of provocative singers.

Reading in the Bulgaria *Lonely Planet* book makes me want to see more of Bulgaria. There is a lot of history here going back to 4000 BC. Plovdiv is described as the Paris of the Balkans.

There are many small medieval towns and lots of monasteries. We are not allowed to travel on our own until after six months, and then we do need to give notice where we are going. This is basically for safety reasons. To go out of country we need special permission.

I don't think I will do that at least during this first year. Perhaps next summer when school is out, but will see. First it makes sense to me to tour Bulgaria. On the weekends I hopefully will be able to make small bus trips to various cities.

I am also reading a book on Bulgarian history which supplements the talk that was given to us by a history professor at one our meetings in Vratsa.

Tuesday is our language test. Thursday we find out our assignment as to where we will be placed by the Peace Corps. Then on Sunday, June 21 we travel by train or bus to visit the site and sleep over in a hotel. We come back to Banitsa on June 24. It will be an interesting week for sure. If all goes well we are sworn in July 24.

That's all for now. I will read until 10 PM.

LETTER WRITING

Dear Liv,   **27 May 2009**

Here I am one week in Bulgaria. It is more difficult than I thought it would be, especially the language and being able to communicate.

Learning the new letters and sounds of the Cyrillic alphabet is probably the hardest thing I've ever had to do in my life. My memory often fails me. As it turns out, I am the oldest of the 62 Peace Corps volunteers that flew over from Washington D.C. last week. There is a couple in their late 50's and two other retired women somewhere around 60 years old I suspect.

Now we (PCV) are scattered around villages and towns near Vratsa. There are four to eight people in a group, each assigned an individual house except married couples who they try and find housing together.

My group of four meet at the local village school each morning at 8 AM and goes to 5 PM with an hour lunch break.

Our teacher is Lazar both in language and cultural norms. He teaches Bulgarian literature at a high school in Vratsa during the regular school year. His students are out of class already; a private school I think as Peace Corps mentioned students go to school here until the end of June. We also meet on Saturday.

This Friday I need to present a lesson to the 4th grade. My other classmates are much younger. The young man in our group turns 29 in June. He has lived in New York City the last five years and writes. The two young women are only 22. All are very smart.

My family is an elderly widow, 73 years old who gardens and cans fruits and vegetables. Her married son lives in Vratsa and was here yesterday. He knows a little English. The widow doesn't know any English. She uses a summer kitchen which is separate from the house. It is very simple with very few utensils.

The shower is also a separate little room located away from the main house with only one hook and a small shelf. It is a challenge to arrange my things. I put my clothes in a bag and hang them on the hook, and then my towel over that. The family also has things on the shelf, so there is barely enough room for my soap and shampoo. There are also buckets and other items in this small space so that leaves just enough room to stand. There is a small window on the door which does not lend itself to privacy but as the room is in the back of the yard I feel quite safe.

There is a latch on the door.

Oh, the shower is hooked up directly to the hot water heater and I need to remember to turn it on at least fifteen minutes prior to my shower in order to have hot water. It is a challenge to be sure, but as the weather as been quite warm I have needed to take a shower almost daily. The alternative is a sponge bath, but as the sink is in the middle of the entrance hallway this too presents its own unique challenges, especially when Boris is visiting. And usually when he visits he stays overnight and sleeps in a room directly across the hallway from my room.

The Peace Corps requires that we have a lock on our room. I lock it every evening and when I leave for class.

The toilet also is its own separate room away from the main house, sharing one wall with the outdoor shower room. It is quite primitive. It does not flush, but there is a sort of rinse that you can use. This is hard to explain. There is a faucet you can turn on with a hose connected to it and you can rinse the floor area or put some additional water down the toilet. It does smell. It reminds me of my early years in the country in Wisconsin when our family did not have indoor plumbing. Diana is at a house that is more like our American early out houses and she doesn't even have a shower. Albin has the most modern house, with an indoor toilet that flushes and another room in the house with a shower.

The school bathroom is more modern, but today at the municipal building I discovered their toilet also is very primitive. It was of the Turkish variety, and there was no place to put your bag. There was a hose that you could rinse the area with afterward. (This is basically a hole in the floor. A woman has to carefully hold up her dress or pants to prevent them from getting soiled. It was a maneuver that took me months to learn.)

We met the mayor and police of our village of Banitsa. The mayor served us tea and cookies and spoke some English.

I do have a cell phone now as it is required by Peace Corps so that they can keep in touch with us and that we can call them as needed. I only bought the number of minutes required by Peace Corps as an emergency contact for them. But if you can call me, that would be great. On the Bulgarian phones only the person calling is charged for the minutes, not the person receiving the call. My phone number from the U.S. is 98765321. There might be a zero between the 9 and 8 but I don't think so. Our time difference is 9 hours I think, so sometime after 9 PM my time would be great. This will be my phone number for my entire 27 months, but my mailing address will change around August 1.

I need to buy some writing paper. I had printed this out using paper with information on Bulgaria that I had brought over with me off a library data base I had at San Juan. This Friday I'll be retired four weeks. What a month this has been.

Please make a copy and/or save this letter for me. It'll serve also has my journal. I hope this finds you well. I wish we could have talked before I left.

Your friend, with love, Louise

Address until August 1: Central Post Office, Vratsa 3000, Bulgaria

Note: Up until the swearing in ceremony Peace Corps set up secondary offices in Vratsa for training purposes of the new volunteers, including a central mailing address in Vratsa. This was the only way to receive communication and packages during those first crucial/traumatic weeks when we arrived from the United States.

The headquarters of Peace Corps in Bulgaria was in Sofia and once we were assigned our permanent locations all medical, communication, finances and other paperwork would take place from the Sofia Office. There were computers there for volunteers to use, a library exchange both of books and media, education materials and meeting rooms. It was a combination of U.S. staff and native personnel hired by the Peace Corps. All Bulgarian staff persons could speak English very well. The men hired to transport personnel or materials to various meetings that were held around the country spoke a limited amount of English.

Tomorrow night I will write my long-time high school friend and one of my sisters. Then I want to write another friend from Pittsburgh and one of my cousins who was interested in my Peace Corps experience. I have several cousins who asked me to stay in touch with them; I would like them to share the letter. I might do that also with a group of my college friends and ask if they would share a letter. Other possibilities for letter writing are my nieces and nephews.

I should also write to Janet, the woman who shared her home with me my last week in Farmington, and my group of friends from Farmington who called themselves the Ha-Ha Gang.

There are others I know. Many folks were interested in my experiences and that I was going to be leaving my family for over two years. So far I've the only mail I received is a card from a dear college friend and my children.

I replied to an email from a friend back at San Juan College. I have always enjoyed keeping in touch with family and friends and I'm hoping that even though sending mail takes a long time it is certainly appreciated when I hear from folks back in the U.S.

This week I've had a chance to be on email a little bit more. As I've heard no word that things are not going okay with my house, I will assume the best. Saturday while at a HUB site I had a chance to borrow a PC and emailed each of my children and asked how things were: jobs, health and house at 2907. Hopefully I will hear from Marcus soon. Everyone is busy with their life which is good.

Having some years alone probably helped me have this time alone, and know that people are busy with their lives, children and friends. I'm not connected to any one person, but connected to all. I believe my children are happy which is good and all for the best. I really hope that David finds a regular position soon and that he is enjoying life in the mountains of Colorado.

Peace Corps is giving me time to explore more of this world, meet new people, discover new ideas and become acquainted with a broader world view. This Peace Corps time hopefully will also help me develop my character, my skills at a language and do a service for America. I don't think it will feel like a vacation.

Everyone said the training is the hardest and certainly it has been a challenge for me. Language is the most difficult. I find trying to carry on a conversation next to impossible. I find asking for the simplest item a challenge. Trying to figure out what's going on is like a guessing game. It seems I recognize only a few words in a conversation, and keep forgetting basic ones, like "What time is dinner?" or "I need to be at the bus stop at 7:30." This is all just ordinary conversation, yet so difficult for others to understand you when verbs and nouns are missing from your vocabulary. It amazes me how I never gave general conversation so much thought before in my life.

About twenty years ago I was in Germany. I knew German vocabulary and could speak some German. This was in part from growing up with my Dad and his attempt to teach me German, even though at the time I resisted learning German as I thought it unnecessary. In college though I started thinking differently and took German classes and a few times since then I have studied German through several Adult Education programs.

I came to Bulgaria with no prior introduction into the language, and many of the symbols are different and similar symbols have new sounds. Then there is gender, singular and plural all thrown into the mix to add to my confusion. My brain is totally confused.

Diana came over this afternoon and we worked with verbs. It seems to come so much easier for her and the younger students. They don't have as much history in their brains. Saturday at our HUB there was a group session for slow-pace learners. Only a few of us attended this session.

It included another older volunteer and Albin from our site. He seems to catch on, but is working hard to do it well. And to my surprise Stephanie attended. She is a young woman in her twenties who spent a year teaching in Thailand. She told me while there she was basically at an English school through Brandies University and thus did not learn the Thai language very well. We just all need practice, practice, practice. But some like Diana and Anna, and many of the other younger ones just snap it up from my perspective.

I keep remembering the words from a psychologist friend in Farmington who had served in the Peace Corps a number of years ago: he told me I would be taking baby steps and for me to just hang in there and one day it would start to click. So that is what I am trying to do. I get frustrated with myself for not learning quicker. I have always relied on being a fast learner, but this is a whole new ball game for me.

Nikolai, a tutor for the Peace Corps has come out several times and worked with me.

He is a very good teacher and explains it in a clearer format then just using the lessons in our book. Each day we go fast and faster whether we understand it or not. The concept of the Peace Corps is as Nikolai explained it, is that the fast ones pick it up and the rest the Peace Corps will tutor extra. He said that about half fall in each category. He has very good English skills, and often explains a word or gives an association that is good for memory.

Nikolai has a Ph.D. in Bulgarian history and has worked with the Peace Corps since 1997. He has been to both Boston and New York City for conferences, but did not get a chance for much touring. Both conferences were in February and he mentioned that he hardly had any free time and the weather was very cold.

I need to study hard yet tonight as he is coming back tomorrow to test me. Diana came over and we reviewed, but not thoroughly enough. On Tuesday, Danni comes from the Peace Corps main office to see if we are ready to pass the basic competency test. I have my doubts. With Diana we reviewed many things that I don't think will be on the test and now my mind is a jumble.

Hopefully tonight I can review it. I have my computer set up in Todora's winter kitchen. This kitchen in her house was much bigger than the one where I was served my meals. And I am hoping to show her the pictures of Bulgaria I downloaded on my PC Friday night.

She was coming to the kitchen, and then became upset with Boris and his friend who were watering her garden. I think they were not doing it to her standards. She is very particular with her garden and it is all very neat in carefully laid out rows with not a weed in sight.

Todora's son Boris is a pensioner, having worked with the National Rail Service for 25 years. He is about fifty years old. He drives his motorcycle back and forth to Vratsa, but often sleeps over here. He has a home in Vratsa and a wife and two sons. One son is married. He speaks about his sons driving cars. He mentioned a Nissan and a Ford. The one son and wife, and Boris' son were here for dinner one evening. I showed them pictures and we took pictures of each other.

Rakia is a favorite drink here in Bulgaria. It is the national drink. It is very strong fruit brandy, usually made from peaches, plums or apricots. It's often served with *shopska salada*, chopped up tomatoes and cucumbers. I could only drink a little or I'd been under the table. It has very high alcohol content and most Bulgarians do not mix their drinks with water or a soft drink or even use ice.

It is getting dark and Todora still has not come in from the garden and dealing with the watering. She was quite upset about it all. So perhaps it might not be the night for pictures. I will wait a few more minutes.

Todora came in shortly and I was able to show her the pictures. Just as I was finishing Boris comes in. Todora was excited about the pictures and told him that I had some of her and of Boris. So, I had to start at the beginning all over again. I probably could have skipped the pictures from New Mexico as they were not so interesting to them, but they really wanted to see the pictures of themselves. Then Boris had questions. But, I told him quite clearly I was tired and needed to sleep. It was nearly midnight.

Hi Mom, Greetings from Boston   **June 6, 2009**

It sounds like you're going through a big adjustment, and the language does look difficult. To not use the Roman alphabet I know I would have a very hard time with that. Stick with it, it will come . . . .

Your letter arrived yesterday; pretty speedy it seemed. It was nice to get it.

Things in Boston are good. Nell and I went to the movies this evening; before that, I was in my garden for a few hours, watering, weeding, hanging out with my fellow gardeners (this is our third summer at it together), thinning the sprouts. I feel so bad pulling them out indiscriminately killing some so that others may live; before that, I worked with my public art project clients to run a puppet making workshop in the neighborhood town square.

We're aiming for a Bread-and-Puppet sort of thing; the puppets and banners and fish on sticks and other things we made today will be used in an environmental justice "parade" next Saturday, as part of the "River Revel" festival that celebrates one of the rivers/marshes that defines one of East Boston's watery borders. Today was fun – all ages out there making stuff. Some of "my" E3C high school kids made an 8-foot-tall "trash monster," with 20-foot arms. Hilarious. When your email connection gets more reliable, I'll send photos.

And while this grassroots attention getting stuff is delightful to watch, there's a more serious undercurrent, too. When they're not doing public art installations with me, the high school kids are working on policy change at both city and state levels around issues of littering, air quality, and the availability of healthy food choices. I'm working with their corresponding adult counterparts, the Chelsea Creek Action Group, pursuing a multi-million dollar federal grant for wetlands reclamation.

The river that the River Revel celebrates has been used for heavy industry since the 19th century, and still is. On one site, a big oil company moved out a few years ago. Since then the land has been partially cleaned up, and the marshy wetland has begun to come back. Long story short, we think that this land should stay a marsh, permanently; the land should not turn into industrial production again. Having community support is critical to get this sort of funding, so events like today's puppet making and next week's parade and River Revel help to raise awareness and build that support.

The really interesting piece is that apparently the other big competing idea for the site is to turn it into a solar-panel factory. Competing "green" uses I think that a solar panel factory is a fine idea, though there's lots of other places where they might go in East Boston that are not a tidal marsh.

Spanish is the language on the street in East Boston; many spoke it today. Actually, I suspect that everyone there except me spoke Spanish. Later this summer there's going to be Spanish classes for professionals for people like me, and I think I'm going to take it.

Tomorrow morning I'm going to go for a three hour bike ride with some friends up on the North Shore, the Ipswich, Salem, Gloucester area. This is near where Nell and I lived back in 1992; after that, I will head to the studio.

What is the landscape there like? I know it's a small village. What does it look like? Colors?

Smells? Sounds? Describe it for us. Have a good Sunday, too.

Love, Gretchen

An email letter to my children around this time, June 6, 2009:

Today we have a cluster meeting with other groups in a town about an hour by bus from Banitsa. We had to wait an hour for the bus to come. Another of the volunteers here is letting me use his computer for a few minutes before our next meeting. I've been writing letters by hand, as the Internet is very erratic and usually I don't have much time. Some volunteers have it at their school or town. Our village is fine, but small. There are only a few small cafes, the school, a church and a park with a pool.

Marcus, has the rent been paid for June? I am wondering about the house in Farmington? I have not heard from anyone. Did my retirement check come from Santa Fe? And this week should be my first Social Security check on the 10th.

Also, I hope you found or called about the Citi bill and also my Dell computer bill. They are not set up with auto payment. Once Citi bill is paid it should be okay, as I only used it that one time in DC to buy that new small carry on suitcase. Just thinking, that was only three weeks ago.

I hope all is going okay in your lives . . . jobs, friends, health . . . I am anxious to hear from each of you. Maybe you have written a letter.

Monday we go into Vratsa and hopefully I will have some mail. For two days this week I had a tutor to help with my language, slowly it is coming, but still when I try to remember later it is difficult to think of the correct way to ask to pay the bill, buy something, where is something? I manage with body language, but wish I could say it.

I hope I will do okay to pass the Peace Corps exam and then can go at my own pace. I think living on my own will be different. It should give me more flexibility especially when I eat and wash. Please excuse the mistakes; I'm writing this in a rush before my time runs out on the computer.

The weather is warm today; tomorrow I will do my laundry and take a walk around the village with my camera and study. The countryside is very pretty.

Last night my landlady got a pig. They want to raise it and have it to eat for New Year's. Oh my.

That is the custom here. Time for Bulgarian history class. The class is in English.

Please take care; I love you and missing you all, With loads of love, Mom
P.S. Next week is our language test and the swearing in on July 24. I don't feel ready for this next stage of my life, and yet it seems so long ago that I lived in the U.S.A.

Email to my son Marcus who was taking care of my accounts and my house in New Mexico, June 9, 2009

Today is an unusual day here. We are being observed teaching English in our classes and also meeting with the Peace Corps staff discussing our fall placement. It was a good discussion and she said not to worry too much about the language. I must pass the test, but I think they will work with me. They are happy to have an experienced teacher.

I could also teach English to the teachers perhaps, do some craft classes in a village, maybe some music classes for students, so lots of possibilities. There will be a teacher in the village who has some English background, so that is good. It will probably be a village, but hopefully within an hour bus ride of a bigger city, plus I will have my own apartment. I mentioned that I would like to be near the Black Sea. That may be a possibility at least within an hour or two. We find out around June 20 I think.

A few other items I thought of to send in the package: sleeveless embroidered dress, sort of beige or gray and white sundress with jacket I think is there. Hair pins, or barrettes to help put up my hair. It's long now so that I can pull it back in a pony tail but I need more sizes of berets or pins. Blank note cards for language words. A few of the small games that I left there, they might work with the students, the yellow music book that has folk songs in it. Other music books, easy to play, I could use with students. Plain pencils and an eraser would come in handy. I have a hand pencil sharpener but no pencils.

You may want to send these items in two packages, some now and some later. Whatever works best for you. Be sure to mark it, "items for personal use – no commercial value" on outside of package. Perhaps it makes sense to wait now until I get my permanent site and address. I might have the new address by the end of June. Then you could mail the package directly there and I would have still received it before school begins near the end of August.

Many, many thanks. I served on jury duty in November 2007 and should have three years off, plus of course I'm out of country. Did you put a note with it?

I will look up the CITI phone number tonight and hopefully can get on email again tomorrow. I never know if the room will be open when I have a break.

Big hug, Mom

Hi Mom,   **June 8, 2009**

A new language never comes quickly, so hope you can be patient and stick with it. It will develop and one day you'll realize you are understanding people. I'm sure it is a struggle for now, and it might seem like everybody else is doing better; but I can guarantee that is not true. Everyone is feeling overwhelmed.

You won't be in this village necessarily for New Year's right? Maybe your landlady will invite you back so you can enjoy the pig.

It's good you can get on email regularly. The world sure is a lot more connected than it used to be. I bet you are still more connected than most people in the Peace Corps. Enjoy this time, it won't come again.

Good to hear from you. Vrasta is the main nearby town? What is that like?

We're getting a package ready to mail to you. Which shoes do you want? I have a note to send red, brown and black shoes and orange boots. We found (1) a dark red pair of medium dressy heels; (2) red pumps with a heel; (3) black flats; (4) brown suede zip-ups; (5) brown loafers; but no orange boots. Our guess is that you would like #2, 3, and 5. Could you describe the boots more? Are there other things you left that you would like?

Love, Marcus

Hi Marcus,   **June 9, 2009**

Thanks for the encouraging words on the language.

Yesterday I met several other older volunteers, and they said they basically learned what they could, and told Peace Corps that's all they could do and felt they would manage okay. I am anxious about the language test later this fall in Plovdiv. There are quite a few of us who will be taking the test review at then.

I found out yesterday that this is the first group in Bulgaria where we are scheduled most all Saturdays thus having a full six day week and crunching the learning into ten weeks. The groups before us had thirteen to fourteen weeks to learn the language and assimilate all the new culture. Because of budget cuts a full three weeks was cut out of our training. No wonder, it feels like a crash course. I feel better knowing that and understanding that I'm not imagining it all.

I'm glad to hear the papers arrived. There are several things that were sent to 1605 (This was my address for the six months I lived in an apartment when my house sale fell through.) I should have put a forward on that mail, but maybe forgot to do that. Go to a post office and get a form and fill out to forward my mail sent to 1605 E. 21st. St. to be sent to your Berkeley address. I think you could sign my name.

Well, I want to send this off. Yes, I'm happy to be able to send this to you via email. I can't help but think how different things were for you at age sixteen when you were over in Belgium going to a new high school, living with a strange family and having to do it all in French.

In another email I will explain more about the shoes and other stuff to send me. Much love.

Big hug, Mom

Hi Marcus and Stacey,   **June 9, 2009**

Please mail: Brown loafer shoes and the red dressy ones with a strap, wedge type of heel. Perhaps the orange boots are in a different suitcase. I bought them from Land's End for the rainy season here and took them out at the last minute. I don't think they got to D.C., but if you don't find them perhaps check with Gretchen if she remembers them.

Also did you see a pair of suede strap sandals? They're from L.L. Bean I believe. They would also be nice. I've been wearing my Birkenstocks almost every day as my toes get blisters from the leather sandals I was hoping to wear.

The other items would be my purple bath robe. Felicia had an extra one which she has loaned me to use and I'd like to return it to her. A light-weight bath and/or hand towel would also come in handy. Some small jelly beans would be super if not too heavy.

I don't think I locked the big red suitcase, if I did just break it open. I left the key somewhere on the desk.

Much love . . . and many, many thanks. How is the van doing?

Love, Mom

Email letter to my children: **July 6, 2009**

I tried to call but did not want to leave a message. Then I found out that it was going to use up all the money on my phone. I only put 15 lev on and just trying to call it went down to seven lev. I think I will buy more minutes when I go to Vratsa later this week. But for now will just email or try another text message. They are quite cheap. When I get to Topolitsa I hope to figure out Skype. Now I just use the school computer when the room is open and we don't have class. Calls inside Bulgaria are cheap, but international calls are very expensive.

Yesterday was a very different Sunday. I did my hand laundry as always, and then we four volunteers were invited by a woman here in the village for lunch, called *nagosti*, translated, be a guest.

She speaks several languages, including English quite well. She served us a very nice lunch and has a well kept home. She has lived in France and Italy I think, and now is here. She is looking for a job. She asked us lots of questions and I think was hoping we'd have some contact information to share with her. She seems interested in developing tourism in this area. Next Sunday we may go visit again and she will show us how to make *banitsa* which is similar to baklava I think.

Then I went to the pool. They have an Olympic size pool here and just filled it with water. Volunteers from the neighboring village also came over. We played volleyball with some of the students from our school.

Back at the house I made Todora spaghetti for dinner. I bought a bottle of wine at the local magazine for under 3 lev. It's hard to figure out costs. Just dialing Gretchen's telephone number cost 7 lev and wine was 2.6 lev.

Now it's time for class.

Enjoy Montana . . . there is a Montana here too, way up north almost to Romania.

Love, Mom

Hi Louise,   **July 27, 2009**
Nice to hear from you again, I am not sure if my email goes to everybody that you send your email to so I was not sure if I should respond, but I will do so anyway. It has been a busy summer here.

Norway was nice and the day I came back you and I were at O'Hare, Chicago airport at the same time. What a surprise that would have been if we had seen each other walking through the terminal

Mom is doing fine and has a permanent place at the nursing home. She really likes it there. Her brother is just a few doors down so she sees him every day.

I find it interesting to read about your life over there, but I know it is not for me. I hope you will learn the language well because that will make the whole stay a lot more enjoyable.

Bob and I are planning another trip to Norway this fall. Mom turns 90 on November 1 and is expecting us there. Next summer we are going back to Canada fishing.

Love, Liv

PEACE CORPS PROJECTS

Friday night the four of us here in Banitsa had to prepare a Bulgarian meal for our host families. We also invited both of our language teachers, Lazar and Nikolai. We had it at Albin's place, as his house is the biggest and best equipped. His *baba* has a beautiful garden and a gazebo where we could hold the dinner. His family readily agreed for us to host it at their home. She also has a bench swing by her garden and many lovely flowers in her yard. The house has a big kitchen, living room and generally more amenities. But we mainly used a gas burner which was set outside on a table, and the oven in the kitchen which held only one pan at a time. Peace Corps wanted us to prepare a meal that would be a typical Bulgarian meal. We invited all our host families. Todora came for a short while, but neither Annaor Diana's host families came. The host families had not known each other before being chosen as Peace Corps host families.

Peace Corps had advertised around the villages looking for homes. Families had to interview with Peace Corps to be considered for the program. This was the first time that Banitsa was a village chosen by Peace Corps. As a program under the U.S. government there are many guidelines and forms to fill out. The families are each given a stipend to off set the food that they are expected to provide for each volunteer and also a stipend to board the volunteer.

The four of us worked on the meal plan together. We needed help from Lazar on the translations and where we could buy the food. Much to our surprise, it turned out that we could get everything we needed at the small magazines in the village. Not all the food at the small magazines are put out on display like in our American stores, but need to be asked for from the clerk.

The day of the dinner we met at Albin's house after class. Our meal plan had grown as we tossed around ideas. We first decided to have French fries, bread, and a *shopska salada*. We bought olives which are a big favorite in Bulgaria. We had small peppers from the garden and fresh butter for the bread. I made Bulgarian meatballs and a tomato sauce. I made a sauce from fresh tomatoes. Todora gave me three fresh eggs from her chickens, plus parsley and onions from her garden. I bought the tomatoes and chopped meat from one of the magazines here in town. Diana made the traditional Bulgarian salad consisting of cucumbers and tomatoes. Albin prepared peppers stuffed with cheese and Anna, French fries with feta cheese sprinkled on the top. Bread of course was served. Nikolai brought along some very tasty yeast rolls which were like cinnamon buns one could buy in the States with pieces of fruit sprinkled in it. We served it for dessert along with the ice cream bars we had bought. Albin's *baba* also provided a cake roll, beer and soda.

We ate outside by their garden in the gazebo. It was a lovely evening. Volunteers who were at a village about fifteen miles away were able to catch a bus from their village and joined us in the evening and we exchanged experiences.

It was my best meal since I've been here and we all had a wonderful time visiting. It certainly helps having English/Bulgarian language teachers around. Otherwise it is difficult to carry on any kind of real conversation. I can make some basic sentences, but not a conversation. Nikolai and

Lazar are both very encouraging, so I think that perhaps I will make it yet.

During the week Peace Corps provides an apartment for Lazar in the village. Generally on the weekends he traveled by bus back into Vratsa. For this special event both Lazar and Nikolai stayed in the village until Saturday.

Another afternoon after class when Diana and I were walking around the village we noticed a lovely garden filled with raspberry bushes. They looked very tempting. A woman saw us peering over her fence and invited us in her yard. It was immaculate. Besides the raspberries she had a big variety of pepper plants, green beans and some root crops.

She motioned for us to sit down at a table under a shade tree. She gave us each a lovely bowl of raspberries and a cool drink of tea. Then we looked and saw that she had a lovely display of Bulgarian folk costumes in a room off her garden. As we expressed interest she let us go over and take a closer look. It included a small flag commemorating 1875, the year of the Bulgarian revolution. I wish I had taken more pictures. Our communication was all in Bulgarian. If we had known the language better I'm sure we would have learned even more.

LIFE IN A BULGARIAN VILLAGE

I have not written much about this village. It must have an interesting history but with my limited language skills I have not learned much.

There are many old worn down houses, but I can see they must have been very lovely at one time. Time has not been kind to Banitsa. It does have natural mineral water, which many people still come to and fill up their water containers. I have not had any problem with drinking it. I was told at one time they also had public baths, but they were closed some time ago. Understanding how difficult in each home it is to set up a bathing area, the baths must have been very important for the village folks.

I was also told that many of the people here, especially the men have gone to Italy and Spain to find work and come back once or twice a year to visit their families. There is no employment here except working on your farm and/or garden. For some things cash is needed.

Banitsa is about twelve miles from the town of Vratsa. It has a main motor- way running through it so trucks zoom through on a regular basis. It has a village school serving several surrounding villages as well as the children who live in the village. This is where we meet each day for our training classroom.

When we first arrived on May 24 school was still in session and we each had to prepare several lessons for the different grades. We also put on a special skit for the 4th of July. Of course that holiday is not celebrated in Bulgaria, but they knew about it as many American customs are known.

We wrote up a simple story that Lazar narrated while we acted it out. We did the story of Washington crossing the Delaware and Betsy Ross sewing a flag. We found clothes so that we could portray both British and American soldiers. It took some sleuthing to find a United States flag. We were realizing how much harder it was to find items first when you didn't know the language very well and second, didn't have access to a full array of shops.

There is a market day, a community center and natural spring water. In addition, there is a lovely park with a big swimming pool, which makes it very distinctive from most villages. However, the pool is not heated nor does it have a filtering system so it has to be emptied frequently over the warm summer days. It can take a full day to empty the pool, and another whole day to fill it up again. As a result, you may arrive on a pool emptying or fill day and not get to swim. So far, we only came as a group to the pool. Often, the local girls and young women do not go into the water, but the teenage boys gallivant around in the pool.

Women are not forbidden in the water, they just don't go in the water. As Americans we found this strange and so as a group we went in and enjoyed the water. There were tables around the pool and a small carry out food stand where you could buy a *karbashi* (small sausage) *sladolet* (ice cream)and sometimes *kartofe* (French fries).

Beer and soft drinks are also sold. As in most places in Bulgaria beer was cheaper than Coca-Cola, so beer was often the preferred drink with Peace Corps Volunteers.

As in most Bulgarian villages, cows, chickens and goats can be seen wandering through the streets on a regular basis. This does attract flies on hot summer days.

While residents of the village keep the yard around their house very neat, often the town streets are filled with trash. Stray dogs and cats roam the streets looking for the food that topples out of the large garbage bins. There are only several of these in the entire village and generally they are overflowing. The idea of civic pride still had not taken hold in these smaller communities.

Our second day in the village Anna, Albin, Diana and myself met Lazar at the bus stop at 7 AM to go into Vratsa for a Peace Corps meeting. We were all very surprised at the condition of the bus stop. Cigarette butts, empty plastic cups and paper was everywhere. There were no trash bins in sight. The bench was broken so there was no place to sit down.

The walls of the bus stop were plastered with recent political posters covering older political posters and many death notices called *necrologies*. Often a photo of the person who died was also included. This photo is called a *zhaleyka*. A notice is put up not only when the person dies, but often on anniversary dates, especially the three month, six month and twelve month anniversary of a person's death. A community bulletin board often is used for this purpose, but in smaller villages the bus stops are also often used. In addition a notice is at the gate of the house where the person died, along with a large black ribbon. Todora had a big black ribbon on her door in memory of her husband. I do not know how long she was a widow.

Each Peace Corps group had to coordinate a special community project working with the mayor and the town council. Anna, Diana, Albin and myself decided to clean up one of the two bus stops in the village so that as vehicles passed through the town a better impression would be made. Peace Corps Sofia gave us a small stipend for supplies like paint and brushes. It was up to us to figure out where to buy the supplies.

As we were new to the language this was a part of the project we had not thought much about. Where do you buy paint? What is the word for paintbrush in Bulgarian? Is it different to paint a wall, than it is to paint a painting?

These are the type of challenges that a new person in any country runs across.

It is very different than being a tourist where you just need to find a restaurant or a souvenir shop. We were looking at everyday supplies that most tourists do not consider. Living in a country and managing your day to day obligations is very different than visiting museums, the theater or going out to eat. Working with the town officials to get their approval to do it is all part of the goal of Peace Corps to work with local communities and helping them learn to help themselves.

CLEAN-UP DAY

It was an all day project as first the layers of old posters, political and death notes had to be scraped off. Bags of trash quickly filled up. After scraping off the old paint, we applied fresh coats of paint.

It turned out to be a very hot day. We started at seven in the morning and as the day wore on the sweat was dripping down our backs. I wore the "new" paint clothes I had bought at the Used Clothing Store in Vratsa. Lazar our teacher came to help us and stayed the entire day. A few of the Bulgarian teachers and students came to help us as well for part of the time. The mayor stopped by and was impressed by our efforts. He recruited a few of the village workers to start work on the bus stop on the other side of the street. We were very excited about that but before long they left to leave that project for another day.

Several Peace Corps staff from Vratsa stopped in and worked with us for a while. Then Nikolai appeared. He had been tutoring a student at a nearby village and had to catch a bus back to Vratsa. He was impressed with our efforts and decided to join in. He offered to paint the outline of *Welcome* on the back wall. I offered to fill in the space.

In bright red paint he outlined the words *Dobre Duschee,* Welcome in English. I filled in his outline. Before long I had paint all over my clothes and some on my face. Somehow Nikolai managed to paint without getting a drop on his white shirt

Anna had the idea of painting the Bulgarian flag on the side of the bus stop that was seen as buses pulled into the stop. Diana was a very good artist and offered to draw an outline of the flag. We then all helped to fill in the spaces. Before long the bright colors of green and red with the white strip on the top were painted for all to see as they drove through on the highway.

We worked all day with only a few breaks to have cold drinks and snacks to eat. We wanted to get it finished in one day. With the paint running out and our energy as well, we did manage to write in small letters inside the bus stop the word Peace Corps. Underneath the word Peace Corps we each signed our names in small letters. We worked until dark and lined up our bags of trash. The mayor told us he would send someone to pick them up.

Note: Two years later when I went back to Banitsa the flag can still be seen. Sadly, at some point our names were painted over. We had not written in Bulgarian script, so it was probably just seen as graffiti.

FIELDS OF SUNFLOWERS

Diana lived on the edge of town in the Romani district. I sometimes walked her home and then she walked back with me to a junction where the bar was located and the other big trash bin. In this way, she didn't have too far to go alone and nor did I.

On one of these walks we decided to take another path that went out of the village. We were drawn to the field of sunflowers that we could see. They seemed to go on for miles. They were all starting to blossom. Soon we had a bunch of children following us down the road. They were excited to see us taking pictures of the sunflowers. Then we took pictures of them. As we were trying to teach them English we decided to sing some action songs with them. The children especially liked the old folk song *Hokey Pokey.*

Singing the song and pointing to our body part, it was an easy way for children to learn the names of their body parts in English. I don't think either Diana or myself knew the names in Bulgarian of our body parts. I realized more and more the everyday words that you speak with a child become a part of their early vocabulary. When you are sixty-five and learning and hearing these words for the first time it becomes more and more of a challenge.

We told Anna and Albin about our walk. They too were interested and so we decided that as soon as we had a free weekend afternoon we would go out together. It was great fun. We all looked for the biggest sunflower we could find to take our picture. This was before selfies, so we took turns taking each others photo. Later when we shared our adventure with Lazar he told us that we were lucky that we didn't run into any snakes. He said that they often hang out in sunflower fields

The word for sunflower in Bulgarian is pronounced *slunchogled*.

A colleague of mine from New Mexico sent me a wonderful Ziggy cartoon. It shows Ziggy answering the phone and the voice is saying to him, ". . . to continue this call in Navajo, press 43 . . . to continue this call in Bulgarian . . ." Ziggy is shown to reply, "You'd think they'd start in English."

ICE CREAM WITH LUCY

Another adventure we had as a group started when Anna mentioned a woman she had met who lived not far from her house and had invited Anna and her other American friends staying in the village over for lunch one day. Diana, Albin and I met and walked over to meet Anna on a Sunday afternoon and went to this young woman's house. The yard looked more kept up than many of the others in the neighborhood. A young woman was outside in the yard. We greeted her with *Dober Den* and she answered in English, "Hello." We were surprised. This was the first time that anyone in the village had greeted us in English.

She invited us into her house. It was very well kept. And we could speak English with her. What a relief. She wanted to practice her English. She told us how she was studying it in order to get a better job. Did we have any ideas for jobs? She had worked in France, but decided to come back to her native land. The jobs however were scarce and it was more expensive to live in Sofia. She was hoping to find a good paying job in Vratsa. Many of the younger people who lived in the village with their families worked in the bigger nearby towns like Vratsa.

The economy was hard. Many of the other volunteers mentioned that the mothers from their village were traveling to Spain or Italy to find a job as a housekeeper. They often were gone for six months at a time, leaving their elderly parent taking care of their young children. Sometimes it was the father who worked abroad.

While most of the young people were happy about the new freedoms that happened after 1989 they were realistic and realized that with these freedoms, jobs were scarce.

Higher education was available and usually free, but if you did not have an advanced degree a good job was hard to find. And even with an advanced degree a good paying job was scarce. Teachers were a good example. Most teachers did not make more than $300 US a month. It is hard to compare salaries with U.S. teachers as the cost of living was very different, but still on the whole Bulgarian teachers and doctors did not make anywhere near a comparable salary with someone working in the same field as in the United States.

We weren't in the house long when we were invited to sit at her table and she served us a lovely lunch and dessert. We all missed ice cream. Where Diana and I lived there was no refrigerator that we knew of, thus no ice cream. What a treat. We learned that ice cream is only in the village stores in the summer time. Fruit is more the tradition for dessert.

When our new friend found out that we had not been taught how to make Banitsa she was appalled. How could that be? Here we were in the country over a month and we still had not learned to make Banitsa.

She had a friend who made excellent Banitsa and had a bigger kitchen. She would arrange a lesson for us. A few days later we all met at 6 PM near the school including Lazar and went to Lucy's to learn how to make Banitsa. Her neighbor is actually the one who showed us. They seemed like very nice people and had a very nice house. It was very well kept. We were offered *Rakia*. With the heat from the day and very little food I only drank a small glass and was thankful that they offered 7-up as an alternative drink.

In a number of villages some of the families have hosted volunteers for several years already so it was not as foreign a concept as it was for the families and teachers in Banitsa.

MEETINGS, MEETINGS AND MORE MEETINGS

The next two days in Vratsa were special meetings and Peace Corps had arranged for all of us to stay at one of the main hotels in Vratsa. We were meeting our counterparts who we would be working with us once we moved to our permanent site.

My counterpart, Tantayna did not arrive until the second day. She was on an excursion and had to take a bus across Bulgaria and missed some connections. She was very tired. She seemed nice. She had become the English language teacher when the village schools were required to switch from having Russian as their second language in the curriculum to English as the preferred second language. Prior to this she was teaching Russian to the students. This was a big change for her. Her friend Pauli, also a teacher and Pauli's son, Ruslan came to the conference to help translate. Ruslan was 17 and knew English very well. He had been going to Burgas at one of the bigger language schools in the country. Many of his classes were in English. He was a great help in translating so that we could work on the programs we were to develop. This was the first year that Topolitsa was assigned a Peace Corps volunteer so it was a big learning curve for everyone.

Ruslan went with me to pick up my photos. I had left them at a photo shop the day before, but wasn't sure if I understood the costs. I found out that it is quite expensive to develop photos. I had to pay for the negatives as well as the prints. It made me thankful that I had brought a digital camera along, as well as my film camera. I quickly realized that I would be printing very few pictures. I had brought along quite a bit of film but decided that I probably wouldn't be using that camera very much or at least getting the photos developed while living overseas. I would need to learn how to use my digital camera and download my photos on my laptop computer. A new age was here.

Ruslan helped me again at the telephone store as I needed to buy more minutes for my phone. I realized that this would be one of the main ways that I would be staying in touch with the other volunteers. Peace Corps required that we always have our telephone with us in case of an emergency and so that they could stay in touch with us. Most of the volunteers at this time also had computers, although it was not required. We did not all have Internet connection so this still could present a major hurdle, especially for reports that we had to fill out.

The town of Vratsa had a Computer Internet store which many of us took advantage of when we were in Vratsa. We could pay 5 lev and connect to the Internet for twenty minutes to be on one of their computers. Peace Corps also allowed us some time to use staff computers during our lunch breaks but as there were only four computers and 61 volunteers, the chances of getting even five minutes on a computer were slim.

It was nearing the end of June and the weather was very warm. The second day in Vratsa I felt I needed a break. I wanted to just walk around town on my own before lunch. And who do I meet on the street? In front of me less than five minutes from the hotel I meet Boris. I was surprised and a bit frustrated as I just wanted some time to myself and to look around in the shops. Boris wanted me to tell him all that had happened and of course I could not do that due to the language barrier. Also, it appeared to me that he assumed that I must have free time. I agreed to sit down and have a Coca-Cola with him. He wanted to see my contract. It was in Bulgarian and English. I showed him my new contract. Then I told him I needed to return to the Hotel Hemus, which I did indeed.

When I came back lunch already had been served. But I took a bread roll and also had the ice cream cake for dessert. The food has been fairly good – generally warm – and very plentiful. Breakfast has been a mixture of Bulgarian and English: cheese, bread, yogurt, granola, tomatoes, and cucumbers. The second morning we were offered scrambled eggs, bread and espresso.

The meetings were about working together and coming up with projects to do in our community. At night the young volunteers used the time to go out and celebrate. On the third night I walked up the steps to the museum at top of the hill with Ruslan. It took about fifteen minutes as there were over 800 steps to the top. I was glad to know that I could still do that. I took a few pictures, and then Ruslan and I met his mother Pauli. Ruslan left to watch a movie at the hotel with some of the younger volunteers. Tantayna, my counterpart and several others including another Bulgarian teacher who had spent a short time in Pittsburgh joined us at a bar for some drinks. We stayed and talked until midnight. It was fun to have this casual visit. The conversation was a combination of English and Bulgarian.

LEARNING TO COPE

July 2: the topic of food came up today in our class, which it has before but for some reason today Lazar paid more attention to what he heard me say. I mentioned how the toaster oven was broken so now I was only getting cold bread with cheese in the morning. I also mentioned it was usually the same for lunch.

Meat came up and I mentioned that I seldom had meat. Really? He was surprised. I said I had been gone a few days, but hardly any meat has been on the menu; maybe once a week at the most. He was surprised and asked if I was a vegetarian.

I said no, but that Todora just hardly ever served meat. He said I should say something, and I said how I thought it was Boris' way of saving money.

Lazar mentioned that the families receive money to feed us. I knew that, but I think Boris controlled what Todora did with the money. For Todora living on a pensioners' income housing a Peace Corps Volunteer was an economic windfall.

Lazar said this would not show a good report for Todora. I said she was sweet and meant well, and that I was managing. He said he would speak to her. Then he had to teach our English class. I then told Lazar "It's OK, Todora means well." I left it at that.

Lazar must have spoken to her later that same day while Albin and I were teaching our English class, as today for lunch meat was served. It was a first for lunch from what I can remember. It was rather too much meat as I had two Polish sausages or something similar and some cold ground meat of some sort. She doesn't seem to believe in serving food hot.

And then she asked me what I wanted for dinner which was another surprise as I don't remember her ever asking me. I suggested cheese sandwiches made on the stove as her toaster oven wasn't working. I thought it was just the timer, but she has indicated that it was broken. I had told Lazar this too and asked him if I should offer her money to buy a new one. He said no, they had money to fix it.

The Peace Corps gives us an allowance to pass on to our host family, 240 lev every two weeks. This is the equivalent of about $150. This is more than the allowance we are given as volunteers. Host families really are well reimbursed for housing us. Some families see it as extra income, while others from what I can gather from other volunteers see it as extra income and don't do extra activities or special meals with their volunteer. A volunteer on Monday told me her family took her on excursions. I don't expect that, but a hot meal is a treat. Excursions could be arranged though as her son Boris has two cars in Vratsa, as well as his motorcycle. He usually only has his motorcycle here. I think his sons use the cars and maybe his wife whom he hardly ever mentions.

An excursion would be nice. I don't think he would even think of it. Albin has been to a family wedding in Vratsa and Anna has gone many times to Vratsa just for the evening. Diana and I seem to be at families where we are left on our own to figure things out and isolated from any world outside of our village.

I don't understand why Boris doesn't go back to Vratsa in the evening and sleep where his wife and sons are living? The first week he ate with us, but now he usually eats when I'm not around. He is intense and at times I'm completely at a loss as to how to speak with him. He wants to know all about my life in America and is convinced I live in California, even though I've told him numerous times that is my son, not me. He has indicated that he wants to come and visit. That would be difficult at best. He seems to think I am rich and have a big house filled with gold. That certainly is the impression of many Bulgarians who only know Americans by what they have seen in movies and on television.

Tonight for dinner, the toaster oven was fixed. It was just the timer button that needed glued. I thought the burner still worked and it does. I did get a feeling that perhaps hot food bothered Todora's teeth and that is the reason she eats her food cold. Oh my! But hot cheese sandwiches are sure better than cold bread with a slice of cheese.

She asked me tonight what I wanted for breakfast, and I said "toast with honey" *toct sis med*. She understood me I think. It will be interesting in the morning if that is what I get. I gave her the time of 7 o'clock. We have to be at school at 8 AM promptly tomorrow to get ready for our July 4 reenactment that we are putting on for our students. Generally classes start at 8 AM but we are given a few minutes leeway. I usually leave the house about 7:50 AM but because of our special project I wanted to get to school earlier.

The idea of eggs for breakfast is a foreign concept. I did have warm scrambled eggs the other night for dinner. The plate of food is always set in front of me, so I have no choice on how much to eat. Usually it is way too much, as a plate of cold stuffed peppers has little appeal to me. I am used to eating smaller amounts and a variety of vegetables even at the same meal, but here it is usually cooked chopped peppers with onions and chopped tomatoes, but then served cold. Sometimes it is peppers stuffed with *siranade* (white cheese) but again served cold.

She is afraid of getting cold. She wants me to wear a sweater to school, and to take a warm shower, but food is served cold. This is a very common Bulgarian trait. Drafts are avoided at all costs. Sweaters should be worn even on the warmest days in case a breeze comes up or a window is open.

And one more surprise. When I went in to take a shower tonight, there was a space cleared off for me to put my soap and shampoo. The shelf was still dirty, but at least there was a small space cleared for my soap. I had mentioned this to Lazar awhile back, so perhaps he also mentioned something to her about it as I can't believe that this is just a mere coincidence.

Last night there was another surprise. She had a little kitten, and it was in her kitchen. She never let the puppy in the kitchen. The poor little puppy died from malnutrition.

I think she and Boris firmly believe in that the strong survive. They expected the puppy to eat regular food, when it really probably needed to be bottle fed yet, or at least milk to lap. The puppy only survived about two weeks. It seemed small, but okay when I left for the week to Vratsa and Topolitsa, but on my return I found out that it had died. I felt so badly. Poor thing.

But now today the kitten must stay outside. It was given a box, but not a closed room so I wonder if it will be there in the morning. It sure is tempting to bring it in the house, but I know Todora wouldn't understand, and when I leave July 23 the kitten would have to adapt to the outside. I think she got it from a friend or maybe even her doctor. She went to her doctor for some kind of shots she gets in her upper leg which I think has to do with her limp. She has showed the shot spots to me.

There are any number of stray cats and dogs around the village. They are constantly searching through the scraps of food laying around the garbage bins. The cats try to climb up to the bins and can be heard meowing pitifully in hunger.

In the bigger cities like Burgas, Varna and Sofia there are neutering laws but very hard to enforce. It is especially difficult when the nearby villages do not have those laws, and in fact many of the citizens feel it is against nature to neuter an animal.

It was a very sweet kitty and must have been kept indoors because it does not appear wild as so many of them do. But, can it stay tame if it's left outside all the time? She named it *Louise* I think. As I understand it, her idea is that when I leave the end of July she will have another *Louise*. Hopefully the kitten will be a survivor and manage with all the machine implements, tools and other assorted equipment around the yard.

The kitten has disappeared for the second time. It has been over a day. It is a very sweet kitten, but of course Todora doesn't allow it in the house, nor does she ever pick it up.

Yesterday it seemed very lonesome and I so much wanted to bring it in my room. But I knew that wouldn't be fair to the kitten for when I left what would happen to it? But now the kitten is gone and I find myself missing it. It was a living being that needed my care. Maybe it will still come back. I can only hope for that. I have always loved pets, especially cats and dogs. Having a small kitten to pet helped stem any loneliness I was feeling.

It has been a busy week and feel I have become behind in my Bulgarian language. We are studying past tense. Past tense conjugation seems even more difficult than future and present tense. I wouldn't even bother, but it is part of our language test so I must learn it. Many of the words end in the "h" sound to make it past tense. That is very strange for my tongue to get a handle on.

Today I think I will review the red book, Bulgarian Language Workbook developed by the Bulgarian Peace Corps Staff and my notebook as much as possible. On Monday Nikolai will be here. Hopefully with his assistance I can learn what is necessary for the test. Sometimes it seems to me a waste of time. I want to teach English, meet the people, but learning the language is certainly a hindering block.

I continue to be amazed, and I guess somewhat envious of the younger volunteers who seem to pick it up without any difficulty. They also have each other to hang around with and support. I know Hazel, another older volunteer, is also frustrated. The older husband and wife team seem oblivious to us and continue to project to me a rather haughty attitude. I don't receive this feeling from the younger volunteers; most of them are just busy with their own lives.

Thursday in our cluster meeting this was spoken of briefly by JoEllen, an older volunteer who is almost ready to COS. This is short for Close of Service. She will be finished with her assignment. She spoke of her time here in Bulgaria. She also mentioned the isolation. She seems to have overcome it, but is ready to return home. Joan, another older volunteer, has opted to do another stint, after a visit back to U.S.A. At this point I can't imagine doing that.

This week was more difficult as there were three trips into Vratsa on three different days for meetings. They all seem rather redundant to me and I wish the time was spent with language classes, but I suppose we can't do that 24/7 but yet it seems we should. Yesterday was Roma Day and we heard from Roma government groups some of the problems and solutions being considered. Then we had a long walk to the Vratsa Roma community in very hot humid weather.

Peace Corps had no water at the school for the walk so that made it even more difficult as it was a very warm day. Only Diana and I went from our Banitsa group. It was very educational and I learned about the Roma family and life style. At the same time, I felt that we were intruding on their lives as though they were on display. The Peace Corps office had permission for the tour, but later I heard that not everyone was happy on how it was organized.

One more item from Vratsa: over lunch time I walked to a second hand store that I was told about. I wanted to find a t-shirt and pants that I could paint in. I was very excited to find the store to get a few extra clothes items. I also found some short sleeve sweaters that would be good for teaching. The clothes were weighed and are bought by the pound. In all, I spent 19.8 lev. It was a real bargain for all the items, costing me only about $14 U.S.

It frustrated me though as I realized that living out in the remote village and being older I was not aware of some of the social things that were going on among the volunteers. It became for me another example of what others knew and only by accident did I find out about it. I realized I was in nobody's circle, and that makes this time period much harder.

I did receive cards this week from several friends and a letter from my sister. The younger volunteers are surprised by how much mail I receive, but then I write letters and they do not. It shows the generation gap. A package came too from David and he included school supplies, towel and a Snickers bar. There was also a small package from Elaine, an administrator who worked with me at San Juan College. She sent me a deck of UNO cards and a small towel.

We had another group meeting on Saturday at a town about twenty miles from Vratsa. Lazar found the bus schedule for us, and fortunately we could catch a bus from Banitsa. It was very crowded.

I feel so frustrated as I am not up on the latest technology gadgets. I cannot do a flash drive, nor do I wear a headset like many of the volunteers. Today I feel lonely. We finished early as they were falling asleep in class. I'm back here at Todora's and it makes for a long afternoon. But now with this written I will go back to studying and look forward to having Nikolai here on Monday to help me with my language lessons.

Today was the first all day rain on a Sunday so I could not do my laundry. I did spend time playing with the kitten, in fact I snuck her into my room. Todora was busy with Boris as she was canning apricots. The empty jars were left outside overnight covered with the red fuzzy blanket that we sit on. As it was already threatening rain, Boris put an old bench seat over the blanket so that it wouldn't blow away.

He had put sugar already in the jars, using a plastic glass from Todora's kitchen. And the apricots were already in the jars. It didn't appear very sanitary to me, but the jars were washed and I know she does heat her wash water. As I understand, Boris bought apricots in Vratsa, or maybe a friend gave them to him.

In the morning I had a quick breakfast with Todora with strong fresh coffee and some pieces of coffee cake. As the kitty was there and it was raining I held it under my jacket and brought her into my room. She settled down on my bed and took a nap while I studied my Bulgarian language words. When I went out to use the toilet, I saw Todora was busy with the jars and had the wood stove going with the canning kettle. She had six jars in it and seven were already finished. She also showed me that she had chicken and rice in the wooden cook stove for our lunch. She indicated it would be ready by one o'clock. The noon meal is usually the bigger meal of the day, a practice very common throughout Europe. I took the kitty back inside with me.

Anna messaged me asking for the bug spray. She would walk over. We went to say hello to Todora and then went to my room to see the kitten. It was good seeing her and she helped me with a few words. Then she went back to her home and I had my lunch. In the afternoon I had a nap and continued with my studies.

I showed Todora how to play UNO. She had fun with it. It went fairly well. I think if we could communicate better we could become good friends. She means well I know.

Later one of Todora's friends came over and I decided to go back to studying sitting outside on the front steps. Too late I realized Boris had taken a shower as he came back walking from the shower door with a towel around himself to the front house door. He was rather embarrassed to see me where I was sitting with the kitten and my study book. Thankfully, he did have a towel around himself.

As it appeared there might be company for dinner, I decided that it would be good to take a shower before dinner as well. It takes about thirty minutes for the boiler to heat the water. Taking a shower is always tricky to me. I have only one hook to put all my stuff, so my towel, bathrobe which

I borrowed from Felicia, soap, shampoo, clothes all go in my Peace Corps bag hanging on the hook. I wear my orange flip flops. How I wish I had brought two pair of flip flops along. At the time I packed it never crossed my mind that maybe I could wear flip flops around the village. Everyone wears them everywhere here. I have worn mine to class, but generally save them for the shower or rainy days. These are the orange ones that I bought last year for the picnic after my son's wedding. I always dress myself completely in the shower room as I would be too embarrassed to be seen in my bathrobe or a towel.

Last night I put my first DVD into my computer and watched a Seinfeld episode. I didn't watch that on any regular basis when it was on television in the U.S. It was funny and a nice change of pace from language study. Tonight I watched another episode. It was a fun diversion.

I also sent a text a message to Dora, my director in Topolitsa and mentioned that I would be buying my bus ticket for July 25. It is only two weeks away now. Overall this time has gone fast. Nikolai will be here four days this week, plus we go to Sofia on Wednesday.

TOPOLITSA AND THE BLACK SEA

During the two day conference in Vratsa we found out where our assignment would be for the next two years. Most of the volunteers were assigned to the central and western area of the country. I was placed in Topolitsa, a village near the Black Sea way on the eastern side of the country. There are several of us in the Eastern region :Anna, not the Anna from our Banitsa group, is in a village north of Burgas, Anna, from our group, is about two hours further north of me. Chris, a volunteer I barely know is in Roma. (And Roma or Romani are the terms generally used to refer to this ethnic group of people. *Gypsy* is the slang word that is often used by those outside of the country. There are many groups of Roma people and all do not speak the same language or dialect. It is not to be confused with modern Romania or ancient Romans.) It's a community near Burgas in a community development program. Andrea, the youngest Peace Corps volunteer is assigned to teach at two schools in Aitos and will be the closest in distance to me. Laura, another young volunteer is not too far away from Topolitsa is assigned to teach in two high schools in Karnobat. Her counterpart has lived in the United States for a short time and it was interesting talking to her afterwards.

This is the first year that the Peace Corps program was trying out the idea of a volunteer teaching or working at two sites. It did present some problems. The main problem seemed to be on how to divide up volunteer duties. Each school wanted the volunteer as much as possible. The Bulgarian schools compete for students in the same town and also from neighboring towns. They compete for recognition and also for funding, as the education money is divided in the district based on how many students a school enrolls. Students are free to attend any school they choose even outside their municipality.

If a school is known having a successful English program more students will gravitate to that school as many parents in Bulgaria see this as a very desirable educational goal. Thus a volunteer assigned to two schools in the same town was actually competing against herself. A volunteer walks a very fine line dividing her/his energies.

In the morning it was time to catch the bus for Aitos. It left Vratsa at 7:10. There was a fifty minute layover in Sofia and then on to Aitos. I was on my way to my new site. Several other volunteers were also on the bus to their placement sites. They got off in towns along the way. My big suitcase was taken by another counterpart from Aitos in her car which was super. This is my new favorite word that seems to be understood both in English and Bulgarian. What a help that was. Andrea also rode with her. Her name was Vesala and in time I would get to know her and also work with her on some projects. She loved Bulgarian history and in the future would be showing me some of her favorite historic places. We got into Aitos about 4 PM my school director, Dora and her son George was there to meet me. Thankfully George knows English. Dora is studying it. Both are very nice.

We went to a café for a cold drink and then they took me to my motel, Road Star. This was the newer, very modern motel in town. It even had a television which could get CNN. This was my first English TV since coming over a month ago. I was given some time to rest and then picked up for dinner at 7. We went to a very modern new restaurant called the Waterfalls. What a wonderful surprise. I had spaghetti, French fries and wine. George's girlfriend, Toni was also there with us, and another of Andrea's counterparts, Annie. Everyone was very nice and welcoming.

The next day I was picked up at 8:30 AM. I was down in the café at 7:30 AM as breakfast was included with the lodging. It was coffee, open faced cheese and ham sandwich with a slice of tomato and cucumber on it. It was the same for all three mornings, a very standard Bulgarian breakfast.

After being picked up by Dora, my future school director, we went down to the center of town and met up with Andrea and her counterparts. A meeting had been arranged with the mayor of Aitos. He was a very distinguished looking man. We sat around a big oval table and were served coffee, cold water and cookies. The meeting lasted about an hour. The meeting was in Bulgarian, but several of the teachers in Aitos, namely Vesala, Pauli and Brandi translated for us.

Then we walked around the town a bit. It seems like a nice town. I was surprised that we ran into Todora's mother. I found out she lives in Aitos. Later I found out she actually lives in the same house as Todora, in the downstairs floor. Her brother lives on the third floor. This is very much the custom in Bulgaria where families all live together in a big house or close by to each other.

Then it was time to drive to Topolitsa about 20 kilometers away. At the school there was a welcoming committee of teachers and students and the traditional Banitsa was served. A piece is broken off and then another person holds a salt jar where you are expected to dunk your piece in before you eat it.

Svetlina was an old, but well kept village school. I met the teachers in the teacher's lounge where *ayran* was served, a refreshing summer drink made with mixing an equal amount of cold yogurt and water. Soon afterwards the children sang some traditional Bulgarian folk songs with their music teacher who played the accordion. They were very good. I was told they have won many prizes for their singing and I can certainly see why. They have beautiful harmony.

Then it was time to see the apartment I would be living in for the next two years. I will be living on the second floor of a renovated house. The steps are marble to the second floor and appears very clean. The kitchen appliances still need to be put in, but it has an indoor bathroom including a bathtub.

I can also use the landlady's wash machine. She is a widow and her children no longer live in the village. Her husband's family still lives in the village. Everyone was very welcoming. Milka, the owner is 69 years old and has a friendly smile. She had two grown children, a son who lives in Spain with his family and a daughter who had lived in Germany, but came back to Bulgaria a short time ago and married a man from Aitos. She is of Turkish origin as many are in this area of Bulgaria.

Dora took me back to the Road Star motel where it was nice to see some English television. I found CNN. It was good to hear English spoken after working most of the day on my Bulgarian language communication skills. Overcome with exhaustion I took a nap and then showered in a modern shower to get ready for dinner.

Dora picked me up around 7:30. We went to her house to eat where I met her husband. He is a retired history teacher, and appears to have some slight handicap with his one hand; a very nice man and loves history. Her son George was also there and his girlfriend Toni who appeared very young and was very sweet. She knew a little English. George was the most fluent English speaker.

For dinner, Dora prepared a tasty green salad, chicken breast, French fries with ketchup and of course, *Rakia*. It was a superb meal; the best meal by far that I have had in Bulgaria. We talked long about history and literature with George doing most of the translating. I had brought a bottle of wine, which was served after the main course, and then she came out with a plate of salami and cheese. Bulgarians do not serve liquor or wine without appetizers. It was almost midnight when she took me back to the Road Star motel.

In the morning Dora picked me up about 10. George and Toni were in the car, along with Annie a school director from Aitos. We were on our way to Burgas. Via car it couldn't have been more than thirty to forty minutes to get to Burgas. It is a lovely city located on the Black Sea with a beautiful beach and a lovely Sea Garden running along the border of the beach area; the weather that day also was warm, but not too hot.

We dropped Annie off at the education building and then went to the city center where we walked down the streets looking in shop windows and just taking it all in. It is a combination of resort town and university town. Two major universities are there. George attends the Free University. Free in that it is an open to new ideas established in 1991 after the fall of Communism. It is a private university. The other is the older state university which is free to students who qualify by taking an exam in their senior year of high school.

Most Bulgarians attend Kindergarten and then begin first grade at age 7 and graduate at age 18. During their high school years they follow the program much like many European countries where a student decides whether to pursue an academic or vocational track.

Before heading to the beach we walked inside St. Methodius Church, which is of the Bulgarian Orthodox order. It was good to know that she is religious and I appreciated the chance to see the inside of the church. We lit candles. The tradition is to light a candle and to offer a silent prayer. Hats are removed and as you leave you face forward and back out of the door to show respect.

Then we headed to the Black Sea. It was super. It looked fantastic. The Black Sea was beautiful, way beyond anything I had imagined. We walked near the water where there were many, many cafes. The beach was not too crowded. It took my breath away. It was fun. We stopped at a café and we had *chasa* fish which are small fish similar to smelt, French fries and a Turbog beer. Dora did not drink beer as she was the driver.

In Burgas I mailed my letters from the big regional post office that was located not too far from the beach. It was a beautiful classical building built in 1930, designed by Victoria Vinarova, the first noted woman architect in Bulgaria.

Toni walked with me to see the inside of the Free University. This was a beautiful modern structure with amazing art work on its walls. It was super seeing this very modern university which opened in 1991. I asked to use the bathroom. And happily they had a very modern bathroom.

After that it was time to go back to Aitos. Dora dropped me off at the motel and said she would pick me up at 6 PM; she told me we would have dinner with Andrea, the PCV who was assigned two different high schools in Aitos. She was staying at the older traditional folk motel which is part of the Genger Ethnographical Complex, located next to the town park, Slaveeva Reka. During the day this complex had artisans demonstrating metalworks and pottery. Andrea was staying above the artisans shops. It already had been a super day.

Then there was another surprise. Instead of just going out for dinner, other colleagues from Aitos met us at the park and we walked around the entire park. At one end there was a zoo. It was a pleasant evening. The animal cages were not all the best, but the animals did not appear to be ill-treated. It was fun. Pauli and her son Ruslan were there and other Bulgarian colleagues. A few spoke English. It was great having translators which helped me a lot. We walked and walked. It was a lovely evening. It took over an hour. We ended up at a traditional folk restaurant at the edge of the park. I had pizza. Wonderful. *Rakia* was again served; also some wine, and there were lots of toasts to American and Bulgarian friendship, and our working together in the coming school year.

We also toasted Andrea's 22nd birthday. She was the youngest Peace Corps Volunteer in the group. I did not let on that I was the oldest. Dora drove me back to the Road Star Motel at about 10:30 PM

In the morning Dora picked me up at 8 AM to go to the bus stop as now it was time to catch the bus back to Vratsa, via Sofia and then back to Banitsa for our last month of training. All in all, a super week and I am looking forward to moving there. My main goal now is to get a better handle on the language.

SWEARING-IN CEREMONY

Letter sent to my children, siblings, and friends:

Today I am filled with such a variety of emotions. This past week has been filled with a mixture of emotions and events that it's difficult to know where to begin.

I am indeed at another road of new beginnings, along with 61 other Americans who were sworn in yesterday and was known as the "swearing in" ceremony. We say the same oath that is issued to the President of the United States on Inauguration Day. Wow! Reading and thinking of what I as a person am committed to is indeed daunting and exhilarating at the same time.

I'll recap a bit, and then fill you in with some of the events.

We (the volunteers) all had somewhat different "home stays" as our first 2-months is called. The village and area where we were at is one of the poorer regions of the country. But even in a village, as in America, some have more than others.

My *baba* was nice, but very poor living on an income I think of around maybe 30 euros per month – certainly not more. She basically lives off her garden and spends her limited cash on the very bare necessities, e.g., laundry soap, bread, basic food things that she doesn't grow. She had learned to make do, and so even keeping items refrigerated or reheating food was generally not done. She has a small refrigerator but often had it unplugged. This is the case here for many of the "pensioners."

She has a married son, who lives nearby and he was there much of the time. He too was retired, from either the military or a job with transportation; it never was clear to me. He was convinced that I was from California. And like many misconceptions of Americans, he had the feeling that if you're from California you must be rich.

The reason for the California idea is that I have used Marcus' address for my in-country mailing address so California is on all the Peace Corps information. He also was constantly correcting my speech and so did not help my self-confidence at all.

I always had classes with the three other young volunteers housed in the same village. Now we are scattered throughout the country. And while the country is not large, because of the mountains, rivers and plains and many older highways, two from my group in Banitsa are now over seven hours away from me, and Anna at least three or four hours away.

Most of us left yesterday for our permanent site; the rest leave today depending on their transportation arrangement. I was able to travel with a young woman from Ohio who is assigned to the nearby town of Aitos (pronounced *itos*).

Aitos is only a half hour away from Topolitsa by car. Her counterpart is Pauli, a very nice Bulgarian woman in her mid-forties who teaches English in Aitos. Her teenage son Ruslan is excellent in English and goes to a language school in Burgas. He is also studying German and knows Russian. Your counterpart is the teacher that you are assigned to work with at your school.

Pauli is friends with the director of my school here in Topolitsa. Tantayna who also lives in Aitos and speaks very little English, will serve as my counterpart. Pauli's family was one of the few who drove to Vratsa for the swearing in ceremony. They left Aitos at 3 AM to be there for the 10:30 ceremony.

It was a very hot day, over 100 degrees Fahrenheit. I heard it was 44 degrees Celsius in Sofia.

Andrea and I both had lots of stuff. Besides the items we brought with us, Peace Corps has been supplying us with books and lesson plans, along with a medical kit, fire extinguisher, smoke alarm, and other essential items.

Before and after the ceremony, many pictures were taken and news reporters were around. Official embassy representatives spoke, along with our country director at the ceremony, and we the Peace Corps Volunteers had elected two representatives to speak for us. They had to do their speech, both in English and Bulgarian. The second one who spoke I believe scored the highest on our language examination. He was excellent. I was in awe of the skills he has developed. Everything was done in Bulgarian and English, except the oath was only in English. I'm not sure why that wasn't translated into Bulgarian.

Most of the host families do not speak English and were in the audience as special guests. There were over 300 in attendance. Afterwards there was a reception in the municipal building and we were all given a red rose. I have mine drying today. Obviously even a Bulgarian rose can't survive the heat.

Bulgaria is one of the biggest exporters of rose oil and in the spring there are many fields of roses. Now, all along the way from the car window we saw fields of sunflowers waiting to be harvested for seeds or oil. Most of the wheat has already been cut and put into big bales.

As for my language skills I'm not sure what to say. It's coming, but slowly. Peace Corps passed many of us conditionally, and we are required to find a tutor in our area and continue to take classes four to six hours a week and have another exam in three months. They encourage all volunteers to continue to take lessons. Lessons with a tutor are required if you passed below the intermediate level. I was one step below, novice high. That used to be the passing mark, but no longer. There are 10 to 12 levels.

One person from my village group got a six. So while I'm making progress, it still is frustrating for me to accept how slow my progress is going. I know more vocabulary, but to be able to call on it as needed is daunting. And of course, a person comes in with an American accent, so even though you might be using the correct word, your pronunciation is different. And there are gender forms, like in German and many languages and I often forget the correct form, e.g., bread (*hlap*) for bread is masculine, *domate* for tomato is feminine and tea (*chai*) is neuter.

And the part that really is troublesome to me, if I remember the gender I also need to remember that the personal pronoun is usually added to the verb. So if you are speaking or asking about her the ending on the verb is different from you. It's sort of like a crossword puzzle I guess and hopefully with time I will manage. Past tense uses the H sound at the end of the verb and my tongue just can't get around that sound. The word for bread is still misunderstood by most Bulgarians when I say it. A slice of bread is called *felea* so I often use that word instead.

This last month I was helped a great deal by Nikolai, a special tutor who worked one on one with me at least five different times. But as he teaches at the Sofia University and lives there I need to find a tutor in my new region, the Black Sea area near Burgas. He did come down by bus for the swearing in ceremony and continues to cheer me on.

The car ride was hot. There is a fairly good expressway from Sofia over here, but we were five in the car, an Opel and no AC. Every corner of the car was packed with our stuff.

We left Vratsa around 1:30 and arrived at 8:30 in Aitos. We stopped for lunch at a very modern mall along the way, and later a stop at a Metro store. The Metro is similar to Walmart or a Sam's Club. We bought a few household supplies. We were very limited on our purchases due to space and heat. We did have a drink of cold water and a *lolli,* which is sort of like a fruitsicle. This was the first time I saw such a store in Bulgaria. I understand there is also one in Burgas so hopefully I'll be able to check that out later this summer or in the fall.

At my Banitsa village the magazines had only a small selection of food and sundry items. Beer, wine, *serenade* (white cheese made with either goat or cow's milk), and *bosa* or *boza* could also be bought there. *Boza* is a traditional drink similar to Brewer's Yeast for those who remember that hardy protein drink from the 1970s.

Andrea was dropped off at her apartment in Aitos, where my director met me and all my stuff was transferred to her car. She has been studying English and we managed to communicate fairly well. It's about a half-hour car ride in the country out to my village which is more in the mountains, so it felt a bit cooler.

My apartment I must say is terrific. I had one of the nicer apartments of the volunteers. The house was owned by a Turkish woman whose children are grown. She met us at the door, along with a friend who also worked at the village school where I'll be teaching. They all helped carry my belongings up to the second floor, which was all mine. Peace Corps requires for safety reasons all volunteers have rooms on the second floor or higher in an apartment or a house.

I had five rooms, plus bathroom and kitchen. My director had arranged for the Internet to be installed right away, so that is why I'm able to do this long email. It took her over an hour to get it configured, but here it is. In the meantime, my landlady was serving me dinner. She set six red stuffed peppers with rice and ground meat and fresh cantaloupe before me. I couldn't believe it as I've had very little fresh fruit so far. I also was served *tarator*, cold yogurt soup with cucumber and spices. This is a specialty of Bulgaria. She also served me bread and creme caramel for dessert which is very similar to creme brûlée.

This of course was way more than I could eat at one sitting, but it is the traditional Bulgarian way of welcoming a guest. It would have to qualify as one of my best meals so far. Now of course I'll be doing my own cooking. I do have a nice little kitchen. It includes a small refrigerator. I have really missed having cold drinks. I also have a small two burner electric stove on top with an oven beneath the burners about the size of one lasagna pan. It is doesn't have a rack so not sure about chocolate chip cookies or other things that need space around them for cooking. Later today I'll find the magazine, a small general store and buy some basics for my new kitchen.

On Monday I'll go into Aitos and look for some appliances: coffee pot and toaster are high on my list. I also hope to buy a mixing bowl and a few utensils. It'll slowly come together so when you visit I'll be all set

Two of the rooms have a balcony so this morning I have the windows and doors open and I'm feeling a breeze. As with many European countries, the custom is for closed doors.

In Bulgaria especially the older generation is leery of drafts, so this was a real treat for me to have a breeze blowing through. But flies did come in as I have not screens on any of my windows. But with two balconies overlooking grape vines and garden I cannot complain. I can tell already that it will be a warm day, probably about 39° C, but I will unpack and settle in. Another time I'll describe the rooms more. My main room has an enclosed porch with some windows that open and a few windows that are broken. It overlooks the street by my house.

Having the Internet at my home and to be able to use it in the evening or morning is terrific. It will still be nice to get letters. I don't have a printer, so newspapers and magazines in English for me will still be a treat. Loren, I await your packet. Thank you, thank you.

This has become a long email. I got a text message from Gretchen this morning which was super. If others of you have cell phones that text, I can do that occasionally as well. Talking internationally is still expensive but small text messages are not too terribly expensive.

I hope to get Skype set up so let me know if you have this and I'll figure out what to do at this end. I did try texting a few of you around the 4th of July, but so far have only heard back from Gretchen. Amazing how many people here have cell phones and do everything with it, pay bills, play music, photos, and more. I will look through the photos that I've downloaded on my computer and send a few of them out to you today or tomorrow under a separate email attachment.

The sun is coming in brightly now, so think I will finish this up and get to unpacking. My clothes are in need of some attention. I did not prepare for such warm weather so have limited choices to wear and must launder often. My landlady does have a line on one of the balconies with some clothespins, so I will take advantage of it.

Thanks for all your encouragement. Bulgaria is a very interesting country and the people very welcoming. If I can just manage the language everything else will fall in place.

Hope to hear from you soon. I should be able to use either yahoo or gmail here, so which ever you prefer is okay.

All the best sent with a big hug and love, Louise

Hi Mom,   **July 26, 2009**

Congratulations on your swearing in ceremony. What an honor. From this end, the two months seems to have passed quickly. I'm glad to hear that the people are gracious; that will certainly make the time pass better.

I'm in the midst of packing to move to a new apartment. I will borrow a friend's truck for an afternoon on the 29th to move my stuff up the street to my new apartment. Sounds like your apartment and Internet access are just as good as mine To set up my Internet, I'll have to deal with the local cable company which is always an ordeal.

I also start working under new grants/projects in August. I'm almost entirely back to Antarctic- focused work. I am excited about that.

More later, maybe from my new home . . . Love, David

ASSIGNMENT

Hi David,   **July 26, 2009**

So happy to hear from you. And indeed more changes for you. It sounds like you'll have this apartment by yourself? How big is it? Hopefully it will give you enough room to set up an office and feel like "home".

Yesterday the landlady, Milka came up to see how I was doing. I think she was surprised that I hadn't yet eaten all the stuffed peppers that she had prepared for the night before. I think she had made about ten of them. These are the long green peppers and a few yellow and red peppers stuffed with rice and ground meat. Quite tasty. Todora also fixed them often, but she usually served them cold I have a hard time eating some foods cold.

I tried to explain to Milka that I preferred to eat them warm. The Bulgarian word for hot is *goresht*. I wrote it out then in Bulgarian letters and so she put her hand on the little 2-burner stove in my apartment – no heat. Apparently my stove does not work.

She went downstairs to her apartment and came up with this antiquated electric fry pan, I guess it is. It has no heat controls, just a coil. She placed that over the pan and so the peppers were heated like a broil. Amazingly it worked

This morning I carefully put a pan on it to heat some water so I had a cup of tea and then found a pan that sort of worked to fry an egg with it. Necessity is the mother of invention. I do hope they will find me a stove that works.

I will have to find a coffee pot, maybe a French press style or one of those electric heating kettles like Hyacinth used in "Keeping up Appearances." The only other main item I find lacking is a mirror. I have a little hand one with my compact, so I can manage. Often I lack patience.

The floors are lovely. My hall looks like marble actually and there are beautiful Turkish rugs on the room floors over the linoleum which is over the cement floor.

There is lots and lots of yogurt here, *kiselo mlyako* it is called in Bulgarian. I still have to walk around the village. It feels bigger than Banitsa and certainly is cleaner. I haven't noticed the litter on the streets like was strewn all over Banitsa.

After my lunch Milka walked with me to the magazine and I bought *kiselo mlyako*, oil, vinegar *otsem* in Bulgarian. It must be similar to vinegar because when I look it up in my dictionary I can't find that word, but that is the spelling on the jar and that is what is used for a dressing on tomatoes and cucumbers which is the mainstay salad here.

I think that you will be happy being back in Antarctica research. It takes special people to focus on this and put the time and talent into studying the patterns of our planet earth. I am so very proud of you and the research that you do. I tell everyone about you. "sine me David is ecolog – juveetee stat Colorado grad Boulder."

I look forward for when you come for a visit. Hopefully my Bulgarian will be better and I can get us around. My language tutor who lives in Sofia I know will help us. I think much of his time is spent in writing articles on historical topics, and he too attends conferences much like you do. He has been to Boston and New York City and I think did his Ph.D. in English in Prague. That background certainly helps him in helping to understand Americans such as me.

Good luck with your move. I was so thankful that I had so much help when I moved. Your box came in handy. I filled it very full and it served as another suitcase.

In Cyrillic, a special symbol is used for the JU sound, c = s, upside down N is long E. Slowly it's coming to me. And to add to my confusion at times when looking up words in the Pons dictionary their letters are in a different order than our English alphabet.

Please take care. I look forward to hearing about your move and more about your new position.

I love you, Mom

Dear Mr. Higgins *aka* **Nicolai,**   **July 21, 2009**

As the song goes "the rain in Spain falls mainly in the plains." I went in with courage to the interview (AKA test) and did get wet, but I did not drown. Without your help this last month I would have failed the language examination. You have helped me see that learning a new language can be a pleasant experience. Thank you Mr. Higgins for your confidence in me.

Last night the "Banitsa group" met at the pool and we all had *perjane kartofe*. We taught Lazar how to play UNO. It was great fun. We played almost until dark. Luben had the water drained out of the pool for cleaning, so there was no swimming.

On Friday I will be going via car to Aitos. Andrea's director is coming to the Peace Corps ceremony and she has room for me and all my stuff. My book bag will be filled with language books, language notebooks (most important), papers from Peace Corps, my dictionary, Bulgaria Lonely Planet, etc. Please recommend some other books on Bulgaria in English for me to read. Perhaps I can find a few in Burgas.

What is the name please of your village? Population? Please describe it for me. I already miss my language lesson.

Elisa *aka* Louise

Dear Louise,   **July 22, 2009**

Thank you so much for email. Thank you so much for the nice words. It was indeed a pleasure for me to work with you and to help you feel the wonderful feeling of learning a new language.

Thank you for the good news with the interview (aka test). I am happy that you did not drown but I had indeed no fear about it. You were really very stable in the main topics and questions which were viewed the last week, so there was no real danger of drowning.

It is so nice that you enjoyed so much your last days in Banitsa. I felt sad that I was not with you, but I hope there will be a chance to learn to play UNO some day.

I will think about possible books to recommend on Bulgaria. Are they to be taken from the Peace Corps office or ordered from Amazon.com? Maybe in Burgas it will be possible to find some useful travel and history guides.

I also miss the wonderful stay in Banitsa and will be looking forward to meeting you all soon in Vratsa at the ceremony. I will travel Friday morning to Vratsa, so we will see each other there.

With best wishes and greetings to all the Banitsa group, Nikolai

Dear Nikolai,   **July 26, 2009**

I was so happy that you could come to the swearing in ceremony. It meant a lot to me. I had not seen your email so I was very happily surprised to see you. The time flew by and I hated to leave so quickly afterwards. It was very kind for Pauli and her family to drive to Vratsa and do the round trip in the same day.

Their car was packed with suitcases and people. Ruslan squeezed in the middle between Andrea and me. Pauli said the temperature was over 40 Celsius in Sofia on Friday is that correct? I didn't know that Sofia got so hot. It has been hot here too and last night lots of wind and several big branches tore off of trees, but very little rain.

After about two hours of riding we stopped for lunch at a restaurant in a new mall. I don't know the name. Andrea and I both had a green salad and shared a serving of potatoes and ham made with butter and milk. We have something similar in the U.S. called scalloped potatoes. It was very good. I also had cold tea with ice. I didn't realize how much I missed very cold drinks, especially on warm days. Then it was back to the hot car.

We stopped again near Stara Zagora at a big store called Metro. They wanted us to see it and suggested we buy some things for our apartment. We could only buy small items as the car already was full. I did buy a few toiletries. Then Andrea saw Heinz ketchup, which she really missed. We both bought a jar of ketchup. Now I will have to make *Purjunee kartofee*.

We arrived at Andrea's apartment in Aitos about 8:30. It was very hot and I think we were stuck together. My director met me there and we loaded my stuff in her car and drove to Topolitsa. My landlady Milka, was here to greet me and had dinner prepared for me. What a treat. Stuffed peppers with rice and meat, fresh melon and creme caramel. Super. And now I have Internet set up in my apartment.

As this is already a long email I will tell you about my apartment and Topolitsa next time. Tomorrow I will apply for my *lichna karte*; (an identity card required of all adults living in Bulgaria and needs to be renewed each year and every time you move to a new location.) Every day is filled with a new adventure.

I would like some ideas of books to buy either in Burgas or through Amazon. How does the postage work? Does Amazon charge "in country" rates? History, biography or novels set in Bulgaria would all be of interest to me. I have Lonely Planet and Rough Guide Bulgaria travel books.

I know I can't find a better teacher than you. I will look for somebody nearby who can help me learn your language so that I can move on to the next level. I am so happy that you were in Banitsa and that we could become friends.

Sincerely, Louise

Dear Louise,   **July 22, 2009**

Thank you for your company and support during our PST (pre-service training) in Banitsa. I really appreciated the time we spent together and also for your sharing your wisdom/stories with me. My first memory of you was in D.C. when we had to do a PSA for Malaria pills: you conducted the buzzing mosquito choir. Can you believe it is now ten weeks later and we're off to our new sites?

I know you'll do great in Topolitsa, the kids and staff will love you and are fortunate to have you there to help. Be confident and strong. I know you have it in you to speak Bulgarian with the best of them. Don't worry so much about it because it will come.

I'll miss you lots and will write and text. You're always welcome in Lom. Good Luck.

Always, Diana

P.S. I'm so glad to have met you and have you in our Banitsa family.

Dear Louise,   **July 31, 2009**

Thank you so much for sending us your letters. I have read and reread yours and am constantly amazed at what you are doing and how much you are learning and enjoying it. I am going to start reading about Bulgaria so I have a better idea of its history. Somehow that never came up in any of my classes. Please keep sending your letters. May you continue in good health and keep on learning and loving it

With our love and prayers, Jeanne and Dick

Hello Jeanne and Dick,   **August 1, 2009**

How nice to hear from you. Now I have email at my apartment so this will make it easier to keep in touch. I am thinking perhaps of doing a general letter every several months. Not sure if I will always have news. For now, I need to learn the language so much better.

Topolitsa is a nice village, but I do feel isolated as it only has two small shops that I've found so far. It also has a cafe, but I have only seen men at them.

The town of Aitos is close by but I don't know the bus schedule yet. It is not very often. That is my project for Monday. Also I need to find a tutor. There is no one in the village who speaks English. My school director speaks a little, but she lives in Aitos.

There are not too many history books in English on Bulgaria, but I think you would enjoy reading *Bury Me Standing*, by Isabel Fonseca. It is the story of the Roma peoples in Bulgaria and other places of Europe. There are some Roma people here, also Turkish.

Lonely Planet Bulgaria is good for an overview and they also have a list of other books to read.

I've invited my director and two teachers from Aitos and the PCV who lives there over tonight for my birthday. I am making a modified version of my heavenly spaghetti using *siranade*. Wish me luck. I have a two burner stove and small oven. I hope this works.

Your prayers and love are most welcome, please keep in touch,
Louise

P.S. PC does not allow us to drive cars, so we need to rely completely on public transport. We can ride with other local teachers if available; a few teachers have cars.

BULGARIA UPDATE, JULY 2009

I have been in Bulgaria over two months. On Friday I participated in the swearing in ceremony along with the 61 other volunteers who came over with me in May from Washington, D.C. We took the same oath as the President of the U.S. takes when he becomes President. It was a very special moment in my life. I hope that I will have the stamina, courage and skill to be a volunteer for America here in Bulgaria.

The ten weeks that we had in preparation were very busy and intense. We went to classes and/or meetings six days a week. Sunday we did special projects and laundry.

It was helpful having three other volunteers in the village of Banitsa with me. We sometimes took walks in the evening, or met at one of the nearby cafés to review lessons, talk about family and what we hoped to accomplish in the Peace Corps. The 61 volunteers of our B25 group were located in 14 villages around Vratsa in northwest Bulgaria. (One young volunteer who flew over with us from Washington D.C. decided to return within two days of coming to Bulgaria. This is not unusual as many realize almost immediately that they are not ready for this type of service.)

At least once a week we took the local bus into Vratsa for a meeting with some or all of the other volunteers. We were given instructions on safety and medical, teaching ideas and planning. We visited nearby Roma neighborhoods to learn more about this culture in Bulgaria and throughout Europe. We discussed ideas for community projects.

Most of our group has recently graduated from college; there are a few in their thirties, and I believe only five of us over 50, including one couple. I am the oldest of the group.

About four weeks into training we left our village one morning at 6:15 AM by car. Anna's Peace Corps "dad" drove us into Vratsa so that we could catch the 7:10 AM bus to Sofia. Lazar, our language trainer went with us.

In the regular school year Lazar teaches Bulgarian literature at a high school. I was also able to have some one-on-one classes with Nikolai, another language teacher who works now with the Peace Corps on an "as needed basis." He speaks several languages besides Bulgarian and English and teaches history at Sofia University.

Bulgarian history goes back to pre-Roman days and is fascinating to me. Sadly not too many books have been translated into English. One day at our HUB meeting we heard a discussion from some of the Peace Corps staff who lived and went to school during the Communist occupation. It was a very repressive time for Bulgarians and they lived under constant surveillance of their activities. Journals and more accounts of this time period are gradually coming out and being translated into English. It was the central place where the entire PCV group met, usually once a week at a language school in Vratsa.

(Additional history from my notes: Since the Wall came down and the Eastern European countries declared their independence its been a big adjustment for Bulgaria and the other countries. Even during the harshest time under Communist rule, most Bulgarians valued family, traditions and their religious heritage even though this aspect of their life needed to be underground. Bulgaria, along with Albania, Denmark and Finland were the only countries in WWII who did not send their Jewish population to Jewish concentration camps as Hitler told them to do. The King worked with the church officials and others in the Bulgarian government and basically helped contain them in Bulgaria, hiding them if necessary. At that time there were about 50,000 Jewish people living in the country. King Boris died mysteriously in 1943 after returning from a visit to Germany. His wife died soon afterwards. The two children, Louise and Simone, were taken first to Egypt and then to Spain and lived there until 1996 when Simone returned to Bulgaria and was elected Prime Minister in 2001. In 1944 Bulgaria tried to withdraw from supporting the Axis regime altogether. It was at this time that the Soviets came in and declared war on Bulgaria. On September 16 the Soviet army entered Sofia and a coup d'etat followed.)

In all, we had about 200 hours of language classes, with other times learning about the cultural of the country, and Peace Corps goals and objectives. While in Sofia we went to the Peace Corps headquarters and had individual interviews with either the country director, Lesley or her Assistant Phil. Phil recently moved here with his family from Colorado. Both Lesley and Phil were former Peace Corps Volunteers. Many of the full time American Peace Corps staff started as Peace Corps Volunteers.

The medical staff, education team leaders, resource library and personnel necessary to assist the 135+ PC volunteers who serve in Bulgaria have offices at the headquarters here at 24 Pirinski Prohod Street, 1680 Sofia. Most of the full-time support staff, language teachers and medical team were Bulgarians.

In Sofia and other larger Bulgarian cities there are language schools, where children can learn and take most of their lessons in English or another foreign language. The plan is to have English lessons for all students in Bulgarian schools starting at grade two. Up until a few years ago, most village schools had lessons in Russian, but not English.

I will be teaching some adult classes in English, as well as the children at the village school. I am also hoping to have a music class teaching the recorder, but I need to find someone or some school in the U.S. or some company to supply me with recorders. I'm open to ideas and suggestions.

Sofia is a modern city with museums, music halls, hotels, traffic, buses and many shops. We had about two hours of free time and visited the historic Aleksandur Nevski Memorial Church built by the Russians as a memorial to their soldiers who helped gain freedom for the Bulgarians under the Ottoman Empire.

We saw the buildings of Parliament and had ice tea at the Academic Café by the University. It was a very hot day with the temperature going over 100. Before long it was time to catch a bus that went back to Vratsa and on to our village. The cost one way was 12 lev, about $9. Unfortunately, the bus had no air conditioning and it was very crowded and very hot. Some people had to stand for over two hours.

After the swearing in ceremony, I went via car with Andrea, another volunteer and her counterpart for the drive to my new home in the village of Topolitsa. It took over seven hours. It was a hot day with the temperature over 100 degrees and again no air conditioning. This was a very nice family, whose teenage son Ruslan, speaks very good English. The dad doesn't speak any English, and Pauli, the mom speaks some English. Andrea is a recent graduate from Ohio University and will be working at two schools in Aitos.

On the way we stopped at a modern mall and had lunch. Near Stara Zagora we stopped at a big store called Metro, similar to a Walmart. Zagora is also the name of a popular Bulgarian beer which is brewed there. Beer and wine are very popular here, but *Rakia* is the national drink. It seems almost every home grows their own grapes and makes their own wine and *Rakia*.

Yesterday Andrea and I along with our counterparts, the director or teacher at school who works with us directly went into Burgas to register for a *lichna karte* (identity card). It is similar to a driver's license, or passport. Bulgarians also need it, but they don't have to renew it unless they move. They can use it in place of a passport for travel between the Slavic and EU countries. Foreigners need to renew it every year. It is quite a process as you have to have documentation on where you live, work, family history and citizenship. It must be carried with you at all times. There is a steep fine if it is lost. If all goes well, it will be ready in several weeks. Then we will go back and pick it up. In the meantime, we have documentation to show that we have applied for it.

I am fortunate to have a very nice apartment here in the village of Topolitsa. My landlady is a Turkish widow woman who is refurbishing her house. I have the entire second floor to myself. I have several balconies where I can hang my laundry or just look out over the countryside. This village is less than an hour from Burgas so it has some commuters living here. Many of the older homes are being refurbished. It is less than thirty minutes from Aitos and sits next to a mountain, which makes it cooler than the city. It has several magazines (small stores) for buying everyday necessities like *hlyab* (bread), *kiselo mlyako*, (yogurt) *domate* (tomatoes), some meat and of course cheese. It's mainly white cheese made from goat's milk, called *seranade*. For more groceries or other sundries, I will travel by bus into Aitos or ride back with the school director as she lives in Aitos. So far, I haven't met anyone here who speaks English. Thus I have had very limited conversations with any Bulgarians who live in my village.

I have Internet in my apartment so that will be helpful. I can walk to the school which is about a half mile away. This morning I turned the wrong direction and ended up at the wrong end of the village. I made my way back to my apartment and started out again. It certainly is helpful to speak a few words to ask directions, but the first man I asked didn't understand my Bulgarian word for school, *uchilishte*.

I now feel more comfortable with the Cyrillic alphabet, but still have trouble on many of the pronunciations and where to place the accent. I'm writing the words out in this letter in the Latin to help in pronunciation. My director might get me a Cyrillic keyboard for my computer. Gender is most important in the verb usage, and the pronoun is added to the verb like in other foreign languages. The ending also changes for the present, past or future tense. I still have a long way to go to feel comfortable with the language.

Tomorrow I will have the opportunity to visit the town of Nesebar. It is a UNESCO site and written up in many of the travel books. I will be going with Andrea and her counterparts by car. As Peace Corps workers we aren't allow to drive, but we can ride in a car. I am thinking of buying a bicycle, both for exercise and perhaps to drive into Aitos by myself when the weather gets cooler.

I will send some pictures separately of some of the events in my previous village. Our community project was cleaning up and painting the local bus stop. It was a full day project and we had people from the community helping us including children, the mayor and school director. For the election held July 5, many posters were pasted around town, including the bus stop walls. Local residents use this as a bulletin board, especially to put up death notices. There is an official bulletin board to do this. Some even erect a special box by their house. The bus stop is also used. With no nearby trash cans, there was litter everywhere. It had not been painted in years. I will send some before and after pictures.

Some days we walked in the fields of sunflowers just outside the village. We walked everywhere and most residents knew who we were. Most could not speak English, but did find a few who had learned it at their job or in school. One young boy of ten spends the summer with his *baba* but attends language school in Sofia and spoke it very well. *Baba* is the word for grandmother, and generally all elderly women are called *baba*. Grandfather is *dyado*.

Many homes have three generations of family living in the same house or with families close by who visit on the weekend. My *baba* was a widow whose son stayed in the village most of the time while his family was in Vratsa. He helped with the gardening and repaired stuff. He was retired serving in the military for 25 years.

My previous village was very poor. I'm not sure how it is figured, but older pensioners receive around $60 US a month. That is why the garden is so very important to them as they have little cash. During the Communist era, many were able to build their home as they were given, or had a plot of land. Also, many of the younger men with families are now working in other European countries as good jobs here are hard to find.

Most items cost about the same as in the United States. The imported items cost much more than in the U.S. Only locally produced items are cheap, like garden produce.

Teachers particularly are underpaid and so the need there is great. Our language teacher said he was the oldest male teacher at his school. He was in his early fifties. Many leave teaching as they can't support their families. Most women work, although mothers with babies do have a year long maternity leave which can be extended an additional year without pay and without losing their job.

It is a beautiful country with many green hills, a wide variety of birds, lovely gardens filled with flowers and vegetables. Younger folks drive cars, but most are older vehicles.

Topolitsa is about six hours from Istanbul. Perhaps next summer I may be able to visit there. First I have to learn the language more and prepare for this coming school year. Hopefully later in the year I can visit many of the fascinating and historical places of this country where I will be living for the next two years.

Several volunteers are doing blogs. For more information on the Peace Corps program go to *www.peacecorps.gov.* If you have interest in working with your school and a school here in Bulgaria, look at the following web site: *www.peacecorps.gov/wws/.*

I hope the Coverdell World Wise Schools Program may be of interest to some of you. I would be happy to link up my school here in Topolitsa with another school or two in the states.

Dovizhdane, Louise

LANGUAGE TEACHERS

Dear Nikolai   **August 1, 2009 (my birthday)**

Topolitsa is a very different village from Banitsa. The streets are clean and there are not many animals around. I have not seen any donkey carts and only one horse. On my walk today I saw a few chickens. Each evening around seven o'clock a parade of cows walk past my apartment so I know I'm in the country. I have not seen many people around. Maybe they are all at the Black Sea.

On Wednesday I went with Andrea and her counterparts to Nesebur. There were many tourists and many shops. We only had time to go into one of the churches. I hope I can go back there with more time and less people. In the morning they took us to a nearby beach. That was fun. I loved watching the waves and splashing in them. Like the waves I wish the Bulgarian language would roll over me and then I would know it like magic. But that is not possible so I keep reviewing my red book and my note book. Danni has sent me phone numbers of tutors in Aitos and Burgas so hopefully I can get someone lined up soon.

I invited my school director, Pauli and her family and Andrea for dinner tomorrow night to celebrate my birthday. I read in the *New York Times* that 59 is the new 30, so I have decided that I am now only 45 years old As you told me in class it is sometimes necessary to be creative. If Sofia were closer then you could come to the party also. Milka, my landlady has been giving me fruit and vegetables: melons, grapes, zucchini, tomatoes and peppers. I plan to make a spaghetti dish something like *mussaka* and of course a *shopska salada*.

I was very happy to see you last Friday at the swearing in ceremony. I miss our visits and language classes. Please keep in touch and let me know how you are doing.

Your friend, Louise

Dear Louise,

Please excuse me for replying with such a delay. I was on a work trip in Northwestern Bulgaria and was away from email connection.

Let me first take the chance in the very beginning to greet you for your birthday and to wish you plenty of joy and happiness in Bulgaria, excellent stay in Topolitsa and to enjoy many inspiring events and achievements.

It was a real pleasure reading your emails about your travel to the Black Sea and to Topolitsa, as well as about the wonderful idyllic environment there. It was indeed very hot in the days of your travel and you were lucky that you were close to the sea. In Western Bulgaria it was around 40 degrees Celsius. Luckily, this happens only in late July and rarely in August.

It is really nice that you like Topolitsa. It should be a marvelous village. Hopefully, if not this year, I may be able to travel to the seaside next summer and will be glad to drop by there and see it. I did not know that Nesebur was so close. It is one of the nicest seaside towns in Bulgaria, although it has become very touristy. It is still a pleasure to walk there. There are other nice small towns there too, so don't miss the occasion of the August period before school begins to visit them and enjoy.

The news about trying to find a tutor in Topolitsa are also great. Take the chance to find a tutor as quickly as possible and to continue smoothly the knowledge that you gathered during PST, Peace Corps Training.

Regarding books ordering from Bulgaria, Amazon should be the best one. Everything is from the Internet, but regretfully overseas delivery is only for new books, not for second hand ones. The guides that you mention are certainly good, though for a more involved reader as you are, they may not be sufficient. As you will have Internet at home, you can easily check about texts and publications about Bulgaria online. This is certainly a more convenient and cheaper option.

Well, this is all from me at this point. I wish you a wonderful celebration today and great time with your guests at the birthday party. In a while, I will send you some of the photos from Banitsa and Vratsa that I took. It was really great that we met each other and became friends. I was happy working with you. Hope that we will meet each other soon and continue our conversations.

Looking forward to hearing from you with warm regards from Sofia.

Nikolai

Dear Nikolai, **August 3, 2009**

Thank you for the warm birthday wishes. It was wonderful to be able to celebrate it here in Bulgaria. I hope that is the first of many that I will celebrate here. I received fresh flowers from my guests, and I checked – they were all odd numbers. (An odd number of flowers are seen as bringing good luck, while even numbers of flowers in a bouquet are for funerals.)

I served my spaghetti dish. Ruslan thought it was similar to lasagna. First a layer of cooked spaghetti, then I mixed *siranade* with chopped onions and peppers. *Siranade* seems like a combination of cream cheese and cottage cheese, which I use back home; cheese makes the middle layer.

Milka, my landlady, gave me many tomatoes and peppers, so I used them to make the tomato sauce and added parsley and another herb I found at the bazaar in Aitos. I sautéed mushrooms and onions and added them to the ground meat and combined it with the sauce. That made the top layer. Everyone seemed to like it. Dora fried potatoes for me. I also had fried zucchini. Milka had given me several from her garden. I made the yogurt topping with garlic like I had tasted in Nesebar and I think you told me about. What is the Bulgarian name for this dish? I need to get a garlic press as chopping garlic by hand is not the best method. Andrea made homemade cookies. Everyone liked them and mentioned how different they were from Bulgarian cookies. I enjoy having people over for dinner to try new recipes, but when I'm by myself I usually don't bother. Do you like to cook?

Counting myself, ten were here in my apartment. Pauli's husband Evan could only talk to me in Bulgarian and the other guests enjoyed seeing if I could figure out what he said. In a humorous way, they laughed at my predicament. It was good that Ruslan was here to translate. I got words mixed up, or forgot the word they told me five minutes ago. Dora told me the Bulgarian word for hot pad several times and I still can't remember it today. I received several of them for a gift as they knew I didn't have any for my stove.

Dora is very anxious for me to learn Bulgarian and I hope I don't disappoint her. I think it is difficult though for her to realize how many words and expressions a new person in a country has to learn. I think that is one of the reasons you are such a good teacher for you are very patient and understanding – most of the time Mr. Higgins

I knew that you had done research on memorials and monuments, but I did not realize that you were getting a book published. That is very good news. And indeed it is a lot of work. Will it be in Bulgarian and/ or English? Your Ph.D. was written in English, right? How many pages in your book? Does it have photos? What is the title? Have you done all the research yourself? I would enjoy reading the manuscript of it if it is in English, or another article of yours.

I hope that you don't mind all my questions.

I found some book titles on Amazon. *The Balkans*, a short history by Mark Mazower. *Under the Yoke, Black Sea* by Neal Ascherson and a new author Rana Dasqupta. Do you know of her? I can't figure out if Amazon mails to Bulgaria from the US or UK or how much the postage would be? All I have to read in my apartment are my Bulgarian language books, Lonely Planet Bulgaria and some novels. A novel by Ken Follett is set in London and St. Petersburg right before WW I so started than one for now.

Sometimes I do need a break from *A3* and *TE*. (Bulgarian I and you*)* Dora wants me to get a Bulgarian keyboard. Can you just switch back and forth in languages then? Dora mentioned that I will be going with her and the Topolitsa teachers and some students to a camp by the beach.

She didn't give me the exact dates, but I think the end of this month.

Your former student, Louise

Dear Louise,

I respond again with a delay, but during the week there is hardly time left for non-working emails. I usually return to my private mail over the weekends. I hope that you are doing fine and the life in Topolitsa runs smooth and pleasant, as in all existing paradise worlds.

I was happy to read that you had such a wonderful birthday celebration, though I regretted that I missed such a joyful event and such wonderful treats.

All the dishes that you describe sound marvelous and it was certainly a great birthday celebration. I do not cook myself and generally do not bother for preparing cooked food for myself, I have always admired people who have culinary skills and who enjoy cooking.

I am very glad that people around are eager to help you in learning Bulgarian. I have no doubt that little by little your vocabulary will expand a lot. Don't forget to keep me updated of how your learning is going and what new things have been learned and used in speech.

As for my research on monuments, it is based on my dissertation, which was written in English and which was strongly recommended to submit for publication. I have updated the text with new materials and photos, and within a month or so I hope I will have it polished enough for a book format. In the meantime I will need to find a good publisher.

The text is long; around 350 pages only text. There are also appendices and photos, which in the original dissertation text were 66, but can be more in the book form. I have not decided about the fixed number yet.

The title of the book is *Monuments between Life and Death: Memory and Representation in Monuments after 1944 in Bulgaria*. The research was done only by myself and currently I am the sole person considered as "specialist" on this topic. For the last research trips actually I traveled with an Italian colleague, who is interested in the topic and helped me in organizing the travel and making new visual documentation of these memorial sites.

The manuscript is English. I will be happy to send it to you. There are several articles that appeared on the basis of this text, which will be even easier to send as well. I will make a selection and will do that in my next message.

The books that you mentioned as ordered from the Amazon are really nice. I have heard of most of the authors, but not Rana Dasqupta.

About posting, I think that they deliver the Amazon books from U.S., but I am not sure. Maybe it depends on the book. The information about postage will certainly appear when you make an order. I have ordered books from Amazon just once and I remember that it depended roughly on the book price, but generally being about $10 US for postage.

Regarding the keyboard, there will not be a problem to switch in between keys. It depends on what combination it is set in. Most often it is CNTRL+Shift or ALT+Shift buttons. You can always do it by clicking on the sign of "EN" or "BG" at your right-hand lower part of the screen list.

Best wishes on the seaside, which I believe you visit in these August days, Nikolai

Dear Nikolai,   **August 13, 2009**

This has been a crazy mixed up week for me. I almost called you several times, but I knew that you were busy and it wasn't a crisis, but I was just so frustrated. I thought I understood bureaucracy to a certain extent, but I think not.

It has taken me three trips to Burgas to receive a package Marcus mailed from California around July 28.

Unfortunately he listed the contents as worth $60 and it weighed more than two kilos. The box had some old clothes, shoes, and a word game I can use with the students and jelly beans for my birthday. I'm still not sure if it was the weight or the declared price of $105 that presented the biggest problem or the red shoes. I had to describe them in detail to one custom official. They are ten-year-old shoes.

And, by pure coincidence a package my sister LeAnne mailed from Wisconsin arrived in Sofia or Burgas, not sure which, the same day. Hers was a smaller package and contained only clothes, but as they arrived the same day, another red flag.

Here I thought when the note came to the Topolitsa Post Office, it simply meant that I had to pay the extra fees in Burgas and I would be on my way.

Not so fast Louise. Forms, paperwork, documentation all had to be filled out and given to the proper person. On the second day, I thought for sure I would get the package, but by the time Dora and I arrived back at the "old" post office, the customs window was closed.

I was so frustrated. Today I took the 8 AM train from Topolitsa to Aitos, and Dora met me there with her car and we were the first to arrive at customs and I got my package. For some reason, the postal woman decided to let me have my sister's package that first day. Maybe she didn't want to see a grown woman cry. Why I ever thought I was a patient person I don't know. It certainly is a virtue I do not seem to have.

Good news: I found out that Pauli and her family are going to Shipka this week end to visit her grandmother and they have invited me to go along. I have read a little about Shipka and am excited to be given this opportunity.

I do hope that you have had a good week working on your manuscript and that you will tell me about it and how life is like on the other side of Bulgaria.

Thank you for "listening" to my tale. I look forward to hearing from you, Warm greetings, Louise

Dear Louise,   **August 20, 2009**

Finally, after a long delay, I succeed in writing a response to your two emails. And, as I believe, you are having a pleasant stay in Topolitsa in this summer period, I am relaxed about any challenge that you may face with life in your new site. For that reason, your frustration with the package from U.S. surprised me a lot. Then, after thinking about it for a while I decided that you are a courageous woman and you will not give up that easily with bureaucratic issues, which generally abound in Bulgaria.

The story about the box contents and about the three trips to Burgas sounded very comic and, although I can imagine how serious it was, it is still worth describing in an essay. I know, it had been quite unpleasant, but situations like this are numerous in Bulgaria. You should not feel too discouraged or surprised with only one of a kind. In any case, I admire your patience, as – honestly, I would have made a huge scandal with such a situation. Not that it would have changed anything, but just for the purpose of therapeutic effect.

As for me, I am doing fine and accomplishing substantial pieces of work. The work on my manuscript proceeds, although with a slower pace than expected. I already have some articles that appeared on the basis of this research and I will send them to you, no problem. For the entire manuscript the publishing will be more difficult, but I will think about this when having finished the manuscript itself. The most plausible options are the publishing houses in Budapest or a German publishing house, with which I am currently in contact. I was delighted to hear about your interest in my story about the salami on Tuesday. It was a really very funny situation, no matter that it too was so sad in fact. It would not be a problem for you to write about this situation, but as you may remember I have already presented it in brief in one of my Bulgarian articles on the communist period and, so to say, it is not a "new" one.

Some of the students who read the article were asking me to expand on the story at one of my lectures, which I may do some day, but even if not, it has already appeared published as a short description. Of course, there will not be a problem to tell you more about it when we meet, as I also enjoy talking about this crazy situation.

How is your tutor experience going? Have you succeeded taking language sessions already? I would be extremely happy to hear about the first steps done in that direction and about the first achievements made. We both know how important speaking some Bulgarian to people around your community is and that is why making progress in the language will help you so much.

Did you go to Shipka area already? How was it?

With best wishes for enjoyment and happy spirit in Topolitsa,

Nikolai

Dear Nikolai,

I am happy that you will let me write about your salami story. I am thinking perhaps of a children's book. I need you to tell it to me again and I would ask some questions about the school, your mother, the students and teacher. This will be a good project for me to begin this winter.

Shipka appears worn as a village, but it certainly has a rich history. We walked up the path to the monastery which was beautiful as it was recently refurbished.

But even more interesting to me was Pauli's grandmother who was 98 years old. She is an amazing woman and had a wealth of stories to share. How I wished you could have been there to hear them. Her grandfather, or maybe it was her great-grandfather, was involved in the fight at the pass. She also had stories about the First World War. During the summer she lives in a small worn house in Shipka with a beautiful garden and in the winter lives with her son in Sofia.

As it was her name day, St. Maria, many villagers stopped by to wish her well. The guests included a linguistic professor from St. Petersburg. Perhaps you know him, I believe his name is Victor , sorry I don't remember his last name.

We had a pleasant conversation in English and he gave me much encouragement on learning Bulgarian. His wife is from Shipka so they visit Shipka in the summer. I probably heard more Bulgarian last weekend than all my time in Banitsa.

I could pick up some of the conversations. Ruslan translated his great-grandmother's stories for me. I did get to see the Freedom Monument and two Thracian temples and vaults. I will send some pictures. I still have difficulty with bread and the past tense verbs. My director means well. She gets many phone calls and as people drop in her office, my language lessons with her feel very erratic. She had me buy a CD called *Bulgarian for Foreigners.* It is OK, but I think face-to-face lessons are much better.

Sunday I am meeting a tutor in Aitos who I hope will be able to have regular lessons with me.

I usually read in the evening for maybe an hour, or while I am eating lunch or dinner. Now I am reading *To Chicago and Back* and enjoying

Konstantinov's descriptions very much. Some things in America have not changed since his visit in 1893

I think I gave you the wrong spelling of the author of the *Solo* book. He is featured on the cover of this month's *Vagabond* magazine and his name is Rana Dasgupta. A quote from the review: In its 350 pages it depicts Bulgaria and what all of us now know as the "Bulgarian condition" better than most Bulgarian-born Bulgarian-language writers have done in the course of years." The book sounds interesting and I hope next month to order it through UK Amazon.

I am also very interested in reading your manuscript and also some of your articles. I am sure that they are very interesting and will help me learn about your country.

All best wishes for your work to succeed and for you to be in good health and happiness.

Your friend, Louise

Hi Nikolai,

Today I had an interview/visit with Ivanka in Aitos about being my tutor. She has tutored other volunteers and now mainly works with a language school in Burgas. I plan to start lessons with her when I return from the summer camp.

Yesterday Andrea and I had a picnic at "3 Brothers" with her counterpart Brandi, her young daughter and her mother. The 3 Brothers is a group of high boulders that resemble, with some imagination, three people. There is a smaller boulder, called "The Sister." We had a long hike up the hill on the outskirts of Aitos. The path was rough. We had a picnic lunch there that Brandi and her mother prepared. They were also our guides.

After eating a very yummy lunch of sandwiches and fruit we walked further down a country road around the town and up more hills to view the "Golden Goat". And then down the hill, through the trees, to a spring and a path out by the city park, called Slaveeva Reka Park. It was a fun day, but I wore the wrong shoes and now I have a blister on my foot.

Tuesday Andrea and I will go by train to Sliven for a regional Peace Corps meeting. It will be nice to see some of the other Peace Corps Volunteer's and hear how they are doing.

Your friend, Louise

Hi Nikolai,   **August 27, 2009**

My Internet is back up. It turns out that I had not paid the bill I did not realize that it was due as Dora set it up, but now I know that by the 25th of each month I need to pay her the 25 lev so that the company in Aitos does not turn it off

You may think that this is silly of me, but I must say that I'm rather scared about this whole camp thing. I am looking forward to be near the water and "just relaxing" as they say, but going with 28 students who do not speak English and seven teachers who also do not speak English scares me a whole lot. Hopefully they will all be patient with me. I have a quote on my desk by Georgia O'Keefe, an American artist,

"I've been absolutely terrified every moment of my life and never let it keep me from doing a single thing I wanted to do."

That is me this morning.

I hope that your research and editing continues to go well. It is a very big project and I think always takes a much longer time than is realized. I am looking forward to hearing more about your research and other projects that you are working on.

Warm wishes, Louise

Hi, Louise,   August 27, 2009

I am glad that your Internet is back now. Sometimes, you know, they may cancel it abruptly, without warning, so one should keep a constant eye upon it. With me interruption also happens from time to time, as they change their deadlines for payment. But they always restore the connection back, which I do appreciate.

I almost laughed when I read about your worries for the camp. No need for such; you are simply invited for a vacation and you need to enjoy it to the fullest. Please relax and make the most of it – sunbathing, walking on the beach and enjoying the rest. How long is the camp? When do you exactly come back?

Looking forward to hearing from you and wishes for a courageous and extremely enjoyable camp

Enjoy, Nikolai

From a postcard I mailed a friend back in the U.S.:

The camp was in the resort town of Sunny Beach. It was established in the 1960s. It is very popular especially with families and tourists and they offer many package holidays. The beach area is about five miles long and is very pretty. It became overdeveloped and many of the apartments built near the beach stand empty or are waiting to be completed. Our camp was really in a small family hotel on the top of a high hill overlooking the town. An old van was used to drive us down to the beach in two separate trips. After lunch the students rest briefly and then dress up to walk down to the center of town for some shopping and snack food.

Hi, Nikolai,

The camp was a day longer than I had expected. We left this morning by bus arriving back in Topolitsa around noon.

For the most part it was good, but several times I became quite frustrated with my lack of communication skills. I don't think when I've traveled before in a foreign country I had really thought about how different it is to travel and be the person who cannot speak the language. I was always with someone who I could talk to in English.

Some of the children knew a little English and I did teach them UNO. Also I played volleyball in the water with them as sign language in sports really speaks well but, at night with the teachers around the table chatting it was hard for me not to be able to express myself.

The saving grace was meeting a young woman who is a history student at Sofia University. Her mother is a teacher in Topolitsa. We had several nice conversations, including the bus ride home today where she told me about her studies at the University.

The days at the beach were sunny and pleasant. I think it was just different for me too even without the language as I have not often taken a vacation to just "lay at the beach". Also I was not really told what expectations were for me.

Even when I have taken youth groups camping, I had the day all organized with activities. Most of my vacations have been touring ones, always trying to see many things. The beach was a good exercise for my brain also to just "be still." Tomorrow I have my first language lesson with Ivanka.

Best, Louise

Dear Nikolai,

I have been saddened about the death of Edward Kennedy. I have long admired the Kennedy family and their dedication to public service. It is mostly due to JFK that I am in the Peace Corps. I'm not sure if I told you, but some years ago I heard John Kennedy speak, shook his hand and followed his career and then his brothers.

My daughter has sent me several links from Boston and I was able to listen to Obama's eulogy online and the memorial service held at the JFK library. Thankfully there are others in that family following his lead. The U.S. and all countries are always in need of great leaders. Of course not all feel about the Kennedy's as I do, but that is part of the freedom of opinion.

Caroline, John F. Kennedy's daughter, told a wonderful story of how Teddy always arranged each year a family outing to a historical place in America for all the Kennedy children to visit together. That is something I always have done with my children, wanting them to learn about history and the importance of it and how many different people all played apart.

What is your topic at the seminar? I really would like to learn more about it. Have you other seminars scheduled?

You asked me once in Banitsa, if or what I miss about America. And I believe I answered, that I miss meeting with friends, having conversations, talking over ideas and having them over for dinner. And that I guess is still it. So for now, emails will be for me my conversation with you. I hope soon we can meet and visit in person when I need to come into the Peace Corps office in Sofia and then arrange to meet for dinner. There is so much I would like to talk about with you.

At camp I read Wallace Stegner's book, *The Big Rock Candy Mountain*. He writes about a father in search of a dream and giving his family a transient life of poverty and despair. It is similar in some ways to *The Grapes of Wrath* by Steinbeck. My brother is sending me some Bulgarian history books and I hope they arrive soon. I think tonight I will attempt to order the *Solo* title I mentioned to you through Amazon UK.

As always, I look forward to hearing from you.

With warm wishes, Louise

Hi Nikolai,   **September 6, 2009**

Don't want to be a pest but wondering if I phone you later this morning you'll be free for a few minutes to chat?

Dear Louise,   **September 9, 2009**

No problem, of course, but if possible, please call in the evening – around 8 PM. I will be around the city during the day and it will not be convenient to talk while I am on a bus or tram for example.

Looking forward to hearing from you. Nikolai

Dear Nikolai,

It was a big morale booster for me to talk with you on the phone last evening. I needed to hear your positive outlook. I'm not sure how you maintain that. And I'm not sure at all who this brave woman is that you referred to – it certainly does not feel like me.

Your role-play of me at the camp table and not being able to participate and seeing the humorous side of it helped me tremendously to place it in perspective. Thank you.

Today I went to school and actually laughed with the teachers as several of them enjoyed looking at the red Peace Corps book and helped me pronounce words. One teacher who was not at the camp and I had not met before started acting out some of the words. Another told me she has been studying English for ten years and when she heard I had only been learning Bulgarian for three months she thought I was doing well. I couldn't believe it. And to top off the compliments I was told that with my new hair cut I look much younger. Wonders never cease.

This afternoon I went with Dora to Burgas to pick up my Lichna Karta. Now I'm officially in your country until next August. That's a good feeling.

I did some revisions on my DOWN list and then worked on an UP list yet last night. It was good to do and also I hope will help me especially on the DOWN days. I managed without too much difficulty to make the UP list much longer than the DOWN. It is not just a list of projects, but all the good things that have happened to me since coming to Bulgaria; meeting you is on my UP list. Learning Bulgarian is on both my UP and DOWN list.

Dora told me today that on October 30 there will be a special celebration as the school building will be 125 years old. There has been a school in Topolitsa for over 300 years if I understood her correctly. Sometimes communication does get lost in translation.

What is the topic that you are presenting in London? Do you need a passport to travel to England? Or maybe now with Bulgaria as part of the EU you only need your Lichna Karta.

Have a safe journey and say hello to sunny England for me and give the Queen my best regards

Warm regards, Louise

Dear Nikolai,   **September 9, 2009**

I don't know where to begin. Your articles are fascinating, insightful and absolutely not boring. I did not have the time to read them all yet, but plan to in the next few days. I am also filled with more questions to ask you about, but will wait until you return. Your papers present such an important topic and you make it so very interesting. I can see why you're always busy traveling to give lectures.

In the midst of reading I decided to make a pie from the many peaches that my landlady gave me. I had it in the oven, and not knowing what temperature to set the oven on I estimated what I thought would be okay, and went back to reading. Well, the peaches didn't burn, but my crust was "well done."

On a related topic, can you tell me the word of either the Bulgarian name for baking soda (bicarbonate of soda) or baking powder? They are similar, but not the same. It is used to help cakes and cookies rise. It is similar to yeast in bread baking. I can't find the Bulgarian word for it in any of my books or online. Where and what would I ask for? As the weather becomes cooler I'd like to do a bit of baking, but need one or the other of these ingredients.

Your analysis and insight of monuments and memorials in Bulgaria makes me want to read and learn more and discuss with you. It is by no means boring. The idea of memory and how and what is kept is of particular interest to me and is the theme of Lois Lowry's book *The Giver* which was written for young adults about 15 years ago. A friend is mailing me a copy which I will pass on to you. This also continues the seed of my idea of expanding your "Tuesday was Salami" story into a book.

I have always liked the title of Carl Rogers's book, *On Becoming a Person*. The road we travel on day-by-day, what opportunities happen, what windows open and how we continue to grow if we are open to it. I feel very fortunate that I met you on my journey.

With warm regards, Louise

Notes from my Journal:

The Peace Corps Staff in Sofia encouraged all volunteers to continue their language lesson, even after they passed their initial exam. Gaining proficiency in the language would help any volunteer be able to communicate better with their Bulgarian colleagues, students and community. Volunteers were required to turn in a time sheet for any formal lesson with a teacher. Peace Corps provided names of teachers that they recommended for these classes. Once I settled in at Topolitsa I contacted Ivanka from this list and she became my regular teacher for the next sixteen months.

In addition to giving me formal lessons to help improve my Bulgarian she became a wonderful resource and friend to help me learn more about the Bulgarian customs and habits, practical advice of where to shop in my region and interesting places to visit. She arranged for me to participate in several excursions with other teachers, students and adults.

Once or twice a week, I took the train from Topolitsa to Aitos after teaching at Svetlina and walked from the train station to her home where she lived with her parents. It was about a mile walk and usually took me about twenty minutes to walk. There was a grocery store near her house and sometimes I managed to stop there on my way back to the train for groceries that our small magazines didn't usually carry in Topolitsa. This included fresh meat, produce, and a bigger selection of toiletries. There was also a bigger store near the hair dresser's shop with a wide selection of items, and occasionally I stopped there. Of course all of these groceries had to be carried back in my bags to the train station in Aitos and then carried to my apartment on the second floor in Topolitsa.

The Opening Day of School is celebrated. There are speeches, music and a flag ceremony on the front steps. Many parents come for these opening ceremonies. Many students bring flowers for their teacher, especially the first grade (class) students. They do special activities involving their parents and helps ease the parents and the child's transition into the school program.

Students are dressed in their special school uniform. They are encouraged to wear the uniform every day. It consists of a blazer, pants for boys, skirt for girls, white shirt, and a Bolo tie for the boys. The medal aglet has the school emblem on it. The girls may also have a tie, but it was not often worn. There are both summer and winter fabrics for the students. Some students also had a V-neck sweater or vest that they could wear under their blazer. The emblem was often sewed on their blazer. On very warm days, the students could take off their blazer and for some outings they were allowed more casual dress. The school incorporated the uniform a number of years ago to show pride in their school and that all students would be seen as equal. Not all schools in Bulgaria have a school uniform.

Louise,   **November 2010**

I have a question to you.

You have sent a form for reimbursement which says that you are paying 12 lev per hour. Your Tutor Registration forms say that you agreed to pay 10 lev to your tutor. The last payment was also for 10 lev per hour. Have you changed the amount per hour or it's a mistake?

Thank you and have a great week,

Radka

Peace Corps Office

Hi Radka,

My understanding from a memo that came out earlier this fall was that the new reimbursement fee for tutors had been raised from the 10 lev to 12 lev. So with this last set of lessons that is why I paid her 12 lev. I didn't have the new form, but it was in a memo that Danni sent out.

Thank you, Louise

Thank you Louise,

I just wanted to know whether you changed the payment. I understand now and I will change it in our documents here as well. Your answer is very helpful. I will sign the form and give it to Administration for payment.

Have a great day, Radka

Hi Louise,

I hope that you have your Internet connection. The hairdresser called me yesterday to tell me that on Monday she is not going to work because of the weather. Can you go on Friday? She wanted me to explain to you something about your hairstyle. She worries about your curls because how she told me your hair is too soft and she is not sure how long a time your curls will be preserved. If your hair becomes straight again after a week she wants to repeat the same procedure without any payment.

Ivanka

Hi,

No, you don't need a visa. (This was in regard to the day trip to Greece. It was required to carry your Identity Card with you at all times by the

Bulgarian government.) Greece is a part of the European Union so even for Bulgarians it is very easy to cross the border by only having an Identity Card without an international passport. You prepare all of your documents just in case to be calm.

Hi Louise,

You are right, the weather became cold and you need a stove. All day I am close to mine. I hope that you will have heat and not to be frozen, If you have an electric stove use it.

About the trip you have to send me or bring tome on Wednesday a copy of your ID card and passport. The trip starts on31 October (Saturday). The departure will be at the circle by bus at 5 am. We will arrive back around 10 PM at the same place.

The traveling expenses are 45 lev. The passing of Bulgarian-Greek boarder will be through "Kapitan Petko Voivoda," Svilengrad city. Arriving at Alexandropulos will be round 11 AM.

Sightseeing: the coast alley with the popular Alexandropolis Lighthouse; the harbor, the church "Saint Nikola" with the healing icon of the Virgin Vesala "Trifotisa" from 13th century.

There will be about an hour and 30 minute free time for shopping, visitation of the shop Jumbo and the shop LIDL.

I prepared a list on the course of several evenings the items that made me feel DOWN about being a Peace Corps Volunteer and adjusting to living in Bulgaria and another list of the things that made me excited and happy about being a Peace Corps Volunteer. This I called my UP list.

Down List:
- Not knowing what's happening that day, or when it is happening.
- Camp – finding out as we leave that it's six days, not five.
- Camp – finding out that Dora is not going.
- Camp – getting bunked with two young girls.
- Having to pay 52 lev for a phone bill, because I was not given Andrea's correct phone number.
- Having to buy the stove before the report could be made to PC on the need for one costing me 150 lev.
- Buying the *Bulgarian for Foreigners* CD because my school director thought it would be helpful to me; not realizing that the cost of 100 lev was 25 percent of my monthly stipend from PC
- Dora wanting to give me Bulgarian lessons when she really doesn't have time for it
- Having no one to talk to here in Topolitsa.
- Needing a mirror and shelf in my bathroom.
- No screens or blinds on any of the windows or doors and with a

garden just below the windows the flies and other bugs come into my apartment.
- Not being able to afford cable TV.
- Feeling incompetent – what a huge change from my job last year, when I was the director of the college library and president of the New Mexico Library Association.
- Not having any "down" time between my job and the Peace Corps.
- Not selling my house.
- Moving back and forth from my house to apartment and back again; all the extra energy, time and expense this involved.
- Dealing with all the assorted house issues back in NM; having two different families asking me to rent my house and at the last minute both changed their mind.
- The expense of joining the Peace Corps.
- Having to buy a new stove for my apartment.
- The mind set that I would just sail through PC and adapt easily.
- Having to study so hard to speak very elementary Bulgarian.
- Coping with buying basic food so that I can cook and bake some familiar dishes.
- People asking me if I'm enjoying the adventure.
- PC adaptation style, "sink or swim".
- PC procedures and policies on vacation and travel.
- Being an older volunteer, this was supposed to make it easier, not harder.
- Younger volunteers have more things in common with each other.
- Couples have each other to share experiences, and younger volunteers are drawn to each other.

Up List:
- Getting to live in a foreign country.
- Getting to learn a foreign language in depth.
- Meeting new people.
- Having Nikolai as a teacher.
- Having Lazar as a teacher/
- Meeting Tatyana and visiting Yambol and Burgas with her.
- Meeting Ivanka and learning more about Bulgarian language and culture.
- Time spent in Banitsa with Albin, Anna, Diana and Lazar.
- Visiting new historical places, e.g., Shipka, Nesebar, Sozopol.
- Having time to read many books.
- Having time to write in my journal.
- Having time to write long emails.
- Having time to write letters to friends.
- Visiting Bulgarian libraries.

- Visiting a hairdresser and adopting a new hairstyle.
- Learning new styles of clothing.
- Learning to be more patient.
- Living in a modern apartment with lovely carpets.
- Living in an apartment with a wash machine.
- Living in an apartment with two balconies.
- Living in an apartment with a refrigerator and a new stove.
- Having lots of fresh fruits and vegetables to eat, and most of them given tome.
- Having my basic house and food expenses covered.
- Getting to travel by train all over Bulgaria.
- Having time just "to be".
- Learning to type on a Cyrillic keyboard.
- Learning to be more independent.
- Learning that it's okay to be alone.
- Working with children from another country.
- Laying on the beach at the Black Sea.
- Living near the Black Sea.
- Camp – time to relax and lay on the beach.
- Camp – getting acquainted with many of the students in grades 6, 7 and 8.
- Camp – teaching some of the children how to play UNO.
- Camp- playing "water volleyball" with some of the students.
- Camp – getting acquainted with the teachers at my new school.
- Having music to listen to on my iPOD and PC
- Having the Internet in my apartment.
- Having time to do "hand work" in the evenings.
- Learning about a new culture.
- Visiting many beautiful churches.
- Visiting many interesting museums and historical sites.
- Getting to visit new cities, e.g., Burgas, Aitos, Yambol, Sliven, Vratsa.
- Having the woman clerk at the magazine sell Avon.
- Living in a country that enjoys beauty and culture.
- Living in a country that appreciates and applauds education.
- Living in a country with respect towards religions.
- Living in a country with freedom of expression.
- Living in a country with equal rights to women.
- Having independent children who are happy and supportive that I'm serving in PC
- Having Marcus willing and able to take responsibility for my financial affairs.
- Having family proud of me that I'm willing and able to serve in the PC

- Having friends send me CARE packages and just happy to be my friend.
- Having the ability and health to be able to serve in the Peace Corps.

BIRTHDAY IN TOPOLITSA

Note to myself, 31 July 2009

Here it is the night before my 65th birthday. I certainly don't feel 65, or how I imagined 65 would feel. I feel like I am at the beginning of a new life, or the second stage of my life.

I think thirty-five is closer to what I feel. I'm not sure what age I look, but I don't think I look 65. I think that in the village I will tell people that I am fifty-five. How would they know differently? At fifty-five I could have a 35-year-old daughter and two sons thirty and thirty-three. I would like to think I look even younger than that, but I think it feels much better saying fifty-five. I just read an article in the New York Times that talks about fifty-nine being the new thirty. It was talking about a golfer who at fifty-nine years old almost beat the younger guy. It was just by chance that he didn't make the last hole a par or he would have won. So for now, I will be fifty-five years old.

Now to review:

Nikolai came on Monday to help me review for the test. And again on Tuesday. But on Tuesday morning, Boris was extremely difficult. I was telling Todora about going to Vratsa and Boris runs into the kitchen from the chicken area and starts berating me on how I say Vratsa. "Nay, nay, Vratsa." Then starts shouting "Nay Louisa, nay Louisa, nay Vratsa" for over five minutes. I guess he hears me insert an "r" where it shouldn't be. I really don't know what I do wrong. I find hearing those sounds difficult. I was almost in tears, but I wouldn't let him see me cry. Todora sat there upset and said something to him but he was so intense he didn't hear her. She put her hands over her face, and he finally leaves. I'm sat there stunned. What a scene.

I had been having my usual breakfast, toast and coffee when this all started. I finished as quickly as possible leaving some food and left. I knew I had to leave the house. I went to my room and start to cry, but felt I just had to leave the premises.

Fortunately, I had my things together ready for school. I decide to go get water at the village spring thinking that maybe it would help me settle down. I think I'm ready for school. As I walk up the steps Albin says hello from the computer window. That was all I needed. I said, "Oh Albin, what a morning." He is sympathetic, and said to come around to the other door.

As I approach Albin he gives me a big hug and I start crying. Then I tell him about the morning breakfast scene with Boris. He can't believe it.

His home is so warm and loving. Todora is nice, but Boris is not.

Apparently the entire village feels he has problems. I heard he had run for mayor once and received only two votes, his and his mother's. He is always hollering to people on the street. He has a mean look about him and then tries to act like he's your friend. His wife was only there once with his son and his wife. I never met his other son.

Albin has met all of his *baba's* assorted family as has Anna, but not me. Boris also thinks I'm rich, because I'm from California. At least he thinks I'm from California. I used Marcus' address for the Peace Corps and I can't convince Boris otherwise. I think he would like to come to the United States and have me be the viaduct. Well, he just blew it this morning.

After spending some time with Albin, I decide to go in to the school and there sits Lazar in his usual place on the bench just inside the school building. I feel I need to tell him what happened. This is not the first time I've mentioned Boris to him and how difficult he is. But this time Lazar is very upset about the whole scene. He assures me he will report it to Peace Corps and that they will not have the chance to host another volunteer. The other time Lazar was quite upset and surprised was when we were discussing meals. I had mentioned that I hardly ever had meat, and that my meals were generally served cold. I feel bad for Todora, but know that I need to give Peace Corps the facts. Also her health is not good, so I don't see how she really is capable of hosting another volunteer in the future.

In addition, the kitchen, bathroom and shower are not all that clean, and there are so many flies always about. There are other families in the village who would be great host families. Pauline, who gave us raspberries, and Lucy, and her neighbor showed us how to make Banitsa. I think Boris had Todora apply just to get the money. Very little extra money was spent on food for me. Peace Corps reimburses the families quite well, 120 lev a week.

The Peace Corps Staff sought supportive families for all the volunteers. Occasionally a volunteer moved to a different family when it was clear that the family chosen wasn't working out as hoped. I was asked about this option, but I told them I would try to cope and make this work.

After my talk with Lazar, I go in to see Nikolai who is waiting for me. He says, "What's wrong."

And then I related the whole story to him. He too was very sympathetic. I guess I wasn't expecting that. He was a very good listener. To be so understanding took me by surprise. We talked for over an hour. After a while we got to the language lesson. I had planned to tell him my idea about going to dinner over the weekend as a thank you, but now did not seem the time. He mentioned that he would be returning on Friday, or even Thursday afternoon already so I realized I could discuss the idea with him then.

Wednesday was our day to go to Sofia. It was a very hot day. But I was so happy to be out of the village for the entire day. Todora overslept, and so when I left the house at 6 AM she was still in bed. She woke as she heard me at the gate. I just said, "no problem" and left. I had to catch my ride. Emile, Anna's dad, was going to drive us to Vratsa. I never again say "Vratsa's" name again in either her or Boris' presence. I did have to hurry as we had to catch the 7 AM bus to Sofia.

We arrived in Sofia around 9:30. It is a very modern bus station. We checked some on our tickets to our various towns where we would be moving to soon and then went to get the public bus to go to the Peace Corps headquarters.

It turned out we had to catch both bus Number 7 and then walk a few blocks to catch bus Number 5.

It all seemed confusing and it would have been nice to have the route explained more, but I was happy to be in Sofia. What a fun city. Even though Sofia is somewhat run down, it felt marvelous just to be in a big city, with buses, a subway and a tram system. Looking at the house facades, I could see the grandeur that it once had. The University, the Aleksandur Nevski Church, St. Sophia's, the National Theater all had been restored and were beautiful. People were enjoying the warm day and sitting outside by the cafes enjoying a cup of espresso.

At Peace Corps headquarters we took a tour and met a few more folks. Also, I was called in for my blood pressure. I was not surprised to see that mine was higher than usual. I told the medical doctor what had happened the day before. She listened sympathetically. This morning I took it and it is back down to 117. It was 153 the morning after the Boris episode. Peace Corps loaned me a home monitor to check my blood pressure on a regular basis.

I also had an interview with Phil, the assistant director. I have no doubts about being able to teach and work at the school for the most part. It is learning the language and communication that has me concerned. Phil didn't seem too upset about it.

I also was able to get on email and found a few books to read.

Then we went with another group of Peace Corps Volunteers to take a walk around Sofia.

Hello dear ones,   **August 9, 2009**

I did not do much studying this weekend. Yesterday I vacuumed the rugs in my apartment. The landlady has a vacuum cleaner for me. They are pretty rugs, laying on top of the linoleum which does give the room character and a bit of installation. The walls don't have any installation thus making my house hot in the summer and cold in the winter.

In the afternoon I was waiting at the bus stop to go into Aitos. There are only three buses each day; in the morning, noon and around 4 PM As I was waiting my director and her husband appeared in their car and so I drove back into Aitos with them. I met Andrea there and we sat at a cafe and had tea and studied.

Cafes are very popular here. Folks sit at them and order a cup of coffee or tea and then often visit for an hour or two. There is no rush by the restaurant staff for you to leave. We did walk around the shops a bit, and I ended up buying a 2-piece white cotton skirt and top. The clothes are not that much different here, yet different. They look more European; lots more tight knit tops, lower cut blouses, brighter colors and short skirts and long swirling dresses. It's fun to observe the local people walking down the street. This is definitely not a tourist town, but an everyday look at everyday folks making the best of their life.

Depending on whom I talk to and how good their English is, I am learning how the generation over 40 is aware and appreciating the freedom of their life. It is very different from how their parents grew up under Communism and being part of the Eastern Bloc nations controlled by the Soviet Union.

Many of the older generation, those over 60, from what I understand are generally more nostalgic for those former times. Life was more controlled, but also more predictable. They were assured a job. The schools were run efficiently. And while they didn't have a big variety of food, generally they did not starve. Now many of these older folks see the younger generation getting wild and expecting too much too soon.

This morning I walked to the train station. It is a 15 – 20 minute walk on the outskirts of the village. Andrea got on in Aitos and we went into Burgas together. Chris, another Peace Corps Volunteer who is working in the Romani community on the outskirts of Burgas, met us at the train and we walked to the beach. It was a beautiful warm Saturday and the beach was filled with folks soaking up the sunshine on one of the last days of summer weather.

At the beach we met another Peace Corps Volunteer who will be finished in two months. We played some ball and had a small lunch of fresh fish and chips. There are cafes everywhere along the beach walk. Italian ice cream is another summer treat with vendors in small carts set up at almost every intersection.

Burgas is really a neat city. It got quite breezy. Late in the afternoon waves were really rolling in. All too soon it was time to walk back to the train station about a 25 minute walk. It was a great day at the beach, and spend it with other Peace Corps Volunteers who also were adjusting to life in a new culture.

On the train I had an interesting conversation with a Bulgarian man who had lived in Pennsylvania for two years and had also lived in England, but now was back in Bulgaria. People always seemed interested in finding out why I came here, what I am doing here and what brought me here. Very few have heard of the Peace Corps. Right after the fall of Communism many religious groups came over to recruit and convert Bulgarians, so many persons assume that as an American I was another religious zealot. We are told very implicitly by the Peace Corps during our training to make it clear that we are volunteers from the U.S. supported by our government and have no religious affiliation whatsoever. On the way in on the train I talked in Bulgarian to some people. Walking with Andrea always gets a reaction as she is a very pretty young blond woman. Many take her for German. There are very few American tourists in Bulgaria. Most of the tourists come from either England or Germany. Japan, Germany and England and other northern European countries are the governments that have generally invested and brought new factories and hospitals to this region.

Surprisingly, the train only costs 2.80 lev which is about $2 US to go into Burgas, the same price the bus ticket is to go from Topolitsa to Aitos. The distance to Burgas is at least three times further. As a Peace Corps Volunteer we are allowed only to use public transportation. We are allowed to ride with one of our Bulgarian colleagues. It's an old train but it works. I'll probably be taking the train to Sofia, but not for awhile as I'm only allowed one overnight out a month for the first 90 days, and for Sofia I need at least two nights away from the village.

My village has a mosque, so there is always the "call for prayer" five times a day. I have not noticed any persons paying any special attention to it.

The assistant director of Peace Corps Sofia will be visiting me here this week. As a Peace Corps Volunteer I have lots of reports to do on almost every aspect of my life. Tonight I fixed myself a tomato/cucumber salad with their white cheese on the top. My landlady keeps giving me tomatoes, so I could easily eat five tomatoes a day.

Oh, you might be interested in how I fix coffee here. In a small pot with a lip you heat water and add two heaping tablespoons of coffee. This is not instant coffee, just ground coffee, but generally finer ground than I've seen in United States. You bring it to a boil. Then turn off the heat and pour it through a sieve into your cup. The grounds stay in the pot

This is how "my *baba*" did it in Banitsa too, except instead of heating the water on her stove Todora used a little electric coil to heat the water. When the water boiled she poured it through a sieve into your cup. The grounds stay in the pot. It's basically the same idea as the French Press. I was in a big store looking for coffee pots, and this seems to be the way it's done in homes here. The restaurants have espresso machines and lattes like Starbucks. It's much like in Italy at a cafe where you get only a very small cup of coffee unless you ask for a big one or *Americano* and then they put in a bit more coffee. You have to ask and pay for cream another 10 or 20 lev. Sugar is free.

Well, that's it for now.

The weather is a bit cooler and that feels so good. Oh, I found out Bulgaria has only three golf courses in the country, two of them are in Sofia.

Love, Louise *aka* Mom

I received a number of birthday cards from family and friends. One of my favorites was a Dr. Seuss card from Stacey and Marcus that I taped to my bedroom wall in Topolitsa.

In part it said, "Another year older? You ought to be proud. You ought to get boisterous, noisterous, and loud. Just think of the things that you know how to do. The sorts of things no one can do except you. Your brain's full of wherefores and who's whos, and whys. You think someone else could be nearly as wise? You're one of a kind, you're uncommonly rare. You can't be replaced 'cause there isn't a spare." Happy Birthday to the only Mom we know in the Peace Corps.

Love, Marcus and Stacey

SEPTEMBER 2009: THREE MONTHS IN BULGARIA

Here I am, three months in Bulgaria. This week my emotions have gone like a roller coaster. Sometimes I feel quite happy to be here, and other times I wonder "What in the world am I doing with my life?" It's probably not necessary to review it all, but I will give some highlights – and low lights.

Last week it was dealing with the package that Marcus mailed me from California. As it showed a value of $105 it could not be delivered to Topolitsa. This came in the same day that Phil, from PC Sofia was visiting my school and Andrea's in Aitos.

He was late. It was decided that Dora would drive me to Burgas to get the package. I thought it just meant going there, paying an extra tax and picking up the package. Oh, if it would have only been so simple. What a process it took to obtain my package.

First we went to the wrong post office. We needed to go to the Old Post Office located near the train station. Finding a place to park was a challenge. As many of the streets were narrow people often parked their car on part of the sidewalk. At the Post Office there was a line. By the time it was my turn, it was closing time. I did manage to get the package from LeAnne. That should have been delivered to Topolitsa, but apparently because it arrived on the same day as Marcus' a red flag was raised.

The postal woman did give it to me after I paid a tax of around two lev; but for me to retrieve Marcus' package we would have to return tomorrow.

The next morning I caught the early train from Topolitsa to Aitos. Dora came to the train station to pick me up about 8:15 AM. Her friend Marianna also came along. She drove us into Burgas. By car it is about forty minutes. We had to first get a document number. Just getting your number it turned out would take about two hours.

While waiting for our number, Dora suggested we go shopping and then perhaps the beach. I ended up buying a Bulgarian letter keyboard and some other items at the "technique" store. Then she took me to a bookshop that sold some books in English as it was near the University. Dora wanted me to buy the Bulgarian for Foreigners CD. I wish I had said perhaps next month. It was 100 lev. After I took it back to my apartment and listened to it, I realized it was not very well done. It's more for someone visiting and wanting to know some phrases, but the lessons don't go into detail. I felt I had wasted 100 lev which was 25 percent of my total income for the month After the CD purchase we went to the beach. The weather was grand.

Persons, young and old are not as Victorian as persons in the United States. Everywhere people were soaking up the sun. Bathing suits in Bulgaria are much more revealing than anything I've seen in the States. No one seems to pay any attention to it, so it's not like you're really revealing anything or creating a sensation. Earlier in the summer I've noticed this with different videos that are played on the buses back and forth from Vratsa to Banitsa. Calendars in school hallways are similar to Playboy. It's all appears very nonchalant. On the beach many women are topless. People change their suits out in the open. For many Americans I think they would think this was all scandalous, but here it seems to work.

We then had a salad at a beach café before heading back to the Post Office. It was now three in the afternoon. The documentation number was assigned, and then I had to go to another office to have a report typed out.

It appeared that the red shoes in the box were somehow seen as a problem. I had to describe them in detail. These were the shoes I bought in Spain ten years ago. I had the heels repaired earlier this spring in Farmington. Finally the form was done and the man who filled out the form charged me 16 lev. First he was going to charge me 25 lev. I'm not sure why he came down in price. Then we all went to another customs office. There was a problem. We had to go back to his office and do the form over again. Back to Room 102. Finally they accepted the form with minor revisions. Then down the hall and the papers were given to another person.

It seemed to take forever to be acknowledged at the postal window. And when I started talking to Marianne I was told to be quiet by one of the office people. By this time, I was so very frustrated as now it again was almost 4:30 PM Dora took the payment which was another fee upstairs to a cashier. Finally we were done and hurried down the street back to the Old Post Office.

The buildings were close to each other but we had to cross several different streets and wait for traffic lights. And once there, it took some time to go down the right hallway and find the right door. Then it was back to the first office. And by then, we arrived too late back at the Post Office. We saw the woman from the customs Post Office on her way down the street. We would have to make a third trip back to Burgas in the morning. I was so terribly frustrated. I spent a whole day trying to retrieve one package sent from home.

I couldn't believe it

In the morning I again took the train to Aitos. Marianne came along and I found out that we would go shopping afterwards to Kaufland. This was a big store similar to a Target or Walmart back in the United States. There was one more tax to pay, bringing the total now to about 40 lev. The package contained a big jar of jelly beans, my red shoes and actually another pair of brown loafers which I hadn't remembered, a pair of Bermuda shorts, long pants, a day back pack and a book, *The Memory Keeper's Daughter.*

My children were thinking of me. It felt good to have these items sent to me. It was a connection to home. Marcus knew how important that would be for me.

When Marcus was sixteen years old, starting his third year in high school, he was a foreign exchange student in Belgium. As the program had no more openings in France they found a home for him in Belgium. This was before the age of the Internet, ATM machines and email. I remember how lonesome he was those first months and how he had to do all his communication completely in French. It was much more complicated to make a telephone call back in 1988, the fall he flew from Pittsburgh to Brussels. The entire year he was there we only talked on the telephone three times. I've thought of Marcus' experience often my first months here living in a foreign country.

We went to Kaufland's. I decided to make the best of it and decided to stock up on food. This was turning out to be a very expensive month. Thankfully I could charge the food at this store as my cash was gone. I don't think Dora realizes how very little money I have. She is under the impression that Peace Corps covers all these extra expenses. They don't.

Finally we drove back to Aitos. In the Center we met up with Brandi and Andrea and I had an ice cream and some had beer. The others had ice tea. Then it was time to go to Topolitsa. What a day, but not the end.

Andrea called me and I found out about the trip to Shipka that Pauli and her family were taking. Andrea had plans to go to Burgas to attend a rock concert with Chris, another volunteer on the weekend. I really wanted to see Shipka as I had read about the beautiful monastery there and the town's historic significance but I had already made plans to go to Yambol to see Tatyana. After numerous phone calls, plans were changed and I would go to Shipka. Pauli's family would pick me up at 7:30 AM in Topolitsa.

I realize now that it would have been helpful had I dated each entry when I wrote. I certainly have gone through the full gamut of emotions. For me, I think Bulgaria is the place to be in the Peace Corps. I handled having outdoor plumbing for two months, a primitive shower, no place to brush my teeth except at the outdoor garden sink, doing all my laundry by hand and swatting flies while trying to eat meals. While not exactly primitive, at times it was trying on my soul. A more rugged environment would have been difficult.

The hardest part was dealing with Boris. My blood pressure is now back to normal. I realize the stress I was under at her house. I found that he made the home stay in Banitsa much more difficult than it needed to be. I don't think he did it intentionally. It shows though, how careful home families have to be screened for new Peace Corps volunteers. He always seemed to be "in my face" and then when I tried to talk to him he was constantly correcting me, or asking what felt like to me very personal questions. A person comes to serve and understands there are risks involved in addition to home sicknesses and transition anxiety. Where you stay your first several months in a new country can help make the stay pleasant, or can cause undue anxiety.

I have thought of Todora and wonder how she is doing. I expect she's managing fine. I hope I gave her some joy while spending time with her. The last few weeks we spent little time together as she liked to watch her television serials rather than eat dinner with me. It was lonely. If it had not been for Diana, Anna and Albin, Banitsa would have been even lonelier. Lazar and Nikolai also were bright spots and I am thankful for their support and encouragement.

I must say that the PC policy of three months at our permanent site before being allowed one day off a month is a bit difficult to swallow. And that includes weekends. Apparently this is the only Peace Corps country where that policy has been initiated. I'm not sure why, but have been told by others that they heard it was due to a incident of several years ago where PCVs got out-of-hand, or five of them did anyway. As a result the current director was brought in to bring more discipline and supervision to the program.

She is certainly competent, but as an older volunteer this restriction seems unnecessary. But so it is. Now there are only two months to go, and regular vacation policies will be in place. We earn two days off a month, but of course can only take them with our supervisor's approval which I can understand. Being in the school program most of my days off will be during the school vacations, e.g., Christmas, spring break and then after June 15.

I think there is a summer school program for July but hopefully I still will have time for a vacation either somewhere in Bulgaria or another European country.

Topolitsa itself is a pleasant village, but a bit lonely. The teachers of the school all live in Aitos. I have yet to meet any adults in the village who can speak English to me. There are a few students who do know some English. Hopefully I will use this time to write, read, do some needlework and just reflect. Thank goodness for email and the Internet. I find myself going online more than I ever did in the

Also for the first time, I did a Skype chat on Saturday. This was my first conversation with anyone back in the States. I have sent out text messages a few times, but so far only my daughter has been able to receive them. This weekend was my youngest niece's wedding in Madison. I mailed her a Bulgarian wedding card, hopefully it arrived in time. I'm glad that Gretchen was able to go to Wisconsin for the wedding.

How is the language coming along? It is hard to say. I know more than I did a month ago, but haven't had a real chance to use it much other than with train conductors and at the local magazine. This week at the school camp will be the big test. I should be thinking about what to take along, but I still have two nights to figure that all out.

Tomorrow is a regional meeting in Sliven. I will take the train at 8:12 AM Andrea gets on at Aitos and then we travel together. Coming back will be a bit tricky as it will be dark outside and I don't like walking that country lane from the train in the dark, but I have no choice. The train gets in around 8:40 PM Full moon isn't until next week. I will take my flashlight along. There is a light by my corner, but not sure how it is at the train station. I've never come back in the dark. Every week seems to be some kind of new experience.

I still haven't written about Shipka, but I will. I have many pictures and that will help me remember the weekend.

Nikolai and Lazar were both very good teachers. It was their caring attitude when Boris berated me that morning, and coming to help paint the bus stop on that very hot day when I realized how helpful both of been and what an asset to the Peace Corps organization. Later that same day Nikolai still took time to study with me. We were out at the table by the village pool. He knew I was worried about passing the language examination. It was then that I mentioned, for a thank you for all his time and effort, before I traveled on to Topolitsa I would like us to go into Vrasta via bus to have dinner together at a restaurant. He would be out in the different neighboring villages tutoring the following week; perhaps there would be time. It would be a nice change from my usual stuffed pepper dinner by myself.

The following week after the regular lessons Nikolai and I took the bus in to Vrasta. It was a pleasant summer evening. First we walked up to the mountain overlooking the city. We sat there and talked awhile and just became acquainted with each other as friends. Before the walk we took pictures, which was fun. I can't remember what made me decide to bring my camera along but I did, and Nikolai had his. So we both took pictures of each other and of the sights of Vrasa from the mountaintop. On the walk back down he got a phone call from Danni at the PC office. It was about the swearing in ceremony I think. Nikolai mentioned that he thought it was in Sofia but found out it was in Vratsa. He wasn't sure he could make it, so I figured he wouldn't be there.

We went to the restaurant and ordered our dinner. We both had fish, salad and I had wine. And we talked and talked. We talked mainly about his research and some about his life growing up in Bulgaria. He told me a bittersweet story about his early experience in school where everyone in this class was required to bring the same thing to school so that all would be the same, no favorites. And on Tuesday the selection was salami. And it was of such a flavor that he just could not eat it. So rather than eat lunch that day, he skipped lunch altogether. Finally his mother spoke to the teacher as she felt it was important for him to eat. So the teacher agreed to make an exception. But in doing that, the class noticed and now he was picked on.

He also told me about his dad wanting a car, and that finally after waiting over eight years his name got drawn for a car in a lottery. It was the least desirable car of the three that were being given away, but it was a car. And as I remember the story, his parents still have that car. We were talking away, and then his phone rang again. Here it was Lazar wondering what had happened to us. We had lost track of time, and it was about 11:30. Nikolai told Lazar we were on our way and would be back to Banitsa shortly.

We easily found a cab and the ride was less than thirty minutes. We were dropped off at the center. Nikolai walked me back to my house, and we were barely at the gate, when the light goes on and Boris comes out the door. Boris was acting like an overbearing father. He started questioning Nikolai. I went in the house. The next day he had to teach in another village and I wondered if our paths would cross again.

The surprise was that he made it to the swearing in ceremony in Vratsa. He knew many of the current Peace Corps staff having worked with them when Peace Corps was very new in Bulgaria. I did not receive his email that he was coming. As I was standing outside, just having greeted Pauli and her family, who walks across the plaza but Nikolai. I was delighted. We did not have too much time for uninterrupted conversation, but it was so good to see him and I was so thankful that he had put the effort to come. We were able to visit afterwards at the reception. Soon it was time for me to leave with Pauli and her family and Andrea for the drive to Aitos and my new home in Topolitsa.

Using the analogy of Mr. Higgins in Pygmalion I have tried to convey some of my feelings and frustrations to him. I told him in class when I was practicing the sounds of the Bulgarian words with him that it reminded me of Mr. Higgins' and Eliza, "*the rain in Spain falls mainly on the plain.*" He had not seen *My Fair Lady,* but he knew the *Pygmalion* by George Bernard Shaw.

This week we have Monday and Tuesday off due to a national holiday, Independence Day (from the Ottoman Empire). It was Nikolai who suggested I make a list of all the things that I can do when I get down; I told him I had made a list of the things that happened that made me get down. He thought it was better to make an "up" list. I laughed. He is a very positive teacher;

Last night I went with Ivanka, my new Bulgarian tutor to her English class that she teaches in Burgas. The entire class was made up of engineers. It was very interesting and I totally enjoyed it. Most of them were in there thirties. It still surprises how readily everyone gives their age in this culture. I want to hide my age. Who wants to meet a 65-year-old woman?

The engineers all had gone to different cities in Bulgaria to earn their University degree but then came back to their home region. They were surprised and had many questions about family life in the United States. It is a very different concept with families being so spread out in the U.S. Many of them live in the same flat as their parents or grown siblings, or live nearby that they can see each other on a regular basis.

How would I feel about the Peace Corps without being able to talk to any Bulgarian? For the most part I think I would feel even more devastated. Now at least I have met a few Bulgarians who have kept in touch with me via emails that have given me joy.

HISTORIC TOWNS ON THE BLACK SEA

October 4, 2009

Yesterday Vesala drove me to Sozopol. It was a very nice day. I walked to the train here in Topolitsa and took the 9:55 train to Aitos. She was there to meet me. Then we left in her car.

Her English is very good, but sometimes things do get "lost in translation." Her parents live in Plovdiv. They were here last weekend visiting. She is divorced and has a son living in Aitos and a daughter in Sofia. In August she stayed with her daughter to take care of the granddaughter who is about 2 years old.

We talked some about family, children being on their own, needing help but not interfering and other concerns about parenting. We also talked about economic conditions here. For a talented teacher it seems very difficult to make a living here in Bulgaria. She speaks four languages fluently and knows several others. She has taught students at all levels and does many additional projects at the school, These include writing grants for special projects in her spare time. She has taught for about thirty years and makes only 400 lev a month. She rents a small apartment and pays around 150 lev a month plus utilities. That doesn't leave much extra. She bought a used car from her brother and loves driving. Last week she had to buy two new tires and mentioned that she put them on her credit card. She does sewing on the side for extra income and also other several other part time projects to bring in some extra income.

Last summer she had four months in England as she wrote a grant for a special education project. She has traveled in most of the Eastern European countries and also France and England. She would make a good travel companion.

I told her a bit about my economic situation; especially how I hope these two years will not deplete my funds for retirement. So much of my future is dependent on keeping my house rented and in good condition.

The young family and an older brother living in my house have not paid their rent going into the second month. This is very disconcerting to me. I'm not sure what to do. If I do not hear from Marcus in a day or two I will have to call him. I get minutes on my "American" phone again on the 8th.

Why should I have these problems? So much centers on money. I do not want to have to take out my retirement savings in order to manage the Peace Corps. Then I would have been better to stay working at San Juan College. It seems all a big muddle to me.

Back to Sozopol, it's a very interesting old historic city. Vesala was very happy to take pictures of me, but not too many turned out. Perhaps I had the setting wrong.

At Sozopol we walked around the old ruins. I talked to a man who lives in an ancient house which is now partially an art gallery. He gave me a traditional Bulgarian bell. He has a son in Florida So many people who I meet here have children in America.

Then we went to another museum which was only recently excavated. It has old Roman ruins. We walked along part of the old wall, which is right next to the Black Sea.

Another very unique and beautiful item found in the many artisan shops is the pottery. Artisans display their wares all over the country but especially in these historic towns where many of them live. It was hard to resist buying a full set of dishes. However, as it is breakable it is difficult to transport back to the U.S. They come in a variety of beautiful patterns, but all have a very unique design found only here in Bulgaria. I bought a few small traditional Bulgarian ceramic dishes including two small glasses, two small bowls, a small serving bowl, and a salt and pepper shaker in the traditional style. The traditional style is two bowls connected together, where you use your fingers rather than shake the salt and pepper out of the top. That is what Todora had in Banitsa and I have seen it many places.

Vesala took me to a Greek restaurant where you could sit out on the terrace overlooking the Black Sea. I should have had a picture taken there It was rather expensive for Bulgaria as it costs 21.5 lev. I had fish, bread, Greek salad, beer and a cappuccino. In most restaurants in Bulgaria you ask for bread and there is a small charge for it.

After that we walked some more through the old streets and came back to the more tourist area where I bought three lovely icons at a shop, which the owner discounted for me, 50 lev rather than 66 lev. They are of Mary and Jesus, St. Nikolai, and another of St. George slaying the dragon.

Then she drove us to the new area of Sozopol where there are dozens and dozens of hotels. Apparently most of them have been built in the last five years. This would be a great town to have a week's vacation in and I am thinking of doing that.

Walking down the almost deserted streets, one store had a few clothes out on a rack. I noticed some jeans with a price of 15 lev. I couldn't believe it, especially as the jeans fit me. I had looked in several second hand shops for jeans, but all I had seen had been in very small sizes. And in the historic, old Sozopol at one shop they wanted 50 lev for jeans. So I felt very lucky to find a pair, as I have none here except for the pair with some embroidery on the leg that I found at a second hand shop. Now I am pretty well set with clothes, except for maybe a dark pair of pants for the colder weather. I have corduroys but they might be too warm for the classroom.

I heard from Nikolai and he is now at a conference in Bucharest. I mentioned to him about having a dental appointment in Sofia later this month. Hopefully it will work to meet him there. There are many things I would like to talk to him about, and meeting in person would be so much easier than via email.

Last weekend I saw Felicia, Anna and Albin at a PC meeting in Kazanluk. I wish we had had time for sightseeing, but it was good to visit which is very important. The next gathering is for Halloween which I will have to decide about. It is not my favorite holiday at all, but I would like to see the others, plus it is in Veiko Turnovo, which I am told is a very interesting historic city.

I finally have my train card which gives me a fifty percent discount on train tickets. It took almost a month. First I tried to purchase it in Aitos. I asked there three different times, before a woman finally said I needed to go to Burgas. One woman at the counter told me it was illegal to sell to me because I was an American

My first trip to Burgas the office was closed, but this week I made it on time, paid my 45 lev and now I am set until August 1, 2010. She would not make it for a year because my *lichna karta* expires also on August 1. That also had taken a month to receive.

Just going back and forth to Aitos I will save 45 lev by the end of January I estimate, so with trips to Sofia or Plovdiv I do save 50 pecent. I need to save somewhere because each month I have had to use my own money to have enough to buy my supplies. I understand not having Peace Corps money for books, but for travel and medical is a problem I had not figured upon doing.

That's it for today. I do hope my Internet gets back up soon. Not sure why I'm having these problems. It was also a problem last week.

NEW FRIENDSHIPS

Hello Tatyana,   **July 30, 2009**

We met at the Peace Corps Counterpart Conference the end of June in Vratsa. We walked around outside together and had a pleasant chat.

I am now here in your region in the village Topolitsa. It is a lovely village, but very small. It is also different for me as the teachers of the school all live in Aitos. So far I have not met anyone in the village who speaks English and I am still very limited in my Bulgarian language.

Perhaps we could get together sometime in August. I know the train goes from here to Burgas, and perhaps also to Yambol. I haven't been on it yet but my landlady uses it frequently so I'm sure she could help me figure it out.

I hope this finds you well and that I will hear from you soon.
Louise Hoffmann

Hello Louise,   **July 31, 2009**

I'm so glad to hear from you. I do remember you of course and I've been thinking about you. These days I've spent a lot of time with Vanessa and Nathaniel. (Newly wed Peace Corps Volunteers assigned to Yambol.) We went to the police twice to register and we've done some things to their apartment so they can feel at home. Tomorrow they are going to a camp in northern Bulgaria with Vanessa's counterpart for ten days.

I can guess how you feel. I'll be glad to see you. I'll think of something and call you. The train goes from Aitos to Yambol. It takes about an hour and a half to get to Yambol. Bye for now.

Tatyana

Hello Tatyana,   **July 31, 2009**

How very nice of you to call.

I would be happy for you to come tomorrow also if that would work in your schedule. I should have thought of it when I sent the email off to you or on the telephone.

I have a big apartment here in Topolitsa and you would be welcome to sleep over. I have an extra bedroom. I've invited Pauli and her family, my director Dora and Andrea. They all live in Aitos. They are coming around 5:30, but if you could come earlier that would be great.

First I thought I would just forget my birthday, but then I decided I would probably get too lonesome. If you could come too, that would be wonderful.

I know the train station can't be very far from my house as my land-lady walks to it, but so far I haven't seen it. Just let me know what time to meet you at the station.

Hope to see you, Louise

Hello Louise,   **August 1, 2009**

I had just read your letter when you called me. So it's a sort of telepathy that you called because I was thinking of you.

It's great that you are going to have some guests; One should celebrate birthdays and in Bulgarian we say Честит рожден ден и за много години. When we meet you'll tell me about your colleagues. I'm sure you'll get greetings from U.S.A., too. (Pronounced *chektek rose den den mnogo godina:* happy birthday and luck for many years.)

I looked at the map and I figured out that trains pass by Topolitsa so no need to go first to Aitos, but this refers to the so called "fast" trains or пътнически влак. Fast trains don't stop in your village I think. There is a slow train I think from Topolitsa to Yambol.

I'll be in Yambol most of the time and would be glad to see you and take you round the town. It's not something special, but it's quiet and we can talk, which matters. Now I have time but during the school year it's different. So it will work to get organized together soon. I'll let you know and call you.

Have a nice day, Tatyana

Hello Louise,   **August 2, 2009**
I hope you are adapting and settling down to your new environment. It takes time, that's for sure.

I'm going tomorrow to Burgas only for a day so I'll take a train at 6:55 from Yambol and it will be in Topolitsa at about 8. 15. It arrives in Burgas at 9. If you want, you can come with me. We can have a walk and chat but I'm not planning on going to the beach. We'll take a train back sometime between 4 and 7. This is only a suggestion so don't worry if you can't come.

I'll give you a call tonight at 9 probably so I hope you will see this message and decide. You can write of course. I'll check my e-mails tonight. Anyway, if you have other plans for tomorrow we'll organize it after August 10th and you'll come to Yambol.

If there are changes I'll tell you.

Have a cool day, T.

Hi Tatyana,   **August 2, 2009**
Dora my director will call you to discuss the idea.

She wants to be sure it fits into PC requirements. I do need to learn how to walk around Burgas as Hotel Bulgaria is our emergency meeting site and also will probably have other meetings there so it would be good for me to learn the city.

(Each region of Peace Corps workers had an evacuation site set up in case of emergency. This would be if something happened in the country and the Peace Corps office or American Embassy no longer felt it was safe for the volunteers to be in the country. It could be a natural or man made disaster. For those of us near the Black Sea, our meeting point was a hotel in Burgas, and from there we would be given directions and probably go to Istanbul. We were to keep an American $20 bill with our passport at all times as that is what was needed to obtain a Visa for entrance into Turkey. As far as I know, evacuation never was needed in Bulgaria, but a number of times PCV have been evacuated in other countries while serving. Sometimes they were able to stay in a neighboring country, and sometimes they were flown back to the U.S. Often they were able to return to their country and finish their Peace Corps commitment, but not always. Sometimes Peace Corps Volunteers were reassigned to another country. Peace Corps has volunteers in over 120 countries.)

Hi, Louise,   **August 10, 2009**

Today I was a bit late at the information office; tomorrow I'll check and write again. Friday is okay with me.

No surprise about the fare from Topolitsa to Aitos by bus. It's more expensive than the fare by train. 20 km. by bus cost about 2.20 lev. The price depends on the bus company. I'll be able to check timetable and cost from Aitos to Sofia by train but about buses you better ask Dora.

When we meet we'll look at the map of Bulgaria and it can be useful for your orientation. We can also go round some shops and look for a bathing suit for you at a reasonable price.

You seem to have a busy week. Good luck

Bye for now, Tatyana

Hi, Louise,   **August 12, 2009**

Finally I checked the trains and time. The train arrives in Topolitsa at 6:55 AM and gets to Yambol at 8:05 AM You see this is what we knew in advance. The train back leaves at 4 PM and arrives in Aitos at 5:27 PM I'll tell you when we meet on Friday about other trains that go to Sofia.

Please answer and tell me if there are any changes in your plans.

Hello Tatyana,   **August 12, 2009**

Thank you for being so understanding. I am looking forward to visiting you in Yambol. I heard of this opportunity late today to ride with the Aitos counterpart and her family to Shipka. I thought it would be a good opportunity for me. We will leave Friday morning and come back Sunday.

I have no special plans next week. Please let me know what will work in your schedule. Next week would probably be best as August 27 is when the Topolitsa teachers do the camp with their students.

The last two days I have been in Burgas with my director at the Customs office trying to get the package my son mailed me. Hopefully tomorrow I can have it. It weighed over four pounds and the value listed on it was $105 so that is what is causing all the delay and extra paperwork.

Thank you again for understanding the change of plans to visit you in Yambol.

Louise

Hello Louise,   **August 17, 2009**

I'm glad you're coming on Wednesday. I think the ticket costs about 3 – 3.50 lev. As I told you the final stop of this train at 6:55 AM from Topolitsa is Yambol. You can't miss it and at 8 I'll be at the station. The only thing is you should get up early to catch the train.

I'm looking forward to having a chat with you and hope we'll have a nice time. I'll have my cell phone with me as usual of course.

Bye and sleep well, Tatyana

Hello Tatyana,   **August 18, 2009**

I am so happy to be coming tomorrow. I was quite discouraged yesterday with my language skills. I had not thought it would be this difficult for me to learn.

It will be good to visit and walk around your town. I think that you also mentioned a park. Today Dora reviewed with me how to look at the train schedule online.

See you around 8 AM

The official Bulgarian train schedule, *www.Razpisanie.bdz.bg,* lists slow trains and fast trains. With practice I learned to read the schedule and how to figure out where a station change was needed. Some of the schedule was translated into English.

The bus system was more complicated as there was no central bus web site. Only a small local bus came to Topolitsa and went to Aitos, mainly for the convenience of the teachers and for the folks to shop in Aitos. In Aitos each bus company had their own store front. A person had to check with each one their schedule when they went to Burgas or Sofia or another city. The bus usually stopped either at the Roundabout or the small bus station about two miles from the train station.

Hello,   **August 18, 2009**

I just got your message. This evening I accidentally met Vanessa and Nat. I told them about you and they said they would like to see you tomorrow. We'll go to the park, sure.

Bye till tomorrow, T.

Hello Louise,   **September 7, 2009**

You see how the weather turned cool. I walked through the park in the rain. It looked almost enchanted this evening and I gathered some chestnuts.

I hope you enjoyed the camp at the seaside. Now back to work. We've been busy these days, organizing our work.

How about you? What classes will you be teaching? How do you feel? Looking forward to hearing from you.

Bye, Tatyana

Good morning Tatyana,   **September 8, 2009**

Thank you for your note. Yes, I cannot believe the weather. Is this typical? I'm hoping that the wind stops blowing soon, and that the weather will calm down and that there will be some pleasant fall days.

Camp for the most part went okay. The difficult part for me was the language. Fortunately, a daughter of one of the teacher's came along who could speak English and I had several chats with her. She too loves history and will begin her second year at Sofia University. I thought my director was going, but I found out only as we boarded the bus to leave that she was not going.

Every day we went to the beach and I enjoyed lying out on the sand. The children were well behaved, all around 12-14 years old. There were thirty students in all, seven teachers with several other teachers' children who came along to the camp.

In the afternoon time was free and the children could play in the small pool at this family hotel up on a hill. I taught the children UNO and also played some volleyball in the water with them.

Later in the day we walked down to the center where the students could buy souvenirs and just walk around town. Most also bought snacks as the meals served were very small portions, which really surprised me.

I have found a young woman in Aitos to be another tutor for me. And then last night my director's son called me and suggested another name to me. My director has realized he said that she will not have the time to help me very much in my language skills due to her busy schedule.

I am anxious to schedule regular lessons, hopefully 2 – 4 hours a week. It appears I will have about 14 hours a week of English classes to teach. I am hoping to speak more with my counterpart on this, but at this time she is busy with other items. I've been going to school each day and studying on my own and chatting with the teachers as they have time.

As your schedule permits I would love to come to Yambol again for a visit on a weekend. Or, perhaps you and Peter would like to come to Topolitsa. There is a long walking and car path that goes up the mountain and the view is lovely.

When Phil, the Peace Corps assistant director was here Andrea and I drove up the mountain road to the top with him. In the fall it should be lovely. There is a small restaurant in town, but I also would be happy to make lunch or dinner for you in my apartment. I have an extra bedroom if you would want to stay the night.

I have ordered the book titled *Solo* online through Amazon.UK. It should arrive next week. I was so happy to have *Vagabond.* (This is a magazine in both English and Bulgarian and covered news about Bulgaria with travel ideas, literature, and art from around the country.) There was also an interview with the author Rana Dasgupta in the online Sofia News. I will forward it to you. It is near the end of the news stories, under "Interview."

All the best for a wonderful school year, I look forward to hearing from you, and hopefully seeing you yet this fall.

Please give my regards to Peter, Louise

Hi Felicia,   **October 4, 2009**

My Internet was down again. I'm not sure why. And then my landlady had me come down to visit. Sure wish I could speak more with her. She really means well and she is always offering me food. She was in Istanbul this past week and suggested I could come with her sometime. That would be interesting. She buys and sells at the bazaar. She brought back blankets and scarfs and I think sold some of her almonds and walnuts.

Anyway, it seems as if my school director has not paid her any rent since I've been here. She has mentioned this before, so now I think I will call PC and see what is what. My director has hardly been around all week.

Yesterday, Andrea's counterpart Vesala took me to Sozopol, a neat historic town on the Black Sea. She is nice. Andrea was not interested in going. Laura also came with us. And we lucked out with the weather. Cloudy, but it only started raining as we drove back.

I finally got my train card. I had to go into Burgas; there was no problem getting it there. When I went to buy my train ticket in Aitos on Friday, the woman ahead of me was buying a train card. But, that same woman would not sell one to me in Aitos, because I was not Bulgarian. I don't understand; but I went to Burgas and as I had time before going back on the train. Yes, I wonder too about the language. When will I ever catch on? I decided to try and listen to the CD I bought and now think maybe I should do that every day. It is hard to speak the language, because people who know some English will speak English to you, and the others are too impatient to try and listen to your Bulgarian. I don't have a solution.

I think you mentioned going to the Halloween bash. Some PCV were arranging an informal get together as now we were able to leave our site for a weekend with the appropriate signatures. They were arranging a group rate to sleep at a Youth Hostel and a gathering at a nearby restaurant. On medical trips to Sofia PCV got reimbursed only the amount that a youth hostel charged for lodging. Tricia (another PCV) mentioned an English couple near her place where I could stay. I would rather stay there than at the Youth Hostel. It would be nice to see the other volunteers and I would like to see the town as it should have some interesting historical sights.

If not tonight, I'll call you early this week. I'm sure you're relieved about the apartment. It will be a hassle to move, but then you will not have to think about it anymore; sometimes things do have a way of working themselves out.

I also have no heat yet. I don't understand what's going on at my school or with my director. She is hardly ever around. That sounds like a worthwhile project for a video. I do wish there would be a project that you could do here; maybe something about small village schools and what they need to do to be relevant for the EU Bulgaria

Talk to you soon, Louise

October 4, 2009

Just checking in to see how you are doing this weekend? It is all wet, rainy. We were lucky to have such a nice weekend last weekend.

Journal entry, October 15, 2009

This has turned into an eventful week. My counterpart Tantayna was sick. I only found out when I went to school Monday morning. That meant I had to cover all the classes by myself. This would not be so bad, except the students know that I don't know all the rules, all their names, and all top of that the entire school is undergoing a renovation for the 125th anniversary celebration, which is occurring on October 30.

Fifth and sixth classes go okay, but seventh and eighth classes are a disaster. Boyko especially pushes and pushes to get attention. And then yesterday our class was downstairs in the kitchen with tools all around for the renovation.

Boyko managed to take a big shovel and started running around with it. The other students just laughed. I was so frustrated. I finally decided to go upstairs and see if any other teacher was around, because I was not teaching anyway. Marianna and Krassy were there. Krassy came down and talked to the students, and they settled down somewhat and I managed to get through the class. What a disaster. Afterwards, Dora was upstairs and had heard what had happened. I just told her that I wasn't expecting any of this, and with the refurbishing some of the students were taking advantage of the situation.

She was sympathetic, but again mentioned how busy everybody was. I realize that, and I really didn't expect them to do anything. However, I did mention that there seems to be no rules in place, which makes it difficult to teach.

Then she asked if I had seen the new upstairs rooms, and I had not, so I went upstairs to look at them. It is amazing what all has been done in the last several weeks. But why do this project after school starts and disrupt all the classes? And of course what made it worst this week is that Tantayna was not there. When she is there, there has been hardly any communication between her and I because of the language barrier but the students do behave better when she is around.

After the look around upstairs, I did have a break until the 5th class. I told Dora that 5th and 6thgrades were fine, and for the most part they are. So I would be back for the 5th grade class to teach and decided to walk home.

I was hardly home and my phone rings. It is Dora asking me where I was. I told her I had walked home as I didn't have a class until the sixth period. Well, 7th grade she said had a surprise for me. Apparently she had talked to them. She said not to worry, just come for class 6. So I left it at that.

When I got there, several students greeted me from class 8 and apologized for their behavior. I was surprised indeed. So we will see what Friday brings when they meet again. Several more students came up to me in the hall and apologized. I would like to think their behavior will improve. I really don't want to make a mountain out of a molehill. Having a Peace Corps Volunteer is a new experience for everyone at this school. I wonder if Tantayna will have a chance to attend to the Counterpart Conference that is scheduled in November. It would be helpful to have both of us there. The location is still to be announced.

When I think about it, I really have received very little support from the teachers or Tatyana. They just say they can't speak English so do not even try to communicate with me. I realize my Bulgarian is poor, but they could try to say a few things to me. I have to ask:

"Where is class 7 meeting today?" "Is Tantayna here today?"

Knowing the "what" and "where" helps me understand what is going on. Dora has hardly been around due to all this renovation.

Well, this morning another surprise.

The phone rings about 7:30 and it is Tantayna. She said I didn't need to come in today. Is she okay? I know she really was sick, and I expected to go in and cover the classes, but Dora must have talked to her and decided I needed a day off. I'm not sure what to think. I don't want to feel like I'm getting special treatment, but at the same time I do want support. Well, tomorrow should help me figure it out. Today it is cold and I still have no heat in my apartment. I am wearing three layers of clothing.

I have a new door. On Tuesday evening a man came and did some measuring.

Milka's daughter had indicated that somebody would be coming, but I didn't know when. She called me about four o'clock and sure enough around 5:30 someone was at my door.

It was very difficult to close and lock my door. A "make do" door was put on I think after the renovation and Peace Corps required a locked door to my apartment. There was an entrance door downstairs which was kept locked also due to the Peace Corps requirements. There was no doorbell, so the only way that I knew someone was at the bottom outside door was for them to call me on the phone. This procedure worked with my School Director and the other volunteers, all of whom had my telephone number. It did not work for a student who wanted to visit or someone from the village. It did give me a layer of protection, but still was cumbersome and a doorbell would have really helped.

Sometimes Milka let a person in downstairs and I would hear a knock on my door.

"Who was it?" I wouldn't know. I wanted a door upstairs that had a lock and a window. Sometimes Milka came up and knocked and told me "someone" was waiting outside for me. Of course she was gone a lot so this method didn't always work very well.

It was rainy and cold outside. He did the measuring. He did not understand my question as to when it would be installed.

Yesterday while waiting for the train in Aitos after my language lesson with Ivanka I received a phone call from Dora. The technician was at my apartment with my new door. Would I let him in please? As I have no doorbell, this is how I usually find out if someone is at my door.

I explained to her that I was getting ready to board the train in Aitos and I would get back as soon as possible. I knew it would take at least twenty minutes or more. I never expected him to comeback the next day with my new door.

Fortunately, she was able to relay this message to him and he was waiting in his truck as I walked up the path from the train station. I let him in.

He worked until at least seven o'clock taking the old door down which is now sitting in my hallway and installed a new modern door which has a window and a lock, and I can open and close it easily. What a big improvement. It is not all finished as the framing needs to be done. Who knows when that will happen? Milka is in Istanbul again so maybe when she comes back I will find out more.

Today I did some laundry and hung it outside to dry, but it did not dry so I brought it in and now is all over my apartment. I really have to buy a clothes rack so that I have a place to hang my clothes inside. This will really become a necessity as the weather gets colder. Maybe next month I will buy that and an ironing board. Hopefully either Vesala or Dora could bring me back in their car as it would be very awkward to transport a clothes rack on the train.

It is interesting to see what people do all transport via the train. For many folks in Bulgaria it is their only means of transportation. There are buses between many of the towns but the buses generally cost more money. Not many folks can afford a car. The teachers that have a car have bought it used. It was explained to me that only the mafia in Bulgaria have new cars. I am not sure if that is true, but cars are very expensive for the average worker. And the roads between the villages are in constant need of repair. This is a problem that still needs to be addressed.

I received a short email from Nikolai and he is planning to meet me at the train station next Thursday in Sofia. His Friday is really busy, but perhaps on Saturday he will have some time to show me around. If not, I will have to manage on my own. Plus I also hope to call Svete, the young woman I talked to at camp who is a student there at Sofia University. Perhaps we will be able to meet for coffee.

It's funny, or strange, whatever the word to have a whole day just in my apartment. Not sure what to make of it. I really don't mind it seems, as long as I have something to look forward too. I'm a bit concerned about tomorrow and school, but will just have to wait and see. I'm also concerned about my house back in Farmington. The tenants are now two months behind in their rent. What to do? I have not heard from my friend in Farmington who offered to talk to the young couple who are staying at my house.

Maybe after talking to Marcus I'll have a better idea. Each month I purchase one hundred minutes. I want to also talk to Gretchen and David. One hundred minutes can be used up very quickly, but I am so glad that I found out about this telephone program to America.

I emailed Sandra at San Juan College and asked her about the adjunct faculty member who seemed interested last spring in renting my house. It turns out he is now renting a room from her. Of course the house rent would be more, but I have not heard back from her. Again, my time is so different than people back in United States going along doing their regular jobs. My job seems to be just trying to cope, teach a bit, and try to keep all the loose ends afloat.

One more item to write about tonight, I am so thankful for Ivanka my tutor. She is a gem. She couldn't believe how I have been treated at the village school. She feels it does happen even though she disapproves of it she was not all that surprised. So we discussed my situation for a short while. Ivanka had been a tutor to several Peace Corps Volunteers before me. They taught in Aitos. I was the first PCV who was placed in Topolitsa. At this point, there were no other PCV in any of the other nearby villages.

Ivanka has become a good sounding board. I guess it is her and Nikolai who I have most been relating my life too and how I'm trying to manage. They seem best to understand how difficult it is when language is a barrier. I am so impressed with both of them and how well they speak and understand English. Of course I've only been at it five months but that doesn't help me feel better about it when I'm trying to deal with the students.

Ivanka also mentioned the possibility of going with her and some other teachers to Greece for a day trip the end of the month. That would be fantastic. And then on October 26 there is a theater performance in Aitos. It is a Wednesday so I should be able to go with her. That would be so terrific. This makes up for not being invited last Saturday to tour some ship in Burgas that the teachers from Topolitsa and Aitos visited.

Andrea was there, and also my director and other teachers, but I guess they just didn't think of including me. Andrea called me around lunch time and asked what I was doing; I knew she was on a school excursion. Apparently someone did ask about me when they saw Andrea there. As it turns out, I was in Yambol visiting Tatiana and Peter. What a wonderful couple they are. It was a great visit. We walked around the City Center, and then up the hill overlooking the city and had lunch at a small outdoor café. Tatyana met me at the train station at 8 AM and we walked to Peter's apartment where he served us breakfast. All in all, it was a very pleasant day.

Hello Dora, (Peace Corps Education Director)   October 19, 2009

I have been invited by my language tutor Ivanka from Aitos to go along with her and some of the other teachers from Aitos on a day trip to Greece. It is to the city of Alexandria.

This would be on October 31. We would leave at 5 AM and return that same evening. Due to the early departure Vesala my other language tutor who is also going on the trip said that I could sleepover in her apartment the night before. She is coming to the Topolitsa celebration and I would ride back in her car to Aitos.

(As it turns out Vesala couldn't make it to Topolitsa for the celebration. I managed to get a ride with another Aitos teacher. They dropped me off on Vesala's street, but as it was raining and I had not been there before it was a challenge for me to find the correct Bloc building and what entrance to use.)

What paperwork do I need to fill out? It is OK with my school director, if PC approves for this day trip opportunity. The day before, October 30 is when the school celebrates the 125th anniversary. Perhaps you have already received the invitation.

The school is still in the midst of a complete renovation, so classes are constantly changing and moving about. It has been interesting and challenging. This Thursday I am coming by train in to Sofia for a dental appointment which is scheduled for Friday morning, so if need be I could come into the PC office.

Thank you, Louise Hoffmann

Hi Louise,   October 19, 2009

It sounds like you are having an exciting weekend. You need to send us a Leave Request Form signed by your school director or counterpart as soon as possible. You can find a copy in your Volunteer Handbook, attachment F. I attach a copy of the Leave Request form just in case you cannot find it.

Best, Dora

October 29

Last night I went with Ivanka to the theater in Aitos. It was a comedy called something like, "The Gentleman from Spain." Of course I missed most of the lines, but the costumes were fun and the facial expressions great.

On Saturday when we travel to Greece I hope Ivanka will translate more for me. As the performance went until 8 I decided to take a taxi to the train. Before my language lesson at four I had done some shopping and left it at Ivanka's house. Besides needing the time to retrieve it and my red bag being very heavy a taxi seemed best. First it seemed we might not even find a taxi. Luckily as we were about to give up, one appeared. Another passenger was in the front seat, but the driver was willing to also take me. It cost 2 lev from the center to the train, about one kilometer. (Bulgaria printed a 2 lev paper note. It also had a 5, 10 and 20 lev paper note. They were printed in different colors and varied in size. They did not have a 1 lev paper note. They did have a 1 and a 2 lev coin, plus a 5, 10 and 20 lev coin. Occasionally I had a 50 lev coin. They too were of different sizes.)

Then I walked back to my house from the train in the dark, but thankfully I had my flashlight. I have a kitty. I had brought her home the other day with me from school. She was very sweet. As it turns out today I gave her to a student who had asked his mom about the kitten and seemed to really want her. So what could I do? It would be difficult to keep a cat and travel, and deal with the litter, so while it was fun having the kitten for a day I think it is for the best.

TEACHING

Friday, October 31 was a very special day for the Svetlina School in Topolitsa. It was celebrating the 125th anniversary of its founding, 1884. The entire month before faculty, staff and students were very busy in preparing for this special celebration.

Additional monies were received from the district education office to help offset the special expenses. All the classrooms were freshly painted. Some classrooms received new chalkboards. The mural in the hall between the primary grades of Snow White, Winnie the Pooh and other favorite storybook characters was redone, led by the art teacher and students she asked to assist her.

The outside grounds were also included in the refurbishing. Before the school ball field begins the school has a lovely park area filled with trees and benches. It also has several flower gardens and these were all replanted. The special outside drinking fountains were cleaned. These are three ducks whose mouth became the stream of water for children and adults to enjoy fresh spring water.

The outside front of the school and the entrance hallway were also painted. Several parents helped with this project along with the older students. The cement steps were repaired. Everyone was excited to see their village school get a fresh new look.

The day of the event, a Friday the weather turned much cooler. All of October had been fairly warm. Now the wind started to blow and by mid-afternoon the rain came pouring down.

The Community Center, a building across the street from the school, was packed with students, parents and friends. There were also many special guests invited from the region and from Burgas, the Regional District Headquarters for the festivities that evening. Speeches were given and awards given out. The school children performed musical numbers featuring traditional Bulgarian folk songs. Other students sang some of the current musical popular songs. In addition, several special performers were invited from neighboring schools and recent graduates of Svetlina School also performed.

After the special program all were invited to the school to see all the improvements that had been worked on so diligently these past weeks. Plates and plates of food were brought in and served. It was catered by Happy's. In addition to the restaurant they have in Sofia, they have a restaurant in Burgas. It was a very special evening for the 125th Anniversary of the Svetlina School in Topolitsa.

While the school faculty, administration, and students were all getting ready for the big celebration classes continued on a fairly regular basis. This first semester, I was asked to teach grades four through eight. The higher grades met four times a week, grades three and four three times a week. There were on average fifteen students in a class. Eighth class was the biggest, with twenty eight students. I taught 15 classes a week.

First I had to learn their names. I found some of their names a challenge as they were new to my ears. Many of them had Turkish names as that was their family heritage. Radostein, Borko, Julian, Valya, Dimitar, Seid, Valentina, and Chavdar were some of the easier names for me. There were familiar names as well, to name a few Peter, Krassi, Ivanka, Astri and Andrew. I had the students print their names both in Cyrillic and in the familiar English letters.

With the younger grades I found that singing songs was a great way to have them learn. We sang and performed songs like "The Hokey Pokey," "Head and Shoulders," "Put Your Finger in the Air." Children all over the world love to sing and dance and be involved. This is a wonderful way to also learn the different color names. I would bring in pictures of the world, the sky, and sometimes food items. These were all different ways where they could hold up a pictures and say the same first in English and then Bulgarian or vice versa. We could act out small dramas:

"Inviting a friend to lunch" *"Buying a ticket for the train"*
"Shopping at a food store" *"Not feeling well"*

These were all short little skits, and depending on class time and the number of students, each child usually would have a chance to participate several times.

Sometimes, I had the students write on the chalkboard. Younger students especially love to come and write on the board.

A friend had given me a set of letters. I would pass these out and ask the students to make as many words as they could with the letters. Maybe they could even make a sentence.

In addition to using the assigned lesson book, day by day, I tried a new variation of games and songs to help the students in their English skills. In the Upper Classes, more time had to be given to the assigned lesson book. The books were from an English (Great Britain) publisher and at times, a discussion was encouraged to explain the difference between American and British English. For example, *flat* for apartment, *lift* for elevator and so on.

Some of the older students still liked to come up and write on the chalkboard, but not all. Sometimes, word puzzles were used. Or, I would hand out a variety of words for two or three students to share and see if they could create a sentence from the words in front to them.

A few times, I brought in American music for them to listen to and then interpret. We discussed television shows and different styles of clothing and eating habits. They loved to see pictures of my family, and I let them ask questions in English about what they wanted to learn about my children and where I lived. They were interested in college life, city life, magazines and television shows. Most of the children wanted to learn to speak English, but they did not want to sit quiet and just read sentence after sentence from their text book.

All the students loved to have their picture taken, and occasionally I would bring my camera to school and take a picture of the different classes, or take photos of a particular lesson or event. Sometimes, I had my camera on the playground and took pictures of the children playing with a kitten, throwing the ball, chatting with a friend, or just "hanging out." Later, I would be able to take some of these photos and make a photo album to give to the school.

Every classroom was different, and classes could be different depending on who was at school that day. The classes were never dull. I was fortunate to have my years of experience in the classroom, which helped make up for my lack of Bulgarian expertise.

On an early spring day I learned of a special outing. We were going

"Up the Mountain." Topolitsa sits on the foothills of a lovely mountain. There are vistas on the way up and many lovely trees and birds to observe along the way. Hiking is a wonderful pastime in Bulgaria and sleeping huts are provided on many of the routes. Today the students and teachers were celebrating spring and walking up the mountain. We walked through the streets of the village, passing some cows in the field and the village restaurant with its lovely flowers along the way. Then the ascent began, up, up and up. We walked for about an hour when we came to a lovely vista where we could either sit on the grass or on some worn monuments. Lunches had been brought along. There was some mountain spring water to drink. It was a day to relax and to enjoy being outdoors. Students of all ages enjoyed the camaraderie. We didn't see any storks, but seeing your first stork in spring was a sign of good luck, and it was a fun way to welcome spring.

Some of the students had singing practice once or twice a week. They were learning the traditional folk songs from a music teacher who came in from Burgas. Week after week they practiced. These students also had special traditional dresses to wear depending on what region of Bulgarian their family originated. They also learned some of the traditional dances. Several times a year the students had a chance to perform for the public.

Most of the students were female, although a few boys participated now and then. They performed at a special regional Christmas show in Aitos. Students came from different schools all over the region and performed for parents and friends in the Community Theater.

In the spring the students performed in the Plaza in Aitos to celebrate the founding of the city. And later in the spring the students went to Burgas to sing and dance in a competition for the region and then participated in the afternoon parade.

Two other very special highlights at the school need to be mentioned: the mural and the museum. While sometimes Americans think of some of the popular animated story book characters as American, many of them have European beginnings. Winnie the Pooh and Snow White and the Seven Dwarfs are two examples. Children all over the world love these stories and they both have European origins.

On a long wall between the primary classrooms is a lovely colorful mural that was designed by Yura, a very talented teacher in Topolitsa. On it are many of these story book characters painted in bright colors. The characters and the entire mural was drawn freehand. Some of the children helped paint them once the design was on the wall. It gives brightness and a sense of pride to the children to have this very special painting in the hallway.

While I worked at the school, I was allowed to use a bulletin board by the entrance to put in any announcements or special notices that I wanted to share with the students. Teaching and learning styles are shared the world over.

Another highlight of the school is the Folk Museum located on the second floor. In it are objects from earlier eras in Bulgarian history. It gives the student a chance to see clothing, kitchen utensils, fabric, furniture, and many other everyday items from their grandparents day and earlier.

The school serves about 120 students from Topolitsa and several smaller nearby villages. There are thirteen teachers, counting myself, the Director and her assistant and a school secretary. In addition there is a kitchen staff who prepare and serve lunches to the students, a full time custodian and two women who keep the classrooms very neat and tidy.

My friend Felicia started working with another volunteer to develop a national spelling bee program in Bulgaria. It took lots of coordination between the different teachers in each school and the different schools in each district. With much effort and careful planning this has become a very successful program that has continued throughout Bulgaria.

TRAIN TO SOFIA

I walked to the train about 6:40 AM Thursday, October 22. It was still dark outside. Other people were also walking as many high school students take the train into Aitos. But I only had a window of ten minutes before the fast train left from Aitos to Burgas. The train this morning was late. Oh, I couldn't believe it. I thought there might be a later train, but it still was very frustrating waiting. I wasn't sure what I'd be able to arrange as I was to be in Sofia for a medical appointment early the next day.

The train finally showed up about 7:20 and I was able to tell the conductor my dilemma. He called the Burgas / Sofia train and asked them to wait for me. Thank goodness. What a relief. This was the only fast train for the day from Aitos. If the train to Sofia had left without me on it, it would have been difficult to rearrange all the appointments.

The conductor actually took my bag for me and handed it to the other conductor on the fast train. Fortunately I had bought a first class ticket as it gave me an assigned seat. (Second class train seats are not assigned. Slow trains only have second class wagons. Only on my trips to Sofia could I purchase a first class ticket and have an assigned seat.) In reality it costs only about 4 lev more, but for many Bulgarians that is way too much money. As soon as I boarded the train it left. I was off to Sofia.

On the train, I mainly read my book, did some language study and watched the scenery. Nikolai had sent me a text that he couldn't meet me at the train, but could meet me at 6 PM at the National Palace of Culture (NDK). This is the big performance hall that was built by the USSR in commemoration of the 1,300th anniversary of Bulgaria as a nation.

He was concerned that I didn't see the text, so he also emailed me and gave me directions to get to my hotel. This was my first train trip to Sofia. I recognized what I thought was the bus station and decided to walk over there to see if I could find the Vagabond magazine and use their toilet facilities which I remembered as being clean.

After the bus terminal I had to figure out where to buy my ticket. Without too much difficulty I managed to find the ticket booth and buy two tickets for two lev. Lazar had told us that if we had a suitcase with us, we needed to buy a ticket for it as well as for ourselves as it took up extra space. I needed to board either tram number 7 or 1 as they both went down the main street, Vitosha. The tram stop was near the ticket booth. But what I didn't do is get my tickets punched as soon as I boarded. As a result, I got fined 10 lev by a very insistent security person who boarded the tram after a few stops. These are random checks to see that everyone has bought a valid ticket. First, I thought I would have to leave the tram and walk the rest of the distance. A young woman offered to help interpret. Since I paid my fine, I found out I could stay on until my stop. She ended up helping meal so locate my hotel. It was called, The House / Restaurant. It was off on a side street of Vitosha, near the NDK.

I was very happy to see the sign, The House/Restaurant. It was a converted house made into a restaurant with rooms on the second and third floor. I was welcomed by Evan. He spoke English. I had a very nice cozy room and I would stay here often on my trips into Sofia. It became my home away from home whenever I visited Sofia. It was now only a little past 3 PM.

I walked over to the NDK and tried to figure out where I was to meet him. It was a very big plaza, with gardens and some fountains and many entry points. I saw him come up some stairs. It was good to see him again. We had a very long walk around the center of Sofia. He was tired after a busy day of teaching. I had so many questions to ask him. He couldn't visit long as he needed to catch transportation back to his village. On Friday he had a busy day with several classes to teach.

We sat for a little while at the outdoor garden café by The House. I gave him the books I brought along, *Solo* and *The Giver*. I also gave him the book of poetry that was included with *Vagabond*. I had a copy already as it had also been included in the previous month's edition. Depending on his schedule he would contact me about a walking tour of Sofia and meet up on Saturday.

On Friday I walked to the dentist's office. I found it without too much difficulty. It was in a five star hotel about just a mile away from The House where I was staying. The cleaning and check up took over three hours.

They greatly recommend that I come every six months. Hopefully Peace Corps will agree that it is necessary. For now I have to pay for the extra cleaning, 100 lev. The dentist also put a coating like substance on my one tooth where the gum seems to be wearing away. I had mentioned this to my American dentist some time ago, but he didn't know of anything to do. Hopefully, this will prevent further wearing and also look better. I needed to get this in writing from my U.S. dentist for Peace Corps approval. Whenever, we traveled for medical reasons, educational meetings or other valid expenses, forms needed to be filled out and turned in for approval in order to get reimbursement. This often took two months or longer before the reimbursement money appeared in our banking account.

After the appointment I stopped at the City Center Mall that Felicia had mentioned to me. I found a pair of black jeans at Mark and Spencer's, a chain department store based out of England. They cost 65 lev which was the most I had paid for a pair of pants since my arrival, but I felt a need to treat myself to some new clothes. I also found a knit cap and a narrow brown belt. I found several candles on sale in a kiosk. I left messages with Felicia, but did not realize they were going to her old number. She had lost her telephone. I was trying to ask her if she could come back to Sofia. It would be great if her schedule permitted. Felicia lived about an hour away from Sofia. It took me until much later when she sent me a text that I found out she had not received any of my messages. She had bought a new phone and had a new number. She had already decided to come.

I seemed to be finding my way around okay, but as yet I had not made it on my own to the Peace Corps headquarters. As it turns out for this first time on my own in the city, a Peace Corps staff was traveling near the NDK and would meet me there and bring me my mail and other reports that had accumulated in my mail box in Sofia. I would face the challenge of finding my way to 24 Pirinski Prohod Street on my next visit.

I got a text message from Nikolai Saturday morning while I was touring the Bulgarian art museum. He wondered if meeting at five at the NDK could work. Felicia had also contacted me about coming to Sofia around lunch time. It would be a fun filled day.

Felicia and I walked around Sofia. We wanted to get better acquainted with the city. We went into St. Nedelia's church, the historic round church where Communist activists planted bombs earlier in the century and 150 persons were killed and over 500 injured on the April 14, 1924. The terrorists had hoped to kill the monarch Tsar Boris III but he was not in attendance that day. Many other political leaders were killed as they were attending a funeral of a noted general.

We also went into St. George, the old Roman church considered the oldest building in Sofia built by the Romans in the 4th century. Bulgarian

Orthodox services are still held there on a regular basis.

Nearby is the TZUM market. It gets its abbreviated name from the Bulgarian, TZUM Central Department Store (magazine). It was built during the Communist Era in 1956 as a mall for the common people. After 1989 it was public property and then sold to a Hong Kong developer who turned it into an upscale Mall. It almost felt like being back in the U.S. A.

We had lunch at Happy's. This is the most American type of restaurant in Sofia. It was started after the fall of communism in 1989 by a group of Americans anxious to bring some American cuisine into the country. They serve hamburgers and French fries, pizza and pasta as well as a variety of popular Bulgarian dishes. The menu is both in English and Bulgarian which was not generally done before 1989. It is a popular stop with Peace Corps Volunteers and tourists when they become hungry for American cuisine. It is one of the few restaurants in Sofia where the name is spelled in English letters. The story is told of an unsuspecting PCV thinking the name was in Cyrillic letters and thought the name was Narro's.

Not too far away is the Ethnological Museum which I had started to tour before Felicia arrived. It is housed in the former Royal Palace. It has been somewhat restored and is now filled with thousands of objects, including woodworking, clothes, embroideries, and many other Bulgarian artifacts.

We met Nikolai at 5 PM at the NDK which is about a 30-minute walk from the museum. It was a pleasant fall day. We walked through lovely neighborhoods and park gardens and around the big soccer stadium. He was more rested than Thursday night and in very good spirits. It was fun. He needed to catch a bus at 7, so the time again would be short. It was a good weekend and fun to be in the city. I just wanted it to be longer.

I made numerous trips for medical concerns to Sofia. I tried to schedule them on Fridays if I could. I needed a full travel day there and another day for the return back to Topolitsa. Several times I needed to visit the dentist. He was in a separate office in a hotel on the 14th floor about a mile from where I stayed at The House. Another time I needed to see a specialist about my arthritis as Peace Corps was concerned about my fingers as they had become swollen and very noticeably bent on several of the joints. For this I went first to the Peace Corps office in Sofia and then a staff person went with me for the drive by a Peace Corps driver to the specialist office in another part of Sofia. The Peace Corps medical personnel scheduled these visits. I also needed to see an eye specialist as my eyes were bothering me. For this again, I went with a Peace Corps staff person from the Sofia office.

And one time I had a test needed that was given at the new hospital in Sofia that was built with grant monies from Japan. It was a "state-of-the-art" hospital. Again, a staff person went with me and we went via Peace Corps transportation.

For routine items, like a cough or cold, blood pressure check-up, PC had two doctors on duty in the Sofia medical office most days. Supplies like band-aids, allergy pills could also be picked up in the medical offices. For any prescriptions that a PCV was taking when you began your service, a copy of your prescription was given to the Peace Corps office and they filled them under the U.S. government PC guidelines. If you were ill and it was not life-threatening, PC provided a room at the office for you to stay in while being treated. Fortunately, I never had to stay overnight in the sickbay office.

All PCVs were given a first aid kit when we arrived at our Orientation in Bulgaria. It contained all the basic items we would need for routine ailments. At our regional meetings, Peace Corps staff often brought along some medical supplies. I was given a blood pressure self monitor to keep track of my blood pressure and had to report it to the medical staff on a regular basis. Only in an extreme emergency did Peace Corps allow a volunteer to go to a doctor in their neighborhood. In this way, they felt they were giving PCV the same care as if they worked for the government in the United States.

FRIENDS NEAR AND FAR

Monday, November 2, 2009

Today I received the pictures from my friend Irma that I had asked her to print. It is so terrific of her to do that for me. I have so many good friends back in the U.S. Irma sending pictures, my sisters sending clothes and other essential items and my brother Loren mailed me special books on Bulgaria that I requested and my children all have mailed assorted things.

Many of my friends throughout the United States have sent books to help me start an English library for the students. They include: Sharrey and Nancy, friends from high school days; Sharon, a college library director in New Mexico; Jim, a colleague at San Juan College; Trish, another librarian friend has sent me numerous packages including CDs and DVDs; Dana a former colleague sent me some knitting supplies; Susan, another dear friend and librarian who I worked with in Pittsburgh mailed a box of books; Donna, another good friend from Pittsburgh and women from Trinity Church in Farmington all sent books for the school English library. More books continue to come almost weekly. They are all keeping the packages small so that they will be delivered directly to Topolitsa so that I don't have to go through the Customs hassle. The exception to this rule is a charity set up in the United States to donate used books to disadvantaged countries as long as the proper forms are filled out. They sent several bigger boxes of used books for the children to read.

I have another kitten. I saw her last week in the school yard and the children suggested I take her home. The children liked her and I asked several of them to consider her. The next day, Krazi said he would like her. I thought that would be good, even though in a way I hated to give her up, but knew that would make my life easier.

Well, today returning to the school to get some apples that were being given out, there was the kitty. I don't know if Krazi had brought her over, or she was just there. But I recognized her and right away she let me pick her up. Well, I decided to take her. I didn't want to leave her outside in the chance she would disappear and it was cold out. She snuggled up in my coat and I took her for a walk. I had decided I needed to take a walk. Even though it was cold, the sun was shining. She seemed quite content.

I am so glad that I had saved the box of dirt that I had prepared last week for her. And she knew the house. She walked right to the kitchen looking for food. She was hungry. Fortunately I had some chicken. Now she is sleeping on my lap. So we'll see how this goes. I mentioned to Krazi about watching her when I was gone. But I know most families here do not let cats in the house. They like pets, but see them only as outside pets. Hopefully, Milka would take care of her if I'm gone more than a day.

I listened to the CD *Bulgarian for Foreigners,* read *Under the Yoke* and my history of Bulgaria. Crampton, the author, will be on the panel with Nikolai at his seminar in Dublin. What a small world indeed.

Late fall 2009

It was another nice weather day and I did more laundry. I could hang my clothes outside on my deck. I actually have two decks, one outside a door of my living room and the other outside a bedroom door. Only one has lines to hang my clothes. I have a small wash machine in my kitchen. It is very convenient in the warm summer months and the fall season. In the winter I have to hang my clothes in the house in my dining room area as that is the only room with heat. It often takes two or three days to dry my laundry in the winter as the heat usually goes off during the night.

When I first came to Bulgaria I had to do all my laundry by hand. The water had to be heated with a small electric coil. I plugged it in an outside outlet near the outside shower room where I could get the water for the bucket. Then I placed the coil in the bucket of cold water. It took about fifteen minutes to heat the water. The hot water was then carried and poured into the outside wash tub, which was closer to the house. I added some soap, which I had bought the previous week in Vrasta with the help of Lazar, the Peace Corps teacher who was assigned to Banitsa.

The other side of the washtub I used cold water to rinse my clothes. My clothes were hung on the lines that were strung around the outside of the garden plot to dry. This was like my childhood on days when I helped my mother hang out the wash back in Wisconsin. There were many things while in Peace Corps that reminded me of my growing-up years in the 1950s back in rural Wisconsin.

I'm waiting to hear from the Kelly's and the Federwitz's. These are friends that I've known since my undergraduate days at Concordia. They are getting together in Philadelphia today and are going to try and reach me via Skype. It's 10:15 PM here already.

It is amazing to me how many people here use Skype. Many use it in place of telephone service which is comparatively more expensive. It is the way that many keep in touch on a daily basis here in Bulgaria.

I was so tired that I laid down and set my alarm. I wish I could sleep late, but I usually wake up early and don't sleep all that soundly. I'm sure it's also my bed. It's like sleeping on a board. I'll be happy to have a softer mattress again.

Bob and Ellie moved back to the East Coast. They were ready to retire and wanted to be closer to their children and grandchildren. All three of their children live within an hour of Philadelphia. Ellie is glad to be nearer their children but misses California and all that sunshine. The transition is always difficult I think when you move, especially cross country.

When I teach English classes to adults over here that are amazed how much Americans travel and how many of them leave their home base. In one particular class to a group of engineers in Burgas it was mentioned that even though they might go away to the University, after they finish their course work and have their degree they expect to find a job back near where their parents and other siblings live. Many of them move back to their childhood home to live in the same house with their parents. The houses are designed for three or even four generations to share. Once married, they often have their own floor or flat (apartment) but would share the same entrance door and at least once a week have a meal together.

I made some chocolate chip cookies tonight. I could have used more butter if I had it, but they turned out quite good. I find it very hard to get the oven temperature just right. I plan to take some cookies in to school tomorrow. The teachers often bring in treats to share with each other. Earlier in the year I brought in a plum pie made from the plum off of my landlady's plum tree.

Well, I'll send this off and turn on Skype. I hope it works tonight. Sometimes it crashes my computer; I will wait and see what happens today.

Hi Louise,   **September 16, 2009**

Tomorrow one of my students is going to give us a lift by car to Burgas. He is from Karnobat so it's not problem for him to do this. The meeting with him will be close to the traffic lights (the circle there, the rounded traffic) at 4:30 PM. If you'd like, I can wait for you straight there or earlier at 4 o'clock near the post station. You decide how is better for you.

Ivanka

Hi Louise,   **September 22, 2009**

According to my schedule I have time for Bulgarian lessons in the following days: on Monday – I'm free after 1 PM (you can choose what time) on Wednesday after 3 PM on Friday – I am off from my regular teaching duties so you can choose the time Tell me which day is convenient for you.

I'm sending to you the photos from your special visitation of the English course in Burgas. I am so happy that you agreed to do this. It was very kind of you. It was very interesting and helpful for my students there and for me.

Greetings, Ivanka

Hello Louise,

I haven't heard from you for ages it seems but I do hope you are fine and feeling well.

I've been so busy since school started. I had many entry tests to mark. I'm also a class teacher and have many duties that go with it. It is always the same at the beginning – a bit hectic.

I hope things have settled with your schedule. And now comes the routine. I'll be looking forward to your reply. Sometime in the afternoon after 4 I can usually be reached.

Have a nice forthcoming week, Tatayna

Hi Tatyana,   **October 4, 2009**

I was hoping to email you earlier today, but have had Internet problems. Everything seems to be working OK now. I also had to have Excel installed to do a report for Peace Corps.

Yesterday I had the wonderful opportunity to visit Sozopul. What a fantastic historic city. I went with Vesala, who is one of Andrea's counterparts, and also is going to be helping me with Bulgarian lessons.

I also have been meeting with Ivanka who speaks English quite well. She had me come to Burgas with her to speak to a group of engineers who are studying English. That was a very nice evening for me. I talked about the U.S., travel and my family. I do want to come to Yambol and just visit with you, and maybe a little shopping or the art gallery and a walk in the park.

Maybe the new *Vagabond* is out on the newsstand. Would this Saturday work for you? Or Sunday, October 10 or 11? The following weekend could also be a possibility.

I finally was able to get the train card so that will make my train travel half price. I had to go to Burgas for it, as in Aitos they said they could not sell it to a non-Bulgarian.

Louise

Hi Louise,   **October 6, 2009**

I was glad to hear from you. I think Saturday October 10th will be okay with me. I can meet you at the station at 8 AM and have a similar nice day in Yambol as the previous time. Days are getting shorter and you'll have to get up early but there isn't more convenient time. I'll let you know if something pops up. The art gallery is not open on weekends but we'll compensate somehow.

Hi Tatyana,   **October 7, 2009**

It will be nice to see you on Saturday. But if you feel too busy just let me know and I can come another time.

It can be a quiet day. It's good to visit and perhaps a walk in the park. I have no special shopping needs, except *Vagabond* if it's available. I always like to look in stores, so if you would like to that is fine with me. One other possibility are second-hand shops. I have found a few bargains at them in Aitos and Sliven on the day we had a meeting there. I'll also bring some of the books along that I've finished. Now I've started *Under the Yoke*. (A Classic Bulgarian novel about the freedom struggles in the 19th century from the Ottoman Empire.) I know it will take me some time to read.

This morning I am waiting for the technician as I have no hot water. Monday this was also a problem, but was fixed for a day. So we will see what will happen next. Unless I hear from you otherwise, I will plan to be on the train arriving at 8:05. And the train back is at 6:52. If you have other plans in the evening I can just wait at the station by myself so not to tie up your evening time. I now have a train card so it will not be very expensive to ride the train.

Louise

Hello Louise,   **October 8, 2009**

Yes, Saturday remains as we have already planned it. I hope we'll have more time to talk. The weather will be the same as today's but next week it's getting cold according to the forecast.

I'm not sure which train at 6. 50 PM you mean for the journey back but we can check and decide when you arrive. I have to prepare for tomorrow. See you on Saturday at 8 at the station.

Tatyana

Hello Tatyana,   **October 10, 2009**

Thank you for the wonderful day. It was so great to see you and Peter again. I enjoyed the walk, shopping, breakfast, lunch and especially the conversation.

It was a very pleasant day. I made it back just as planned. The train made up some of the time to Karnobat, and then the Burgas train arrived right at 6:03 and pulled out again at 6:15. I made it back to my apartment before dark.

Thank you again for the loan of the movie.* I plan to watch it tonight, having a piece of bread with the rose hip marmalade and tea. I hope that you make it to the conference. If not, we will visit soon again either in Topolitsa or Yambol. In a day or two I will send you some of the pictures that I took.

With warm regards, Louise

We started to exchange some English movies. My computer allowed me to only watch those formatted for U.S. screens.

Chat via Google transcript, October 7, 2009,
12:45 PM

Laura: I made it home but will not take the night train again
Me: was there a problem?
Laura: There was an old man who was drinking a lot on the train after you left – kept trying to get my attention little girl, little girl and then when I was getting off the train there was another man who got uncomfortably close to me and just stared me down.
Me: Oh, yuk . . . I was wondering . . . there did seem to be some "seedy" sort of people around Laura: so, no more night trains
Laura: yeah, there were.
12:46 PM

Laura: and the lights went out so 1/2 the train ride was in the dark
Laura: so, sticking to the buses from now on me: next time for sure the bus. . .
Laura: yeah me: for sure
Laura: anyway... thank you for meeting me today, it was really great.
Laura: It was extremely relaxing for me – I needed it
12:47 PM

Me: We will do it again soon . . . maybe on a Sunday for a longer walk on the beach . . . . and please think of 17th in Topolitsa, and December break in Istanbul.
12:49 PM

Laura: yes to all
Laura: thank you for the invitations

Me: I would so love to have you come with me and David. . . do you know Diana in Lom. . . perhaps she would come too

Laura: I'm thinking I probably will join you for the new year – I'll give you a definite answer in a day or two

12:50 PM

Me: super. . . that would make me so happy. . . .

Laura: :) me too, really.

Me: and would it be OK with you to extend invite to Diana? Laura: of course

12:51 PM

Me: I'll send her a message

Me: I can call her with my phone also. . . so she'll feel doubly invited :)

12:52 PM

Laura: haha

Me: Sweet dreams. . . hope teaching goes OK tomorrow. . . . now I'm hungry for a Big Mac

Laura: true

12:53 PM

Laura: haha ME TOO

Me: next time

Me: sweet dreams to you, too.

Me: Take care of yourself . . . .

Laura: you too, Louise

Me: let me know if you need anything

12:55 PM

Me: Thanks Laura . . . I'm glad you're my neighbor. Sweet dreams and good luck tomorrow

Laura: you too –

Me: sweet dreams to you too Laura: good night :)

Hi Louise,   **October 17, 2009**

You are right – the weather became cold and you need a stove. All day I am close to mine. I hope that you will have heat and not to be frozen. If you have an electric stove use it.

About the trip you have to send me or bring to me on Wednesday a copy of your ID card and passport. The trip starts on 31st October (Saturday). The departure will be at the circle by bus at 5 am. The arriving will be round 10 PM at the same place. The traveling expenses are 45 lev. The passing of Bulgarian/Greek boarder will be through "Kapitan Petko Voivoda," Svilengrad city. Arriving at Alexandropulos will be round 11 AM Sightseeings: the coast alley with the popular Alexandropolis Lighthouse, the harbor, the church "Saint Nikola" with the healing icon of the Virgin Vesala "Trifotisa" from 13th century. There will be about an hour and 30 minutes free time for shopping, visitation of the shop Jumbo and the shop LIDL.

About the theater in Aitos: on 28th October at 6 PM in the Culture Centre. Entrance is free.

Ivanka

Hi Louise,   **November 3, 2009**

Congratulations! So exciting to hear about Marcus and Stacey. You will become a grandma about the same time as I will and Loren a Grandpa. Hard to believe, but I'm ready for it.

I bet you are getting very excited for Marcus's and David's visit.

I have been thinking about you often, and have read all the letters you have copied me on or sent to Loren. I've enjoyed reading about all your experiences. It sounds like you have had many challenges, and have really done a great job adapting to the situation there as well as take advantage of the many possibilities to explore the culture and country there.

Over Halloween here, I heard something about one of our local stores that specializes in costumes; they had an order to send some to Bulgaria. I was surprised, and am curious, what do people do over there during that time. Is there some similar celebration or something?

What did you do over Thanksgiving? Was there any sort of getting together with other Americans or did you still have to teach during that time?

We had Thanksgiving at our house with my sisters and Rebecca and Mark. I had a nice long stretch off of work, so I was really happy about that. Due to the poor state of Wisconsin economy, as a University of Wisconsin State employee I have to take eight furlough days a year for the next two years. I like having that extra time off, but of course don't like the reduced pay that goes with it.

Interesting to hear you are now teaching younger children too. How many classes do you teach between older and younger? Is it all teaching English? Sounds like a very full day

How is your heater working for you? Just how cold does it get there?

We don't have any snow here yet this year. The longer the better, as far as I'm concerned well, it is almost time for bed here. I hope you are having a good week. Take care.

Love, Anita

Hi Laura,   **November 8, 2009**

I hope that you will plan on coming to visit me here. I suggest Tuesday. There is a train from Karnobat at either 9:36 AM or 11:05 AM. It takes only about 20 minutes. Let me know which train you come and I will meet you.

I looked up Pomorie in both the Rough Guide and Lonely Planet. Neither thought they were worth a visit. I think maybe in the summer to the beach there perhaps, but they indicated that with the fire in 1906, the old lovely buildings are not the same and it is a small modern town but nothing outstanding. Vesala told me that often in the winter the buses run much less frequently to these resort towns than in the summer.

What I suggest instead is to come to Topolitsa. We can walk, talk and play Scrabble if you like. It will be a quiet kind of day visiting. But if the weather's nice we can take a long walk around the village. You can plan to sleep over if you like. I have an extra bedroom with two beds and in the morning either go back to Karnobat, or come with me into Aitos. We could have lunch together and perhaps Andrea could join us.

Hope you get your phone fixed on Monday. It really is much safer to have a working phone. You also have to meet my kitty.

Hope that you will consider it. While I love beach towns and old towns it doesn't sound to me from what I've read that it is worth the effort to visit Pomorie now. We could plan to do that next spring sometime as the weather gets warm and the days get longer.

It will be so nice to see you again. I do hope that you will come.

Louise

Hi LaVerne,   **Veterans Day 2009**

My back feels a bit better today. At least it doesn't hurt with every move anymore.

Regarding lifting, the PC makes no concessions on age, or on what we are expected to do. And as they only require your site (my school) to provide me with one room that has heat, they meet the regulations. As far as explaining "kindling wood" I've yet to find a dictionary with that word.

I have three dictionaries but how we describe something and how another cultural describes is not always the same. I think she understood "small wood" but that isn't necessarily the word that they use to describe the wood to start a fire.

My landlady is more sympathetic, but doesn't speak a word of English and even has a hard time understanding me when I speak Bulgarian to her. Two of my dictionaries go at it from Bulgarian to English, so unless you have some idea of the word it is challenging.

When I get to Plovdiv and speak to the woman I know from Yambol I will have her write it up for me in Bulgarian. She is very patient and understanding. She has worked with PC for a number of years and is much more aware of various situations that arise. She also has a daughter-in-law living in London and understands more adapting to a culture.

This is the first year for Topolitsa to work with the PC so everything is new to them. My counterpart, who should be the interpreter, speaks less English than the school director. Because of the above is why I was so disappointed when the site visit from PC was canceled last week due to the flu. At the same time, now that the school gave me this tiny space heater, about 4 by 6 inches. I know the PC will not reimburse me for the bigger space heater that I bought. I saw this tiny one in the store and was about half the price, but the language teacher from Aitos who was with me, thought that the bigger one was much better and I agreed.

It's like the stove situation earlier in August. If I wanted one that really worked, a new one, I would have to pay for it myself. My new stove has two oven racks; the old stove had no oven racks, and the burners didn't heat. So, I'm trying to take it all in stride. Most PC workers have different but similar stories. What PC emphasizes is to adapt and to be flexible. I probably could write a book already about assorted items; but that will have to wait for several years.

Today I will go to Aitos for my last lesson before the test next week, so need to study this morning.

Love, Louise

Dear Grace,   **November 23, 2009**

It was so good to hear from you. It was about a year ago that we celebrated Thanksgiving together in New Mexico. That was such a good time. I always enjoyed having you and Mike over for good conversation. And I was so glad that you were able to take the time to stop in for tea the following week.

It is hard to believe that I've been here now six months. It is a good country I think for me to be in. I love the history and the topography and I'm gradually learning the language, but I can't imagine ever knowing it well.

This past weekend I had the opportunity to go with a group of teachers from a neighboring school on an excursion to several historic villages in southwest Bulgaria. It involved quite a long bus ride, but it was worth it. We were near the Greek border.

The two main towns were Bansko and Melnick, and a monastery called Rozhen. The roads to these historic towns reminded me of the mountain roads to Silverton and Ouray in Colorado.

It is very different scenery than where I live here near the Black Sea. It was over an eight hour bus ride one way. We stayed overnight in a small hotel in Bansko which is now quite well known as a ski resort in the Pirin Mountains. Its early renown is as the home of Nikola Vaptsarov, a poet and activist. These towns go back centuries. A few of the teachers on the bus spoke some English so I managed. On the way back the history teacher played his accordion and sang Bulgarian folk songs.

I have been trying to get a fire going in my little wood stove, but guess I had too much wet wood. It just won't catch, so now I have on my little space heater. Fortunately, it is not too cold out tonight, about 50° Fahrenheit.

I hope to write a Thanksgiving / Christmas letter email soon so I will fill in some details of life here. Yes, walking is still done quite a bit, and train and bus travel is used extensively. Some people do have cars, but two-car families are rare. Most Bulgarians buy a used car. A new car is out of the price range for most people. Bulgaria doesn't manufacture their own car so all the cars, new and many used cars, are imported.

I was told Bulgaria did not have enough population so there isn't a company interested in investing here. Given its location in Europe, German, French and Swedish cars are not that far away. Ford has a plant in Turkey and Germany I believe.

I've been busy reading history books and some memoirs of those who grew up under Communism. For a change of pace tonight, I picked up a mystery novel by Carl Hiaasen. I had never read one of his books, and needed something light; a hurricane, murder, bribery, all the great stuff out of Miami.

Well, I need to turn in soon; it was late last night, getting home after midnight with our bus excursion and we left shortly after 4 AM Saturday morning.

Marcus and David are coming for Christmas. It will be so terrific to see them. Marcus can stay for only for a few days, but David will be here until New Year's Day. We may go to Istanbul with a few other volunteers while he is here.

I hope this finds you well, and taking some time for yourself. I hope you have a chance to visit your parents, and maybe an extra day or two just "to be."

Your friend, Louise

Dear Sisters,   **November 23, 2009**

I'm trying to remember what travel I wrote about. The back and forth to Aitos is how I do my grocery shopping and banking as there are only a few small stores here in the village and no bank. We get our money from the PC through an account set up like a credit card which we can pull from. All transactions here are in cash. Only in Sofia and a few stores in Burgas accept credit cards. It is so different from the United States where I was using a credit card for just about everything. Here it is certainly still a cash economy, even to pay bills.

The travel over the weekend was fun, but the bus ride was very long. We got back about midnight last night. We were only about ten miles from Greece and very close to Macedonia.

I roomed with a daughter of one of the teachers; she didn't speak

English, but we managed. We stayed at a small hotel and paid only 20 lev a night so I certainly can't complain; plus it had heat and a hairdryer.

We went to several house museums of Bulgarians: the poet Nikola Vaptsarvo and founder of their education system, Neofit Rilski and the Rozhen Monastery. We also toured a very old winery and tasted what is considered some of the best wine in Europe and the world. The winery has caves like in Champagne, France. We had dinner at a very traditional Bulgarian restaurant and danced the *hora*.

On the way back one of the teachers played the accordion on the bus and sang some Bulgarian folk songs. A few of the teachers spoke some English.

I can't get my wood to burn tonight, so have my little space heater going. I think my wood is just damp; the paper burned, but even that struggled as it's been so damp.

I finished a very insightful book about life in Bulgaria from the mid-1930's to 1965, called *Dreams and Shadows*. (The author, Radka Yakimov, tells the story of her mother, a research scientist, attending a conference in Denmark. Her most memorable impression was the modern toilets. They were led to believe in Bulgaria that other European countries did not have these modern conveniences. She began to wonder more about what life was like in the free-world countries.)

It's hard to imagine living under such changes. During Communism, very few people were allowed to travel. If they traveled it generally was to other Eastern European countries, not the free world.

Dora (Peace Corps Education Program Director) is coming this Wednesday so I need to prepare for those classes and our meeting. I wonder how that will go. I wonder what she will think of my ancient wood stove known as the Bulgarian miracle.

Well, time for bed. I have an 8 AM class tomorrow.

Love, Louise

THANKSGIVING

Hello Felicia,   **November 23, 2009**

How are you feeling? Hopefully you are over your cold and back to work. I've been trying to get a fire going for about an hour now in my "Bulgarian miracle" and guess I've give up. My kindling wood is gone, and most of my matches. Tomorrow I should get more kindling wood. I hope it's dry. I can't even get some of my paper to burn, everything is so damp.

I had wanted to check on the bus schedule to Istanbul on Friday but Vesala was busy, so will do that this Wednesday with my other language tutor.

I'll plan to take the Friday early train to Sofia and hopefully arrive around 2:20. I'll check your email, but I think that works out with the train you mentioned. Do you want/need me to bring anything? It doesn't seem possible that Thanksgiving is this week already.

Talk to you soon, Louise

Hello Ivanka,   **November 23, 2009**

I passed my language exam. Thank you for all your help. I would like to continue my lessons.

Is this Wednesday at 3 PM okay?

Also, if you have time this Wednesday would you come with me to the bus station to inquire about the bus to Istanbul? Could I have a lesson from 3 to 4 and then go to the bus?

Thank you, Louise

Hi Louise,   **November 23, 2009**

I'm so glad to hear that you have passed the exam. Well done to you. I am proud of you. Wednesday is OK for me and it's not problem for me to come with you to the bus station. You will explain to me what exactly you want to do when we see each other on Wednesday, to buy ticket or something else.

See you soon, Ivanka

Hi Felicia   **November 28, 2009**

Hope your day went well. I would have loved to come, but I realized that I really was exhausted from the last two weekends, so thought it was best I stayed here. I did go into Aitos today and spent the afternoon with Andrea and Anna. We played UNO and just had a quiet time. Andrea roasted a chicken, I brought along mashed potatoes. I wish you a Happy Thanksgiving.

After talking to Andrea we decided it would be good to travel together to Istanbul. With her boy friend and David I think taking the night bus from Aitos on the 29th would be safe. That would get us into Istanbul around 7 AM. We could return on January 2nd. Would that work for you? I can look for lodging tomorrow, so that we can get our forms to Peace Corps. I've sent an email to Diana to see what she is planning; hope she can make it.

I'll call you late morning tomorrow.

Hope that you had a good day, Louise

Hi Louise,   **November 29, 2009**

I see, just like a man, you dumped me for a younger woman. haha.

No, I really wish you could have been here. I have tons of food, but we are going to have round two today, so I hope that puts a bigger dent in it. Also, Tricia and a friend are supposed come this morning. She missed her train stop last night, or would have been here earlier. I hope they bring an appetite.

I will try to touch base with you later this evening. I'm going to Sofia tomorrow for a Junior Achievement training, so worse case, I will talk to you tomorrow night or Tuesday.

Hi Felicia,

Did you actually find a turkey? Amazing. Andrea found a chicken, and we thought that was doing well. I think it was the ten minute train ride versus the eight-hour journey that made my final decision not to travel to Vershets at this time. I was home before seven last night. Anna decided to sleep over. She is north of Burgas, near Sunny Beach I think. Laura was invited, but decided not to come. She doesn't have her phone fixed. I'm concerned, but not sure what I can do.

Last night my son and his wife did a Skype chat with me from Hawaii and their happy news is that Stacey is pregnant. The baby is due in June. Will that make me a *baba*?

Oh my, I'm going to try and find a hotel in Istanbul today and tomorrow deal with my cat. If the student doesn't want him back I think I may just put him out on the street. What do you think I should do? Enjoy all your goodies. I do wish I could just take wings and be with you all there.

Louise

BOOKS, BOOKS, BOOKS

Dear Peggy,

I am a Peace Corps volunteer in a small village in Bulgaria near the Black Sea. I teach English to students in grades 2 – 8. The school has approximately 120 students in these grades. It also has a first grade, but English begins in the second grade. Several other villages bus their students to Topolitsa. I have been receiving some books from friends in the U.S., but as you know, postage is very expensive. I was so happy to hear about your program. Other than their textbook, the school students currently only have the English books that I've been able to have my friends and relatives send me.

I have the full set of the Harry Potter books, some of the older classics like *Oliver Twist, Moby Dick* and *Tom Sawyer* and some old Golden books. Some of the newer classics I think would be terrific for the students here to read, e.g., Judy Blume, Lois Lowry, L'Engle, Dr. Seuss, and *Winnie the Pooh*. Perhaps the *Little House on the Prairie* set. I think the students here could identify with Laura. Also books on heroes and sports figures would be enjoyed by students. And I would like books on the U.S.A., geography, teen life, European countries, culture and the environment. Some alphabet books for the second grade would be helpful as well, perhaps a few books on popular music stars, or pop culture, but not at the expense of the other types of books.

This is my first year here in Topolitsa. I will be here until the end of July 2011. Thank you very much. I was so happy to learn of your program. My address is: Louise Hoffmann, Peace Corps Volunteer OU "Svetlina," Celo: Topolitsa 8549 Ob. Aitos Obl. Burgas, BULGARIA.

Dear Louise,

I got your request for books and there is sufficient information in your email for me to type up your request. I'll send an email when the books leave Darien.

Peggy Minnis, Darien Book Aid Plan, Inc.

Dear Sharrey and Nancy,   **February 2010**

Thank you again for your wonderful support of mailing books to the students here in Bulgaria. The students that I have shared them with have been very excited about them.

As I'm here through next school year I know having these books for the students is a big incentive for them to learn to read English. I hope to come up with some kind of project idea to determine who will receive the book bags. That may wait until next school year.

Everyone here is waiting for springtime, especially me. When it snows the roads really are a mess. Last weekend we had some rain and then it turned colder, so the roads were covered with ice. Today it is melting and I am very happy about that.

This coming week I travel to Sofia for some medical appointments. It takes me almost eight hours going by train. I need some tests done, including testing for rheumatoid arthritis. It has especially affected my fingers.

While I'm in Sofia I'm hoping to see a movie. I have not been to a movie theater since I've arrived here. Only the bigger cities have theaters so hopefully there will be a movie of interest playing. I know Avatar was advertised but I am not sure if I want to see that or not. Have you?

Well, I need to do some reading. I hope this finds you both well and thank you again for sending the books.

Your "old" friend, Louise   (*We were high school friends in Wisconsin.*)

Louise,   **December 15, 2009**

Today at my domino's Christmas party the group gave me a donation of $50 to continue "Books for Bulgaria." I was very pleased that we are able to continue our mission. I will be sending another box tomorrow I will also in the future when the Christmas rush is over include the names of my domino's friends and would appreciate a thank you if that's not too much trouble. You could send it to me and I will pass it along either via email or snail mail. Again, I wish you and your family that will be visiting along with your new family of Bulgarian friends a very Merry Christmas and Blessed New Year.

God Bless, Nancy

Thank you Nancy.   **December 16, 2009**

After the Christmas break I will work with the students to compose thank you letters. It will be a good writing project for them.

I will look for this next box of books. If you want to wait to mail it until after the Christmas rush at the Post Office that is fine too.

Just let me know the date you actually mail it.

Many thanks, Louise

Hi Debbie,   **January 17, 2010**

That was very generous of you to send all those books for the students English Library. Six packages have arrived. The easy to read ones I can use now with some of the students. The Harry Potter books will be a great set for them to have here. Now I have only a few students who can read at that level. There are several girls who are doing fairly well, so perhaps by the end of the year they will be able to read them as well. If not this year, then next year I'm sure they'll be able to enjoy them. Thank you very much.

The weather here now is quite cold; it's usually around freezing or even colder. And without central heating it is hard to keep my apartment warm. Today I have my wood stove heating up my one room very well, but the rest of my apartment is cold.

Yesterday I went with several other volunteers to Burgas. It's fun to look at the shops there. We also ate at a Chinese restaurant which makes for a special treat. Then they came back to my apartment and we watched Fiddler on the Roof. Marcus brought the DVD with him at Christmas time. David brought me some Jimmy Stewart movies too, and they too will be great to watch.

This week I have to go again to Burgas to get a flu shot. The PC is requiring it of all of us. Usually we have to go to Sofia for such type of medical arrangements, but they made special arrangements to have them at several places in Bulgaria, which certainly helps as Sofia is a minimum seven to eight hour train ride.

Thanks again for the books. It was fun to open all the packages. I showed them to the teachers here in Topolitsa. They make a great start for an English book library here at the school in Topolitsa.

I have one more request: when you come, could you perhaps bring some of the coloring books that your dad did at Modern Color? I don't know if you have any extra copies, but it would be a good way for me to share with the students another look at the United States, especially the desert and Indian life.

Before you come, I may also ask you to bring along several toiletries.

Love, Louise

Hi Louise,   **February 3, 2010**

I sent off a package to you February 10th. Hopefully you will receive it in two weeks. Let me know when it arrives. The Readfield Post Office questioned the combined English and Bulgaria address. So I hope it doesn't come back to me.

We have lots of snow here for the children to enjoy.

Take care, Rogene

Hi Rogene,   **February 12, 2010**

I'm looking forward to receiving the package. I've received several packages this way. I think it's only in the U.S. where the Bulgarian letters throw the postal people a loop.

As long as BULGARIA is spelled out in English (Latin) letters it gets to Bulgaria. And in Sofia where the mail is sorted, Bulgarian letters (Cyrillic letters) are what they read.

One package from a friend took six weeks, but the average time seems to be two to three weeks. I'll let you know. Loren sent me some books in the fall and they came without a problem.

I have a cold this week so did not teach yesterday nor today. I've been fortunate as generally I've been healthy. Today the weather is warmer. Thankfully, today it has been in the low 30s. I'm looking forward to spring.

Monday I travel to Sofia to see the PC doctor. I need some annual tests and also need to have my arthritis analyzed. My two index fingers are really getting bent out of shape. Generally my fingers do not hurt, but they are very stiff especially in the mornings.

Enjoy your snow. We've had some big snow banks here. It reminds me of when we all were in grade school at Zion and made forts and trails in the snow. Very little plowing is done on these village roads. The walk to the train is a challenge. It is covered with ice and packed snow. Thankfully spring is on its way. I'm looking forward to receiving the package.

How's the piano playing coming along?

Love, Louise

Hi Felicia,   **October 27, 2010**

Other than the Darien Book Project I do not know of any companies donating books to volunteers here in Bulgaria. When I asked PC about help with the book project I was told about the same as you received in your reply.

I had thought maybe there would be help with postage, but again it seems not to be set up that way. I decided just to ask friends to donate books if they would like, but that it would not be a tax donation, just a gesture of good will on their part. I suppose that is why the projects with the funding going through PC is so important as then it becomes a tax donation for companies and individuals. I know this is not the answer that you want to hear. It is very difficult to raise money for individual projects it seems.

Frank suggested that perhaps Rotary Clubs would be interested in helping library projects and maybe that is an avenue you can explore. Wish that I could be of more help. I still haven't had a chance to talk with my son and need to sort out the situation in NM with him. I was told to expect snow tomorrow.

Talk soon, Louise

Hi Caroline,   **January 26, 2010**

Today I received a package from a friend in Buffalo and she used the Bulgarian address and it worked fine. She put a value on her package of $10 and paid $27 for postage. She sent me some spices, candy canes and a few personal items. Thanks again for caring. I really appreciate it.

Louise

Hi Louise,   **January 29, 2010**

I sent your package yesterday through the U.S. Post Office. It should arrive in 7-10 days.

Enjoy, Caroline

Hi Louise,   **January 30, 2010**

I gave the correct address to the Business office and Don is sending your son a NM Tax Book and forms. Sorry you're still having problems with your tenants. Did you ever find an attorney to assist you?

I'm glad the books got there We have some others but haven't packaged them up yet to send. We're busy getting our house ready to sell – again. Hope this time it works.

We loved your post card. Beautiful. Take care, Sandra

Hi Sandra,   **January 31, 2010**

Thanks for all your help. I'm glad to hear that the post card arrived. One idea for a project for students, maybe English as a Second Language, (a program that many schools in the U.S. offer to help students coming in from another country to learn English) would be to send postcards to me of New Mexico that I could share with students here in Bulgaria. Students hear me talking about New Mexico and also other places in the U.S. and postcards are a fun way to share. Perhaps even a short note on the card, like I'm learning English too.

My first language is Spanish. And then I could have students send post cards from Bulgaria. I'm off to my Bulgarian language lesson. Today the weather is warmer; I think it's over 30, Louise

Domino's friends and Louise,   **December 17, 2009**

Today I sent out three and a half pounds of books to Bulgaria. Thanks to all of you for your donations. I found out from the postal person on how to save money sending the books. She was very helpful. I have spent about $200 sending about twenty pounds of books. She told me how I can send fifty pounds for the same price.

Louise, if it's okay with you when I have money again, I will send about fifty pounds of books. The postal woman told me if they open the packages now with only three to five pounds, what's the difference if they open a fifty pound package? I don't know, but I don't want you to get into trouble over there so let me know if you will be able to get the fifty pound packages. I have to fill out the forms either way.

Watch for the books that I sent on December 16. If you could write me back that would be appreciated, I know we have discussed this before, but I can't remember your reason why not to send larger amounts.

Nancy

Hi Nancy,   **December 17, 2009**

I'm sorry to say that the reason for not sending the heavier packages is not because they open them, but because they do not deliver the heavier packages to the village. I would need to travel to Burgas, via train and then go through enormous amounts of paperwork at the customs office there and pay extra taxes and fees on the delivery. And it would be very difficult to bring that heavy a package with me back on the train. I doubt that postal regulations here allow us to receive a fifty pound box, but perhaps ten pounds. Let me check and see about the possibility.

I will talk again to the Peace Corps office and to another volunteer in Sofia and see if she has been able to get heavier packages sent to her. If she can, then perhaps I might have you send books to her address. But this must wait until after the New Year. School will be closed for two weeks, and I will be traveling in Bulgaria. This volunteer is also having company from America. She's from Ohio.

I am anxious for you to send on the books, but I have been learning that all good things take time and patience. I will be here for two years, so even if the books come in 2010 that will still give me plenty of time to share them with the students. Please for now keep the books in Wisconsin and I will get back to you ASAP in January and see about the weight on packages. Thank you Nancy for being patient, I am very appreciative of your help. Sending you Christmas greetings and all good things for the New Year, Louise

Hello Pat and John,   **July 15, 2010**

I'm LeAnne's sister. She gave me $25 cash for the check that you gave her for my projects here in Bulgaria working in this village school. Thank you so much for your support. It is always wonderful to have such good friends. With the money I was able to buy some school art supplies for my classes.

The students are expected to furnish their own materials as the school does not have a budget for such supplies. Students in the upper grades also have to buy their own workbooks. As a result all of them don't have the supplies, which makes teaching even a bigger challenge for me.

For the most part I am enjoying my time here in Bulgaria and learning so much about the history and culture. It is a beautiful country and now the gardens are busting with many vegetables. There has been a lot of rain this year, so the weather has been a mixed blessing.

I'm fortunate and have been able to arrange a trip with another older volunteer to go on a ten day trip and see a bit more of Eastern Europe this summer. First I have to take the seven hour train ride to Sofia. We'll meet there, as Hazel serves in another area of Bulgaria. Then we're flying to Prague to begin our adventure.

In August we both will be teaching again. I hope to write up a special project through the Peace Corps program which will deal with renovating their school playground. Hopefully Peace Corps will approve the project and I will be able to raise the necessary funds.

Thanks again for your help and support. It is so good to have such wonderful friends.

With warm regards, Louise

Hi Nadia,   **April 12, 2010**

It was so interesting talking to you on my last visit to the PC office. I want to let you know that I found those two books on Bulgaria through Barnes and Noble online (used editions) and my brother is mailing them to me. Also I found a book called *King's Ransom* by Jan Beazely & Thom Lemmons. It is a novel based on the story of King Boris saving the Jews during World War II. I know I was to email you several more titles, but not sure if I can remember which titles, so here is a short list of books that I have found interesting that tell about Bulgaria:
*   *The Balkans, A Short History* by Mark Mazower
*   *Fairy Tales* collected by Ran Bossilek. These are Bulgarian fairy tales,

translated to English. I found a copy in a Sofia bookshop on Vitosha Street.

- *Bulgarian Rhapsody – The Best Of Balkan Cuisine* by Linda Joyce Forristal
- *To Chicago and Back* by Aleko Konstantinov
- *Contemporary Bulgarian Plays* Introduced by Anna Karabinska
- *The Price* by Marko Semov written in 2003 by a Bulgarian who lives in Sofia I believe.
- *Cultureshock: A Survival Guide To Customs And Etiquette* (Bulgaria) Agnes Sachsenroeker. I think you found this online when I was there.
- *Street Without A Name* by Kapka Kassabova. This one also I think you perhaps found that same day. Another book that I recently bought, so it may not be available used is
- *Best European Fiction 2010.* Edited by Aleksandar Hemon. It looks very good. Short stories from all over Europe, includes Bulgaria, Romania, Macedonia, Russia, Estonia, Bosnia and Hungary.

I would be happy to give a short book talk about books on Bulgaria at our mid-service, or for the PST if you think that would be helpful and interesting to the group. Louise

COPING VIA TELEPHONE AND EMAIL

Often I had long telephone conversations with fellow Peace Corps Volunteers in Bulgaria. We shared joys and the perplexities of dealing with our everyday lives. Sometimes many of us felt overwhelmed. It was hard to explain this to our family and friends back home. A few times we poured our frustrations into email.

December 10, 2009

Hi, friends and family. I had written this to my Mom and then I realized I'd like to get other opinions on it. If you don't agree with something I have written or my ideas, please tell me. I didn't get an Education degree from college, so I'm doing this all kind of blind.

If you have ideas, please let me know.

Love you.

Hey –

Sorry I haven't been writing. I feel like I've been so busy with schools and projects lately. There was another student murder a few towns west of us and I'm getting so fed up with the Bulgarian Ministry of Education. Students have no sense of consequence and no sense of achievement.

I have been thinking about this and thinking about this, and I have decided that in my opinion, the four worlds of children are: home, family, school, and friends.

It's clearly obvious that the worlds of home and family are destroyed and corrupted for these kids. The generation that is rearing children now is the first out of communism. These parents are in the midst of that political pendulum swing from strict and obedient ways of the old system (communism) to chaos with the new system (democracy and capitalism). Either their parents are caught up in the 20 year "communism is over I can do whatever I want attitude," or they are simply not home because they are forced to go to bigger cities or in some cases, other countries, to find work. In short, the worlds of "home" and "family" are anything but stable and supportive for children.

So, where should children turn for some kind of constant support? School. When all the classes have been taught, all the ten minute breaks have been sat through, and all the vacations have been had, teachers end up spending more time with children than their actual parents do.

We, in many cases, know more about them, their talents, their troubles, their hopes, their dreams and their fears. We have a unique opportunity to be a guiding light for them, even if only during school hours. But, what do the vast majority of Bulgarian teachers do about this? They dress in fancy outfits and stand on a stage (the classrooms have small stages for the teachers to stand on) in an attempt to create the biggest relationship gap between adult and child as possible. They teach their materials like robots, they don't allow for emotional conversations and if they do, they are ignored. They allow cheating, they aid to the lack of self worth, and they watch their kids leave school perhaps more hurt and disconnected as when they came in.

The world of school, that world which is meant to be a safe-place, is destroyed. So, what do children have left? They have the world of friends.

Unfortunately, most at risk youth gravitate to other drifter children. These are children whose only world in which they can try to breathe in is friends. These are children who have lost the safe worlds of home, family and school. The problem is, when these drifter students cling to each other, they drown in those deep waters they unfortunately have to call life. They ultimately destroy each other with drugs, alcohol, sex, gambling, stealing and whatever else is around.

I know nothing I have written is new news to anyone. But, what can be done in all of this?

Should people sit back in their chairs at home and disregard it as "our troubled youth" with no hope or purpose? Should the schools continue to put the blame first on the family and then the child, disregarding the sacred space of their own bureaucratic impersonal systems?

Should the parents continue to put the blame first on the schools and then the child, disregarding their own inability to successfully and lovingly raise their own offspring? In either case, both of which by the way, are happening as I type, the child is ultimately put at blame.

I had a slightly heated discussion about all of this with my counterpart yesterday over coffee. The more I talked, the more upset I got. As all of you know me, that means I talk faster, louder, and I tend to use my hands to help get my point across.

Surprisingly, she listened to me. As I let all of this and more pour out of me, she lit cigarette after cigarette, sipped her coffee, and bounced her foot to the English Christmas music which played in the background. Happy Holidays, I believe it was.

When I finished, I made a point to say, "Look, I don't want you to be angry with me. I realize that I am a young American coming into Bulgaria with a fresh outlook on the world. I know you have lived this life for too long, that you are disillusioned and tired. But, do you at least understand what I'm upset about? "I understand that one of the main reasons why we are in this situation is because of a lack of money. But, you don't need money for some of my ideas. My ideas are sustainable. All you need are teachers interested and passionate enough to give them a try again"

She replied, "We had some of your ideas during The Old System. Here I'm talking about an honor role, detention, cheating consequences, a "goodwill hall of fame" board, and a few after school activities, summer school even, since the teachers do get paid during the summer".

I replied, "So, why can't we try to start them again? You see that these kids are suffering. They are murdering each other. Don't you think they need somewhere safe to go? Or are you okay with just watching your children, almost all of them, fall through the cracks as you patiently wait for retirement?"

I winced when I said this, knowing it was rude. She didn't say anything for awhile. She put her cigarette to her mouth, inhaled, and closed her eyes as she exhaled the smoke from her body.

The music had changed to "Jingle Bells" and then "So This Is Christmas". I sat and sipped my coffee. When she was ready, she opened her eyes again and said, "Alright, so how do you think we can make it work?" I smiled, and went on again about all of my ideas, pulling out a notebook which had them all messily written down.

"We can do it, you and I, I know we can," I said. "We just have to start small in our classroom and then, when we have our ideas worked out perfectly, we can introduce them to the director and the rest of the school".

She looked at me strange. She either thought I was crazy or she was thinking something like, "I hope she's right". Maybe it was both. Either way, I made some kind of progress.

After our conversation I went to the bookstore to buy neon colored poster boards for Goodwill charts and Student of the Day charts. Today, I'm going to school early to help her set some ground rules with my children about cheating. There will be a test and my counterpart has agreed to work with me in not tolerating cheating. We have a game plan and we're going to see it out at 12:15.

So, that's what I've been doing.

I'm also trying to start some Life Skills programs in the other school for the students. On Friday I kicked one of my students out of class, He was misbehaving, it was Friday, I was tired, and I lost my patience. The whole situation has been weighing on my conscience since Friday. If I see him today, I would like to sit him down and hopefully we can both apologize for the events in class. He's one of those kids who has lost all four worlds. It's hard, but as long as I'm here, I can't give up on him.

Anyway, the weekend is just around the corner. That's always a plus.

I love you and I'll talk to you soon, Laura

Hi,

I want to respond to your letter, but need some time to absorb it all. I'll try and call you this weekend. I understand your phone is working again. That's great.

Next Saturday I go to Sofia as both my sons are flying in on the 19th already, and then we come back to Topolitsa.

Hang in there. It's a different culture and so that makes it more difficult to try to sort it all out.

Big hug, Louise

Hi, Louise,   **December 12, 2009**

I know. The e-mail had a lot in it. I wrote it right when I woke up. I didn't even get out of bed and it's a bit of a rant. I don't mean to bombard mailboxes, either, anyway, my apologies for that.

I love working with my kids, I do. But, I'm finding myself wanting to reach out to all of them and I just can't. It's impossible. I don't have the resources or the energy. So, then I get frustrated with the schools for not doing more when I feel they have money to do more than they're doing currently.

Sometimes I think I get through to them, and other times I feel like I'm trying, but not achieving anything. I know that they maybe feel as if they have no where to go for support and in many cases, maybe they don't. I know many of their lives are difficult. I wish there were more resources for them at school. I want to do so much for my kids, but I'm not really sure how to achieve it all.

I'm doing well, I am. I feel good and my kids are such a bright light for me. I just don't want them to fall through the cracks. They are such good people. I promised my 8th and 9th graders in one school that we can start a Film club where we will watch films in English with Bulgarian subtitles, eat snacks, and then discuss. They are excited. I hope to start in January.

I'm working on projects to bring more English books into the school libraries. Something I would like to talk to you about actually. I know you have your library connections in the states, but if you're interested in getting additional books for your kids I have found a few organizations that donate for free. I also started team-teaching on Wednesday nights with a new teacher about Life Skills. So, I'm trying to use my youth as an advantage to easily talk to the high school kids about drugs, HIV / AIDS, friendships, relationships, decision making skills and so on. So far so good.

I had one girl kind of gaze into my eyes afterwards, play with my scarf, and say, "thank you . . . thank you." I've also made "Goodwill hall of fame" and "student of the day/week/month boards" for one of my schools. I'll try to use them starting January, too.

So, I have good things going. But, I know there's more that can be done. I guess I just need to *spokoino*? (A favorite Bulgarian expression we would hear often, it basically means, "to relax" "take it easy" or "sit back.")

Louise, as a teacher, how do you compartmentalize all these problems? I look at my class and they have told me so much about themselves and their problems at home and I feel happy that they feel safe with me, but I feel so sad at the same time because I know I can't always be there for them and I can't hold their hands. They need to be strong in order to make it and I know some of them just won't make it. So, I guess I'm asking you, from your experience, how do you deal with that fact? Do you find it challenging as well, or am I just too emotional? Anyway, that's great about your sons. Can you believe it's time for them to be here already?

That's very exciting. Enjoy your time with them. We will talk soon.

Big hugs back. Laura

Hi Laura,   **December 12, 2009**

I just came back upstairs from spending a few hours with my landlady. It's snowing like crazy here and the wind is blowing. The terrace off my kitchen is filled with snow because of the wind blowing through the broken windows. But I have a new wood burning stove and it works quite well. It keeps the heat better and is much easier to start a fire. We will have to meet soon and have a good talk. You raise many good points and concerns that teachers have had for many years. These problems will not be solved overnight, nor by one teacher.

There are similar problems in America's school also. I think one of my most frustrating times in America was when I worked in an inner city parish as education director. I worked there for about four years and had all ages from infants to older teens, plus did parenting classes. There were many children from broken homes, mixed racial ethnicity, varied incomes.

I was sad to learn on a visit back to Pittsburgh just a year or so ago, that one of the "better" families' daughter, now in her thirties is dealing drugs and her brother was in jail. They had moved out of this inner-city neighborhood into one of the "better" neighborhoods. It was an affluent Pittsburgh suburb, but apparently the problems are also out in the suburbs.

The minister at this parish often had some of the teenagers stay at his place for weeks, sometimes a month or two, in the hopes that a different environment would help. Sometimes yes it seems to help, but often no. There were kids that I knew who stole from their mother's purse for drug money. When I first worked there it too was overwhelming, and it was easy to get burned out in such a situation.

Why am I telling you this? As a teacher you need to step back a bit. You have to take it one day at a time, and then do your best job that day. Some days you will feel that you reach no one. Other days you feel that you connected. You cannot reach every child, every day. Some children, no matter the age, you will never reach. It's not because of you, it's just part of how the world is. This may sound harsh, but it's not meant to be harsh. It's just realizing that as a teacher we cannot do it all.

Is it the parents fault? Sometimes, yes, but not always. I know of many examples where a family has three "successful" children and then the fourth child, no matter where in the group, youngest, oldest, middle, just throws the theory of the parents fault out the window. Children have their own make up, and have inner and outer influences; they all have an effect on how they view the world.

Yes, Bulgaria has gone through big changes, but just because the discipline isn't as severe as it was, does not mean that teachers don't care. Talk to some Americans who went to Catholic schools. While the students behaved in class, afterwards many of them turned away from the church and felt the school rules were totally a sham. While discipline, or polite behavior, makes teaching feel a whole lot easier, it doesn't always mean that better teaching and more learning goes on or is necessarily better. I can't give you the answers. I think trying several ideas like you mentioned: after school clubs, films, discussion groups are all good. Do one or two at a time or you will wear yourself out. Do the best job you can every day, but don't expect every day to be a ten.

Your students will know that you care for them just by your demeanor. You cannot solve all the prejudices overnight. Just by your caring you will show them that there is another way to view the world. Just by being a kind American there in your town you are changing perceptions.

The first goal that any teacher/parent/worker has is to take care of them self. Give yourself time to relax, read, play, prepare and just try to take a day at a time. I hope this helps a little bit. I know it's hard. Even with my years of experience I've had frustrating teaching days.

The students don't know my style, it is different than what they are used to, so to expect them to change in a week or two is very unrealistic. And yet some days that is what I expect. It will be good to have a break and then go back in January and do the best you can. And I look forward to you visiting me early in the year in Topolitsa.

Big hug, Louise

Hi Trish,

Thank you so very much for your letter and the magazines and DVDs. It was such a nice surprise. I really enjoy getting "The Week" magazine and catching up on the news. It has a nice variety of articles. I especially like the book reviews. They are great.

I ended up not traveling this weekend after all. I decided I was just too tired, so basically just rested and worked on my Christmas letter. I hope to get it off soon. It's rather long, not sure what parts to edit out, or if I should send it in two sections.

I took in a little street cat, and now I wish I had not. I decided it is too much work and expense. It keeps me company, but being a kitten she gets into everything. And while I didn't notice any fleas I think maybe she has a few and now I have some flea bites. YUK I'm going to ask some kids tomorrow and see if anyone is interested in having a kitten. If not I just made put him/or her back out on the street. A nice kitten, but difficult with traveling and with living on the second floor.

That is so good that you were able to help your friend out. I'm sure she's very appreciated. It would be great if she could get a job in Farmington.

I saw some snow in the mountains on our excursion last week, but none here so far. I think it must be *Luminarias* next weekend. It sure seems more than a year ago since I was there for the last one. Well, time to get ready for bed.

All the best, Louise

(*Luminarias* is a New Mexico tradition from the early Spanish and Mexican immigrants. Sand is placed on the bottom of a brown lunch-box–size paper bag. Enough sand has to be on the bottom of the bag to hold a candle. Then on Christmas Eve the candles are lit to await the coming of the Christ Child. Many homes in New Mexico line their driveway with these Luminarias. San Juan College started observing the tradition 38 years ago on the first Saturday in December. The Luminarias are placed on all the foot paths and around the special gardens and line most of the parking lots. The week before local school children come to help fill the thousands of bags with sand. The Friday before, faculty, staff and students of the college place the Luminarias along the paths. Starting in the early afternoon SJC staff and local people come to help light the over 50,000 candles. People all over the region come to see this special display. There is a path for cars to drive slowly through the lighted area, with their car lights off, or people can walk around the campus and enjoy this special evening. Hot chocolate and coffee are served and Christmas music is played.)

BULGARIAN JOURNAL

The beginning my second 6 months in Bulgaria, December 12, 2009

The first intensive winter storm arrived today. Snow came down hard and the wind blew all day. With several of my windows broken on the porch that's off the dining area, snow came inside the porch. There is no insulation on any of the outside walls so all my rooms are cold. The temperature outside is around freezing. My little stove is doing okay, but tomorrow I'll be out of wood. I told Dora, that I would need wood by Monday. Hopefully she will remember.

The school is to supply my wood. They have an enormous room of it down in the basement by the furnace. So far the students have been bringing it over in old plastic bags and stacking it outside. But I can see that will not be a very good method if snow storms continue like this through the winter. The wood will have to be carried upstairs and stored on my porch and some even in my living area so that it can dry out enough to burn.

I know if I run out completely I could get some wood from Milka but I'd rather not. When I can go down to her apartment she likes me to stay for a long visit. I generally don't mind, but sometimes I would rather stay up here so that I can read, embroidery and just do my own thing.

Today I went downstairs in the afternoon and had coffee with Milka. I haven't gone down very often just on my own. It is hard for me to carry on a conversation as I know so few words. We talked a little about sewing, traveling, and children. She was very pleased I had come down.

She ended up serving me boiled eggs and then baked potatoes. They needed only about thirty minutes to bake in her stove as it was so hot. Then she gave me some juice from apricots. She remembered that I liked juice, so she opened up a jar of her canned apricots just so I could have the juice. She really is nice and I know she would visit me a whole lot more if I spoke the language.

School has been going along okay. Now I am helping out with the younger grades which I really like to do but this gives me less time with the older students. Tantayna, the regular language teacher is sick. In prior years she taught Russian. She translates the lesson well in the written format but has a very difficult time speaking it. It has been a challenge for both of us to communicate with each other.

I think Tantayna will be back in the New Year. I'm working with Yura now and is very nice. She is younger. She has a daughter going to the University in Sofia who speaks English well. Yura doesn't know English at all yet somehow we manage. Unless her generation and older went to a language school, their second language most likely was Russian. It is only in the last twenty years that English was offered as a second language in the regular school curriculum, and then only in the bigger cities. English has been mandated as the second language for students to learn in all the Bulgarian schools starting in the second grade.

I've also started teaching the teachers, but I think that will not be on a regular basis as they all are so busy with other projects, it is difficult to find a set time to offer the class. Hopefully in January a class will start in the evenings for community members. Dora, the school director is to set it up. Peace Corps wants us involved in community projects. This seems like a natural fit. If I knew Bulgarian better it would all be so much easier.

I mainly work with the more advanced students in grades 5, 6 and 7. To me it seems I should be working with the students with problems, but perhaps that is a losing battle. To spend more time with those who are advancing does make sense as they will probably go on to Burgas for high school and to have good English skills is very important.

My two sons are planning to visit me around Christmas. Their schedule is very tight. I really hope that they can meet Nikolai and my Aitos language teachers, Vesala and Ivanka. Maybe I could arrange a dinner together in Sofia upon their arrival and another dinner in Aitos.

Peace Corps requested that we fill out an expense sheet to help them access whether the monthly stipend we receive from the U.S. government covers all our regular expenses. It was an interesting exercise.

I feel it would be very difficult to live within the modest budget that they allocate for us. It would mean eating even more frugally that I already do, buy no clothes even at the thrift stores and certainly no travel excursions to see other Peace Corps Volunteers or go on an arranged trip with Bulgarian teachers.

I could not afford the telephone to call back to the U.S. to speak to my children even briefly on a monthly basis. Fortunately, I have some savings that I can use but as I have to cover my house expenses back in the States and other debt that I accumulated when my house sale fell through I find this dilemma quite frustrating at times.

The money values are in Bulgarian *lev*. The coins are called *stodinki*.

Expenses/Tracking One Month Bulgaria B-25/Village Topolitsa

Food	77.49
Toiletries	22.11
Household	62.70
Communication	168.30
Travel	82.60
Recreation	41.05
Clothes	79.80
Total	534.05

CHRISTMAS IN BULGARIA, 2009

Dear Family and Friends,

Many of you have asked me, "Is Peace Corps what I expected it to be?" And for this I say it depends on the day. I have had many unique experiences and have met many very nice people. Students I think, by and large, are the same everywhere. Some like to study, some don't. Some are polite, some not so polite. PC has high expectations of the volunteers to get involved in the community. Some communities are easier to adjust to than others. Some volunteers have better living conditions than others. We all have different situations to adapt to. It is great when we have meetings and see our co-workers from the U.S. and can share our different experiences. It is certainly different for those who are younger. The biggest majority are in their early twenties just out of college. A few are in their thirties and forties taking a leave of absence from their career or thinking of switching careers. There are five of us over fifty, including one couple.

It is easiest for me to think of it as my adventure and realize what a wonderful opportunity that I have to live in another area of the world, to learn about a new culture and work with children. But at times when you are in an adventure, it doesn't always feel that way. It feels more like a scary upside down feeling of "what more can go wrong?" or "what could happen next?"

And then, as I mentioned to many of you that it was my dream come true to join the Peace Corps, I think, hmmm, "did I really say that?" We dream so many things, and like in dreams, reality and dreams are not always the same.

This week makes six months that I have lived here in Bulgaria. And as with my life, this is a country of contrasts. I will briefly summarize some of the events that I have observed and also some of my feelings, observations and adventures.

Bulgaria has a long rich history and the book *Under the Yoke* tells about their fight for freedom from under the Ottoman rule. They were under the Ottoman Empire for nearly 500 years. Independence Day is celebrated here on September 22 and Liberation Day on March 3. The memorable battle is similar to our Bunker Hill or Battle of Trenton and was fought in the hills around Shipka. I was able to visit there in August and stayed at the home of a 98-year-old woman. I visited the Shipka Monastery and the nearby Ethnographic Museum which is similar to Sturbridge Village in Massachusetts. That evening in August her friends dropped by to say hello and I had the chance to speak to a professor from Moscow University. He spoke seven languages. He gave me courage to continue my language struggle as we talked about how languages are built and formed and also about Bulgarian / Russian history. An evening such as that is indeed an adventure and a dream come true.

History is rich, and I am enjoying learning more about it every day. I had the chance to visit Roman ruins and go inside the tomb of Thracian kings dating back to before the Greeks. That was extremely fascinating to me and filled me with awe. The geography of Bulgaria is as rich as its history. For a country quite small in size, about the same as Tennessee, it has a rich variety of landscapes that both geologists and hiker alike love and appreciate. Bulgaria is bordered by the Black Sea on the East (40 miles from where I now live) to the Danube River on the North, separating it from Romania and the countries of Turkey, Greece in the South with Serbia, and Macedonia to the West. Mountains and valleys crisscross the country, with fields of sunflowers and roses and everywhere many home gardens of vegetables.

During Communism rule (1944–1989) most of the churches were either closed or used for other purposes. A few were left open for use as general gathering places or historic significance. Many were torn down. Today most of the remaining monasteries and churches have re-opened. While all do not have regular services, from what I have observed people do go to pay their respect, remember loved ones or special holidays, like name and saints' days. The custom of lighting candles to remember a loved one and saying a prayer for family and friends is observed by many. Bulgaria does not have a state religion, although the majority of the population belongs to or observes the traditions of the Bulgarian Orthodox Church.

I live in a predominantly Turkish community where there is a mosque and the call to prayer is heard five times a day. Today and the next several days is a special holiday called Byram (different spellings). The children were all excited in school this morning, as this afternoon and tomorrow special family gatherings and celebrations would be observed, including the giving of gifts. Just a few minutes ago, a young girl who is in my 6th Grade Class brought me a gift of warm fry bread. Picture a flattened donut, deep fried or a crepe, it is delicious. Her younger brother came with her. She speaks very little English, but that is not needed to convey good will and best wishes.

The Peace Corps program director was here recently and she noticed that I had several icons – religious pictures, often of saints to help tell a story – on my wall. She asked if my landlady objected. She had not. In fact, her daughter admired them. It gives me another side of the often mistaken belief that Muslim's are intolerant. This I have not seen here, although I won't say it doesn't exist. I have Saint George fighting the dragon, and Mary holding the baby Jesus, and Saint Nikolai.

Another part of my village life ethnicity is the Romani people who Americans often call gypsies. About 15% of our student population is Roma or Romani. I would compare their acceptance similar to other minorities in the U.S. I especially think of Native Americans, where the stereotypes simply do not hold true. But it is difficult for many to accept them as equally deserving of an education or employment opportunities. Here in the village they are generally employed as the workers in the gardens. But many of the Turkish people also work in the gardens. Only a few of my students have Bulgarian names, most are Turkish and I understand that at home many children speak Turkish, while at school they speak Bulgarian and are learning English. Up until a few years ago, Russian was taught rather than English. Now all schools are required to have English for all students from grade 2 through 8.

Tonight I rode home on the train with a young Roma girl from my village and her mother. She was so pleased when I sat down next to her.

Teaching English in the villages and smaller communities is where most of the Peace Corps workers are here in Bulgaria. PC first came to Bulgaria in 1991 and my group of 61 is the 25th group to come over. There are about 120 Peace Corps volunteers currently serving in Bulgaria. Most of us work in schools. Some volunteers work with youth development and a smaller group with community programs. In all over 1,150 PC volunteers have served in Bulgaria. New groups overlap with the group before, there are some here from B-24 who came over from the U.S. in spring of 2008.

While I am not roughing it, it is not the same as living in the U.S. Several items:

Central heating is rare. Just yesterday my very old wood stove, called a Bulgarian miracle was replaced with a new stove. It was a miracle if I could get a fire started in my old one. It is much better as I don't have to take this one apart to take out the ashes. It is small and still only gives me heat for one room, but I am so happy with this new stove. Clothes dryer. Non-existent. Clothes are hung outside to dry even in the winter. Clothes washing machine. Some of us have them; many do not. My landlady brought her machine upstairs for me to use. It is the small apartment mini-size. In June and July I did all my wash by hand in an outside wash basin when I was in the training program in Banitsa.

Stove. 2-burner is typical with a tiny oven. I find it hard to regulate the temperature, high or low.

Bathrooms. No toilet paper down the drain. That is put in a container next to the toilet. This is everywhere in Bulgaria, even the better restaurants. The school I am at does not have indoor toilets. Similar to what I had as a child, except these are called, "Turkish style". You learn to stoop. The hole is in the floor. Even in many community places and restaurants Turkish style is used, not the seat style that we use in the United States.

Electricity / Water. Electricity is very expensive and often in the village it can go off or on, several times a day unexpectedly. Water too has been shut off and you just wait and hope that it will come back on soon. Once this summer my water was off for two days in Banitsa. People usually have buckets or bottles of water set aside for such times. Some towns have mineral spring water and you can go there to fill up your containers. Most showers I've seen use no curtains by design and you just get the whole room wet. In the summer, I had a separate shower room (outside small room) and you heated the water 30 minutes before you needed to use it. There was about a five minute shower limit for warm water. Now I have a fair sized bathroom, but it has no heat. The ceramic tile floor is cold and my window often has frost and icicles on the inside. Good thing I'm accustomed to quick showers.

Magazines. This is the name for small shops. Many in the villages still keep the items behind the counter and you have to ask for what you want to buy. This is a hold-over from the Communist era when the food sold and other items were very carefully controlled. Families stood in lines to receive their loaf of bread for the day. Now the food is available, but you must ask for it as most of it is either in the back room, or under the counter.

Bigger shops and supermarkets are coming into the towns and cities, but in villages you find only the magazines. This makes it difficult if you don't know the language and have no idea what to call baking soda or flour, or how to ask for vinegar or a nail. They may have it, but you need the correct word for it. At times this is a real challenge for me. I've only found vanilla in a tiny little packet, holding about a ½ teaspoon dry powder. Credit cards are only used in the larger cities. It is still very much a cash economy here although ATM machines are now found in many towns and cities.

Street signs. Many of you have wondered about my address. I have seen no street signs here in Topolitsa. Some villages do have streets with names, but people just seem to know where everybody lives. Topolitsa has a population of about 1,000. But like today, when I walked to the post office to ask for my mail, it was closed. It was because of the holiday I am sure, but it was a surprise to me. Like tomorrow, I found out today that tomorrow will be a vacation for the village students.

Transportation. Walking, taking the bus or the train are the main ways of getting around. Many families here do have a car, but it is not assumed. And cars are not generally bought new, but used. They are shipped in from Turkey and Germany for the most part. I schedule my errands around the train schedule. A mini-bus only goes to Aitos three times a day, early morning, mid-morning and late afternoon. The bus costs twice as much as the train due to fuel costs I think. Fuel is very expensive.

Train transportation is not bad, but some of the train passenger cars are very, very, old so not only do they go slow but are usually dirty. I haven't tried the sleeping car yet to Sofia but hope to do it on my next trip. All my medical appointments are in Sofia, about a 7 to 8 hour train ride away. There is a fast train to Sofia, but for this I have to travel to Aitos or to Yambol on a slow train, and wait for the connection to the faster train, thus saving me no real time.

Language. Many of you have heard my lament about learning the language. This has been the most difficult transition for me. I have never been fluent in another language, although I learned a bit of German at home and I had it in college. Speaking a language on a regular basis and having to communicate thoughts and ideas is quite a different thing.

At first, it was just learning the new alphabet. Bulgaria uses the Cyrillic alphabet which was developed around 900 AD by two monks Cyrus and Methodius to write down the Bible for the people living in the region now known as the Balkans. Their disciple, Clement was the one who actually transcribed it from what I've learned, and it was the fourth accepted translation for the Bible, following the Hebrew, Greek and Latin versions. It is the basis now for the Bulgarian and Russian Orthodox churches. Russian and Bulgarian languages are similar, but not the same.

While English shares some of the letters, only 6 of them actually have the same sound and shape that we use: A like a in far, O like o in dough, and C like s in sit and K, M and T. It is confusing to my brain to see the English P and have it pronounced like the R that I know or the letter X pronounced like our H. Also, they do not name the letter like we do, but rather just say its sound. And they have different consonants linked together and each needs to be heard. To pronounce a word, a person needs to know the sound and where the accent is placed on a word. Think of desert (dry land) and dessert (cake and cookies). We know it in context, but in a new language you have to learn the new context.

I manage to do my basic transactions in Bulgarian, but it is still difficult for me to carry on any extended conversation. Imagine all the various ways that a person uses language every day, from cooking to listening to the radio, to buying a new dress, to traveling.

Telephone conversations present a special challenge as you don't have any body language to help the interpretation and pronunciation is extremely important. All of these factors present a challenge to me on a daily basis as very little English is spoken around me. Some of the students know phrases, but only a few know how to talk in English. It is easier to read a language than to speak it. Hopefully by this time next year I will be able to speak to the teachers in Bulgarian. I will be starting an English class for the teachers and community members soon and I am sure we will learn from each other. I have found though, that it is much easier to learn a language from a very competent bilingual person, as otherwise many things can get lost in translation. Hopefully, I will be up for this task.

It is fascinating to me also that Bulgaria, like other third-world countries, is taking a giant leap forward in technology. Going from one land line phone in the home, to multiple cell phones, computer savvy young folks are moving quickly into the 21st century. There are problems to be sure, but hopefully the young people will decide to stay here and work and sort them out, rather than leave as so many did ten to twenty years ago when many Bulgarians felt very hopeless about their future here.

It is a beautiful country, with flowers galore, medieval and turn-of-the-century revival architecture and with the Black Sea, the Danube, Rhodophe and Perin mountains for skiing. Bulgarian people here can be very proud of this country that they call home.

I must say a word about the music. While many do know the current American and European pop stars, the traditional folk music is studied and practiced. The hora is a favorite dance that often is done after a group meeting or at a school program. Folk music and the gypsy music is all so energetic and stimulating, it is hard not to like it.

The coffee here is great, but many places do not serve milk with coffee. Or if they do, you have to pay extra for it. I can now drink Espresso just black, but sugar helps. People sit for hours in cafes here enjoying a small cup of coffee. There is no rush by waitresses to clear the table for the next customer. If all the tables are filled, you just find another café. There are no real cafes in Topolitsa, but a group of men sit outside of the magazine on warm days. There is one restaurant and a hiking path up the mountain with a hut that campers can sleep in. In Aitos and Burgas there are many cafes. Some serve food, but most do not.

I do have a television, but it gets only three channels and they are all in Bulgarian. I listen for twenty to thirty minutes several times a week just to hear the accents and vocabulary. Generally I don't miss television as much as I might have thought. I do enjoy watching a few movies on DVDs. I can only watch those that have been purchased in the U.S. as that is how my computer is registered. Most of my news I read through the Internet.

I have truly appreciated all the books, newspapers, school supplies and other goodies that many of you have sent. Some things just are not found here, or at least not easily found here. I shop in second hand stores for sweaters, but it seems that jeans are only for those who wear size 8 or less It is difficult to find a size 9 shoe anywhere The lev shop, similar to our Dollar Store, sells assorted household items like small mirrors, kitchen knives, and light bulbs.

What do I do day-by-day? My official assignment is teaching English to the students enrolled in the Svetlina Village School here in Topolitsa. The school has about 120 students.

I teach grades 5, 6, 7, 8. Some I teach four times a week, others three times a week. Also now I will be helping out the Primary teacher teaching English to grades 2, 3 and 4 as the regular English teacher is out until sometime later this winter.

Also, I will be teaching the teachers English, as well as a class for the community members. Earlier this fall, I went to Burgas with my language teacher and spoke to her class of advanced English students, and Engineers who work for an Austrian company with offices in Burgas. I also am expected to initiate several community projects. I have started with help from many of you to begin a small library of English books for the students to read.

PC expects me to integrate in the community as much as I can to visit neighbors, shop locally, and spend time around the neighborhood in an informal basis. I had the opportunity to help out the Topolitsa teachers with the camp for students in grades 7 and 8 in late August and other school trips are planned. I've also gone on two excursions with the teachers from the neighboring town of Aitos: a one-day outing to Greece and another two-day excursion to Melnik and Bansko in southwest Bulgaria.

My meal preparation is generally quite simple. In the summer with the fresh tomatoes and cucumbers I usually had a *shopska salada* for dinner. This is basically cut up tomatoes and cucumbers with grated white cheese on the top and oil and vinegar. For breakfast I often have yogurt, perhaps with some muesli sprinkled in it. This winter I've done some baking. My landlady has been kind and often brings me up donut type pastries. Stuffed peppers or crème caramel are both favorite deserts here. To purchase fresh meat I have to take the train to Aitos as the local little shop only sells some frozen meat. So many days I just have a cheese sandwich, or maybe some bread with salami.

Many people can fruits and some freeze vegetable. They raise their own chickens, both for eggs and eating. Extra food is sold in the local bazaars.

I froze about two quarts of tomato juice as that is all the room I had and didn't have the equipment for canning.

Being the "voice and eye of America" is indeed an honor and a challenge at times. To know that for many in this region I am the first American that they have met is something that I feel is always important to keep in mind. Their first question usually is, "Why did I come to Bulgaria?" They are so surprised that an American would be interested in coming to their country. And when they find out that I am a volunteer and living in a village, they are even more surprised. Some Bulgarians have met British folks, but know they are usually here for a holiday. Some British folks have bought homes here, especially in the Black Sea towns. But there are few Americans living here, or even taking holidays here. I think this will change. With being part of the European Union many industries and other programs are being developed, roads are being improved for travel, and the young generation is growing up bilingual or trilingual, Bulgarian, Turkish and English. Some at the university know four and five languages.

I would be remiss if I did not tell you about some of the wonderful Bulgarian teachers who have been such a big help to me. PC hires very talented individuals to teach each new group of volunteers the Bulgarian language. The 61 of us who came over May 20 were divided into groups of four to six and lived in small towns near Vratsa. The language teacher also moves to each particular village for the nine weeks of language immersion. Once a week or more several groups met together to learn about PC policies, education dogma and assorted topics. We had classes six days a week.

In Banitsa, Lazar was our regular Bulgarian teacher. His regular teaching job was Bulgarian literature at a high school in Vratsa. Besides teaching the grammar and vocabulary, he told us about every day life, translated with our host families as situations arose, spoke about traditions, history and food. The teacher has to be well versed both in English and Bulgarian so that when expressions and situations arise it can be handled in either Bulgarian or English.

Some times we were divided into smaller groups and another tutor came in to work with us individually or in groups of two. This was a big help as even in a group of four people have different learning styles. Several tutors came over the course of the nine weeks. Like with any skill, a good teacher is a gem. Nikolai was one of the special language instructors who came to Banitsa and could dissect the grammar in simple context to help me understand it better. He has a degree in linguistics and also a Ph.D. in history and another in anthropology. He teaches at the New Bulgarian University in Sofia and speaks and writes five languages. Without his extra help and patience I would have probably given up on being able to learn Bulgarian at any level.

I also met Lucy, a young business woman in Banitsa who moved there recently and had lived in Italy and Spain. She speaks Italian and Spanish as well as English and Bulgarian. She taught our group how to make Banitsa, a favorite Bulgaria *filo* (phyllo) bread usually filled with cheese.

All schools now are required to have a bilingual teacher for English. Many of the older teachers know Russian, but not English. For many years there were special language schools in the bigger cities, but in the village schools most only taught Russian and Bulgarian. In Topolitsa the teachers want to learn English but it is as difficult for them as Bulgarian is to me. There are 14 teachers at the school divided by subjects except for grade one. Like in many countries, it's the older generation that is not bilingual. Education has always been valued here, and the country has a 98.6 literacy rate. Attendance is mandatory from age seven to sixteen. In 2003 4.9% of the national budget was devoted to education.

I am now studying with a language teacher, Ivanka in nearby Aitos. In addition to helping me with grammar she helps me with everyday items like going to the hair dresser, basic school instructions to use with students, conversation language to use when shopping and general support. She is working on a Master's Degree in linguistics. It takes a very good bilingual teacher to help a person adapt to the cultural and learn the language. A few times I've also met with Vesala, another very talented bilingual teacher in Aitos.

If I were to go to school again I would study linguistics. Communication with other cultures I feel is the key for better understanding. The world has become smaller and so being able to speak to people in their own language is a way to break down barriers.

Bulgaria is a country that many Americans know very little about or perhaps not even aware of it. When it was part of the USSR most of those countries were not studied individually in high school history classes. And unless you were a European history major you did not have Eastern European history. The Black Sea and the Danube River is the extent I think that most Americans know of Bulgaria. I am very happy to be here and to have the opportunity to share with my family and friends my experiences and to tell them about Bulgaria's rich history, its beautiful landscapes and varied culture. While I know there are problems here, I feel that with time many of them will be overcome. All countries and governments face problems on how best to serve their people. Twenty years of being independent is not a long time for all the changes that need to happen in a country that has been under a controlled government for nearly fifty years. I still have much to learn about this country, but I have met many very nice people willing to help me adapt.

In some ways it reminds me of my growing up years in rural Wisconsin.

Family ties, hard work, living off the land were all a part of America's rural landscape. And sometimes in the progress of moving ahead some values get lost. I hope that Bulgaria can jump-start to many of the modern conveniences that many in the Western World are used to, but at the same time not lose old traditional values. It is a fine line I think.

When I was asked what surprised me the most about Bulgaria I would say two things: how well they know Western music and how well they know Hollywood pop stars. I feel sad though because I think many do not really know much about average Americans and only have the ideas from old Hollywood B movies and third rate television shows. I only wish I knew the language better so that I could talk with my students more about the everyday American. Hopefully after two years here it will happen.

With love and warm greetings for Christmas and the New Year,
Louise

Mera, Shtasliva e Nadezhda   Peace, Joy and Hope
МЕР ЩАСТАЛЙВ НАДЕЖДА

Vesela Koleda   Merry Christmas
ВЕСЕЛА КОЛЕДА

Shtasliva Novogodishno Vercher   Happy New Year
ЩАСТАЛЙВ НОВОГОДЙШНА ВЕЧЕР

Dovizhdane   Good-bye for now,
ДОВИЖДАДНЕ

ЛУИЗ Louise
НАЗДРАВЕ *Nazdrave*   Cheers

Blagodarya   Thank you
БЛАГОДАРЯ

Pronunciation using Latin alphabet. When Bulgarian words using the Cyrillic alphabet are converted to English there is often a variance in the spelling. I have attempted to be consistent with conversions, but please excuse any inconsistencies you may find.

EXCURSIONS

Hello again,   **November 29, 2009**

I went to Expedia and have found several possibilities for hotels in Istanbul. One is called City Otel, It's a 3 star, includes breakfast, Internet and would cost us each around $30 a night. I looked into booking for three nights: the 30th, 31st and January 1.

Another place a bit cheaper is about $26 a night, called Anzac Wooden House. I don't think this one has an elevator.

They both include breakfast. They both are around historic sights. I'd like to book today, and then have a phone number to give PC for the leave request form. Then I think, if need be, we could change the hotel if we find something else, but this would give us what we need for the form.

There are several others in the same price range. I have not heard from Diana. I looked into a room for three. My feeling is that if she decides to go to Istanbul with us, the hotel would most likely have availability, and then we'd just get two rooms, or get a cot in the room. David would only be there for two nights.

Louise

Hi Felicia,   **November 30, 2009**

After I called you today I remembered about your trip to Sofia. You are lucky to live relatively close to the big city.

Diana is planning on coming for Christmas and Istanbul. I will check in with you tomorrow night, and then plan to get a hotel. The Expedia site mentions that you can cancel up to three days before without a penalty so that is good. I will see what kind of four person room rate I can get. I gave my kitty back to the student, but I'm not sure if he'll keep it. He was talking about trading it back and forth week by week. Something about his dad being allergic, so we'll see . . . .

Today I taught grades 2 and 4. Now I'll also be doing grade 3. I like teaching the young ones better than the older ones. The 8th grade girls are fun to talk to, but have very little interest in learning English.

Louise

Hi Louise   **December 1, 2009**

The lobby pictures look a little sleazy to me and it is a 2 star rather than a 3 star, at least I think I saw that on one site. Golden Palace was the name of the other hotel I saw for 4 people. It was $118 to $120 a night US. I couldn't find the forward information, but it was through Expedia. I may or may not have the Mystic reserved. I didn't give them my cc information, but I think this one looks better. It appears to be the newest . . . that could be good. . . but then again . . . maybe no . . . .

Hi again,

Okay, I wasn't able to find anything different than you, These three look similar and close to each other. I put the links to their actual websites. I was trying to get a better idea of what we are getting. Even though they mention they sleep four sometimes that is still on a sofa bed or roll-away bed. It seemed on Expedia it would not let us specify the type of room.

Felicia

Hi Louise,   **December 27, 2009**

Thank you for the invitation for the dinner. It will be very nice group of people who I can see, so I don't want to miss it. During the Christmas holiday I eat all the time and rest. Maybe I'll become overweight and weigh as much as a little elephant. It doesn't matter. One dinner more is a good thing because I will share it with nice people who will be there. I would like to come on Tuesday.

Greetings, Ivanka

Every time we left our village for an overnight, whether it was required by Peace Corps or we arranged it as a personal visit, we had to fill out a leave request. This had to be signed by our immediate supervisor. In my case my school director, Dora signed it and then I submitted the form to the Peace Corps Education Director for her signature. As I lived across the country and the mail might not get it to Sofia in time, I was allowed to submit a photo copy of the form signed by my director.

At the end of October several of the teachers in Aitos mentioned a day excursion to Greece. They thought I would enjoy it. We would be leaving early in the morning from Aitos and return late at night. As it was out of country it counted as a vacation day, even though it was on a Saturday and I would not be staying overnight in Greece.

We would be visiting a Bulgarian Orthodox Church and a museum filled with famous icons. Then there would be a stop at a Jumbo store, similar to a Walmart in the U.S.

HOLIDAY REVIEW, 2009

Hi Hazel,

I'm really excited about the holidays coming. Both of my sons are planning to fly over to spend a few days with me. Marcus is flying to Europe earlier in the month as he is attending the Climate Conference in Copenhagen. It would be great if you could join our excursions that we're thinking about and then come back with us to Topolitsa.

I would love to see the Rila Monastery. Felicia has been so I have not mentioned this to her. Diana is interested. I had asked the tour guide I found on the Internet about the cost for two or three persons. I was hoping that both my sons could go, but now it appears only David will be here on the 24th. So you could take Marcus' place. David and I are staying the night of the 23rd at The House,* the small hotel that I mentioned earlier near the NDK.

The tour guide would pick us up in his car at 8:30 AM to go to Rila. If Diana and/or Felicia would like to go I will have to check and see if he will keep price the same. It is about a two hour car ride to Rila.

Taking public transportation is much more complicated, especially to get back and forth on the same day. We would have a three hour tour. Then we'd stop for lunch on the way back to Sofia. We get back to Sofia around 5:30. That evening, December 24 I hope to go to the Aleksandur Cathedral to observe how the Bulgarian Orthodox church celebrates Christmas Eve.

On the 25th we would travel to Topolitsa. I'm thinking of taking the fast train which leaves Sofia around 7 AM and gets to Karnobat around 2:30. Then we have about a 90 minute wait to catch the slow train to Topolitsa or take a taxi. I don't think a taxi should be more than 20 lev. Hopefully we could find a taxi that could hold all of us and our luggage.

The other possibility is taking a later train from Sofia. We'd still have to switch trains in Karnobat and means that we wouldn't get to Topolitsa until evening. From Karnobat to Topolitsa is about a 30-minute taxi ride.

In regards to Istanbul, please check with the Oceans 7 regarding availability. Yes, we are all non-smokers so having your own room is probably better. But then for the last night in Istanbul, if you want to room with us we should have an extra bed.

Regarding the official form for leave: look in the PC Volunteer handbook, I think it's page 87 or 92. You also need your Lichna Karta expiration date, phone contacts and date of travel. I did two forms, one for In-country and one for International. You can start the process without the hotel information, but Dora will ask you for it. This afternoon I will look at my form and send you more details.

I'm using the school computer this morning as I had a break, but now need to teach a class. Hope this helps. I'll call you over the weekend.

Cheers, Louise

*The House was a small friendly hotel that I found on my first visit to Sofia. Now other Peace Corps Volunteers who needed to be in Sofia for a day or two also stayed there. In general it accommodated many European travelers who came to Sofia for meetings or a short holiday. Many of the staff spoke English. In addition to a small bar, it had both an indoor and outside garden restaurant. It was located directly off of Vitosha Street, the main upscale shopping street in Sofia and was very accessible as the tram ran only a short block away. The cost for lodging was about ten lev more than staying at the hostel, but The House provided a private room and shower and a discount for two or three persons staying in the same room. They would also call a taxi for any of their guests and arranged a fair price so that further negotiation was unnecessary. Taxi drivers in Sofia were known to scam outsiders. PC had warned us to be wary of unscrupulous drivers and many PC workers had stories to tell of paying extravagant fares. Few companies were licensed and a person needed to look carefully at the taxi window. Many companies used the same colors or letters, but only "<u>OK.</u>" – underlined with a dot after the K – was a legitimate and fair taxi company. There was another company who used the letters OK, but did not have the blue dot next to the K. The taxi driver waited at favorite corners and tried to entice unwary travelers.

Hi Hazel,

So good to hear from you, I'm glad to hear that you like your new place. I know that was an unexpected move and really was unsettling.

Felicia and Diana are planning to come and it would be great if you could make it too. I've already made reservations for us at a hotel called Oceans 7 Hotel. I made it for four people. Perhaps it will work for you to get a room for 2 nights there by yourself, and then come in with us for the 3rd night as David flies back to the U.S. on the 1st already. I found it first through Expedia, but ended up calling Expedia through Skype and made the reservation that way. It doesn't look like they would allow five in the room, but hopefully another room is free.

Another possibility is that Diana may want to move over to the hostel as that is cheaper and you could be the 4th person. I believe it's costing us each $36 a night. As for coming to my place for Christmas that would be great. David and I will be traveling to Topolitsa on Christmas Day from Sofia. I've reserved a tour of Rila on the 24th. Perhaps you would like to join us.

I'm quite sure I could get the same price from the guide for three persons as for two. Would you be interested? I found this contact through Lonely Planet and emailed them. The guide's fee is about $200 for the day. When I looked at going there on public transportation it sounded very complicated so took I looked at this option. He is English speaking and would give us a 3 hour tour. I'm actually coming to Sofia on the 23rd with both sons, as Marcus is already leaving on the 23rd to fly back in time for Christmas with his wife.

Both nights we're staying at a hotel called The House/Restaurant. It's right near the NDK, off of Vitosha Street. I stayed there when I went to a dental appointment and really liked it. The House is 37 euros a night (single person rate). It's a small hotel, very friendly staff and the price includes a great breakfast

I was planning on making a Christmas dinner either on the Saturday or Sunday or both. We can go to Burgas on the 27th or 28th, and take the night bus to Istanbul. The bus leaves at 11:30 PM and arrives about 6 in the morning. So we'd be at a hotel the 30, 31, and January 1. I'll look for the contact information for you. The round trip via bus to Istanbul is 70 lev. I'm suggesting traveling on Christmas Day from Sofia. I haven't had a chance to write Diana about it yet. It's been a busy week. I just finished my Christmas email to friends back in the U.S. and I have lots of classes to teach this week.

I look forward to having you visit and if you could join us for Rila that would be great. My landlady has offered part of her downstairs to me for guests so I have plenty of room. I might run out of silverware, but I'll have dish soap handy.

Hope this all makes sense. Please call or email with any questions. I just photocopied the form from the Handbook and emailed it to Dora. It needs to be signed by your immediate supervisor.

I suggest getting the form to Dora on Monday to start the process. Peace Corps wants a two week window for International travel. I also noticed hotels getting booked, so I suggest looking ASAP. Diana mentioned to me that she might stay one more night at the hostel and come back on the 3rd rather than the 2nd from Istanbul. Andrea and her boyfriend will also be on the bus with us to and from Istanbul.

There are tours we can take in Istanbul or just walk around on our own. I'd love to take a boat ride on the river. Maybe we can even consider a dinner cruise if it's not too expensive.

Talk to you soon, Louise

While my Christmas was different, it was fun. A brief recap – I took the train into Sofia on 19 December leaving at 6 AM from Aitos. Marcus and David were both flying in that day. As often happens in December weather played a role.

This is when I realized how important cell phones were becoming. Marcus sent some text messages, but we did not know what happened to David. I checked in at the Czech airline counter and the agent noticed David was scheduled to be on the afternoon flight from Paris, but it did not appear that he checked in. It turned out he missed the flight by about ten minutes, most likely due to either the weather or the extra security checks in Paris.

David left a phone message on my Bulgarian phone using a calling card. He found out later that this call cost him $36. I ended up calling Gretchen back in Massachusetts who then emailed her brothers. My friend Felicia was with me at the airport. Thankfully she had her computer with her which was a very big help. In this way we managed to pretty much know what was going on.

Felicia and I thought Marcus had made his flight, but after waiting for a couple of hours at the Sofia airport, we found out via email from Gretchen that he had not. Marcus was in Copenhagen for the Climate Conference. He planned to leave Saturday morning. There were various delays as many heads of state and delegates from around the world were leaving around the same time, thus causing numerous flight complications.

David was coming from Denver via JFK, Paris, and then Sofia. We found out from the airlines that David's flight was delayed. He was flying Air France. His was a weather delay. Even with well thought out plans weather and air traffic plays an even bigger role to make travel work.

Nikolai was returning from doing research in Turkey. Earlier we had arranged to meet at Happy's for dinner that night. As it turned out it was just me as both Marcus and David missed their connecting flights. I returned to The House briefly to get ready. Felicia had to take a bus back to Varshets. I met Nikolai at Happy's. The restaurant was very crowded. We managed to get a table without too much delay, but conversation was difficult as it was so noisy. As we were leaving the restaurant and walking to the bus stop my phone rang. It was David. He was at the Sofia airport. His flight had finally come in. He was waiting for his luggage, hoping it'd be on the next flight coming in from Paris. Then he'd get a taxi and meet me back at The House. We estimated it'd be near midnight. As he is a seasoned traveler I knew that he would figure out the logistics of coming to The House via taxi from the airport.

A few minutes later Nikolai caught his bus and I walked the 30-minute trek in the slushy snow back to The House. Around midnight I went outside and walked over to Vitosha Street looking for David. And there he was, nonchalantly walking down Vitosha Street towards the intersection where I was standing.

It was so good to see him. Wow! It seemed unreal to me to have my youngest child here in Bulgaria with me. It was a tremendous moment and I was very thankful that he had arrived safely.

It turns out that with the delay and the weather David's suitcase with his clothes for the next ten days did not make it. The suitcase he had packed with items for me arrived. He had brought along assorted vitamins and make up I had asked him to purchase; also he had some clothes from my sister and books for the school English library and special treats for the students. Air France said to be patient with his suitcase. As we planned to go out to Topolitsa the next day we had our fingers crossed. We hoped that both Marcus arrived with his bags and David's luggage with his clothes. I have always believed in miracles.

We had breakfast at The House the next morning and then did some walking around Sofia. I had arranged to meet up with Sveti, Yura's daughter who was at The University. This was a chance for David to speak English and meet a Bulgarian university student.

Marcus ended up spending the night in Prague. He arrived in Sofia Sunday afternoon. By the time his flight landed the city was in the midst of a major snowstorm. Both David and I were there to greet him with our suitcases ready to leave for the eastern side of the country. Our time table was very tight to make it back to Topolitsa yet that day.

We managed to make it to the main bus station from the airport via taxi. It was too late for any trains going to Aitos or Burgas. The taxi driver from the airport wanted to drive us all the way to Topolitsa for a mere 175 euros. Train fare from Sofia to Topolitsa is about 14 euros and bus fare about 20 euros. He was trying to convince us that we wouldn't be able to find a bus leaving that night. Fortunately, we managed to catch one of the last buses leaving that snowy afternoon to Burgas. It would drop us off in Aitos the town closest to me. I say fortunately as the bus was just getting ready to leave. The woman at the ticket counter told me we should hurry and board and pay the driver directly. The cost was only 20 lev each, quite a difference from 175 euros. Sixty lev for the three of us would come to about 30 euros.

Due to the outside weather the bus driver turned the heat on full blast making the bus interior very hot. It snowed the entire way and the driver only stopped once for a bathroom break. It was confusing as we had no idea when or where he would stop. For this reason, I really prefer the train. The trains do have bathrooms and often they are dirty, but available. The slow train bathrooms are especially bad, and usually the stoop style, so I try to avoid them if at all possible. The fast train bathrooms are generally cleaner, but on a seven hour trip they often run out of water. It's hard to know what the best choice is. But you can walk around on the train and you have more leg room so generally I prefer them.

A stoop style toilet, or Turkish as it is often called, has the opening on the floor. Usually it is in the shape of a triangle, sometimes with a wood rim. The newer ones are often cut out of a stone slab. A woman has to be skilled to use them without getting her dress or trousers wet. Hopefully, there is a hook to hang your purse and/or coat. Your clothing must be held up and you carefully stoop down. Paper should be ready in your other hand. With practice, a woman learns how to skillfully manage. Some of these toilets have a flush mechanism, others sometimes have a hose nearby where you can rinse off the area, and sometimes there is a bucket with water in it to rinse the floor area. Many places, including restaurants and hotels had this type of toilet. Sometimes, there was a choice and both were in the same facility. The used paper was always put in a can set nearby for this purpose.

The bathrooms at the bus stops are often at a small cafe. Some have several stalls as they are prepared for a bus load of passengers and you may have to pay ten or twenty lev. The train stations bathrooms are a mixed bag. At the bigger stations, like Plovdiv and Sofia they are kept cleaner, and you can usually find both the Turkish style and American.

Many of the smaller stations do not have bathrooms, and those that do leave much to be desired. The toilets on the fast train were the seat style and generally were clean.

While on the bus Dora, my school director, called me and told me that school was canceled for Monday and that the road to Topolitsa was already closed due to ice and snow. She would call the Road Star motel for me in Aitos so that we could stay there that night. We arrived in Aitos about midnight. The bus let us off at the town Roundabout. The bus was on its way to Burgas. One road led to the shopping area, another to the train station and the other to the bus station and the other to Burgas. I wasn't sure which of these roads led to the motel as I had not seen it since my first visit to Aitos back in June. As I was trying to orientate myself, I saw some headlights. It was a taxi. We stood in the middle of the road and hailed it down. Lucky for us, I managed in my Bulgarian to convey that we needed to go to the Road Star Motel. It was so great to see lights on at the motel.

Before the taxi driver took off, I asked him if he would take us to Topolitsa in the morning. And then I thought to ask him, also perhaps he could drive us down to the shops so David could get some clothes and we could buy some food. We agreed on 9 AM as I figured shops wouldn't be open before that time.

A big advantage of staying at the motel I realized was that it had heat. I knew my apartment would be very cold. Also, I had planned to buy food the day we arrived, thinking that we would arrive at least one day prior in the daylight and also have time to visit the school and go into Aitos on the train.

We had a hot cup of espresso and a Bulgarian breakfast of cheese on bread and a boiled egg. The taxi arrived on time. We would come back for our suitcases after shopping. He drove us to the center of Aitos where I was hoping a few shops would be open. It was about 15 degrees outside, very snowy and icy.

Fortunately, we found a few shops open and David got a few essential items. We were hoping his suitcase would arrive by the time we made it back to Sofia on Wednesday. I remembered a wool sweater I had seen in a second hand shop a few days earlier and had thought of buying it for David as a gift. I had decided I better wait and see if he really needed one and laid it back on the stack with the other sweaters. Again we were lucky. The shop was open and the sweater was still there. It was worn immediately. Actually, David wore it until we got to Istanbul where it was much warmer. I've bought most of my clothes in the second hand shops, as have most of the volunteers. They are very popular here, like the Good Will stores in the U.S. There are at least six or seven in Aitos that I have shopped at the few months that I've been here. It's a favorite pastime with Peace Corps Volunteers.

The same taxi driver took us back to the motel to pick up the suitcases. Both Marcus and David brought an extra suitcase with stuff for me: clothes, toiletries, DVDs, books and Christmas gifts. Finally about 11 AM on Monday we made it to Topolitsa. The road was very icy, but the taxi managed. He told me he was a professional driver. The distance is about ten miles on a rugged country road.

The road to Topolitsa was very icy. It was a mess with lots of ruts now covered and filled with snow and ice. This was especially true in Karageogievo, a village that we had to drive through on our way to Topolitsa. They have been repairing their main street since I arrived in the summer. I never did learn how to pronounce it's name very well. I was told it meant Black George. We got to Topolitsa around noon I think. It was so good to have David and Marcus in my apartment. If I had not taken some pictures I think I would have dreamed it all. The time went so fast.

My apartment was very cold. It had no heat for the past three and a half days. The first thing we did was get a fire going in my little stove. It was over an hour before we could feel some warmth coming into the room. There was no heat in the other rooms. As school had been called off it gave us more time together, but both Marcus and David were disappointed as they had been looking forward to meeting my director, the teachers, and the students. Luckily one of the women custodians was at the school and we were able to go inside and I could show them the classrooms. We spent the remaining day light hours walking around the village.

I had a small tree that I bought at the magazine near my school. Before opening our presents, Marcus moved the tree into the living room and we added some decorations he had bought in Aitos earlier that day. He also moved the little space heater in there so the room warmed up somewhat. Then we opened presents. Marcus and Stacey made a beautiful wedding album that Marcus brought along for me. They had bought the album in Nepal. They also gave me a photo album made out of a New Mexico license plate filled with candid shots from the past year.

Marcus fixed the fish we had bought in Aitos. We were busy every minute, but such a good feeling of busy. I realized how much I missed them all and wished that I was not so far away.

The time flew by so quickly. I called on Marcus' phone to the United States and talked to Willow the young woman who was staying at my house with her husband and toddler. She said they would be paying the money that they owed me soon; they could borrow it from her mom. I said okay, but I did need the money.

The next day we had to head back towards Sofia. We took the train into Aitos, and from there a bus to Plovdiv. This would put us over half-way to Sofia. Marcus was flying back to the U.S. on Wednesday afternoon and so we needed to be closer to Sofia. It is about a 7 to 8 hour journey depending on traffic and weather from Topolitsa. The first train from the east doesn't arrive in Sofia until almost 3 PM so the train directly from Aitos would not give Marcus enough time to go to the airport to catch his flight back to the U.S.

I had made arrangements earlier for us to spend the night in Plovdiv. Plovdiv is a very historic old Roman city. We got there about 2:30. And surprise – they did not have snow! Walking around that night in Plovdiv I mentioned how nice it would be to have our photo taken with the three of us by one of the historic buildings or at the recent excavation. Perhaps I could ask someone in Bulgarian. And then a voice out of the blue, says, "I'll take your picture Louise." I turned around. Who had called my name? Here was Stephanie, another Peace Corps Volunteer walking around Plovdiv. She was with her dad who had flown in the day before. What a pleasant surprise. She took several pictures of us, as we did of her and her dad. We continued to walk around the beautiful and very interesting old city. We found a lovely Italian restaurant for dinner and walked back to our hotel that was heated

We left too early to enjoy breakfast there as we had to be on the 7 AM express train to Sofia. We were in Sofia about 10 AM. We took our suitcases to The House Hotel, and there met Nikolai. I had asked him the night at Happy's about coming to The House to meet my sons and if he could give them a brief tour around Sofia. The snow was beginning to melt. The sidewalks were still a mess from the recent snowstorm.

We had a great walk around the City Center and Nikolai talked about the history of Sofia and made general conversation. This would be Marcus' only chance to see some of the city. By noon we headed back to The House to pick up Marcus' luggage and go to the airport. Nikolai left to head back to the University. He was coming back to The House at six and would go out to dinner with David and me.

We took a taxi to the airport with Marcus. At the airport David checked again about his luggage and it seemed they had no record of where it might be. He was told he could buy up to 100 euros and would get reimbursed by the Air France airline if he would go to their main office in Sofia. He was becoming very concerned about it as in a few days we would be leaving for Istanbul.

Marcus' flight was a bit delayed, but appeared like he would make it to Frankfort but most likely not catch his connecting flight back to the U.S. He ended up staying the night in Frankfurt and getting to Pittsburgh the next day where he met up with Stacey. His flight being delayed by nearly two hours gave him the unique distinction of seven different nights in a row sleeping in seven different cities.

David and I took the bus back into the city from the airport and went shopping for more clothes. Lots of shoppers were out which made it fun. The snow was starting to melt and everyone felt in a holiday mood. I found a Christmas tablecloth, buying it from a vendor on the street.

David wanted to find the Air France headquarters. He was told that their office was near the NDK. At the last shop the clerk told us that it was the street by the NDK and it turned out to be closest to the side that we were walking. The NDK building is on a very big square with park area, gardens, cafes and sitting area. It is at least six blocks long on each side. We found it.

David filled out the forms to put in a claim for his lost luggage. I was anxious to get back to the hotel to get ready for dinner so I left the airline office before David. But as the streets still confused me, I took the longer way and ended up getting there the same time as David.

We had dinner with Nikolai at a small restaurant. He brought me back a gift of candy from Turkey and I surprised him with a Bulgarian T-shirt. As it turned out, unbeknownst to me that the map and the names on the T-shirt were for a certain radical Bulgarian political party. I had bought it as a neat T-shirt, not understanding the ramifications.

As we were leaving the restaurant and walking towards the bus stop that Nikolai had to catch my phone rang. It was a man from the airport with news about David's luggage. He wanted to know if he should have it delivered to The House. The House did not have David's name on the register. Nikolai talked to him on the phone and sorted it out. Nikolai finished the phone call just in time as his bus arrived. David and I walked back to The House from the restaurant and retrieved his luggage. What a relief as it included his sleeping bag and of course his clothes for his almost two week visit. His suitcase also contained some presents that I had ordered online delivered to his apartment in Boulder.

The next morning, Christmas Eve Day we met up with Diana and Hazel for the trip to the Rila Monastery. We were picked up at 8 AM. First we had an early breakfast at The House. The staff there always served a fantastic breakfast. We could order eggs any way that we liked them, cereal, toast and fruits in addition to hot sausages or bacon, cream cheese and jam. Orange juice, coffee and tea were also available. This was all included in the cost of the lodging.

We left for the two hour ride south to Rila. The driver turned out to be a woman. She was very well informed and spoke excellent English. It is a beautiful monastery set in the mountains dating back to medieval times. Rila is an UNESCO site set in the Rila Mountains and forest preserve in southwest Bulgaria. It is filled with intricate icons and the setting of the Rila Mountains with the snow was a beautiful sight. It is one of the few monasteries that did not get ruined by the Communists during their occupation years. After walking around for over an hour, including taking many photos of the beautiful icons, David and I went into the museum. It included many precious items that were used in the monastery over the centuries including Rafail's Cross. This is a wooden cross made from a whole piece of wood (81 x 43 cm). It was whittled down by a monk named Rafail using fine burins and magnifying lenses to recreate 104 religious scenes and 650 miniature figures. Rafail worked on this cross nearly 12 years up to 1802. Sadly he became blind doing this intricate work and died shortly afterwards.

We went into the Monastery gift shop where we bought some crosses and also some post cards. It was now after 1 PM. We stopped at a small restaurant that the tour guide had arranged and had a delicious lunch with fresh fried fish and all the fixings. I remember my fish was delicious. We were told that it was caught in the nearby Rilska River. After lunch we were on our way back to Sofia. We arrived around 5:30 PM It was already dark outside. Felicia had returned and joined us for the walk around Sofia on Christmas Eve.

We decided to walk around and see the city lights. I was hoping also to attend services at the Bulgarian historical church, Aleksandur Nevski, but the service wasn't until later. As we had the long train ride back to Topolitsa in the morning we just walked around the church and took pictures. It was beautiful with the snow and the Christmas lights.

On Christmas Eve, the city was very quiet, a big contrast from earlier in the day and the day before. On the 23rd everyone was out shopping buying Christmas trees, presents, and special foods. By 6 PM on the 24th everything was quiet. This is a family celebration here and people also attend later church services. A big meal is prepared without meat on the 24th and on the 25th another huge meal, this time with meat.

It was a beautiful clear night with stars out and the moon shining. It was very pretty. I had wanted to go inside the Aleksandur Nevski Memorial Church but the doors weren't open yet for the late evening services. We decided not to wait around as we didn't know what time the doors would open.

We thought that perhaps restaurants closed early as Christmas is observed by families with celebrations in their home and attending services at midnight. We were getting hungry and started looking for an open restaurant. All seemed to have closed very early for Sofia, even Happy's. Oh my. We thought certainly something must be open on Vitosha Street. Finally we found a Pizza Restaurant/ Bar. When we went in we were the only customers. A few more people came in while we were there. The food was good. We enjoyed a great pizza and a Bulgarian beer.

I had mentioned taking the early train to Topolitsa but no one seemed in favor of that idea. So we decided to have breakfast at the House and take the 10:45 train. It would get us to Topolitsa around 7:30 PM. Felicia was going to Whitney's for Christmas Day. The train was not too full and we had a room (6 seats, not the whole coach) to ourselves.

Riding across the length of the countryside on the train was a new experience for most of my friends. We did some sleeping, talking and of course eating. A vendor came around selling food. That had not happened to me before on the train. A woman stopped in and started talking to us about computers. She was very curious about where we lived, and what we did. I gave her my phone number and as it turns out I ended up meeting with her in Aitos in January. She still occasionally phones me, but I really can't help her with her project.

We had to get off the train at Karnobat to switch to the slow train. I had thought of hiring a taxi, but there were too many of us and we had too much luggage. And surprise, there was Milka. She was coming back from Serbia. She travels so much. We waited with her, talked and just spent the hour and twenty minutes in the rather dingy Karnobat train station. It's actually only twenty minutes from Topolitsa by car, so it seems a person should be able to walk it in that amount of time. But it was cold outside so that was not a very practical idea and no path other than on the train tracks.

We finally made it to Topolitsa. The train has two very quick stops at two small villages, Klikach and Chemograd, on the way. It was now very dark outside with no illumination at these village stations. I always counted the stops on the train from Karnobat so I would know when to get off. The conductor does not generally walk through the train and announce the stops. The passengers are expected to know their stop. My first few times I would ask the conductor to tell me when my stop was coming. Eventually most of the conductors knew me and knew I needed to get off at Topolitsa. The slow train from Burgas to Topolitsa had many more stops and with little illumination at them. It was very important to watch for landmarks. A few of the bigger villages had some lights on that I learned to recognize. In the darkness, I was always very concerned about getting off at the right station. In Burgas and Sofia it is the end of the line, so getting off at the right station was not a problem.

At a village stop, it can be very tricky getting off the train, especially when it doesn't stop directly in front of the cement platform. The conductor doesn't pull out any steps to use. The passenger is expected to open the latch on the door and jump off. This Christmas Day night, we got the latch up and the door open, but the train stopped just past the platform. There was snow on the ground making the jump down of several feet rather precarious. David went first and quickly helped the rest of us descend. The conductor watched to see that we all got off, but no time is wasted. In a flash the train took off. We had arrived in Topolitsa. The road to the house from the train station was covered in ice and snow. Walking back to my house was another adventure. Thankfully everyone was dressed in warm winter coats, scarfs and mittens. I had my trusty flashlight to help lead the way. Milka and my group were the only passengers that got off Christmas Day night in Topolitsa. It was cold in my apartment. David quickly tried to make a fire but it always takes at least a half hour for the fire to really make a difference in a room. We found the small space heaters. I heated some water to cook some pasta. I can't remember what else I made for dinner that night.

I had bought a chicken and set it out to thaw. In the morning I would start preparations for our Christmas dinner. We had a great time visiting. Thankfully, the weather turned warmer and snow was melting. On Monday it rained and the weather got a bit warmer. This greatly helped the sleeping situation as my little wood stove only heated one room and that room only had one bed in it. My two tiny space heaters were put to good use in the other rooms.

Marcus had plugged in one of the heaters in the kitchen as it was quite cold in there, and then turned on my two-burner stove. That combination blew a fuse. So we decided to keep the kitchen cool and only use the space heaters in the evening when nothing else was turned on. The fuse box was in my hallway, but they were fuses the like of which none of us had never seen before. My sons figured out how to reattach the fuses, but I didn't want to have to deal with them again so we were very careful on what electrical combination of devices we used.

Monday we took the train into Burgas to see the Black Sea. Felicia traveled from northwest Bulgaria and met us there. Now I had four guests sleeping in my apartment. On the 29th we went on the last train into Aitos in late afternoon and had dinner at a traditional Bulgarian restaurant. I had invited my school director and Ivanka, my language teacher, and Andrea the young volunteer from Ohio with her boyfriend. He had flown in from Ohio. Brandi and Vesala, her counterparts were also there and her school director. It made for a fun dinner; there was some Bulgarian spoken, but mainly English.

Vesala baked special holiday bread for the group. It celebrated the New Year. A lucky coin was hidden inside it. Whoever gets the bread with the coin is especially lucky for the next year; we toasted "Nazdrave," "Cheers." It was a joyful celebration with a wonderful feeling of friendship.

After the dinner we went to get our suitcases that we had left in Andrea's apartment with her little dog. Then it was time to walk to the bus station. It was about a twenty-five minute walk. We waited and waited for the bus to Istanbul. It was cold outside. We hoped we had not missed it. We were told that it should be there about 11:30 PM. It was now midnight. There was no heated bus terminal to wait inside. You needed to stand outside and wait to make sure that the bus stopped for you. The bus was late and it was cold waiting for it at this time of night. Finally we saw a big bus approach. It was a few minutes after midnight. It is about a six to eight hour bus trip. The time it takes depends on the border crossing and how much traffic once you reach Istanbul.

We had our luggage loaded underneath by the driver. The passenger seats were quite full. It was impossible to find seats together for the seven of us, Andy, Andrea, Felicia, Diana, Hazel, David and myself. We broke into two groups. Finally we were off. Of course we were too excited now to sleep. When we approached Burgas the bus pulled into a gas station. We followed the other passengers lead and went inside to use the bathroom. We did not know how long it would be before it would stop again.

We can do some traveling now with special permission. School teachers should only travel during school holidays, but it's still considered part of your vacation days. About fourteen volunteers from our B-25 group went to Istanbul over the Christmas break, other volunteers went to Germany and a few of our group went back to the village to visit their host families where they had spent their first two months in Bulgaria.

At the Bulgaria/Turkey Border everyone's Passport is checked inside the building where the Border Crossing agents are waiting for you. As American citizens we also had to fill out the form to obtain a visa at this time and pay $20 USD. Bulgarians were allowed to enter with their *Lichna Karta*. We had to show our ID, and we also needed a valid U.S. Passport. Peace Corps is under the U.S. Department of State and when we were accepted as a volunteer for the government we filled out forms and were issued a Passport that was valid for three years. This is in addition to the Passport that a U.S. citizen usually obtains for travel outside of the U.S. We could use either one for travel outside the country, but it was recommended to use the one issued for us when we became a PC volunteer as we were continually under their jurisdiction while serving in the Peace Corps. David and Andy did not need an Identity Card, but they did need to show their Passport and pay the $20 for a visa.

Finally we arrived at the center bus station in Istanbul about 8 AM. We were anxious to find a bathroom. The only other stop we had made since boarding around midnight besides the quick stop near Burgas was at the Border Crossing. We did use the toilets there. They were not the best, but we had no choice. Once we located the toilets, we discovered the matrons wanted Turkish money which we did not bring with us. Finally a woman near my age accepted American coins and allowed us to use the facilities.

After living in Topolitsa for five months now, the traffic in Istanbul really surprised me. There were people, cars, trucks, and buses everywhere. You can definitely see that Turkey is richer than Bulgaria. They were independent while Bulgaria was under USSR from 1944–1989. Then we caught a small bus which would take us closer to the historic part of the city. This ride was almost another hour. When it stopped we realized we still were not in the historic part of town or near our hotel where we had reservations. We needed to board their modern transit system. But first we needed to convert our money. David found a bank machine to obtain some Turkish money. A small hitch happened. The machine swallowed his bank card. Fortunately the bank was open. David decided to stay by the machine and I would go inside and see what could be done. Many in the business world speak both English and Turkey so they understood me when I explained what had happened. A bank official was able to retrieve David's card after he showed his Passport. This is a good reason to always use a bank machine by a bank when traveling overseas.

Before long we found our way to the very modern transit train that would take us into the heart of Istanbul. We would use this several times in the next few days. On New Year's Day, David took it the entire way to the Istanbul Ataturk Airport for his flight back to the U.S.

Istanbul is an amazing city to visit. It is a city of over fourteen million people. It is filled with many bazaars, beautiful mosques and other historic sites. Restaurants and shops are everywhere. We took a boat ride on the Bosporus and hiked up a small mountain to an old castle. Everything was more expensive than Bulgaria, especially the food and eating in restaurants. It appears you have to bargain for everything you buy. Also at some of the restaurants, proprietors were outbidding each other to get the tourist trade. They would follow us and rattle off the menu. In the Bazaars vendors would follow you to encourage you to buy from them and not the next booth. It could prove quite tiring to a tourist for as the saying goes, "they could see you coming." We had three days there and by the third day I was getting the hang of it on how to avoid eye contact, but at the same time try to look at some of the merchandise. It was all very beautiful and very tempting to buy, especially the scarfs and decorated bowls.

We went inside the Blue Mosque, also known as the Sultan Ahmed Mosque. We visited the Aya Sofia, or Hagia Sofia which interpreted means Holy Wisdom. We had a five hour round-trip boat ride on the Bosphorus Strait. We stopped at an island and had lunch and then hiked up to see the Rumeli Fortress ruins and amazing views of the water which divides

Europe from Asia. We also walked up the Galata Tower in old Istanbul and visited the Basilica Roman Cistern from the 5th century. We visited the Grand Bazaar with over 4,000 shops spread over 61 covered streets and the Spice Bazaar with over 85 shops of many exotic spices. They were both very interesting, but a bit overwhelming.

On New Year's Eve, David, Felicia and I walked with thousands of other people down Independence Boulevard strung with bright Christmas lights. It would be similar to being in Times Square on New Years Eve. David had researched restaurants and we found the one he had earmarked. It was crowded, but they squeezed us in and we had a delicious Turkish dinner at about 11 PM. Hazel had decided to spend the night at her hotel, and Diana was with the other Peace Corps Volunteers visiting Istanbul.

David left the next morning for the U.S. from the Istanbul Ataturk Airport using the modern transit system. The rest of us took the day to go back to the Grand Bazaar and just walk around again this very ancient beautiful city. On January 2nd it was time for us to return to Bulgaria. We left around 9 AM making it back to Burgas just in time to walk to the train station and catch the last train back to Topolitsa. Fortunately in most cities the main bus terminal and train terminal are fairly close to each other. In some of the bigger cities there are two bus terminals, or a bus may leave you off on a street and you have to sort out your own way.

My friends stayed in Topolitsa one more night and the next day we caught the early train into Aitos in order for them to catch an Express bus back to Sofia. From there they were going their separate ways, back to their towns in Northwest Bulgaria. I am in the Southeast corner so we do not see each other very often. Others live in the Southwest in the mountains and a few in the far North. Besides the sightseeing this was a good chance to catch up with our various Peace Corps experiences. Hopefully later this year I will have a chance to visit them in their neighborhoods. Over 100 Peace Corps volunteers were in the country, but never did we all meet as a group. On our First Year Anniversary most of the 61 of us who flew out together from Washington, D.C., would gather in Vratsa.

This month seems rather quiet. Hopefully I will manage and start a quiet routine of teaching and learning more Bulgarian. I have two trips to Sofia coming up. Late in February I plan to meet with Felicia and work with her on a tourism project.

Shortly after that, I'm going with Laura and we're going to a concert in the NDK with Brandon. He's known as a RPCV (Response Peace Corps Volunteer, a person who has served in the Peace Corps previously and signed up for a short term for a special project.) He will be here for five months with the Peace Corps working at the University Library in Sofia. He worked at a library in Phoenix. I had met him on an earlier medical visit I had in Sofia. At that time he mentioned the concert featuring Alla Pugachova, a famous Russian singer. The tickets were rather expensive but sounded like it would be a good experience. The teachers in Topolitsa I've mentioned it to are all excited as she is very well known in Europe. Wikipedia has a write up on her. It surprises me again how few artists from Europeare known in the United States. Sometimes I think we feel that all art and celebrity comes from the United States. And that is absolutely not true.

In April I will be going to Sofia to meet Belinda. She is flying in April 2 from Japan where she is a librarian on a U.S. military base. We will have a short stay in Sofia and then come to Topolitsa, go to Plovdiv and then fly from Sofia to Warsaw. This is over my school spring break. I am so glad that she is able to come. Otherwise I'm not sure how I would have handled this vacation time.

In summer I am thinking of traveling on my own to some Eastern European cities, e.g., Vienna, Budapest and Prague.

The Internet is down again tonight. The weather was clear today, but cold. I got more wood from school. This past weekend it was very cold in my apartment.

NOTES FROM MY BULGARIAN JOURNAL

Mid-January

I am sitting in my apartment with my little wood stove trying to keep warm. Today I think it was warmer outside than in my apartment. The cold air comes in and it is hard for it to leave. Insulation is very poor. When it snows or rains and we've had both this week, the moisture collects on the walls. My bathroom is particularly cold on those days. I need to build up my courage to take a shower.

There are no shower curtains in my bathroom. Some volunteers have rigged one up, but my ceiling is so high I can't figure out how to do it. The entire bathroom floor gets wet. In the very cold weather all the hooks that I had super glued on the wall to hold towels fell off. So now I keep towels outside the bathroom which is rather inconvenient, but I figure come spring I'll hang the hooks back up. My water is hot, so once I manage my courage and get the water going I am fine.

School started again this week. Now I am teaching more often the lower grades, but I still help out in grades 5, 6, 7 and 8. The children are fun, but often communication breaks down.

Hi Donna,   **January 2010**

It's Friday night for you and Saturday morning here in Bulgaria. It's a very cold and windy day. Probably one of the most windy days I've ever experienced. This past week my Internet was also down and most likely will go down again.

I had my hair dyed in the fall. I hardly recognized myself. The following morning Milka did not say anything, so perhaps it wasn't as drastic a change as it appeared to me. The gray is covered. My gray hair is what really showed up in pictures. Now it is more auburn, but still brown. The volunteers at the last meeting were all amazed when they saw me. I received lots of complements.

Yesterday I went into Aitos as I usually go twice a week no matter the weather for my Bulgarian language lessons, but also thought I should get a permanent. That was a big mistake. I want to wash it today, but hesitate. My hair looks like it was fried. I can't believe it. It is a mess. The hairdresser cut it even shorter on the top – yuk!

If you know the picture of Einstein where his hair is standing straight on edge, well that's me. I'm not sure what I can do except let it grow out. Tomorrow I may try to wash it, but my apartment is so cold. I have icicles on the inside of my bathroom window. I will have to figure this out. She is a very good hairdresser I know, but apparently my hair does not like Bulgarian perms.

I can't believe how strong the wind is blowing. When I was walking back from the train about six o'clock last night I could barely stand up. Fortunately, there were other people, and one young man from the village took my arm and became my support the entire walk back to my apartment, at least a half mile. It was bitterly cold. I had four layers of clothing on under my heavy winter coat and could still feel the wind through it all. I had a wool hat on and my hood jacket.

Today is more of the same. It's not snowing now, but the wind is blowing the snow all around from the storm on Monday. I have been having trouble connecting to the Internet.

Thanks for listening.

Big hug, Louise

Hi Grace,   **January 2010**

It has taken me awhile to reply, but I remembered that you were gone over the holidays. How was New Orleans? How is the recovery from Katrina? Can that be five years ago already? That doesn't seem possible. It's hard to believe that it's 2010.

In some ways time seems to fly, even though January was a very long slow month for me. It's always a let down for me after the holidays. David was able to stay until January 1st. It was so great to have him visit.

Marcus was only here a few days, but his visit too helped make the holidays extra special. The weather for the most part was cold and snowy.

Both of their flights were delayed into Sofia, and the bus ride back to Topolitsa was a snowy windy night. The road actually to my village was blocked so we had to stay in a motel in a nearby town.

Several other Peace Corps Volunteers also came to Topolitsa over the holidays so I had a full apartment. There were seven of us including David, who took a bus to Istanbul. That is a very interesting city, but don't think I'd like to live there. Having a boat ride on the Bosphorus River and seeing the historic mosques made it all worthwhile.

Tomorrow starts the second half of the school year. I'm to get a new teaching schedule. But like many things here, you don't know until the moment what it will be. I guess that keeps life interesting. Classes are forty minutes in length with a ten minute break. After the second class, there is a longer break to allow students to have a snack and go to the toilet. These are outside and so the longer breaktime is really needed. Then there are two more periods before lunch. There is an hour break at noon time, which gives time for the students who live in the village to go home for lunch. I usually do that as well. Then there are two more regular classes in the afternoon. Many students then can have study time, music, or sports until 4 PM when the bus comes to take them home. Besides Topolitsa, students come mainly from two other nearby villages, Chemograd and Kikach.

Sometimes it would be nice to know a bit more what's going on. The language is slowly coming, but often I find it frustrating here in the village as I really have no one to talk to. I do go into Aitos and see the other volunteer and she has several teachers at her school who do speak English. Also, that is where my language teacher lives, and she is great to talk to.

My biggest news is that yesterday I took home a cat. I had had a kitten for a few weeks, but decided it was too much hassle and got a student to take it to his home. There are many strays around on the streets.

Yesterday this black cat walked up to me. It let me pet her and then I picked her up. I think she must be about a year old. I noticed a bunch of healed scars on her body and I think she must have been hit with a car. As I was holding her and when a car approached she froze. She actually reacted to it before I even saw the car. She seems very gentle, so for now I'll keep her. At least she has it nicer than being out in the cold snowy and rainy weather we've been having. Last weekend was so windy it felt like a tornado to me.

I had to walk back from the train and I could barely stand up. Fortunately a young man took my arm. The wind blew all weekend. This weekend is milder and today we are having rain. Now the walk to the train is slush. The walk to the train takes me about twenty minutes. I try to allow myself thirty minutes as sometimes it's early, or I meet students on the way and sometimes I just try to walk slowly and enjoy and appreciate the natural setting around me.

It is important to get there ahead of the train as the door only opens on the other side of the track. Several times I've had friends here and the train came before we had crossed the track. There is nothing a person can do, but check the schedule and hope that there is another train later in the day. That is generally okay if you don't have a connection to make or a class to teach.

The train to Aitos where I go for my language lesson, general shopping and the bank machine makes three trips in the early morning and three mid-morning to late afternoon, all about an hour apart. The return trains are also spaced out about an hour apart. The train schedule is not like the New York Subway where another train will be coming in the next ten minutes. I need to plan my day carefully when it includes a train trip whether to Aitos, or Burgas which is an hour away by train or to Sofia. For that train, I usually take the slow train to Karnobat (east) and wait for the fast train to Sofia. From leaving my apartment to arriving in Sofia is over 7 hours. I generally use the time to read or study.

The Hiassen book I read was *Stormy Weather*. That's the only one I have here. Maybe when I make it into Sofia and the Peace Corps office they'll have some more of his books. It's a good change of pace. I've mainly been reading history books. I also read a good science/literature book called *The Age of Wonder, 1780-1830* by Richard Holmes. It is about Joseph Banks going to Tahiti and William Herschel discovering the planet Uranus and relates also the discoveries of his sister Caroline. Holmes narrative shows how poets who were writing in that time period knew many of the scientists and how their lives were woven together. They inspired each other. Holmes is a marvelous writer.

Now for fun, I picked up another Alexander McCall Smith book in Burgas and also one by Sophie Kinsella. Her books are like "crazy fun" very light, some romance, basically young women trying to make it in business. *Shopaholic* is the name of the series of books she's done.

Do you know *French Women Don't Get Fat* by Mireille Guilliano? I found a follow up book she's written, *French Women for All Seasons*. She really has some good basic eating tips for people. I met her once at a library conference. I think she has the ideal life, married to an American professor and spends half her year in New York City and the other half in France

While a wood stove can be romantic, it certainly isn't very practical from my point of view. I can't believe how much wood it needs to keep a fire going twenty-four hours a day. Once it gets going you're very warm, but as the fire goes down the air cools off, and the cycle starts over again. Without a fan, it's really only warm by the stove, not six feet away. There is also much soot in the outside air from all the wood burning stoves in the village. The nice clean snow gets dirty quickly.

It's getting late here, but I wanted to get off a reply to you before the end of this month. Several times with our bad weather I've been without Internet. Then I really do feel isolated.

I'm glad you enjoyed the pictures. I can't remember if I've sent you any of Christmas or Istanbul. Let me know if you'd like more sent.

Have you seen any good movies lately? What's out there? David brought me some DVDs that I can watch on my computer: Jimmy Stewart classics and old Dick Van Dyke television shows. They are fun to watch.

Big hug Grace and please write soon again, I love hearing from you.
Louise

Hey, Louise,   **January 3, 2009**
Yes. I'm sick. Well, getting better now –

I had bronchitis, strep, and double ear infections all at once. I was in the Peace Corps sick bay for three days and two nights. I got home New Year's Eve but I shouldn't have made the long trip on the train so soon. Oh well. Feeling a bit better so we'll see how the week goes. I wish I could have met your son but I do hope you had a good visit anyway. I also hope you figured out the transportation to Topolitsa okay. I realized I never got back to you with that information. I'm very sorry. Talk to you soon and have a good week.

Big hugs back, Laura

HAPPY NEW YEAR

Hi Louise,   **January 6, 2010**
How are you doing? What was your holiday like? I just can't imagine being away from home, much less the United States during Christmas. I hope you survived with glorious experiences. Any adventures? I'm sure you will write all about it when you get a chance. How much time off do the children get from school, if any?

If the children do not go to school, do you get time off also or does the Peace Corps require that you keep busy? I hope you had a splendid time during the holidays. Today was our first day back with students. It was exhausting. I am so tired. I am going to bed early. Just thinking of you, and wanted to say, "Hi."
Trish

Hi Trish,   **January 11, 2010**
How are you doing? There was total confusion at our school today. I never seem to know what's going on. Today I found out that the first three classes were shortened. I was scheduled to teach Grade 6, period 3

to start at 9:40, but today it had started at 9 AM. Nobody bothered to call me. And then when I came in nobody was around. Where was everybody?

It turns out they were showing the upper grades a movie. It was to deal with aggression. The director was concerned about some of the behavior going on at the school. I figure it must be a documentary. Well, it turned out to be the Kevin Spacey movie *Pay Forward*. By the time I found the group and figured it all out the movie was half over. She showed it with Bulgarian sub-titles and English turned way down. Oh my . . . so it goes . . . .

I think you mentioned about mailing a package before Christmas. Do you remember when you mailed it? Nothing has come so far. It could be part of the holiday package delay, but I was just wondering. Perhaps you had said you were thinking of mailing it and didn't actually mail it.

That's it from me. Today the sun was out, but so frustrated with school I guess I didn't appreciate it like I should have. Over the weekend there was a heavy downpour of rain.

Always like to hear from you, Louise

Hi Louise,   **January 12, 2010**

Sounds like a bad day. I've had those. Hang in there. I'm quite certain I mailed those packages (there were 2 of them) on December 9th. Nancy was with me. It was the Wednesday after we had our cookie party. I'm surprised you haven't gotten them yet. Maybe somebody in the post office ate all the cookies.

Darn. I hope the packages show up eventually a lady at the post office said they should arrive in about ten days. Evidently she was wrong. There was a little article about Bulgarians in the latest *Week* magazine. I forgot what it was about. My brain is dead now as it's too late at night, but I'll try to remember to send that magazine to you some time. Bye for now, and I hope you have a better day tomorrow.

Try to stay warm, Trish

Hi Trish,   **January 12, 2010**

Guess what? Both packages were at the Post Office today. What a pleasant surprise? I opened them at school and shared a few of the cookies with some of the teachers. They were very impressed. The little Christmas tree is still up in the teacher's lounge and so the cookies of the tree with a star on the top were very appropriate. I was glad to see some of those also in the other box and I saved all of those in that box for me to eat.

Most of them arrived in pretty good shape, except the ribbon candy. That is rather all broken-up, but I will use it in tea. This afternoon I downloaded the DVD and watched the Cookie Movie. It was great. That was so nice of you to do that; I really appreciate all your efforts. The

package coming in January was good as I really needed a "pick me up."
I can play it now whenever I want to cheer myself up or rather you all
will be cheering me up.

Of course I remember Randa. Is Vickie also a librarian? And Linda?
What does she teach?

That was so nice of you all to share your goodies with me. There is
nothing like it here.

Sometime soon I want to bake chocolate chip cookies but I haven't
found chocolate chips. Some volunteers have chopped up a chocolate
candy bar. David brought me vanilla, and I have flour and sugar. But the
brown sugar here is granulated, so not quite the same. But that project
can wait now until I eat up all the cookies you mailed me. I want to
spread out the days to enjoy them. What a treat, thank you so very much.

And I look forward to watching the DVD movie too. I tried to explain
to the teachers why you sent me some brown paper bags. I'll have to look
online and see if I can find a picture of the Luminarias.

Big hug to all of you. I miss you. I'm in my 8th month. Sounds like I'm
pregnant I'm just looking forward to when I'll see you all again.

With many warm wishes for the New Year, Louise

Hi Trish and company,   **January 23, 2010**

This weather is unbelievable. It is cold and very windy. It is even wind-
ier than the desert winds in New Mexico. Walking to the train yesterday I
could barely stand up. I couldn't believe it; the wind continued all night,
and now all day. Not sure about the temperature, but with wind chill I'm
sure it's below zero.

And to help make life exciting here, the road to the train, about a half
mile I estimate, was covered in ice. On my way back the wind felt even
worst and it was dark out. Thankfully a young man offered me his arm
and I took it. There are a few street lights on timers but there were some
sections when I was walking where it was completely dark. I always carry
a flashlight with me and I used that also when I reached my house to see
the key hole. The bottom door is to stay locked at all times. I am on the
second floor and usually the light works in the hallway so that I don't
have to walk up the steps in the dark.

My little wood stove is working like crazy to keep this one room warm.

School was canceled two days this week due to the roads being blocked
by big snow drifts and now it looks like more is coming.

Oh my, I'm enjoying the cookies and so glad I have DVDs. Electric and
Internet has been intermittent.

Keep warm, Louise

Hi Louise,

Brrrr! I can barely tolerate the winters here in Farmington. I can't even imagine what you're going through. I hope you have some warm snow boots to walk in.

Believe it or not Farmington got eleven inches of snow last week, not all at once, but we had two delayed school days and two closed school days. The entire mall closed down for one of those days. My daughter who lives in Flagstaff got between three to four feet of snow. Both Interstates were closed running through Flagstaff.

My Spanish class was canceled due to not enough people signing up for it; I was bummed about it. I still plan to study all the vocabulary I can so next time it will be easier for me. What about you? Are you learning more of the Bulgarian language?

Take care and keep in touch, we miss you.

Your friend, Lola.

Hi Louise,   **January 23, 2010**

Oh, I am so glad the cookies arrived. I was getting a little worried about it. As you said, it's probably even a better treat in January. You were busy traveling around during December. January is always a letdown after the holidays. Actually, I think February is worse for me. I always think spring should be coming by then, and it's still cold. Tonight it is raining, our first rain in a long time. It might turn to snow, who knows?

We have an early morning staff meeting before school tomorrow. We no longer have what they called "early outs" where students are dismissed early so we could do "professional" things such as plan, workshops, and hold staff meetings.

Oh, we have a new restaurant in town. It used to be Johnny Carino's, and then turned into a Texas BBQ place and now: Taverno Greek Grill. It is a real Greek restaurant. It's good, too something for you to look forward to. Well, as usual, it's late so I better move along the e-mail list, and get it all done, before I fall asleep at the keyboard.

Take care, Trish

Oh my gosh, Louise,

Try to stay out of the cold. It sounds like blizzard conditions. We've had our share of snow this winter. Well, last winter we had a lot of snow also. However, it came more in one week this year. The TV weather report this morning said Farmington has gotten 13inches of snow the last few days. We had 2-hour delays on Tuesday and Wednesday, and then complete SNOW DAYS (no school) on Thursday and Friday. That has never happened, according to my memory, in the ten years that I've been here.

However, unlike you, I don't have to walk a half mile in it, nor do I have to worry about electricity and a warm heater We are so fortunate in the United States to have reliable infrastructure for the basic necessities of life. You are sure seeing a lifestyle and culture unknown to most of us. I wouldn't be surprised if you write another book, this time about your Peace Corps days in Bulgaria.

So, be keeping notes and memories, so you can have a lot of information, should you decide to write a book about it It may be miserable now, but after time has passed, I bet you look back on it as a great accomplishment on your part. Anyway, thanks for writing.

Stay warm, Trish

WINTER DOLDRUMS

Today I am home with a cold. It probably was worst yesterday, but today I decided to call in sick. I have been blowing my nose quite a bit, took Tylenol Severe last night and slept fairly well. I've been sleeping now in the room with the stove. It's a more comfortable bed, but I have to make it up every day and sleeping in the same area as my computer, television, and table makes the room feel very claustrophobic. Hopefully by this time next month the weather will be warmer and I can move back into my regular bedroom.

Yesterday in the package that arrived from LeAnne was a thermometer. Taking some quick readings, it showed my kitchen and bathroom around 42 degrees Fahrenheit. And it was a warm day. It's probably ten degrees warmer in my apartment than outside. In my heated room I can get it up to 60 degrees and it feels fairly warm. The air is still cool as I type on the keyboard. My fingers feel cold. It rained last night and it seems to be melting some of the ice and snow that is around. The walk to the train yesterday was horrible.

There was ice and packed slippery snow, deep ruts with water and crusty mud. As I approached the station area a car was stuck in the slushy frozen mess. I had to walk on shear ice to get around the car. At least the wind wasn't blowing. I really don't know how people put up with it. Why isn't some sand put down? At the platform waiting for the train a tiny bit of snow was sprinkled with sand in a few areas, but not really enough to make it noticeable. I did manage to go in for my regular language lesson.

And this morning the black cat that I picked up several weeks ago was meowing so pitifully I decided she wanted to go outside. I opened the door by the balcony which is off what I call the guest bedroom and she jumped up and went on her way. I looked for her several times later in the day, but she was not to be seen. Hopefully she finds a home. She had a big breakfast and is really healthy. But I miss having her around. She was a very gentle cat and I had named her Alice. Krazi, the student who took Oscar the kitten, indicated to me that people at the corner magazine in the village had a black cat. Perhaps that's where Alice has gone. Yesterday I bought another bag of litter and a kilo of cat food at the little corner shop in Aitos. I guess I'll save it, as it appears cats have a way of coming into my life.

I still want to write about Christmas, perhaps tonight. The Internet is down again. I want to do some embroidery while it is daylight. Christmas time went so very fast.

Marcus only actually stayed in Topolitsa one night. The next day we took the slow train into Aitos in order to catch a bus to Plovdiv. I wanted my sons to see this historic city, plus it helped the schedule so that we could be in Sofia in time for Marcus' flight back to the U.S. the next day. It was a short visit. We tried to make the best of it. The bus was late leaving Aitos. We caught it at the Roundabout, the same place where we were let off at midnight on our way from Sofia. The bus driver to make up time dropped us off at a gas station on the highway rather than take us all the way into the bus station in Plovdiv. We had to call a taxi that would take us into the city. Fortunately, another woman who could speak English explained this to us about five minutes before it all took place. We got the number for a taxi from the woman. I had the taxi driver take us directly to our hotel. It was further away from the Old City than I realized. The weather was cold, but not windy so we walked to the City Center. We found a nice Italian restaurant for dinner and we walked around the old city. Marcus bought some souvenirs and I bought a lovely hand knit wool vest. That night they both had work to do on their computer. It was nice staying in a warm room. We left the next morning on the 7 AM train for Sofia.

Finally now, March 9, my tenants seem to be getting their act together. Al is going to school through the GI program as he is a veteran. They owe me over $4,000, and hopefully they will get it paid off. I have not heard from Marcus as to whether he discussed new terms with them.

Marcus is busy flying back and forth to D.C. working on assorted programs dealing with clean energy. I will need him to do my taxes for me this year. He may have to hire someone as mine appear complicated this year.

More later . . . no electric today . . . again wind and snow . . . .

Dear Irma,   **January 23, 2010**

I thought instead of a regular email I would attempt to make my notes and ideas in a letter to you. Also, as the Internet is interment this will save it. It was good talking to you and I appreciate you taking the time out of your busy schedule. I don't think I realized that with joining the PC how far removed it would make it seem from most people back in the states.

My life has changed so drastically, while family and friends back in the

U.S. may have some changes much is the same – where people shop, who they talk to, the language they speak, the church they go to – that is the same. For me, that is all changed. I guess that's why it's difficult for me sometimes to even reply to some of the emails people write me and why Peace Corps staff have mentioned that it is a big transition going back to our home in the U.S.

My niece Debbie, Lyle's oldest daughter emails me occasionally. She wants to come to the Passion Play in Germany this summer and is thinking about coming to visit me as well. I emailed her some suggestions. Depending on her time perhaps we could do a week together touring some capital cities, e.g., Budapest, Prague, Vienna and then time in Bulgaria. Hopefully that will happen. If not, I may decide to do it on my own. We do get vacation days with PC and hopefully I can use them this summer when school is out. In April a friend from my library conference days may come and spend a few days. She works at a military base in Japan as librarian and loves to travel.

Generally now we can travel one weekend a month inside country. I'm not sure how much outside country I'll be able to afford to do and have the time to do. Some Peace Corps Volunteers plan to travel before they return to the U.S. after their PC time is finished, but I know I will be anxious then to come back to the U.S. and see the new grand baby and my children and other family and friends. I think it is different when you are older as to how you view time away.

Not sure why I'm telling you all this, just want to share with someone. I thought there would be more camaraderie in the Peace Corps. I think there is perhaps with the younger folks. The two young women who are closest to me in miles are very nice and I try to get together with them as much as our schedules allow. They are 22 years old. So while they both are very nice, they are at a completely different stage in their life. They were born in the mid-eighties. I wonder if I am like a grandmother to them.

The other two single older women in the Peace Corps are quite far away in miles and their life back in the states while some similarity to mine, appear quite different. Not sure exactly what the difference is, maybe just our personalities. One has her daughter and grandchild living in her house while she is in the Peace Corps and has another daughter who lives nearby. Both seem to have their plans set for when they return to the states. As she relates it, she was looking for something to do in retirement and just happened to see the PC poster at the Arizona State University campus in Tempe.

One other aside as I muse about people, I'm so happy that Trish is keeping in regular touch with me via email. She is the school librarian who took my position at Heights. This is the junior high school where

I first worked in Farmington. Trish has mailed me DVDs, magazines and organized the cookie exchange at her house. This group of friends sent me a batch of homemade cookies and surprised me with a home-made video that was really fun to watch. Besides her regular librarian job at Heights, she devotes much of her time to her elderly dad.

The weather here has been truly awful. I expected most of it I guess, but still when winter happens it is still somewhat of a shock. The wind started again on Friday.

Walking to the train around noon on Friday was truly challenging. The road from my house to the train station was all ice and the wind was so fierce I could barely stand up. Aitos was windy, but somewhat better. The sidewalks were still all covered with snow and the roads weren't much better. There was some sand thrown here and there to make walking doable. It wasn't quite as windy as Topolitsa.

My language teacher lives about a twenty-five minute walk from the train station. I've learned the path well. I walk up from the train station; pass some houses and a few small shops. Then I come to the Roundabout. From there I cross over to walk the street to the center of the shopping area. If I have time, I sometimes stop and pay my phone bill in the office which is close by or I get my PC money out of the bank machine. Then I continue my walk up an incline for several more blocks and find her street. She lives in a residential area not too far from the nature park. She lives in the house with her parents and a married sister. Her sister has a young family and they live on the first floor. There's often a pram and other toddler things in the hallway.

Ivanka usually leaves the outside door unlocked for me. Then I go up two flights of stairs and she usually is there to greet me. If not, I ring the bell. I leave my boots in the outer hallway. We meet in the dining area and spread out the papers on the table. She often offers me tea and sometimes a biscuit. I really look forward to my sessions with her. Depending on her schedule and mine, we meet for one hour or two. She really is a terrific language teacher. She makes learning Bulgarian interesting. We hold a conversation in Bulgarian and then work on some exercises of translating, grammar and topics of the day. I just wish I were better at languages and could remember the phrases that I hear each day.

I generally go to Aitos at least once a week for my Bulgarian language lessons and to get the PC money allotment from an ATM. Yesterday though it was so cold that I had to go to three different machines located near the Center before I found one that worked. Thankfully the last machine worked for as far as I know, those are the only three ATMs in the town.

In the winter as it gets dark by five in the afternoon I like to catch the 5:25 train back to Topolitsa. In the spring and summer I often caught the

6:25 train as it was still light outside when I returned to my village. If I have time, I may pop into one of the smaller stores that I pass on my way to the train. Sometimes it's just to buy a Snickers bar. Sometimes I buy one or two hot dogs for my dinner and maybe a beer. In the smaller magazine the woman recognizes me and knows that I'm in a hurry to catch the train. The other store is bigger and has a number of clerks and I often have to wait in line. But its fun when I have time to walk down the three store aisles and see if something special catches my eye that I can add to my dinner. I also bought a light bulb there once, and the clerk tested it to make sure it worked. That was a new experience for me.

Other times, I've stopped along my walk at a tiny shop that only sells pet food. You buy it by the pound. This store also sells cat litter, but I find that quite heavy to carry back with me on the train. The bus stop is another direction from the Roundabout. My hairdresser's shop is near the bus station. She has a very small shop behind a big grocery store. It is in the same neighborhood as the bus station. She is very nice and very pretty. However, between her English and my Bulgarian we do not talk too much. At the beginning, Ivanka, my language teacher went with me.

After Christmas, I got a perm for my hair and now it's worst than ever. It looks like it's fried. You know the picture of Einstein with his hair on end – well that's me. Honest! Tomorrow I will wash it. That will be another challenge as my bathroom is freezing cold. I do have hot water, but can't put the heater in the bathroom because when I shower the water goes everywhere. When I step out of the bathtub shower it's like stepping into an ice box. Actually I think of my kitchen as a walk in freezer. It's probably even colder than the typical walk in freezer having ice around the windowpanes.

Back to the weather – by the time I boarded the train at 5:30 the weather was getting worse. A young man, probably around 20 started to talk to me about English classes. He heard me speak to another man in the train station I guess, or just knew I was the American in his village. He asked me about the classes and then sat next to me on the train. He could speak a little English and was very polite. He works in Burgas and takes the train back and forth to work. At the Aitos train station there is a small waiting room and on very cold days many people wait inside until they hear the train whistle.

Anyway, as soon as the train stopped in Topolitsa this young man opened the door. The wind blew in. It was fierce. Usually the passenger standing closest to the door opens it at the station, not the conductor. Although, when I've been the lone passenger getting off at a stop, the conductor has opened it for me as the door latch can be difficult to maneuver.

I had on my warm long winter coat and four layers of clothing including a down vest and I could still feel the wind through me. It was blowing snow that was still there from Monday and Tuesday's storm. The road was ice. This young man came to my side and took my arm and walked with me back to the house. It's about a half mile walk. It was bitter cold and the wind was so strong that without his help I don't know what I would have done. The wind hasn't stopped blowing since. I think the temperature is around zero, and with the wind who knows?

It's frigid. Last night I slept in my down sleeping bag and covered with all my blankets and I was not too warm. Tonight I'm going to sleep in this room with my wood stove and will use my little space heater also. It takes a huge amount of wood to keep the fire going all night and to feel the heat. I have to add wood about every three hours. Fortunately the electric has stayed on today. The Internet has been intermittent.

Well, dear friend this is probably more than you really want to read. It's just so good to share with you; I truly value your friendship. Your questions about life were so good – it's hard not to think about what the future holds, what are my dreams, what is realistic?

Oh, the book and author I mentioned to you is Paulo Coelho, *The Pilgrimage*. Not sure how to describe his books: mystical, romantic, religious, all elements are in there. *The Zahir*, another book of his I really liked and another I read this fall is *The Witches of Portobello*. That title refers to a section in London. I'm also reading *The Balkans* by Mark Mazower. He was at Princeton and now is at Birkback College in London. It's a very interesting analyses of history and religion in that region over the last 500 years. It's a short book, only 155 pages. I think you would find his comments on comparative religions very interesting, certainly thought provoking. After I finish it I'm going to read one called *Balkan Ghosts* by Robert D. Kaplan. He's a correspondent for the Atlantic Monthly. Somehow the day passes and I manage to keep busy. It's just a very different kind of busy from most folks that I know. Peace Corps is as much a mental challenge as a physical one. I wasn't sure what I expected and every day I seem to find some new surprise.

I did hear from Steve and I sent him a brief reply. (Steve is Irma's son, was a teacher outside Philadelphia. Irma was my college roommate and we've been friends for many, many years.) Hopefully we can be in touch more with Skype. I do hope to work with him and his school project.

I hope you have the chance to enjoy your new grand baby in California. It's a wonderful opportunity you have to spend this time with Jon and his family. I think of how my mom came out to Philadelphia and Vermont. Not sure I always told her how much it meant to me, but I couldn't have done it without her help.

Maybe while in California you will have a chance to get in touch with

Marcus and Stacey. I know it's hard to make the schedules work, but it would give you both a chance to get reacquainted. Stacey is a wonderful woman and I'm so happy for her and Marcus that they're expecting a baby in June.

One more item, if you get a chance visit the Episcopal Cathedral in San Francisco. I'm sure they have some special discussions or other programs that might interest you. I believe right outside the main doorway is a special Circle of Life I think it's called. St. Mary's is the Catholic Cathedral with the high tower and has a beautiful organ. Maybe there'll be a concert there that you and Michael could attend.

Well, before I lose my courage I think I will send this on to you.

Love, Louise

GINNY

Ginny was a dear friend from Pittsburgh. We worked together at St. Michaels' and All Angels and stayed friends afterwards. She was quite a few years older than me, but always young at heart and a joy to be with.

Dear Ginny,   **January 12, 2010**

I was so happy to receive your letter today. It was so good to hear from you. This is the letter that you wrote on November 30, 2009. It took a very long time to cross the Atlantic.

The mail has been very slow this last month. Today in the mail I also received a package of cookies from my friends in Farmington. They had mailed the package about a month ago. I'm not sure why the mail is taking so long. I think there is extra screening on packages and with the holidays everything is taking longer.

I asked Donna to print out my Christmas letter for you so I expect that you have received it and read more than you want to read about me. When I first wrote it, I had it even longer. I hope that she was able to print out some of the pictures also. I am so glad to hear that you are doing better. You have the spirit and the will so I know that you will get better every day. Hopefully you will not need the surgery that you mentioned about drilling a hole to drain the blood.

There are very good doctors there in Pittsburgh, so if it needs to be done, I know that you are in good hands. We have so much to be thankful for. I do pray for you every day and I am thankful for your prayers for me. Some days I get very lonesome and can't figure out what I am doing here.

It was wonderful having Marcus and David here, but now I am all alone again. I knew that would happen, but I still don't like it. I have to go to Sofia for a medical check up and that will give me a chance to visit in the city and maybe meet up with some other volunteers.

On Christmas Eve Day David and I went to a very special monastery here in Bulgaria. It is called the Rila Monastery and it is about 100 miles south of Sofia. It is in the mountains and it had just snowed so it was very pretty. The church has beautiful icons both on the inside and outside the building. It was a monastery since about 1000 AD. The first church burned down, but some pieces from it were saved. Most of the buildings now date to about 1835.

On Christmas Eve we walked around Sofia and admired the lovely Christmas lights. On Christmas Day morning we went on the train and traveled to Topolitsa. It was still quite cold and snow was still on the ground. Now it is warmer again and the snow is melted.

Several other volunteers also came to Topolitsa during their Christmas break. On December 29 a group of us, including David, took a bus and traveled to Istanbul. It took about 7 hours. We left around midnight and got off the bus about 7:30 AM. Then we had to figure out the transportation system. We stayed at a small hotel near the famous mosque called the Blue Mosque. Istanbul is a very big and interesting city. The history goes back to the Greeks. The mosques are beautiful. I couldn't believe how many shops there were lining many of the streets. On New Years Eve we walked down Independence Avenue with thousands of other people.

Turkey is a much richer country than Bulgaria and has lots more people and cars. We also took a boat ride on the Bosporus River and climbed up to an old fortress. It was very interesting but I was happy to be back in Bulgaria where life is slower and not so many people. And while I don't know Bulgarian well, I know it better than Turkish. In the tourist areas we did find people who spoke English. Most of the shopping involved bargaining for the price. I did buy a few scarves and some pretty hand-painted bowls. David flew back to Colorado from Istanbul and I came back on the bus with the other volunteers.

Marcus was only here a few days. It was so good to see him. I wish his visit could have been longer. I expect you saw the news in my letter about his wife expecting a baby. So far everything has gone well. The baby is due in June. Please keep them in your prayers. I will be sorry to miss seeing the baby as an infant, but not to be helped. I am signed up to be here until summer of 2011, so another 19 months.

The time has gone pretty fast, but some days seem long. Especially now in the winter we are having lots of rain and overcast weather. It is like Pittsburgh. Some days there is also lots of wind and that makes it very cold. I don't have central heating. My little wood stove works okay, but is not great. My bathroom is always cold. My kitchen is quite cold too so I don't spend much time in it.

Today they are working on the electric in the village so I have no electric this afternoon. I had not fixed my lunch yet, so just had a banana. They have been working on this project for about four days now. Hopefully they will be done soon. The electric comes back on at night.

I am using my computer to type this as it has a battery. I bought a printer in November so when I have electric again I will print it out. I like to write, but I think you will find this easier to read. I had no trouble reading your handwriting. You are doing very well.

I'll include a few postcards that I picked up as I traveled around Bulgaria.

A big hug dear friend, take care of yourself and please write again soon. I miss you. I'm including a label with my name and address so that you can just tape onto an envelope for your next letter.

Dear Ginny,   **February 4, 2010**

It was so nice to receive your letter. And yes, your handwriting has really improved. That is great. I am so glad that you are feeling better and that you are again out and about. I think that I had cabin fever in January. It was such a long and dreary month for me. It was often like that even when I lived in America, but here it was worse. While this is a pleasant village, I am alone. And then on some of the weekends with the cold wind and snow, I had to stay inside the entire weekend. I have things to do, embroidery, read and write but I still miss conversation and talking to people. Do you by chance have a cell phone? I bought a phone just to call to America. I mainly use it to call the kids as I have only 100 minutes a month on it. It only works to call cell phone numbers.

If you have a cell phone number I could call you on it and we could talk for a little while. That would be so great to hear your voice. So let me know the number to call and also suggest a time and day of week when to call. If I call at 8 PM my time it would be 1 in the afternoon for you. Most nights I am here in my apartment and could make a telephone call. I would love to talk with you even if only a little while. I am 7 hours ahead of you here in Bulgaria.

On the 13th of this month I will be traveling to Sofia. The Peace Corps doctor wants an x-ray and to test my blood to see about arthritis. I really don't think there's anything that can be done, but good to have it on my record and properly diagnosed. The doctor in Farmington just always told me it was old age. Also some medications that might help could perhaps be covered like the *glucosamine chondroitin* that I take every day and is rather expensive. Both Marcus and David brought me some so I am stocked up for now.

I am excited to take a trip into Sofia. The Peace Corps does pay for medical travel. I would be gone almost a week as the tests have to be done on two separate days, plus it takes one day of travel just to get there and another one to come back to Topolitsa.

I miss playing the piano; that really helped my fingers besides just being a relaxing thing to do. I am thinking of buying a keyboard for my apartment.

I am still dealing with the couple who are living in my house in Farmington. I have now asked a realtor to become the manager of the house which should be of help to Marcus. It has been very frustrating dealing with them. They agreed to pay a regular stipend each month, like a rent, and now are over five months behind. I would rather not ask them to leave as I think it's good that someone is staying at my house, but my impression is that they are not being very responsible with the property. I am still thinking of putting the house back on the market when I come back to the U.S.

I have a cat again. This is an older cat than the one I had earlier this fall. I found her on the street last week. She looked so cold that I brought her into my apartment. She's a very gentle cat, all black. I've named her Alice, like *Alice in Wonderland*. Her life changed from being a street cat to being fed and living in a wonderland apartment.

Now though it appears she's pregnant. I'm not sure what to do. I don't have the heart to put her back outside in the cold because she might have kittens. But I think once the weather is warmer I will have her live outside. The biggest problem is when I'm gone I don't have anyone to tend to her. My landlady will help out, but she often is gone as well. I know she will feed her when she's here. Hopefully she will be here next week.

Now my landlady is in Serbia. She travels there almost every other week. She sells seeds and stuff at a bazaar. It seems a long way to travel to me to sell, but she has friends there and seems to get energy from traveling. I think it is at least a nine to ten hour train ride one way. She would like me to go with her sometime, but I don't really think that's a good idea. I am here to teach school and I would have to get special permission from the Peace Corps to go "out of country."

Now it is almost time for me to leave for school as I have classes to teach. I was there already this morning, and came back to my apartment as I had almost two hours between classes today. I wanted to bring in some food to the students to help them learn the English names. I have three more classes yet to teach today.

At night I have been too tired to write. I think this cold weather and cool apartment makes me tired. Now I mainly stay in this one room where my stove is. It stays warmer, and is very cozy as I eat and sleep and do my studying in this one small room.

I bought some curtains so I have more privacy. The windows only had lace curtains and I noticed that it was very easy for anyone to see into my apartment as they walked up the street. It was tricky hanging the curtains. First I had to move my bed. Then I had to put a stool on top of a chair so that I could reach the hooks as the windows almost reach the very high ceilings. I managed to hook the new curtains into the same hooks as the lace curtains. It probably would not pass Martha Stewart's Good Housekeeping look, but they do keep my room warmer. I bought the curtains, more like drapes at a second hand store. They are white with green stripes. They only had 3 sections, so one window is not completely covered, but certainly better than it was.

Later: I'm back again from school. The classes went well. The students got a kick out of seeing the food I brought and saying the names in English. I brought along a boiled egg, cheese, bread, an empty milk carton; milk comes in a box here about the size of a small box of Grape Nuts, orange juice, again in a box, some potatoes, a tomato, an onion, and for a treat, I brought along Hershey's Kisses for everyone.

Marcus gave me several pounds of them for Christmas and if I eat them all myself I will certainly gain weight. So far, I've managed to keep the weight off that I lost last year. Actually I'd like to lose about ten more pounds, but to do that I think I have to walk more. I do walk every day, but now in the cold I only do the necessary walking and nothing extra. It's about a seven minute walk to the school.

How is your health? Does the doctor think that you're healthy again? Have you lost weight? Are you doing any reading? What do you do for fun? How are your neighbors there in the apartment? Any news of Pittsburgh? I know that the Steelers didn't make the Super Bowl.

This has become quite long. I'll try to get it to print on one page. It's always good to hear from you. Please don't forget to send me your cell phone number.

Sent with a big hug and prayers for health and happiness,

Your friend, Louise

Dear Ginny,   **February 21, 2010**

I was so happy to get your letter. Your handwriting is definitely improving. You can see mine is not so good from the last letter I sent you. That's why I'm typing this. I got the idea to send this electronically to Donna and then have her mail it to you. The main reason is that I am out of stamps. They don't sell the stamps to the U.S. in my small post office and I don't want to hold up the letter until I get into Aitos.

I was going to buy stamps last week at the Post Office in Aitos. I was in line waiting when I saw the young volunteer from Aitos standing outside on the street. I went outside and spoke to her. She had had a very bad scare. I spent the next couple hours with her. She had an episode with a "strange" man the night before outside her apartment. She was not hurt and he did not touch her, but she was very frightened. This was not the first time that this type of occurrence happened. Down from her apartment is a small cafe and often a group of men hang out there to smoke and drink.

She is young and this is her first experience of not just visiting, but living in a foreign country. I think when you are young you don't comprehend all the things that could happen. A younger person often doesn't take as many precautions as an older person does. Besides that trauma, she had some medical problems. She has been sick on and off all fall and winter with colds and sometimes a fever. Two weeks ago she had lots of intestinal pain.

The Peace Corps staff came and picked her up and drove her via car to Sofia where she had surgery. She is doing fine now, but all of this together made her decide to go back to Ohio. She missed her family a great deal. I think she talked to her mom almost every day. She is only 22 years old. Most of the volunteers are in their 20s. I could be the grandmother to many of them

Yesterday it was warmer. The temperature went up into the 50s. I couldn't believe it. Our ice and snow melted and streams of water were flowing down the streets. Actually in some places in Bulgaria it is flooding. Today it is raining again. I think it has rained every Sunday since Christmas. And now our electric is off. My computer has a battery so I can use it for about two hours, but it is so dark I can hardly see what I am writing.

Thanks for the picture. You look great. I think I wrote you about my permanent. My hair is a mess. It is kinky. Yuk. I washed it this morning thank goodness before the electric went out. I'm letting it air dry. But I'm afraid to look in the mirror.

At the PC office last week they were all surprised by how I looked I told them when I looked in the mirror I didn't know who it was One woman who I had seen a number of times during our training in Vratsa mentioned that she had to look at me twice before she realized it was me

With covering up my gray hair which had completely framed my face I look very different, especially now with curls. I had this same hairdresser in Aitos dye my hair. It's brown, my natural color and it does feel good having the gray covered. I didn't like being seen as this old volunteer.

Most women here have their hair dyed. It is a very popular thing to do here. It would be great if I could lose more weight, of course, then I wouldn't have any clothes to wear.

Well, dear friend I need to study my Bulgarian. I have to practice some every day or I forget what I learned the day before. My memory has never been good for memorization and now it seems even worst to me. I have to hear and say a word over and over again before I can remember it. I wanted to make myself a cheese sandwich for lunch, but with no electric

I will have to settle for yogurt. That is what I had for breakfast. Hopefully the electric will come back soon.

Sent with love and a big hug, Louise

Dear Ginny, **March 10, 2010**

Spring is definitely in the air. Today I think it is up to 40 degrees and the sun is shining. I even hung some of my wash outside. I miss having a dryer. But now at least the sun is shining and hopefully by the end of the day my towels will be dry. I'm still wearing flannel pajamas at night and sleeping in my down sleeping bag. I bought it with David's help back in Colorado and its supposed to be good for temperatures down to 0 degrees Fahrenheit. It keeps me quite warm. My apartment is about 60 degrees right in front of my stove. It's much colder in the bathroom and kitchen, but it is definitely warmer than it was in January. Then I had ice inside on all my windows.

We had a lot of holidays to celebrate this month. The first one is called Baba Marta Day. *Baba* is the Bulgarian word for Grandma. The holiday is based on a story of a woman called Baba Marta. I will try and find the story and include it with my letter. It is a lot of fun as everyone exchanges bracelets of red and white that you wear on your wrist until you see your first stork.

Last summer I saw several storks in my village, so I am hoping I'll see one or two here in Topolitsa. It is to bring you good luck all year. When you see a stork you have to hang your bracelet or string on a tree. I remember last spring seeing trees with red and white streamers on them.

The next holiday was their "4th of July." In Bulgaria their Liberation or Freedom Day is the 3rd of March. It is when they became an independent country after almost 500 years under the Ottoman Empire. The Russians helped them defeat the Ottoman army at the Battle of Shipka Pass, 1877 to 1878. There are many monuments showing that help. It's kind of like the French helping us win the Revolutionary War. Again in 1944 Russia was the country who helped them get rid of the Germans in their country, but in 1944 Russia was Communist so Bulgaria had no choice or freedom to decide about their country and thus became a puppet of Russia for 50 years.

It took until 1989 to become a free country again. This was right after the Berlin Wall came down. This is a very sad part of their history for when the Communists were here they destroyed many of the churches and other beautiful buildings. People were not allowed to go to church. Many of the churches have re-opened, but many were destroyed. Many dissenters were put in forced labor camps, called Gulags, located all over the country. One estimate is that there were over 100 such camps. Stories just now are being translated into English about many of these atrocities.

I think it is difficult for Americans to understand what it does to a country when for 50 years people are not allowed to go and worship God as they choose. Some people of course worshiped God in their home, but it was against the law. Many of the churches have been restored and do hold regular services again, but two generations of people did not have that opportunity.

There was a celebration in Aitos that I attended and the priest from the church was there who read from the Bible and gave prayers. The Orthodox Bulgarian Church is similar to both the Catholic and Episcopal churches from what I have read. Bulgarians have freedom of religion, so all are not Orthodox. Mormons came here right after their liberation in 1989. I have not met any but I have heard about them. When people hear that I am a volunteer, they sometimes ask whether I'm here for a church group.

The other holiday that is celebrated here, but not much in the U.S. that I remember, is International Woman's Day. Women are given flowers by friends and family. The school children also bring flowers to the women teachers. I think it is a very nice holiday.

April 1st to the 10th we have a school spring break. A friend is flying over from Japan to visit me. She's a librarian there working at a Marine base. She has worked overseas most of her career. We'll spend a few days in Bulgaria and then we're flying to Warsaw, Poland.

We're going to travel to Auschwitz and visit the site of the World War II concentration camp. I know that will be difficult to see, but I think it is an important part of history that is important to remember. We'll also have a day walking around Warsaw. I don't have anyone visiting me in the summer. How I wish that you could come. I've started cross stitching the top pattern for a baby quilt for Stacey and Marcus. Not sure if I'll manage to get it finished before June but it does give me something to do. It's the ABCs with assorted pictures like an elephant and balloons, one picture for each letter.

What are you doing these days to keep yourself out of mischief? Are there any good TV shows on? Do you know of Susan Boyle? A friend sent me her CD. She has a very nice voice. She was a winner on *American Idol* or some show like that. I only get Bulgarian TV, but now I have found *Wheel of Fortune* in Bulgarian. It's not the U.S. show with Pat and Vanna, but a Bulgarian version of the American show. I don't understand much of it, but I find it interesting to watch. I'm thinking of modifying it and using it to help my students learn words in English. I have to fix myself some lunch and then study Bulgarian. I'll probably make myself a toasted cheese sandwich. I usually have bread and cheese in my apartment. Hope this finds you well.

Looking at the calendar I know your birthday is coming. So please accept this also as my special birthday letter to you, Happy, Happy Birthday Dear Friend. I hope this year will be filled with many joyful days, good health, and good eating.

Sent with a big hug and lots of love, Louise

I often mailed post cards to my friends and family back in the United States. A favorite design of a post card was in shape of a lion. The lion has long been the symbol for Bulgaria. When you look at a map of Bulgaria the shape of the lion can easily be seen. Often the lion postcards contain a theme: monasteries around Bulgaria, road map of Bulgaria, sights of Sofia, sights of Burgas, landmarks of Sofia, mountain ranges in Bulgaria, famous churches in Bulgaria. The lion-shaped cards were extra big and I mailed them in an envelope as they could easily be bent out of shape. Postcards were fun to hang on my wall in my bedroom. They were my decorations. Here is the note that I wrote to my friend Ginny on August 12, 2010. She saved all my letters and postcards I sent her and returned them to me when I visited her in Pittsburgh.

Dear Ginny,

I'm at the Sofia airport waiting for my niece to arrive from Phoenix. She will visit me for ten days. The weather has been very hot; over 100 degrees in my village. Yesterday I had to ride the train over seven hours – all across Bulgaria and I thought I would melt.

Thankfully it rained here in Sofia so it is a bit cooler here – about 90 degrees I think. Thankfully the small hotel I'm staying in has AC. It was so good to sleep last night without flies and in a cool bedroom.

Big hug dear friend,

Love, Louise

FRIENDS AND TRAVEL

Hi Belinda,   **January 30, 2010**

I'm finally on Facebook. Have you had your surgery yet? I'm looking forward to April. I have a few more ideas for the trip. Louise

January 31, 2010

Yes, I had the surgery on January 14. I got back from Yokosuka on January 22. I have just been trying to take it easy. I have a 6-inch pin in my second toe to correct my hammertoe. The doctor from Yokosuka is supposed to be here on February 9 to take the pin out.

Belinda

Hi Belinda, **Monday, February 1, 2010**

Guess what? Your Christmas package arrived today. What a great surprise. I really thought it must have been lost. I wonder where it was. It was fun opening it. I've already opened the bag of chocolates and sampled a few. Yummy. The newspapers and magazines are great. I'll share the books with a few others in the Peace Corps. Thank you so very much. I am so glad that it's February. In two months it will be April first! I'm going into Aitos to look for some curtains in the second hand shop. I have a cat. I found her over the weekend. Now I think she might be pregnant; she seems a very sweet thing.

Well, I want to write more and talk about April, but have to run. I need to get to the train and walk through the slushy melting snow.

I hope that you're healing well, Louise

February 2, 2010

Well, it took long enough for the box to arrive. That was over six weeks I think. Think of some other things I could bring with me so that you don't have to go through such a long waiting time.

How much snow did you get? My sisters in Virginia got over six inches this weekend. The six-inch pin in my toe will come out next Tuesday. I can already move my big toe so hopefully with the pin out I will be completely mobile again. Wow, only three weeks this time.

On Valentine's Day a group of us are going to the Club for dinner. Do they celebrate Valentine's Day in Bulgaria?

Keep in touch, Belinda

Hi Belinda, **February 2, 2010**

I just got back from teaching an English class to adults. It is a snowy night here, so I was happy that four people showed up. They seemed very interested. It's when you start teaching and learning a new language to people you realize how many different words and expressions are needed to communicate. I admire so much people who can speak a number of languages. I manage here in Topolitsa, but don't carry on any long conversations.

That sounds like quite an operation that you had. I'm glad it was you and not me. Hopefully your foot continues to heal quickly.

It would be great if you could bring some things along when you come. I will work on a list. Some things I'm sure they have somewhere in this country, but living in a small village it's difficult to find many things and I don't get into big cities very often.

In two weeks I do have to go to Sofia for medical; the Peace Corps doctor wants to check me out regarding rheumatoid arthritis. For some time now several of my fingers have been bent so Peace Corps wants to have them all checked out. It bothers me especially for my ring fingers, as several of my good rings I can no longer wear as my fingers are so swollen. I found a ring in Plovdiv that I can wear so I'm happy about that.

I'm so happy and excited that you will be able to come and visit me.

Another idea I've had depending on how much time you have off would be for you to come to Bulgaria first, e.g., fly into Burgas already on March 28 or 29. Then we could have that weekend here in Topolitsa and do a few things in this area and you can experience village life and visit my school.

I have school March 29, 30 and 31 I think. I have an extra bedroom and by then the weather should be warmer so my apartment should be more comfortable. Then we could decide where all to go in Bulgaria. I know I want to show you several very interesting towns on the Black Sea: Burgas, Nesebar, and Sozopul.

Then we could take the train to Plovdiv, a really neat city dating back to Roman times, and from there we could go into Sofia. There are many nice things to see in Sofia. If you like I could arrange some special day tours. We can fly directly to Warsaw from Sofia. One possibility is for you fly from Warsaw to Italy and I'd fly back to Sofia. I'll take a look at air fares Sofia to Warsaw. The train is also a possibility, but I think quite a long ride. This schedule would give us more time to see sights in Bulgaria and then we could decide what day and how long to stay in Warsaw.

I don't know what the weather will be by then, but for sure the days will be longer which is good. There are several Bulgarian travel web sites. Belogradchik should be very nice, but it's way in Northwest Bulgaria and I'm not sure how it would be to visit in April. Several Peace Corps Volunteers work near there

Varna and Veliko Turnovo are also interesting I hear. Train transportation is quite good, but of course it takes a bit of planning especially if the places are at the opposite end of the country.

I was thinking of the Black Sea area, Plovdiv in the middle and Sofia. But other places could maybe be worked in depending on our time and interest. I know we both like to travel and explore, so I know we will have a great time.

Let me know how long you are able to stay. I can take off from school April 1 to 11. Hope this finds your foot healing rapidly, Louise

Hello dear family and friends,   **April 8, 2010**

I am writing this on a laptop at a guest house here in Warsaw, Poland. I flew in yesterday with a colleague from my library days. She is a librarian currently working at a Marine base as librarian in southern Japan. She had never been to Bulgaria so I was happy to have a few days showing her some of the country. I gave her a walking tour of Sofia, went to a restaurant at the foot of Mt. Vitosha where there was traditional Bulgarian folk dances, walked around historic Plovdiv and visited the Black Sea.

Yesterday we flew from Sofia to Warsaw. It is only a two hour flight. This morning we were picked up for a tour to Auschwitz. It is about a four hour car ride south of Warsaw. The tour itself was about 3 1/2 hours. It is difficult to put into words. I believe many of you have been to the Holocaust Museum in D.C. This is similar, but even more real as this is the place of the largest concentration camp of WW II.

We saw the barracks, the ruins of the gas chambers, the room filled with shoes, another with suitcases, on and on. The pictures that some of the prisoners and some of the guards managed to take are very enlightening. It is gratifying to realize that somehow some of the photos and artifacts survived so that this history can be known. The acres and acres of the camp is humbling. It is hard to comprehend.

On the car trip the university student who drove us answered many questions for us about Poland's history, geography and people. Tomorrow we will go on a three hour walking tour here in Warsaw, and we also hope to visit the Uprising Museum and maybe a Chopin concert in the evening.

On Saturday we fly back to Sofia. Belinda will fly out early Sunday morning to Italy to visit a friend there, and I will go via train back to Topolitsa.

The weather has been good. Today I think it went over 60F. The trees are just starting to bud here. We were told there was snow on the ground here just before Easter.

I will be quite busy in April as I have some special projects for the school, including writing a Peace Corps proposal to help the school raise money for it's playground/sports renovation and to assist another Peace Corps volunteer chaperon her 12th grade class on their trip to Turkey.

I am also working with a friend in Philadelphia to Skype chat with his students. The school year here goes until June 15. I will probably be doing several summer school projects with the students as yet to be decided.

It's getting late, but I wanted to send this out as I probably won't be have Internet again for a few days. I know when I get back to Topolitsa school planning and teaching will again take up most of my time.

I hope this finds everyone well and enjoying spring weather and joyous celebrations of the Easter and Passover holidays.

Love, Louise

Hi Louise,   **April 13, 2010**

It sounds as if you are enjoying yourself in Poland. I'm glad you're getting a chance to travel around a bit.

We talked with David this evening. (Her son David was only in his early thirties and fighting a very aggressive cancer.) He mentioned that he had just come home after having dinner with your David in D.C. Your son David was there for just a day. I'm so happy that your "kids" still keep in touch with us and have sent our David so much encouragement.

David had another appointment with his doctor and an infusion this morning. His numbers are now in the normal range. Praise the Lord! He will have his next infusion in another three weeks, but his doctor said that he really doesn't need to see David for six weeks. David feels fine. He had a fever for about a week, but we're not sure why. His doctor took some blood work, and for now everything was fine. David will have another body scan the end of June. Until any major changes, he continues working and is doing projects as planned.

Hope everything is going well with you. Take care.

Love, Barb

Peace Corps Incident Report, April 20, 2009

Description of Incident: My friend, an American visiting me from Japan (She works at a Marine base there as a librarian) and I were sleeping in the Gangre Motel in Aitos. I had heard of this unique motel located in Aitos, next to the park and zoo.

My friend wanted to stay in unique Bulgarian places. We had taken the train into Aitos in the afternoon and walked around the park. It was a sunny day. The restaurant at the Park was closed due to repairs. So we walked to the town center, about fifteen minutes away and ate at the "Old House" historic restaurant. We were back around 7:30 PM I believe. It was still light outside and there were a few people having beer or coffee.

I was given two keys. One key locked the outer door, and then there was a small entrance, and a room to the left and to the right. Our room was to the left. Around 1 AM we were awakened with a man shouting "Open the door" in Bulgarian. First I thought the person just forgot his key. But he got louder and louder. My friend who was in the bed by the window saw him staggering around. She was peeking out the window at the bottom of the curtain. Our curtains were drawn and our lights and television were off. We had been sound asleep since around 10:30 PM. (Our plan was to catch the Fast Train from Aitos at 7:20 AM to go to Sofia as we had reservations to fly to Poland the next day.)

He was very drunk and she saw him lean over the railing to vomit and also to relieve himself. His voice became louder and louder and he continued to pound on the door. I decided I had better call the police. We had already pushed our small dresser against our room door.

I had two phones with me, the one I bought our first week in Vratsa, and one from the school here in Topolitsa.

The police answered. For some reason, my first call was cut off. I called again, and explained as best I could in Bulgarian where I was and what was happening. There was no phone in the room and I was not aware of any guards on the premises. I had been shown where to leave the key in the morning. We planned to leave by 7 AM.

I was quite sure the policeman understood me, but I decided I would make sure and decided to call my director, Dora Rusanova and tell her what was happening. She lives in Aitos. She answered immediately. She gave the phone to her son, who understands more English. He said he would call the police to make sure they had understood me.

In a short while, he called me back and said, yes, the police had understood me and would be at the motel in a few minutes, which they were. In the meantime my friend also pushed our TV in front of our room door, as the man definitely was very drunk and very angry.

The police came and restrained him, and we think they put him in the room next door to "sleep it off."

My friend did not notice them taking the man away, but perhaps they did. However, I did hear noises in the next room as the bathrooms were adjoining.

In the morning when we were leaving we noticed the broken door handle and door frame and the lock was broken off.

The woman from the motel was down in the cafe in the morning along with another man who both apologized to me in Bulgarian. The incident was a bit scary, but I was thankful that I had my phones with me, and that the police came. I think it took maybe five to ten minutes for them to come.

The door has now been repaired. This happened April 5th during our school spring break.

During our PST time in Vratsa we were given many instructions on safety. This included everything from robbery, vandalism, rape and other personal safety issues like the aforementioned incident. I had been to this area several times. It is a lovely spot and many families come here to eat and enjoy the park setting. I had never been here at night though by myself. I had not taken into consideration how dark it would be for us to stay here. And unlike motels in America, and bigger motels in Bulgaria there was no front desk or any person on duty during the night hours. Anytime a PCV needs to notify a police office, a report is to be filled out. As we were on our way to Sofia and immediately to Poland I didn't file my report until my return. Peace Corps was always very supportive and concerned about our safety.

Thank goodness for cell phones. And I had practiced during our language sessions the emergency words that are needed to speak to the police. These are words like Help, man, danger. I never expected to use them, but thankfully they were embedded in my memory bank. Also, I never traveled without a flashlight, whistle or my Bulgarian dictionary.

I appreciated the apology from the woman and man at the cafe in the morning. I told them, we were not harmed and all was okay. I had called the taxi man the evening before, so he was there outside the gate when we walked towards the street about 6:45 AM. We were happy to be on our way.

COLD WINTER DAYS

Letter to family and friends:

January and February were extremely cold winter months. The wind blew steadily sometimes two to three days in a row, and often the electric went out and my Internet was down. I spent those days in the room with my wood stove.

On a weekly basis students carried wood over from school. The school is also heated with wood but has radiators in each classroom. On the coldest days the custodian slept on a cot next to the furnace to keep the fire from going out during the night at the school. Dora, the school director told me she orders over one hundred ton of wood each school year. The big blocks of wood were too big for my little stove. They worked fine for the big school furnace. For my stove, the custodian or an upper-class student needed to chop them into five or six pieces. I didn't have enough paper or cardboard saved up to burn for kindling wood to get my started. Most days I had to start from scratch as it was difficult to keep a fire going all night. During the day when I was at school it was also a problem to keep a fire going.

I was given old textbooks to use as kindling. These books had been stored in the school basement from the Communist era and were terribly damp. It was difficult to get a fire going with them. I never thought as a librarian that I would be burning books. After struggling with the damp pages I finally found it best to tear the pages out a day or two ahead of time and spread them out on the floor to dry. I always saved my toilet paper cylinders, any tissue box or other scrap paper I might have and all boxes that came in the mail. All of these assorted items came in very handy when I needed to start my fire in my woodstove.

School was canceled a number of times as the students at my school are not only from this village but two neighboring villages and these country roads would be closed due to drifts and often ice. There was still snow on the mountain bordering Topolitsa last week and I also saw snow on the other high mountain peaks in Bulgaria on the train ride back from Sofia. The highest mountains in Bulgaria are about 10,000 feet. Skiing is a popular sport and the bigger towns have ice skating rinks.

I have a television set but get only three Bulgarian television stations. I watch them to help me hear the language, but I still find it more helpful to read the news in English online. One local station has just started the Bulgarian version of *Wheel of Fortune*. I have yet to figure out any of the words, but it helps me learn the Bulgarian alphabet sounds. In the Cyrillic alphabet the letter has no name, only the sound that it makes. There are several Bulgarian English online news sources and one general magazine that I have found in Sofia. Several of our English magazines are published here: *National Geographic, Rolling Stone, Glamour,* to name a few but they are all in Bulgarian. I still am taking language lessons from a tutor, usually twice a week. I generally meet with her at least once a week for an hour. In addition to learning basic grammar and conversational Bulgarian she has helped me figure out where to buy certain household items, answered questions on protocol and tells me about life in Bulgaria. She is a teacher at a high school in Aitos and also working on a Ph.D. in English Literature. While my Bulgarian has improved and I manage, I still have a long way to go to carry on a regular conversation.

Spring was welcomed as the days grew longer and there was less severe wind. We have had several nice sunny days, but today is not one of them. The village people have been busy planting their gardens and I look forward to the warm days and eating fresh tomatoes and cucumbers. I have found a market in Aitos where I can buy fresh produce. In my village store I can find bread, butter, yogurt, cheese and other staples.

Bulgarians welcome the first day of spring with exchanging *martenitsas* with each other.

Wikipedia has some of these legends written up. All over Bulgaria vendors were selling bracelets and dolls. The custom is to hang the *martenitsa* on a tree branch when you see your first stork. It is a sign of good luck for the entire year. It was several weeks before I saw a stork, and I was on the train so did not get to hang up my *martenitsa*.

Storks are quite common here. They make their nests high up on a lamp pole and are easy to spot or else you will see them by a pond or near a river bank.

I'm reading a book now about King Boris of Bulgaria. He is especially revered as he managed to stand up to Hitler and save all of the Jews in Bulgaria from being exported and sent to concentration camps. It is estimated that there were about 60,000 Jews in Bulgaria that he was instrumental in saving.

The school year goes until June 15 and I teach English in grades 2 through 8.

I also will have some summer projects, including one special fund raising project through the Peace Corps. I will be writing up the proposal for the school. It is to refurbish the school play and sports area. It is a mess. Much of the area has broken cement and some is dirt. There is one broken basketball hoop. There is no other place in the village for the students to play so this project is not just for the school students, but for the entire village community.

I hope to submit this proposal to the PC for their approval by early June and then have the next few months to raise the money. The school director is expecting it to cost over $5,000. According to PC guidelines, the community has to contribute at least 25 percent of the project costs. They will probably contribute by giving their labor. I will send out an email when I get this project approved and hope that some of you may be able to contribute. All the funding goes through the PC so it is tax deductible.

I have so many of you to thank for sending me books for the children to read. They are invaluable. While many of the students here want to learn English, books in English are not readily available. The students hear English songs on the radio and know some jargon, but few have actually read any English books until now. My English tutor in Aitos is also looking for books for her high school students, so if you are interested in helping her please let me know and I will give you more details.

I feel so blessed to have so many good friends and your support via letters, emails, and special gifts of candy, school supplies, books and food. It is all greatly appreciated. It would be so much more difficult to be here working in a foreign country without all of your support. When I had the dream of joining the PC I don't think I realized what a change it would be for my life. There are days I feel like the "lonely American," and then a package or a letter arrives. The teachers here are surprised how many gifts I have received. I tell them I have a big family and a big circle of friends. A big hug, and thank you to you all.

The cherry trees are now blossoming and the villagers are all out planting the spring vegetables. I am looking forward to enjoying fresh cherries. In a few weeks I will again be going to Istanbul and other parts of Turkey. I am going with another PCV, and her 12th grade class as assistant chaperon for six days.

Upon my return I'll take the train into Sofia to see my sister and her husband, who are doing an Eastern European tour. Sofia, Bulgaria was offered as a pre-trip extension. It will be so great to see them and to share some of the Bulgarian customs with them.

In Sofia there are many beautiful churches, especially the Aleksandur Nevski Memorial Church. The custom is to light a candle and say a prayer for family, friends, and peace in the world among all people. There is also a special area in the church to light a candle to remember loved ones who have died. I am happy to light a candle for all of you and I ask you to light one for me and continue to keep me in your thoughts and prayers,

Louise

BE A GUEST / NA GHOSTE

In Bulgarian a person is often invited to "be a guest." The Bulgarian phrase used is на гости. English pronunciation is *"na ghoste"* and rhymes with our word *ghost* with a long e on the end.

I have been invited now several times to be a guest and I will try and describe the events. The events that I have chosen were quite different, but yet had some of the same elements to them.

The first one was an invitation extended by a young woman who invited the four of us Peace Corps volunteers who were living in the village of Banitsa in June and July to be her guests for a Sunday lunch. This was the village about ten miles from Vratsa in northwest Bulgaria where we were stationed by the Peace Corps to begin learning the Bulgarian language, local customs and traditions. The very first week there was the annual "Banitsa Festival" so we had all tasted *banitsa*, this very delicious pastry which is made from layers of thin dough.

Lucy was one of the few people in the village who could speak English. She had not lived in this village for very long and wanted to extend a welcome to us and practice her English.

As it turns out, only three of us could make it as Albin, was busy that Sunday helping out his host family during some farm work. We each lived with a different family. I was with an elderly widow, Anna and Diana were with younger families, and Albin was living with an elderly couple, who had a son and daughter living in Vratsa who came to visit almost every weekend.

The three of us, Diana, Anna and me met at Anna's house to walk over to Lucy's house. I had noticed the house on a previous walk as it was especially well kept and had many pretty flowers by it.

We each brought a gift as is the custom. It is usually candy or flowers. She welcomed us to her house meeting us at the gate. The table was all set. We first were served a "шопска салата" (*shopska salada*). This is tomato cut up in pieces, along with a cucumber and topped with сирене (Bulgarian white cheese pronounced *seranade*). It usually has an oil and vinegar dressing. Bread is always on the table. A beverage of either beer or a soft drink was offered, Bulgarians seldom drink beer, wine or other liquor by itself. Most often it is served with a salad, perhaps nuts, s alami, yellow cheese (кашкавал – *kashkaval*) and perhaps olives.

Lucy collected our salad plates and then brought each of us a dinner plate with a large slice of meat loaf stuffed with a boiled egg, potato and cooked beans. It was delicious and very filling.

After we had eaten as much as we could and were offered seconds, Lucy collected our plates and served us a dessert of ice cream and cake. (сладолед и торта – *sladoled* and *torta*). She also served us coffee, кафе, pronounced *café*.

We talked about how she had learned English through watching movies and also some very specific language courses which she showed us. She had studied over ten years already and had also lived in Sofia where there is more English spoken and in Italy where she had a job which required English. She had recently lost her job as a sales manager and now was sending out applications trying to find a new position. My impression was that she did not have a University degree which would keep her from being able to teach in a school. But it was also mentioned how poorly the teachers were paid in Bulgaria and that also many of the manager positions were not very well paid.

She was certainly a gracious hostess. When she found out that we had not been shown how to make баница (*banitsa*) the Bulgarian main dish, and the namesake of the village we were in, she said she would arrange for us to be shown how it was done.

Dates were discussed and it was decided to meet with her the following weekend.

She very generously arranged with her neighbor who had a bigger house for us to be guests there and to actually watch and help participate in the баница (*banitsa*) making.

Lazar, our regular language teacher was also invited to come as well as Albin.

It was a fun evening. Lucy, our hostess, plus her neighbor and another neighbor brought us all into the kitchen. Step by step was explained to us how to put the layers of dough together, along with mixing the egg and water with baking soda and spreading this mixture on the very thin dough. It is put into a large round pan. Between each layer is sprinkled pieces of сирене (*seranade*). There are other varieties, but this is the most traditional recipe. There are nine layers in all. Then it is put in the oven to bake.

While we were waiting for the finished results, we were served a шолска салата (*shopska salada*) and ракйа (*Rakia*). It was a fun evening, with learning a bit more about traditional Bulgarian foods and how to be a guest.

Another на гости (*na ghoste*) I had was here in Topolitsa. It was more informal and rather serendipity. I decided to take a walk up the street in my village. On the way neighbors recognized me from living with Milka. They invited me in, waving their arms in a downward fashion. So I entered their gate.

Another Bulgarian custom is shaking your head from side to side. Side to side indicates, yes while nodding up and down, is no. It reminded me of driving in England. Once I learned to drive on the left side of the road on my return to the U.S. I always had to think about which side was the correct side to drive on. Nodding my head or moving it side to side had to be relearned upon my return to the U.S.

The husband's mother was also sitting in the yard and recognized me from a recent visit at Milka's. I was not there more than three minutes when food was brought out. It is the season for peaches and grapes. A big bunch of grapes were pulled off the vines, rinsed off and served to me on a plate. Then the woman went inside her house and came back with about six peaches peeled and sliced and added them to my plate. In the meantime, I attempted to talk to them in my limited vocabulary.

From the visit at Milka's I knew the mother had come from Russia. I believe they also have a son living in Boston. As I had shown them some of my pictures when I met them at Milka's I thought that taking their picture would be a way to show my appreciation. However, I had not brought my camera with me. So I attempted to explain to them that I would go back to my house and get my camera. They seemed to understand, so off I went.

When I went back to my apartment, Milka was there in the yard and I explained to her that I was at her friend's house eating peaches and grapes (праскои и гроэде – *praskoee* and *grazde*). I got my camera and went back.

While I was gone, the woman had gone into her house and changed her outfit. She was all dressed up and happy that I was going to take some pictures. They knew I had a computer and we discussed the Internet and emailing photos. Then Milka came also to visit and more pictures were taken. The neighbor, who's name was Nina, gave me her email address and I told her that I would send them to her.

And then Milka mentions, на гости (*na ghoste*). I knew her brothers lived in the village as I had been introduced to one of them in Milka's living room earlier in August. Now Milka, Nina and I walked up the street to Milka's brother's house. She calls out на гости. The daughter-in-law was busy placing fresh peppers on a grill, roasting them so that they could be canned. The sister-in-law was sitting on the ground, yoga style, putting the peppers in jars. Without stopping her work, she seamlessly served us candy and then a drink, and then before long, we were served fresh hot roasted peppers, e.g., чушки – (*choshke*). First we peeled them. The peeling easily came off. Then we picked them up in our fingers and ate them. They were delicious.

Their son came over, and saw that we were not served any ракйа (*Rakia*). This was quickly remedied. A toast called наэдрве (*nazdrave*) is always done when *Rakia* is served. The glasses are clinked together with all who have an alcoholic drink and you look into the person's eyes and say "*nazdrave*" (cheers).

All the while, the daughter-in-law continued to put more peppers on the grill, taking them off as they became roasted. We were offered fresh corn-on-the-cob (царевица) to eat. I indicated that I was full. This was no problem, they understood. But rather than not serving me any corn, the son-in-law went into the house and brought out some plastic bags. I could have the "corn to go."

And so for this day, I did not have a long walk but certainly a very interesting one with photos taken, peppers eaten and feeling a bit more a part of the village life here in Topolitsa.

TYPICAL SATURDAY IN TOPOLITSA

Today I decided to take a walk up the street from the school to photograph the Muslim Mosque. In Bulgarian the word is джамия (*djurmya*). On the way there I saw the technician who had come to my apartment to check out my stove and the plumbing. So I waved. He does not speak any English. I had also seen him at school working on some projects so he recognized me and invited me into his yard. There was a very nice garden.

Everyone in Bulgaria seems to have a beautiful garden, well tended with many vegetables and bordered with flowers. He calls into the house for his wife and she comes to the door and invites me into the house.

Before long I was sitting at a table and food was served. Neither spoke English and my Bulgarian is so poor I was not sure what they asked. I think it was about food, храна (*brana*), but I can never say that word correctly. It gives me the same problems as the word for bread, хляб (*blyab*). Coca-Cola and pretzel sticks were served. Something was asked about coffee and I indicated that I liked coffee. His wife went into the kitchen and I attempted to carry on a conversation with him.

Coffee was brought out with sugar. I now have learned to drink coffee again without milk or cream. It is very strong coffee, like espresso and with sugar I can manage it.

At a restaurant I have learned to ask for coffee with cream, (кафе със сметана *cafe sis cmetana*). But you are charged an extra twenty страница, (*stotinka*) is the way it is pronounced. It is about twenty cents. What I have observed here is that most people drink coffee black with sugar.

His wife went back into the kitchen and came out with меденка (*mekitsa*). This is a very good hot cake (similar to Pennsylvania Dutch fry bread or Navajo fry cake). She also brought a small plate of honey мед (*med*). You can dip your fry cake into the honey. It is interesting to me how traditions are so similar. In New Mexico, fry cake is served either with sugar or honey. Since this is the season when the grapes are at their peak, a bowl of grapes were also set before me. They did not eat. What I found out was that they were observing Ramadan, so they did not eat between sunrise and sunset; but they had no problem with serving me plenty of food. Topolitsa is a very Turkish community and every day the call to prayer is heard five times in the village starting at sunrise until sunset. The other times are noon, mid-afternoon and early evening.

She turned on the television and a travel show about Bulgaria was on. I had seen the program before with my landlady so I recognized the opening scene. Today it was about the Rhodope Mountains. I couldn't understand most of it, but the scenery was beautiful.

It's a favorite area for hiking and skiing. The guide showed a museum in the area and interviewed an older man who explained how bag pipes were made. He then played a tune. Another woman showed how she spun wool. Hopefully, that is an area that I will be able to visit. When the show was over, I felt it was time to leave. She was so pleasant. I found out that one of her daughters is a diabetic and she has grandchildren living in Aitos. We are about the same age. I asked her if I could take her picture and she was very obliging. I do wish I had a printer. I think I will ask a friend in America to print out some of these pictures and then I can give them as a gift. It appears to me that while some people have cameras, and maybe computers, very few have printed pictures or a printer.

Before I left I took a picture of both of them outside and she gave me two more *mekitsas* to take with me. Then I noticed what I thought maybe were squash hanging up overhead with the grapes. As I admired them, the man promptly picked it off the vine and gave it to me as a present. He said, "Do not eat." Yes I knew this for sure was a gourd. I will have to look up the Bulgarian name for it. He picked one more for me, and indicated it was to be a "souvenir" for me. Souvenir is pronounced the same as in English.

Another Bulgarian word that is pronounced goblin, had me very confused in the summer when I was going with Pauli and her family to Shipka. They kept talking about seeing the goblins. It was not Halloween. What kind of goblins were they talking about? We stopped in Nova Zagora at a friend's house. I was told to come see their lovely garden. It was indeed a lovely summer garden filled with flowers and vegetables. Then I was asked to come into the house. On the walls were dozens of lovely nee-dlepoint designs. There were flowers, children, religious scenes like *The Last Supper*. They ranged in size from small, six inches by six inches to very big pieces of art, covering an entire wall, 24 inches by 36 inches. The needlepoint was amazing. In Bulgarian the word for this type of handwork is pronounced goblin. Pauli's friend had a shop where she sold patterns and the special wool yarn needed to make a goblin. She also sold some of her beautiful framed designs.

It surprises me how open and welcome the people are to invite you into their home and proceed to give you presents. Perhaps that is why I have been placed in this village.

I continued on my walk and took pictures of the джамия (*djumirya*). Then I saw the magazine where I had gone to my first weekend here. As I needed bread, I thought I would go in and buy it there. I've mainly gone to the magazine right across from the school. The other day on my walk in another direction I found two other magazines. The second of them was definitely bigger, and had a small aisle with items on display that you could pick up yourself. Most magazines are small and items are kept behind the counter and you have to ask for them by name. Magazines (магаэйн) are small general stores, usually selling food, but also a variety of hardware and other household items.

After the magazine I thought I would go down another street which was unpaved but I knew eventually it would have to go downhill back to the center of town. In a short distance was a paved road and I realized I had inadvertently found myself on the road where the only restaurant in the village was located. I had just made a square. If directions would come easier for me, this probably would have been obvious from the start, but I seem to have to walk around more to get my bearings. I passed the restaurant and then saw a young girl who I recognized from both the camp and the school. She ran up to greet me, "hello."

I have noticed in the village, that when the students see me, they like to call out, "Hello." This is an English word that most of them know. I usually reply, back in Bulgarian, "*Kak cte?*" "How are you?" The answer is "добре" (*dobre*, e.g., good). We talked a bit, and then she asked me if I'd like some coffee. I answered, "That would be very nice." So I sat down at their outside table, a tradition, which is found in many Bulgarian homes,

Within minutes her mother brought me a cup of coffee. The dad was also in the yard, and he was busy working on the house. They are fixing it up. He seems very handy and was happy to show me what he had done. I walked to the back of the house, where he was laying cement on top of his brick work. This appeared to be a 4-story house that was being remodeled. I was very impressed as he indicated he was doing the work himself. Then he had to hurry away as I think his cement needed attention.

I heard a "baaa." The young student showed me the sheep that they had in a small stall in the basement of the house. Apparently it stays there all the time. That seems a shame, but I know from my days in Banitsa not all that unusual. It is probably a sheep they are keeping to fatten up and plan to eat it sometime in the future. She told me that they did not have any other animals.

Before I left, she gave me some candy to take with me on my walk and we talked about her helping me with my Bulgarian and I would help her with her English. I knew already from two days of classes that she is probably the best English student in seventh grade.

She told me that she plans to go to Burgas to high school. In the morning I have seen students from the village walk towards the train and I expect that they are going into Burgas for high school which is about an hour away by train.

After her house, I was nearly back to the school where several more students greeted me. They had several big bags of candy. I was surprised. Maybe they were going door to door selling it, I don't know. But they opened up the bags to me and wanted me to take some. So I did. What an interesting walk. Or perhaps it was a special gift because of the Ramadan holiday.

Going on a walk to take pictures, I was invited into two homes and served coffee and warm fresh fry bread. Life here is full of pleasant surprises. I came home with no need to fix myself something to eat for lunch; I already had two coffees, fry bread, pretzel sticks and grapes freshly picked from the vines.

Before I became comfortable in my apartment I decided to pick some tomatoes from my landlady's garden. She has told me many times to help myself. So I took a big bowl with me downstairs and easily filled it up with fresh red ripe tomatoes. I was not upstairs long when my landlady called out to me and here she had a small container with fresh roasted almonds. What could be better? I am always touched by her kindness to me.

Before long, I heard my name called again. At my door was one of my students with her younger brother. I know she lives nearby as I have seen her on the next street near the school. She had in her hand warm fry bread. It was certainly my day to be filled with pleasant food and welcoming voices.

To finish off the weekend, there was a knock on my door early Sunday morning from my landlady. I had just finished making myself some coffee, and I was still in my pajamas.

She wanted me to come downstairs as she had guests. I indicated to her that I was tired and still not dressed. Then she left. Well, before long, another knock on the door. She was insistent that I come downstairs. So I said, "Okay moment." My hair really was a mess as I had planned to wash it yet this morning, but thought I better hurry and get dressed and go downstairs. Her daughter was there and her husband, and her daughter's mother-in-law and grandmother, plus her friend Nina. The table was set with lots of dishes and food. It was the end of Ramadan, so fasting during the day was over and they were celebrating. Fresh fried fish (*reba*), another meat called бапчета (*kobcheta*) something like hamburger, coleslaw, bread, donuts without holes (поничка, *ponechka*), and of course *Rakia*, beer, soda, and water to drink.

I really was not hungry as I had fixed myself an egg and toast just moments before, but it would be very impolite not to eat. In fact, if the hostess sees that you have finished a piece of fish or bread, immediately another piece is offered or put on your plate. Before I was finished I had three pieces of fish, a *kobcheta*, a big plate of cole slaw (зеле), a very big piece of cake (торта, pronounced *torta*) and several glasses of beer. I did not drink the *Rakia*, as I knew that if I even drank a small glass that immediately it would be refilled. Before I could head back upstairs, she filled up a bag with fish for me, some donuts and another glass of beer

In the morning I was to accompany her to Aitos to go to go to her daughter's where another feast would await us. I was asked to bring my camera and hopefully I would be able to find a place in Aitos where I could get some pictures printed for them.

BIRTHDAY GREETINGS

Here are samples of how I sent birthday greetings to friends and family back in the U.S.

честит рожен ден
Happy Birthday
　Dear Otto,
　RoseDenDen is how birthday sounds in Bulgarian. And for Happy Birthday it's *Chestek Rosedenden*
　Честит пожден ден Желая тиздраве, щастие и късмет
　May your year be filled with health, happiness and luck.
　Love, Louise

What number does this make? I know that you look 45 but since I'm already 39 I know we are not that close in age

Hello Mike,
　RoseDenDen is how birthday sounds in Bulgarian. And for Happy Birthday it's *Chestek Rosedenden*

Честит пожден ден Желая тиздраве, щастие и късмет
May your year be filled with health, happiness and luck.
With warm regards, Louise
Please excuse my late birthday greeting.

BABA MARTA

Hi LeAnne,   **February 23, 2010**

Spring is coming. Yesterday I took a short walk and saw some of the fields were already turning green. There are a lot of rolling hills around here so a very pretty countryside.

My landlady means so well. She invited me in and made me coffee. Then she offered me stuffed peppers. Well, I thought I'd be coming upstairs after the coffee, so I said "no thank you, not today." Well, she always feels like she has to feed me. It is part of the Bulgarian tradition.

She had some filo dough and eggs. Then she told me she would go to the magazine quickly, five minutes. So, I thought OK I will wait. She went to the magazine and bought some *siranade* (white soft cheese) and a big bottle of cola. (Bulgarian version of Coca-Cola) And then she proceeded to make *banitsa*.

She made individual ones, rather than one big one in a pan. Before I knew it, she had one done and gave it to me, and then another and another. I indicated I was full. Well, she made four more and decided to keep one for herself, and gave me the other three to bring upstairs. I'll have them for dinner or lunch tomorrow. I think it's best eaten freshly baked, but not too bad warmed up. I told her that you were coming in May.

You would enjoy her company. And I know you would love to see her garden. She's having it cultivated this Thursday if I understood her correctly. Then she'll plant scallions. She has a big pail of seeds ready to go. She also sells the seeds in packages at the bazaars. She mainly goes to Serbia I think, but also Istanbul. She's leaving again tomorrow.

Tonight I have my class for the adults. I wonder if anyone will show up as the weather is very cold. I want be prepared just in case.

If you have room in your suitcase could you bring along a bottle of Oil of Olay face lotion? I can't find it anywhere here, I looked in Sofia too. I really like using it as a base in the morning.

We're also having our mid-service conference in May, but I don't have the dates yet. I think it would be around the 20th as that's our one year anniversary. Some volunteers are thinking that it will be in Vratsa. That's the town where we had our meetings last summer. Apparently a new group of volunteers are arriving in early May. I heard as many as 80 may be coming.

Love, Louise

Dear Louise   **March 1, 2010**

I didn't know Nancy was sending more books. I will see if I can get a little more money to her so she can send some more.

I really enjoyed the email you sent about the Martenitsas. I sent that on to the people I share you letters with so they could enjoy the news.

I hope you got to the movies. I don't go to the theater any more, they're become too expensive. I'd rather just sit home and watch DVDs; they are much cheaper and it's more comfortable for me to sit in my living room to watch.

Take care, Sharrey

Hi Sharrey,   **March 2, 2010**

Tomorrow is Bulgarian Independence Day, similar to our 4th of July.

Another volunteer is looking into a program that might help with getting cheaper postage to mail books for the school library. I will let you know as soon as she finds out more details. It wouldn't takeaway all the expense, but possibly get a cheaper rate. Hopefully this can happen.

Your friend, Louise

Main holidays celebrated in Bulgaria: New Year's Day January 1; Liberation Day March 3; Easter Sunday and Easter Monday; Labor Day May 1; St. George's Day May 6; Day of Bulgarian Education and Culture May 24; Unification Day September 6; Independence Day September 22; and Christmas Day December 25.

Some families observe saints days and other religious holidays; the above is a list that are observed in the school year when students receive a holiday.

Next is an email sent by a friend in the U.S. who was friends with a Bulgarian graduate student.

Hi Louise,   **March 10, 2010**

It sounds like you've been to a lot of places already. I haven't ever heard Alla Pugachova live. This is great. I did my undergraduate work at Stetson University, DeLand, FL in organ performance; now I'm doing my Master's at the Eastman School in organ performance and literature. I used to be a serious pianist, and studied in the music school in Plovdiv.

There are not very many organs in Bulgaria, since it is an Orthodox country, but I happened to be a Catholic, and we have a small organ at my church. If you get a chance to visit Plovdiv again you should visit the Catholic Cathedral.

I still don't know when the next time I'll go back to Bulgaria. I hope I can go during Christmas but it is not very likely. My next hope is the summer of 2011, hopefully before you leave the country.

What exactly do you do at the school? I'm sorry the language is giving you trouble. Are you going to be in Aitos for the whole time?

Silviy

Hi Debbie,   **March 23, 2010**

I enjoyed reading your letter and to hear all your news. I'm glad to hear that you got to New Orleans. I think it is one of the more interesting U.S. cities in terms of character and unique flavor. No pun intended. I know they also have been great restaurants. There are many things I like about that southern coastal area and hopefully when I come back to the U.S. I can travel there more.

You asked about my wood stove. Many in the villages, and perhaps also in the smaller towns still use wood stoves. But for the size of my apartment, I really should either have a bigger stove, or at least have another one in either my bedroom or living room. Peace Corps only requires a school to provide a volunteer with one warm room. So while I have this nice size apartment only one room is warm during the cold winter months. I'm sure some of the newer stoves have thermostats, or at least a blower on them, but mine is very basic. The room is about ten feet by twelve feet and has outside windows on two sides.

My living room was my biggest room, about nine feet by fifteen feet. It had a sofa and a love seat and some built in shelves at one end. One of my two balconies was off the living room and sometimes I brought out a chair to sit here and observe the village. The other balcony was off the guest bedroom and this is where I hung my clothes to dry on sunny days. It had a piece of linoleum over the cement floor. The bathroom was at one end of the hallway, about seven feet wide by nine feet long. It had a toilet, sink and a bathtub. The hot water heater was in the corner by the bathtub. I needed to turn on the electric to it about twenty minutes before I wanted warm water to either wash my dishes or take a shower. I had no mirror or hooks in the bathroom. The hooks I put up with super glue fell down in the cold weather. My bedroom was about eight feet by nine feet and the kitchen about six feet by ten feet. There was a wide hallway that all the rooms came off of about six feet wide by twelve feet long. The walls were all cement so it was difficult to pound in any nails for hanging pictures.

The more wood you use the more heat it generates. It thus is a very uneven heat, which is what I find frustrating. This room has a porch that looks out onto a side street and I store my wood here. The windows are broken so rain and snow come in on blustery days.

Tonight as it's warmer outside it is warm in this room, but without any heat it is cold and damp. I think more and more people have electric heat, but electricity is relatively expensive. The layer of soot in the neighborhood makes you realize that the air isn't as clean as it might appear.

But spring is in the air. When we arrived in Bulgaria it was mentioned about surviving your first winter in Bulgaria. For many volunteers who grew up in the warmer climates in the U.S., it was the outside cold air that was the problem. I had no problem with that usually, except for the wind. For me I must say I miss most having a warm bathroom and a warm kitchen.

Today Baba Marta was celebrated. That is a fun holiday. I think I sent you the information on that. Teachers and children at school all give each other red and white bracelets, or ribbons to pin on your shoulder.

And Wednesday is a National Holiday, like our 4th of July. It is interesting to learn about new holidays. This is the day when Bulgarians celebrate their independence from the Ottoman Empire in the wake of the Russo-Turkish War of 1877–1878, and in Bulgaria it is called the Battle of Shipka Pass.

This past weekend was different for me as I went to Sofia just for the social aspect. I met another volunteer who needed to visit the conference on tourism being held there. We visited and talked to various countries and tourists agencies that had exhibits at the huge NDK (National Palace of Culture) building. This is similar to a convention building in the U.S. It opened in 1981. It was built by the Russians to commemorate the 1300th anniversary of the Bulgarian State.

On Saturday we visited the Boyana Church. It took us awhile to figure out where the bus stop was that went out in that direction. Thankfully, Felicia has a good sense of direction. We got off a stop too soon, but that gave us an interesting tour of that section of Sofia.

The Boyana Church dates back to the 7th century It is an UNESCO site. It is beautiful. For the most part, the building is intact, but the walls have been plastered several times. Some of the icons are from the 5th century, and also the eighth and tenth century. Some are frescoes; it is all very beautiful. I wanted to buy the information and photo book in English but they were sold out. You were not allowed to take pictures, which is understandable. Bulgaria is really an archaeologist's dream world I wish you could come. There is so much archaeology here. (Grace had a Master's degree in Archaeology.)

From the church we walked to the National History Museum which also has amazing artifacts going back to the third to fifth millennium BC. As late as 2005 they have discovered Thracian tombs here in Bulgaria with gold. An amazing find was in 1912. Archaeologists found a very beautiful gold piece. The museum is very well laid out. Coming back on the bus was easier as there was a bus stop not too far from the Museum that went into the center of town.

To top off our day, we went to the Sofia Opera Theater and saw *Prince Igor* performed. We were able to get tickets in the First Balcony for about $15 US. It was a sellout crowd. It was very interesting to watch an opera performed in Russian in Bulgaria

All in all it was quite a different day for me. Riding back on the train is long as it takes about nine hours from leaving the hotel to getting back to my apartment, but I really needed a weekend off. January and February were very long and cold months.

The week prior I had gone in for some medical tests. The Peace Corps doctor wanted to rule out rheumatoid arthritis, which I do not have, thank goodness. My fingers are very stiff in the morning, and it seems that once I bump a finger or a joint, it swells easily and doesn't go back to normal size. I notice it particularly on my ring fingers. Generally, my fingers do not hurt. They do bother me when they get cold but that has been going on for many years. In May I needed to go back for the annual check-up. I find it hard to believe that I have already been living here ten months.

A few more volunteers have returned to the United States, including the young woman that was closest to me in distance. I felt bad, but while I understand why, it still is disappointing. It is a bit complicated to explain and of course Peace Corps administration does not disclose any specific details. I still wish I had an English-speaking teacher / friend here in the village, but I'm managing okay.

Not having that social part here in the village does give me more time for reading and writing which I appreciate.

Now with the warmer months my social calendar is filling up. A librarian colleague is coming over from Japan to see me in April. We have a spring break. She works under the Department of Defense as a librarian at a Marine Base and loves to travel. We'll spend sometime in Bulgaria and then fly together to Warsaw for a few days. In May, my sister and her husband will be in Sofia on a tour through Eastern Europe so I will meet them there for one or two days.

For now, my summer is open. I'm hoping to find someone who would like to go to Vienna, Budapest and Prague with me. Don't you want to come? I'm thinking of flying to Prague and then take the train and work my way south back to Bulgaria. I'm hoping to also visit Bucharest if I can manage to work out the logistics.

I have a full day of classes tomorrow. They are going quite well. I really like teaching the younger students, but it's fun interacting with the 13- and 14 year-olds, also. Today four of the 8th grade boys brought me some more wood. That's always an adventure when they come with the wood. It's become a weekly occurrence. Not sure why I just don't get one big load, but this seems to work. Yesterday I was down to my last three pieces.

Oh, I don't have my kitty anymore. She seemed to want to go outside, so one day I let her out and I haven't seen her since. One student at school mentioned someone having a black cat, so I'm thinking maybe she belonged to a family. She was so gentle, and did I mention I think she was pregnant? So maybe she's busy now taking care of her kittens. I thought she might come back, but I haven't seen any sign of her. I feel bad, but I didn't feel I could keep her penned up inside here either, and it is difficult when you travel.

Some volunteers do have cats, but it does make things more complicated. So, I'll try and not bring any more home. I just had stocked up on cat food and litter, but can take this over to Laura, another volunteer who has adopted two cats, which she named Petrana and Chavdra. These are very Bulgarian names. Pepa is the shortened form for Petrana. She lives in a neighboring town and we visit occasionally. I'm taken the train several times to feed her cats when she was out of town. Even though the town is fairly close by American standards and also here if you have a car, but via train it can be tricky as it runs only several times a day.

I've already had to sleep over at her apartment as the last train had left for the day. She lives in one of the Soviet "block" apartments and going up the elevator in the dark can be daunting. I always carry a flashlight with me. One time the elevator wasn't working and I had to walk up dark dreary steps in the dark to the sixth floor Her apartment is almost two miles from the train station. Usually, there is a bus at the train station to take passengers into the center of town. From there it is rather a maze of streets to her apartment building, but I managed. The first time I took a wrong turn, and then stopped at the police station to ask for her street. Ulista is the Bulgarian word for street. I am always thankful when my Bulgarian is understood. The policeman pointed me in the right direction and I found her block apartment. What a relief that was as I don't like wandering dark streets at night.

Well, time to call it a day. Hope that you are giving yourself some free time, away from work and the stress of reports, budgets, family trauma and other work related chores. Take care of yourself and please write soon again.

Sent with a big hug, Louise

Email letter to siblings, March 18, 2010

Yes, it is starting to warm up but I decided to make a fire this afternoon as it was only about 50 in my apartment. Now I have it up to 62°F so that's fine. My bedroom will be cooler, but comfortable for sleeping. It's around 35°F outside.

I did some laundry today and hung it outside, but brought it in around five o'clock as I don't like to leave it out overnight. It wasn't dry as the sun really didn't come out much today. And now I've decided to wash my assorted bed linens. I have some kind of bite on my skin. I was thinking fleas, but I see no signs of them and I haven't had the cat for over a month and I had never noticed any fleas on it.

After doing a little research online, I think that maybe some kind of mite got activated with all the renovating, dust and dirt that's been happening up on the 3rd floor. I had some bites two weeks ago, and finally got them under control and this morning I had a new batch. They itch like crazy. I vacuumed everything and now decided to wash all my bed linens.

My one blanket is way too big for my little wash machine, but maybe if I hang it outside tomorrow and give it some good shakes that will help the situation. I was also thinking bugs could be in my wood and with the warmer weather they could be coming out. Anyway, my one leg is a mess and it itches like crazy. I just took a Benadryl and have some cream that Peace Corps gave us last year for bites.

Yesterday I went into Aitos for my language lesson. Ivanka, my language teacher, is such a nice young woman. We speak some in English and then I try and talk to her in Bulgarian, or she asks me questions in Bulgarian that I try to answer. I could practice every day, and think if I lived in Aitos I probably would take more lessons. I'm going in tomorrow for another lesson, but it's hard to manage lessons twice a week on a regular basis.

After the lesson I met with another Bulgarian teacher who asked for my help to review her English for a grant that she's writing for her school. They have to submit it in English and Bulgarian. It is quite an involved project. They had all the basic translation done, and then I reviewed it all and clarified some of the sections. There still are a number of pages that I need to rewrite.

Last time I worked on it over four hours; I must say I rather enjoyed doing it, and sure hope it helps their project. She made me dinner and then as it was so late when I got through all the pages, she wanted me to sleep over, so I did. She has a very small apartment, like a studio. She brought me back then this morning as I had an 8 o'clock class to teach.

The road to Topolitsa is sure a mess. There are some really huge pot-holes and other places just rough, and bumpy. It is very hard on any car.

Tuesday afternoon I did a Skype chat with Irma's son Steve. He teaches at a middle school in suburban Philadelphia. Hopefully next month we'll have our students talk to each other. I need to lineup a few more schools to work on exchange projects.

I finished a really good book, although certainly depressing about Communism in Bulgaria. It's a novel written by a Bulgarian who lived during that time period and deals with all the corruption, mind control and concentration camps. It's called *The Mire*. For a change of pace I think I'll read an Alexander McCall Smith book. He has a new series out. Or this might be a stand alone book. It's called *LA's Orchestra Saves the World*.

I also have *The Shock Doctrine* by Naomi Klein to read. It's about economics and capitalism and begins with how disasters are used to stimulate the economy or how certain people and companies have used them or even encouraged chaos to get rich. There are some clear examples that come to mind. I found it in Helikon, a very browse friendly bookstore in Sofia that carries many books in both English and Bulgarian. It is the second book store I found near The House where I stay that carry English books. Sofia has a big variety of shops and I know if I lived closer, I would get better acquainted with the bus system. My favorite plaza is called Slaveykov Square, named after Petko Slaveykov and his son Pencho. Both were writers. Father and son are here in life-size bronze statues sitting on a bench in the corner of the plaza. The square has many vendors selling new and used books, CDs and DVDs. Many are in Bulgarian, but if I have the time its fun to browse. I have found some books in English.

I can't believe, but I only have eight more days of school before our school break. I leave already on March 31 for a medical appointment in Sofia. Each year we need a complete annual physical. On April 2 my friend will be here from Japan. She is a librarian over there working under the Department of Defense. Hopefully the weather will cooperate. People are busy here getting their gardens ready for planting. I know they grow a lot of onions in the spring. I'm looking forward to fresh tomatoes and green peppers.

You asked about the mountains in Bulgaria. From what I've read the highest ones are around 10,000 feet. They have a number of ski areas especially in the Southwest and Northwest areas of Bulgaria. I'm in the Southeast. I'm not sure exactly how high the mountain is here in Topolitsa, but I heard around 4,000 feet. There still is snow on it this late in the season. It doesn't seem as high as Jay Peak, a mountain in Vermont, where I lived when we owned the General Store. The pictures I sent, where I went weaving, is in Northwest Bulgaria, and those mountains I think were in the 8,000 to 9,000 foot range.

Well, that's all from me.

Love, Louise

MARTENITSA OR BABA MARTA CELEBRATION

On the 1st of March Bulgarians celebrate a traditional holiday called Baba Marta (*Grandma Marta* in English) and it is related to welcoming the approaching spring. People all over the world meet spring with joy and new hopes but in Bulgaria it is saved as an ancient tradition.

On that day, Bulgarians exchange, *martenitsi* (*martenitsa* – singular, *martenitsi* – plural) and tell each other, *Chestita Baba Marta* (Happy Grandma Marta). This custom is essentially to wish great health, good luck, and happiness to family and friends. The name *martenitsa* is taken from the Bulgarian word for March, or, as a legend tells, an angry old lady Baba Marta in Bulgarian (*baba*, grandmother and Marta from "*mart,*" March in Bulgarian).

In Bulgarian folklore Baba Marta is a grumpy old woman who changes her mood very rapidly and it reflects in the changeable March weather. When she is smiling the weather is sunny and warm, but if she gets angry the cold will stay for longer and it may even snow. By wearing the red and white colors of the *martenitsa* our predecessors asked Baba Marta for mercy. They hoped that it will make winter pass faster and bring spring.

The Martenitsa is made of twined red and white threads – woolen, silk, or cotton. The white is a symbol of strength, purity and happiness. The red is associated with health, blood, conception, and fertility.

The most typical *martenitsa* represents two small wool dolls – Pizho and Penda. Pizho is the male doll, usually dominating in white color. Penda is the female doll, usually dominating in red color and distinguished by her skirt. There are many other variations and forms. Out of twined red and white threads are also made bracelets, necklaces, tassels, pompoms, balls, squares, human or animal figures. Over the past several decades the tradition has been innovated by attaching all kinds of representations and symbols made of wood, leather, ceramics, metal foil to the thread-made *martenitsas*.

When someone gives you a Martenitsa you should wear it either pinned on your clothes, on the hand tied around the wrist, or around your neck until you see stork, or fruit trees in blossom for the first time in the season. After that you can tie it on a blossoming tree for fertility. It is believed that the Martenitsa bring health, happiness and longevity. Like kind of amulet, Martenitsa was attributed a magic power believed to protect folks from ill fortune, diseases and an evil eye.

The custom of wearing Martenitsa is probably one of the most interesting Bulgarian (pagan) traditions and it is considered to be unique to Bulgaria. According to one of the many legends, this tradition is also related to the founding of the Bulgarian state in 681 AD.

WINTER LINGERS ON

March 4, 2010

This week we again had snow and wind here in Topolitsa. School was canceled both Tuesday and Wednesday. On Thursday the schedule was shortened as the roads were bad. Finally on Friday it was a regular schedule. I still have confusion with what days I will be teaching in the upper grades, but I try to go with the flow. I've hardly been in 8th grade since Christmas; 6th and 7th a few times. The younger grades are doing find and Yura is very adaptable and is willing to go with my plan.

We don't discuss ideas more than minutes before class time, but somehow we manage. I've been teaching the children some songs. They especially enjoy the Hokey Pokey; the younger students also like "Head, shoulders, knees and toes." The other song I've sung with them is "Old MacDonald." I want to look for a few new songs yet this spring. I'm still not sure if they understand the words, but at least they're hearing English (American) pronunciations.

It is as difficult for them to say words like Thursday as it is for me to say bread (*hlyab*) in Bulgarian. Tuesday and Thursday are often confused which is understandable. I often get cooking, talking and working confused as in Bulgarian the spelling is very similar as is the pronunciation. In the evenings the Bulgarian version of *Wheel of Fortune* is on the NOVA television channel. While I don't understand many of the words, I do hear sounds which is good for me and they speak slower so I'm hearing more Bulgarian which is what I need to do. Also with Ivanka she is forcing me to speak Bulgarian; I read it in Bulgarian and then answer the questions in Bulgarian. Slowly, slowly it is coming.

This weekend it is warmer and it sure feels good. While my apartment still only registers 60 degrees that is okay. My kitchen isn't freezing to enter. I washed the areas of floor that are not covered by carpet. Also I washed the hall steps. My wood this time was left outside so I had to make about 20 trips up and down the steps to bring it in. That is okay too as sometimes it is a bit awkward having the students traipsing through my apartment. I can't blame them for being curious, but it does feel a bit like an intrusion. Thankfully, I've had my bedroom door and living room doors shut as is the practice here, when the students come in. Hopefully now I have enough wood to carry me through until spring. I kept a fire going yesterday, but think I may let it die out today. I can't believe the dust and dirt the wood creates; the briquettes are worst as they are dustier than the wood. The television stand was very dusty.

I did my laundry and took the free-standing dryer rack out on the balcony. A few of the clothes actually dried. I also hung some up on my yarn clothesline by the stove. I couldn't find any string, so I took some of my yarn and pounded a tack in the wall to fasten the yarn and ran it zigzag across my warm room a few times. By rotating my clothes close to the stove I've managed to have them dry on these cold winter days. It usually takes two or three days for my clothes to dry in this way. This morning I hung a few pieces outside on my regular balcony clothesline and may take the rack outside again today. I think it's only about 40 degrees outside, but the sun is shining so it feels a whole lot warmer.

This weekend the U.S. changes to Daylight Savings Time, but the EU countries don't change until the last Sunday of the month. I'm happy about that as it's nice being light early. Now it's getting light around 6 AM and dark around 6:30 PM, so by the end of the month it should be similar, but it will stay light close to 7:30 PM I would think. I can tell the difference when I go to Sofia that we get light earlier here on the east side of the country, than in the west.

The summer is still very open. No one is planning to come that I know of. I want to do a train excursion, Prague, Vienna, and Budapest. It would be nice to do it with someone, but I can't think of who might be interested. I have mentioned it to Gretchen who would make a great traveling companion, but she is very busy with her work. I can't think of anyone else in the states who would consider flying over and doing such a trip.

General reflections of the PC experience so far:

I thought learning the language would be easier. It is difficult to motivate myself constantly to practice. It is discouraging when I do try to speak the language at school and then get corrected. I realize that for the most part they are trying to help me, but it gets discouraging. I can't remember the vocabulary, must less the correct form of the verb to use. I wonder how I will feel next year at this time. Ivanka told me she sees improvement, but I really need more time with her, or more time with Vesala just in simple conversation.

It surprises me how easy it seems to come to the younger volunteers, like last week in Chiproski where they spoke with Yulka, the weaver and owner of guest house where we stayed. I can barely make a basic conversation about my daughter and where I live that she understands. Body language has been my saving grace.

On the train to Aitos two women conductors wanted to talk to me, and I thought they asked about Andrea, but then it was something about my sons. I think that was it anyway. Perhaps she saw us on the train over Christmas. She seemed to say the word for Christmas. Many of the conductors recognize me now as I go back and forth to Aitos at least once a week, and have made several trips now to Sofia. I do wonder what they think of me.

Besides the language, living in the village is okay. For the most part I spend the days by myself. Thankfully I enjoy reading and doing handwork. There is nothing really to do in the village except take some walks. I feel so conspicuous. In the cold weather I did not take any walks except to school and to the train station. Now if the weather warms up I will need to force myself to take more walks just for the fresh air and exercise. It all seems so much effort and it goes back to communication. I was thinking that even going to the magazine and having to ask for items by name is a challenge to me. It sure doesn't come natural.

The people here in the village have no need to learn English so the pressure is on me to learn Bulgarian. I don't feel cut out for learning language. And I wonder is it my age or how I learn? When I talked to a friend on Skype yesterday it appears that she too has had little success in learning a foreign language.

She has lived overseas for five years. I'm not sure how much she speaks it and as with many ex-pats does not need to use it on a everyday work environment like I need to do. I must remind myself to be thankful and not dismiss the kindness of the many friends and family who have mailed me packages. It really is more than I expected. If I would add up just the total cost of postage it is probably well over $1,000.

A list of who mailed packages as I remember:

Friends and family from all over the United States mailed me many, many items; a number of them sent two, three and even more packages. A list of names in alphabetical order:

Anne, Avis, Belinda, Becky, Carolyn, Connie, Dana, David, Debbie, Donna, Elaine, Felicia, Ginny, Gretchen, Harris, Irma, James, Joyce, LaVerne, LeAnne, Loren, Marcus, Nancy, Rogene, Sandra, Sharon, Sharrey, Stacey, Trinity Church Women's Group, Trish and Vicky are all part of my network of family and friends throughout the United States.

Personal items I received or for the school:

Packages of school supplies, and other treats for the children, magazines and candy, books to read for myself, UNO game, cards, towel, CDs and DVDs, *The Week* magazine, Christmas cookies, pins, clothes, New Mexico goodies, magazines, books, knitting supplies, comics, coloring books, crayons, candy, shoes, backpack, the *New York Times*, Boston newspaper and various New Mexico newspapers, postcards, clothes, glue, carbon paper, photo hard copies, chocolate chips, spices, candy canes, face cream, assorted food, packages of workbooks for children, socks, cloth shopping bags, plus over 200 children's books for the school library.

This is quite a list. People were thinking of me. I had very positive feedback on my Christmas letter. I wonder how the coming months will develop.

Dear Sis,   **March 12, 2010**

I made chocolate chip cookies and took some to school today. My friend Becky sent me some chocolate chips, the first I've had since I've been here. They were so good. Everybody enjoyed this special treat. I still haven't been able to find brown sugar like we use in the states, but David had brought me vanilla so that helped the cookies turned out.

Plus, I made some chili. Becky also sent me a bunch of spices, including chili powder. I had one package of frozen tomatoes from last summer in my little freezer and a bit of ground meat so I cooked that up with some onion and the tomatoes and used the rest of my landlady's bean soup. I had some noodles so all in all it turned out quite good. I wanted to buy some dill pickles today to go with them as I was in Aitos, but I ran out of time.

I had my hair trimmed and the hair dresser took longer than I planned. I had to rush in the grocery store and bought milk and crackers. Then I took a taxi to the train station rather than my usual walk to the train. It's a mile or more from the hair dresser's/grocery store/bus station area over to the train station.

No plans this weekend, which is okay. I have a big bunch of wood to carry upstairs. The students brought it over and left it by my outside door as I was gone, plus I have laundry to do and I always try to find some time to study Bulgarian.

So I'll probably have three quiet weekends, and then I will go to Sofia for my medical/annual check up and meet my friend from Japan. She flies in April 2.

I'm tired tonight. I already carried up about six armloads of wood. It reminds of me of childhood days back in Fremont. In Vermont we had a wood stove as well and had to chop the wood and then carry it upstairs.

I don't like the briquets, they are so dirty. I carried a bucket full of them upstairs and got some coal on my good white turtleneck. And they smell. When I'm low on wood I use them, or at night to bank up the fire as I think they burn longer, but they are so messy. It's in the mid-30s today, so everything is melting. There is water and slush everywhere.

I heard from Debbie today. Perhaps she still might make it to Bulgaria in the summer. That would be great.

Today I received a nice packet of things from Rogene and Joyce, from Wisconsin, I've known them since childhood, and they were always good friends. Rogene emails me now and then; I don't think Joyce has a computer. Do you ever see either of them?

Love, Louise

Hi Debbie, **March 23, 2010**
Thank you so very much for sending me coloring books for my students, and also for the colored pencils for to use with the books. It will help them understand more about the Southwest culture.

(Lyle, my oldest brother, was Debbie's dad. He died from cancer ten years ago. When I was in high school in Wisconsin he moved with his family out to Arizona and subsequently built up a printing business. This included printing Southwest stationery, maps and very unique Southwest coloring books.)

Years ago when Lyle, started printing those books, I never imagined that I would be sharing them with students in Bulgaria. What a small world that we live in. Did I ever tell you that a museum library near Farmington, NM has several of those coloring books in its collection? It is a museum connected to an ancient site where the Anazai Indians used to live. It is near the Aztec National Park, but this is a site maintained by San Juan County. I helped oversee the museum library. One of my projects while at San Juan College was to have the entire library book collection at the Museum cataloged electronically and tie it in with the full SJC library catalog. I came across several of Lyle's coloring books on Native Americans. Several other companies now do similar books, but I think Lyle's are some of the best. Thank you again for sending them.

How are your summer plans coming? I'm hoping to do the train trip in July; another volunteer might join me, but if not I will probably do it by myself. While I'm living over here I want to see as much of Eastern Europe as I can.

I also am interested in visiting Berlin again. I saw it when the Wall was still up. What a sad and frightening site that was. Now I want to see the united city of Berlin.

Soon I'll be going to Warsaw. A friend who now lives and works in Japan is flying over and I will meet her in Sofia. We'll spend five days in Bulgaria and then fly to Warsaw. We have a school spring break.

School goes until June 15. I'm not sure what I'll all be doing this summer. Officially we're on duty all summer, but are allowed some vacation time. If there's a chance that you can make it this way, that would be great. Perhaps you can come for my birthday, which would be grand. Hope this finds you well and that I'll hear from you soon. Love, Louise

THE WORLD IS BIG

Dear Sis,   **March 25, 2010**

Tonight it is a cool clear night and lots of stars are out. I went into Aitos this afternoon as my language teacher told me that there was to be a movie in the community hall. It was free. It is a new Bulgarian feature film called *The World Is Big and Salvation Lurks Around the Corner*. It was very good. There are not very many Bulgarian films made these days, so they wanted to promote it by showing it in different theaters around Bulgaria. Lots of people came to watch it. The theater was full.

Afterwards I went out for coffee with several Bulgarian teachers and then one of the women drove me to the train station. The last train leaves for Topolitsa at 8:30. Several of the high school students were also on the train and I walked back to my apartment with several of them. One knows English a little bit and recognized me. It was so nice being in the city and just talking with people. I guess that is what I miss the most, living here in this very small village. I'm glad that I know some of the teachers from Aitos; more of them speak English than the teachers who teach in the village school.

Going to a movie was fun. This was my first movie since I've been here. It was about the different countries that make up the Balkan region, and a group of friends who went wind sailing together. Then an English journalist comes who had covered war stories, and he has a Bulgarian girl friend. They start arguing about what makes a Bulgarian, a Serbian, a Macedonian, a Greek, and here they were friends, but because of his questions, it looks like their friendship is over. It was a good story plot. The director was there and answered some questions after the movie. No special plans for the weekend. Tomorrow I'm going to go in to Aitos again, this time for another language lesson. Time to get ready for bed.

Love, Louise

SCHOOL EXCURSION

Hi Louise   **March 26, 2010**

There are several optional tours connected with this European tour and I plan on going on several of those. I hope this will be a fun trip. I was thinking about coming to Bulgaria in August, but probably mid-August for around ten days or so. Sorry, but I don't think I can make it there for your birthday on August 1st.

I would like to see the town you're living in, your school and your home. I'm also open to going to the Black Sea and wherever you'd like. If you would like to go to Greece or Turkey, I would go there also. Just let me know. I was thinking about flying into Sofia. Or I could fly from Sofia to Burgas or take the train. I'm just not sure what you might have in mind. Just let me know. I'm not sure when your school starts back up, but hopefully this time frame will work for you.

Take care, Debbie

Hi Debbie,

Fantastic that is wonderful to hear. So glad you can come for a visit.

I can make those days work. And if it's okay with you, we can stay in Bulgaria mainly around my village and the Black Sea coast. The beach and the coastal area are very nice in August, and mid-August should work. I think there's a school camp trip that I must go on with the students, but last year it was around August 25 that we left.

If you could manage to be here between August 6 and the 23 it should work very well. Ten days sounds good. We can do a few overnight excursions, like up north to Varna perhaps, the biggest Bulgarian city on the Black Sea. Depending on what you can arrange, fly into Sofia or Burgas. I've not been to the Burgas airport. I'll have someone help me figure it out if you decide to fly into Burgas.

If you fly into Sofia, I could meet you there and we could have a day there for a little sightseeing and then take the train across the countryside to my village. Sometimes, I know they run special rates to fly from Burgas to Sofia, so if you don't want to do the train ride both ways, you could perhaps fly from Burgas to Sofia, rather than another day long train ride.

As of now, I have no plans for August, so your visit would be most welcome. The Black Sea is a very lovely area and many people come here for the beach. I'm running to catch the local train into Aitos this morning for some last minute errands. On Wednesday I'm taking the train to Sofia for my medical exam and on the 2nd (Friday) my friend from Japan is coming. We will be here in Topolitsa a few days, and then fly to Warsaw, Poland. I'm mentioning this as I'll be away from email much of that time period, April 2 – 11. I usually don't take my computer with me, but sometimes find an Internet cafe.

Peace Corps allows us International Travel, but it is more of a hassle, and every day counts against our time off, including holidays and weekends. By staying here in Topolitsa and this area I will have someone (you) to enjoy the beach with me plus I won't have to jump through hoops with Peace Corps as I'll be staying at my home base. Just yesterday I agreed to help chaperon a school trip to Turkey with another Peace Corps colleague in early May and even that has to count against my International travel time.

Let me know what you can work out. Mid-August is a good time to come to Bulgaria. The weather will be warm. We can celebrate our birthdays when you come, no matter the date.

Love, Louise

Hi Louise,

Great. I'm glad that this will work out. I'm excited about coming. I think it's probably cheaper and easier for me to fly into Sofia. So, I'll work on my travel arrangements over the next few weeks and let you know. I think I like the idea of flying into Sofia, meeting you there, doing some sightseeing and then taking the train to your village.

Have fun with your friend and your travel to Poland. Also, aren't LeAnne and Willard planning on visiting you in May? You'll be having lots of English-speaking company.

I'll talk to you soon, Debbie

Hi Debbie,

It will be so good to see you and have this time together. I've had been thinking about the summer and how it would all work out. And while we don't have teaching per se, we are required to stay in our village as much as possible.

Last summer when I got to the Black Sea a few days, I was excited. It is such a beautiful spot. So having you here will make it all the more special.

Once you have your flight plans, let me know. There are activities to do around Sofia, so keep that in mind as you plan your flight, but one or two days would give you a good idea of the main city attractions.

Seeing my village and the region here by the Black Sea can easily take up a week or more. It will be good to have you here. And I will plan to go back with you via train to Sofia. We would probably make it a two day trek back. If you can, try for a mid to late afternoon return flight as that makes it much easier on the logistics. There is a very nice city called Plovdiv that we could stop at the first day on the return trek, and then the second day go into Sofia.

That is how I did it with Marcus. We had an afternoon and evening in Plovdiv and then took the morning train into Sofia. We had an early lunch and he flew out mid-afternoon. If you had a morning flight, we would have to go to Sofia the day before. LeAnne and Willard are coming for a weekend in May as part of their Eastern European tour. I feel very fortunate that I am blessed with such a supportive family.

Looking forward to your visit, Love Louise

One more note: if you can make one or both of your flights fall around weekend days would be the best for me.

Hi Felicia,   **March 26, 2010**

Just a quick note, Laura just called me and asked me if I could manage to arrange to come on their 12th grade trip excursion to Turkey. It is the end of next month.

I talked to my director and she said OK. It is missing three days of school, but I will need to take 6 days of vacation time. But the logistics of this is better than to come to Sofia for Jamie's trip.

He had mentioned to me about coming along with his 12th grade class, but I know that I couldn't manage both trips either time or money wise. I will email him and let him know.

It is a spring day here, about 45 degrees and the sun is out. Hope that your meeting is going well.

Talk to you soon.

Hi Louise,   **March 27, 2010**

Where in Turkey will you go this time? That sounds exciting. Yes, I saw

Jamie yesterday and the Greece trip in April is officially off and they are not trying to make it happen, so that is not an issue. Are you helping chaperon Laura's school trip? If so, you should not take vacation, or at least try save some of your vacation time, if possible. I am trying to find a back-up trip myself to take as I think I really need to get away next month.

Well, I'm packing up to leave Sofia and will be back in Varshets this afternoon. The workshop went okay yesterday. I think that most of the volunteers appreciated it. I'm not sure the staff did which carries some disappointment with it since I put so much effort into preparing my materials and presentation.

The speakers were all Bulgarian and not that greatly informative. I had spent a ton of time creating a list of questions specific for each organization. They answered or addressed very few of them. But I think we all just needed to see that for ourselves. Also some people were able to make some contacts with the organizations. Everyone wants to do it again in the fall, so I will take that as a good sign that it wasn't totally worthless.

Talk soon, Felicia

Good morning Felicia,

Congratulations. I think that you should feel good about the meeting. It's not always easy to see all the results at the time, but you started people thinking about issues that perhaps they had, but did not voice or had not even thought about. Yes, take that as a very good sign to have another conference in the fall. And I think that cultural differences do play a part on how items are addressed.

As soon as I have more details on Turkey I will let you know. I know it's Istanbul and Cotton Castle, or something like that. A big resort area, I just found out about it yesterday around 10 AM. Laura said that she needed an answer before school was out today so I said okay. She had checked with Dora (TEFL) and I have to use vacation time. I have to count the holiday and the weekend, as it's not my school. I went over my dates and decided it would be worth it, if my director approved my time off from school. I will only miss three school days, and have to take six or seven vacation days because its out of the country. It is frustrating having to count the weekend days as vacation time.

Now I've off to Aitos to meet Pauli. Pauli is the person who took me to Shipka last summer. I have pictures to share with her. She was very welcoming to me last summer and I really appreciated it.

One big favor to ask you, please could you send me before Tuesday night, directions on how to walk to The Eagle Bridge? I don't trust myself to remember the way. That's where you catch the airport bus, right? I need to meet my friend at the airport, and I will be staying at The House. I don't think I'll remember how to walk there from The House. I've just sent an email off to her as I don't know what terminal she's coming in. She's flying from Japan to Vienna I think, as she mentioned Austrian Air. I will have us take a taxi back to The House. She's coming in Friday evening. I have medical on Thursday, and so Friday I'm just hanging around Sofia. Could you perhaps make it to Sofia for part of Friday?

On Saturday I'm giving her my walking tour which will include museums, shopping, and the pride of Sofia, St. Alekandur Nevski. In the evening I signed up for a tour of the night city, ending up at the restaurant called The Waterfall. She likes arranged excursions. Early Sunday morning we will take the train to Topolitsa. It's going to be a whirlwind week.

I'm off to catch the train to Aitos.

Thank you very much, Louise

The Eagle Bridge was a well known Sofia meeting point. The bridge buttress has an eagle decorating each corner. It was where many buses stopped and also where the bus that took you to the airport stopped. Figuring out the bus system at the beginning was very confusing to me. Most of the street names were only in Cyrillic. To go to the Peace Corps Office from the train station meant taking several buses. I would have to watch carefully so that I didn't get off at the wrong stop. Walking to the Eagle Bridge from The House I could easily get turned around. It was much cheaper to walk to the Eagle Bridge and take the special airport bus than to take a taxi. On my first visit to Sofia I got a city map from the Peace Corps and I took it with me wherever I went. However, the bus stops were not marked on it and I had to watch the street signs very carefully.

Dear Irma,   **March 28, 2010**

I'm getting ready for my trip to Sofia and then Poland. I can't believe it, but I got more bites last night. I sure can't figure out why I'm getting all these bites. These are on my other leg. It is so frustrating.

Laura came by this morning and that was fun. She's the PCV I'm going with to Turkey as an assistant chaperon the end of April with her high school senior class. It should be an interesting trip. She stopped by as I needed to pay for the trip in advance and the deadline is this week. The cost is about $400 USD which includes most of my meals and all the lodging and transportation. Besides the famous mosques in Istanbul, we will also see the Bulgarian Iron Church, St. Stephens. It's famous for being made of prefabricated cast iron elements in the neo-Gothic style. Another special site is to tour the Dolmabahce Palace which was where the Sultans lived up to 1924. Then Ataturk, the founder and first President of the Republic of Turkey used it during the summers. He died here in

1938. It is now a National Museum. We're also going to this place in Turkey called the Cotton Castle, formal name Pamukkale and the ruins of Hierapolis. It is near Izmir. And we are going to Bodrum on the Aegean Sea and we will have a tour of Ephesus. I made Laura a big breakfast, and then she helped me with some computer stuff. Lots of high schools have trips with their 12th graders.

I don't know how many teachers are going. The last time I was a chaperon on a school trip was in Pittsburgh, when I went to Germany with the German class. That's 20 years ago already. As it turns out the school trip ends May 6. The next day I leave to go to Sofia for LeAnne and Willard's visit. I decided to make a fire this afternoon as it's so damp. It was pouring down rain when I walked with Laura to the train earlier this afternoon. You can see some buds starting to appear on the trees now. I want to sort through my clothes for Sofia. The weather is so changeable; it'll be hard to know what to take along. When I go by train to Sofia I only take a very small suitcase. For the trip to Turkey I will take my medium size suitcase along and a big bag on my shoulder. We are going by bus to Turkey.

What a shame the reaction of people to Health Care. They must not know anyone without health insurance and what it's like to manage without it. They live in a dream world. To be without health insurance was one of the major things that always scared the daylights out of me, especially when I was a single mom.

I'm treating myself as I'm going to make some chicken tonight. I bought a frozen package of chicken in Aitos. I hope it turns out. David mailed me some muffin mix. I just had to add water. I made a small loaf of break with it, blueberry. It sure tasted good.

Love, Louise

TALK TO AMERICA

Students from the 7th and 8th grade class were able to talk to students in America this past week via Skype. This special project was set up by Louise Hoffmann, the Peace Corps Volunteer from the U.S. who is teaching English to the students here in the small village of Topolitsa for two years. It was arranged with fellow teacher Steve Kelly in the U.S.A. who teaches technology to his students in a suburban school outside of Philadelphia, Pennsylvania. Both schools have children from grades one through eight.

Arranging the time when both sets of students would be at school provided the biggest challenge as there is a seven hour time difference between the two schools. When the students are arriving for school in Pennsylvania, the students in Bulgaria are preparing to go home.

Students at both schools were excited about speaking to each other so an informal class session was set up by Ms. Hoffmann and Mr. Kelly. The

Svetlina School did not have a camera so the students in America could not see the Topolitsa students. However, they could see the students in their computer classroom in America. With the use of a headset and a microphone they could speak to the students and hear each other.

The students gave their name and age and talked about the kind of music they liked. The students in America held the U.S.A. flag as they introduced themselves so that the students in Topolitsa, Bulgaria could see who was talking. The visit lasted about thirty minutes. The students hope to be able to "Skype Chat" with each other again and share photos of their school and community.

It is also hoped that future visits with more students participating can be arranged in this coming school year. The school is considering buying a camera and a classroom microphone if funds become available. In this way, the students will all be able to see each other and have a chance to ask each other questions. They can learn first-hand how their life is the same and how it is different.

All the students were happy to have this chance to talk to each other. In this small way children across the globe separated by over five thousand miles learn how they can make a difference by appreciating each other's culture and lifestyle.

The school's web site is: *http://ousvetlina.com*

LESSON PLANS

In the midst of all these assorted projects and visitors coming to visit me in Bulgaria, most evenings were spent preparing for teaching my classes the next day. I often brought the students work home to look at even though I was not in charge of their final English mark. I tried a variety of approaches to make the lesson interesting, For the younger students I often used visuals: anything that I could find in my apartment or in the neighborhood store. Friends from home were often sending me items that I could incorporate into a lesson.

I loved teaching music to the younger students and in this way they learned many English words. "Hokey Pokey," "Fingers in the Air," are two favorite songs I taught my classes in the United States that came to my mind and the students here loved it. The middle class students, 4th, 5th and 6th grades, liked doing crosswords, or playing games like "Wheel of Fortune." I found if I could involve the children in the lesson I had a much better chance of participation. I brought in magazines that I received from the U.S. and had them tell stories about the pictures. And I did some writing exercises.

One World Classroom International Art Exchange is another program I had the students of Topolitsa participate in. Overview: Mail colorful, creative, original student artwork that depicts your student's lives / cultures. Attach a student information label (and optionally, a student photo) to each piece of artwork. You will receive one package of artwork that matches your grade levels, featuring the work of students from a variety of countries around the world. If you attach student photos, you will receive artwork with attached photos.

Dear Paul,   **October 7, 2009**

I am a PC English teacher in Topolitsa, Bulgaria – a small village near the Black Sea area. I would like information to register for the art project. In my short time here I have seen some very interesting artwork done by the students. There are 120 students enrolled, grades 1 to 8.

Thank you, Louise Hoffmann PC B-25

Hi Louise,   **October 10, 2009**

Thank you for your interest in OneWorld Classrooms' *International Art Exchange.* I am pasting below and attaching the participation guidelines. You may register your school at *http://www.oneworldclassrooms.org/iaereg1.html,* or send me via email your school name, number and grade level of participating classes, your mailing address, how many exchanges you would like to complete, one exchange is 25 pieces of student artwork, and the rounds you will participate in are Jan. 15, 2010 or May 1, 2010. We look forward to involving your school.

Paul, OneWorld Classrooms

Another project that is set up directly through the Peace Corps National Office is called the Coverdell World Wise Schools, Office of Public Engagement. It matches a PCV who is teaching at a Peace Corps school site with a school in the United States. It is a great way for students from around the world to learn about students their own age and how their life is the same and how it is different.

One day with the 8th grade students in Svetlina the lesson was about the Solar System. It was fascinating for me to see how much they understood as I talked in English and they had to transcribe in their brains, what they knew in Bulgarian to English. I was quite impressed about by how much science my students knew.

Other times I brought in a globe and a map of the world. In the U.S. we have names for all the countries of the world, cities of the world, mountain ranges. In Bulgaria, while the country is the same, they are of course called differently, Turkseea, Etalea, Rusea, are some examples. Peace Corps is pronounced *Corpus na mera* in Bulgarian.

Hello Dora,   **June 23, 2010**

Here is a schedule I worked out for holding English classes at school this summer here in Topolitsa. With meetings and excursions in July I think it is best to wait until August. It will be good to do in August I think before school begins to get them ready for classes.

If possible I would like to meet with you Thursday or Friday about my school schedule for fall and also the Peace Corps special project.

Schedule:

Classes 7 & 8: 1 time each week, always the same day and time.

Classes 4, 5, & 6: 2 times each week, always the same day and time.

Classes 3 & 4: 3 times each week, always the same day and time.

Laura is not able to come on the excursion next Monday. What time will we leave on excursion? What time will we return on Tuesday? Do I have to come into Aitos, or will the bus pick me up in Topolitsa?

Louise

WORKSHOP

This is the outline of a project I did with two other Peace Corps volunteers and presented at a teacher's meeting on a Saturday in Aitos, the fall of 2010.

It was well received and we were asked to do another program the following month, which we did and invited the teachers and directors of all the schools in the region. A lively discussion was held afterwards both in English and Bulgarian.

United States Department of Education:
- Establishes policies related to education funding and administers distribution of funds and monitors their distribution.
- Collects data and oversees research on America's schools.
- Identifies major issues in education and focuses national attention on education.
- Enforces federal laws prohibiting discrimination in programs that receive federal funding.

Qualifications for Teaching in the United States:
- To teach in the United States a person must have a degree in education, either primary or secondary and a license to teach in a particular state.
- At the high school level concentration in a particular subject area is required.
- Some states may have additional qualifications.
  For example, many require a person to have a masters degree before he or she is able to teach certain subjects, especially seen in the high school area.

Attendance at School:
- Neighborhoods or towns are assigned to particular public schools.
- Students do not have a choice as to which public school they will attend.
- When families move, they often decide where they move to based on their knowledge and reputation of the school in that area.
- Parents may choose to send their children to a private school. Then they would incur extra fees imposed by that particular school.
- Many larger cities have magnet schools, which specialize in a particular subject matter and students have to apply and pass qualification tests to enroll.
- Charter schools blend public and private monies, and they cross neighborhood .boundaries.

A School Day:
- Starts between 7:30 and 8 AM, ends between 2:15 and 3 PM.
- Elementary school 1st to 5th or 6th grade; Middle school 6th or 7th grade to 8th grade; high school 9th to 12th.
- All students come to school and remain there for the entire school day.
- All schools have cafeterias and students eat their lunches there either buying it or bringing it with them from home.
- Students can take up to 7 courses in a day.
- Middle and high school students usually have one 15 to 30 minute homeroom period per day.
- Usually, this is the first or second class period. The homeroom teacher takes attendance and makes announcements before the rest of the school day.
- In many schools, the students switch rooms to take different classes beginning at 4th or 5thgrade.
- Students begin kindergarten at age 5 and 1st grade at age 6.
- Kindergarten usually goes only until noon.

A Work Day for a Teacher:
- Teachers arrive before the school day begins and leave at about 4 or 5 PM.
- Teachers have a teacher's room to relax in, have conferences, lunch break or meet with colleagues. Each teacher has a desk in his or her classroom or a shared office where he or she can work.
- Teachers often decorate the walls of their rooms with students work or maps, charts and other study aids.
- During periods where a teacher is not teaching, he or she grades, prepares lesson plans, or is available for students who have questions or need extra help.

Teacher Duties:
- Teachers must be at school while the students are in school.
- Many teachers belong to a union.
- Often, teachers must attend a particular number of conferences or workshops each year in order to remain licensed.
- All teachers are expected to attend regular staff meetings.

Good morning, (to group of college friends)   June 5, 2010

It feels so good to have my computer working again. I still need a part replaced, but for now I am working around it.

Yesterday I had my language lesson. I know I need to study more and keep reviewing the vocabulary. I forget some words so easily, especially the verbs.

I went with my teacher to her class of adult students in Aitos learning English. They have been taking lessons I think for about eight months on weekends. I did manage to communicate with them a bit in Bulgarian. English is not so easy to learn for many of them. I spoke with them over an hour, mainly talking about life in America. They are fascinated with it. Companies and the government has arranged many different classes for adult students to learn English. It is only in the last few years that English has been taught in the smaller towns, but as businesses grow, it is a big advantage to them to have their employees speak English.

I had a few pictures to show them. When I come back at Christmas I will have to make an attempt to find good post cards of historic sites in the U.S.A.; they make great talking points.

I had made a CD of some of the photos I had on my computer, but really don't have many of general scenes of the U.S. Before this new computer, I usually just made a CD of my trips and had some photos printed. Now I download everything to my computer. As a backup with this last computer crash, I made CDs of all my photos. David had backed up most of my stuff when he was here at Christmas, and so now almost everything is backed up. I still have to back up some of my Word docs.

After Ivanka's class I walked in the pouring down rain to Vesala's class. She did have a computer and I showed her class some of my India photos. This is the first time I spoke to Bulgarians about a trip to India. I remember when I was in Germany, now 20 years ago; I went to a slideshow about the Great Wall of China all spoken in German. Ironic I guess, as I never imagined doing this kind of exchange. Usually I talk about life and/or geography in the United States.

After the class I went with Vesala and another English teacher to the park where they were having a spring festival. Fortunately the rain stopped, but everything was quite wet. There were many traditional dancers who

I always fine fascinating to watch. There were a number of different vendors setup selling fries, *kebapche* (sort of like brats) and of course beer.

I stayed over night at Vesala's and came back on the morning train. She lives in a studio apartment. She is always a gracious hostess. She insists on me sleeping on her sofa bed, while she sets up a cot in a small open space in the kitchen area.

I'm taking a late train tonight into Aitos and will sleep at Vesala's. Early tomorrow morning I'm going to the Rose Festival in Karnobat with Ivanka and her colleague Antonea and her students. The train leaves at 6 AM from Aitos. That is why I need to sleep in Aitos tonight, as the earliest train from Topolitsa to Aitos gets in around 7:15 AM. The express train goes through Topolitsa, but doesn't stop, so sometimes it's tricky on how to make travel arrangements.

I hope that my brother makes it over here. I think he likes going off the beaten track. I think it is more difficult to tour here using traditional travel methods, buses and trains as sometimes even getting on the train can be a challenge. The door doesn't always open on the platform and it can be a huge step or jump to get on or off. They are often crowded, hot and dirty, especially in the summer. Early cherries are now getting ripe. My landlady gave me a bowl full to enjoy. I think if I get another batch maybe I'll make a cherry pie. That sure sounds good to me. I still have the pie crust mix David brought me at Christmas. There's a cherry tree outside my balcony, but I can't quite reach the branches.

Love, Louise

Peace Corps Partnership Program Svetlina School, Bulgaria:

"Enhancing the lives of students, and residents of Topolitsa,
and surrounding villages"

Summary:

Topolitsa is a small village of 1,000 residents located in southeastern Bulgaria about 40 miles from the Black Sea. Aitos, the closest town is 12 miles by car. It can be reached by train which stops outside the village six times a day. Villagers without a car have to carefully plan their excursions for shopping, health care, banking, etc.

The students at the school enjoy sports, but the sports field currently at the school is not conducive for safe play. The project proposal is to renovate the current school sports area with new sod, accurate field markers, improved drainage and benches for team players, parents and community members.

With a regular laid-out sports playground Topolitsa could become a center for sport activities with the neighboring villages. During the school year, teachers will more easily engage the students in supervised games.

Students, both boys and girls, will be taught rules for the games, exercise activities for all ages can be given and hazards will be kept at a minimum with a well laid-out safe play area.

As the school budget is given based on school enrollment, currently 125 students, there is not enough money to set aside to improve the outside sports area for the students. Parents and residents knowing the advantage this would give their students and other members of the community are willing to help with the labor to implement this project and to maintain it in the future.

TRAVEL

Hi Hazel,   **April 5, 2010**

Yes, I'm still planning on the train trip, but I haven't done any more investigating. I hope to soon. The end of this week I'm going with Laura and her 12th grade class on their excursion to Turkey. This includes Istanbul and Pamukkale, often called Cotton Castle. It should be very interesting. I'm just a bit concerned about the language and traveling with 26 students. After I return from Turkey my sister and her husband will be in Sofia for a few days.

It's been a crazy couple of weeks at school. I was going to mention the train trip to my director but she has hardly been around. Now think I'll wait until after I come back from Turkey. I did buy a DK book on Budapest and a little tiny one on Prague. I think we if get our plane tickets by the end of May we should be okay. I sure wish we lived closer.

How's your foot doing? I've had a bunch of mosquito or some kind of bug bites. Just when I think I'm all set, I get a new batch.

I'm knitting a baby blanket for my first grandchild but don't think I'll have it done by June, the baby's due date.

Next time I go in and pay my phone bill, I'll add your number to my "favorite list." I have a spot open. Hope we can talk soon.

When a phone was purchased there was an offer for the consumer to have up to five or ten persons put on a "favorites" list depending on your plan. With that offer, these are people that you could text free without an extra charge against your monthly stipend. The Peace Corps Office, emergency phone numbers of the police and fire department, and your school director had to take top priority. After that you could add friends that you contact on a regular basis if you had the plan allowing ten names.

Hi Louise,   **April 12, 2010**

Finally have the dates figured out . . . . We fly out the 6th. We are scheduled to arrive in Sofia the afternoon of the 7th (Friday). We have a walk around the hotel area and dinner is on our own that night.

The 8th we get a motor coach tour of Sofia that evening we get dinner and the folklore show. Perhaps you could join us on that if you would like. On Sunday we can explore Sofia on our own. You can show us around or that's when the optional tour is to the Rila Monastery.

On Monday the 10th I thought we were leaving, but it looks like that is the day we can tour on our own again or take the optional tour to Plovdiv and the Valley of Roses.

If you need to get back on Sunday night, we will do that tour. On the 11th we fly to Bucharest and have some time there and get on the ship the 12th and continue our excursion on the Danube River.

Love, LeAnne

Hi LeAnne,   **April 13, 2010**

Not sure yet what time I can get to Sofia on Friday, 8 PM I think. There's a chance I could get there earlier. You will probably be tired when you arrive. If I make it by 8, we could meet and have dinner and/or dessert together. I made my reservation at The House which is near the NDK, as is the Hilton. So we'll be within easy walking distance from each other.

It'll be interesting to see what they plan to show you on the bus tour; hopefully it includes the Boyana Church and the history museum. Those are a bit further out from the City Center, at least not walking distance from the Hilton. I imagine the restaurant for Saturday night is The Waterfall, near Vitosha Mountain as they do a folk show. I went there with Belinda on our tour that I arranged. It's a nice show and dinner.

Rila is a lovely monastery in the mountains and if you would like to see it, perhaps I could plan to go along with you. I was there at Christmas time with snow on the ground, and it is very pretty there in the mountains. If you have any other free time, we could consider going to the Sofia Zoo. I have not been, but understand it's quite nice.

I know you'd enjoy the trip to Plovdiv and the Valley of Roses. I just found out today that my medical appointments are Monday, so our schedule should work out okay. When you come back Monday evening, we could meet again Monday night. They have my eye exam scheduled for 5 PM, so I will be spending Monday night in Sofia as that is too late to catch a train back to Topolitsa.

Laura, the PCV from Karnobat just called me. I'm going with her 12th graders to Turkey. We won't get back until sometime on May 6th which is a very celebrated Bulgarian holiday called St. Georges Day, going back to Slavic traditions. When I leave on Friday sort of depends on when I get back on the 6th. It looks like I'll be missing a fair amount of school, but students have tests, and assorted Bulgarian holidays in May. I guess that's usual for spring. May 24th schools celebrate Education and Cultural Day and May 11 the schools remember Cyrus and Methodius, the two monks who are credited with creating the Cyrillic alphabet.

It looks like Debbie will be visiting me in August. I feel very lucky to have your visit and then to look forward to another one later in the summer. In July we have our 1-year in Bulgaria conference. I am still am getting some bug bites. They sure do like me

Everyone here is busy planting their garden, and the cherry trees are in blossom.

Love, Louise

Your plan sounds fine. Whenever you get to Sofia is fine. I'm sure we'll be tired that first night. Actually it takes a few days to adjust, but we will be happy to see you when you come. We're pretty well packed, but there is always the last minute stuff. Have fun in Turkey.

Love, LeAnne

May 6, 2010

Hopefully things will go smoothly and we will see in Sofia tomorrow. That hardly seems possible does it?

Love, LeAnne

I was happy to have dinner with their tour group at The Waterfall and watch the Bulgarian Folk Show and Fire Show. We also had time to visit the Sofia Zoo together, going via bus. We got off a stop too early, but managed to find our way to the back entrance. I also had the wonderful opportunity to join their group on their visit of the Rila Monastery. Their last night in Sofia we enjoyed having pizza and beer together, sitting at one of the many outdoor restaurants on Vitosha Street.

Hi Felicia   April 15, 2010

You had mentioned something about an event in Varshets . . . now I can't remember . . . the end of May. Did you get your trip changed with Tricia?

April 15, 2010

Yes, it is the Goat Milk Festival the 21–25 of May. Maybe you could make a long weekend of it and visit during this time. Here is the link, I knew there was something I wanted to send you while you were on vacation and could not remember – *http://novakultura.org/goat-milk/en/*

Tricia and I did change our tickets, so I plan to be here. It cost me more just to change the tickets than they were originally, so I hope I do participate and enjoy this festival.

Felicia

Hi Grace,   April 28, 2010

The Internet is acting up and electric seems to go on and off, but the lilacs and tulips are blooming so that is good.

I'm sorry to hear that your job continues to give you so much stress. That is difficult.

Many days in my career I felt at a loss, or if I could handle it all. Life certainly throws us loops. Even here in the Peace Corps it happens. Last night I talked with another volunteer two hours. She too is frustrated as it seems that Peace Corps / Bulgaria doesn't consider much the unique circumstances of older volunteers or look at our life skills, placement, and other concerns of those of us past 55.

Today she is going into Sofia and talking to one of the older staff members about it. She has wanted, like me, to be in the Peace Corps for many years, but has many frustrations about her placement. I'm doing okay and now with springtime and with several activities on the calendar it seems okay. But certainly village life is pretty quiet. What is an older woman to do in the evenings, but stay home read and knit?

I'm going with a Peace Corps Volunteer from a neighboring town and her 12th grade class to Turkey. Many seniors have a school trip, and this volunteer thought of me and the school approved the idea. But Peace Corps saw it as a vacation, even though through the school I'm seen as a chaperon.

After that my sister and her husband are coming. They are on an excursion with a tour group.

Sofia was offered as an extension trip for three days. I'm happy about that.

I'm not sure what the summer will bring.

Take care of yourself Grace; you are such a special person with so many wonderful gifts. Please keep in touch and write soon again,

Love, Louise

Hi Nikolai   **May 7, 2010**

It has been a long time since I have heard from you. Are you still immersed in all your research work? It would be wonderful to see and talk to you again. Has your book been published?

I hope that maybe this summer you will have a little free time. I went with Laura (PCV at Karnobat) and some of her 12th class on their excursion to Turkey. It was interesting but very exhausting. Several days we were on the bus more than 12 hours

I was surprised that the students were allowed to drink beer on the bus. Fortunately, they could not smoke, but a few of the older adults did. The bus stopped several times so that the smokers could smoke.

We had one night in Istanbul, and then went near Bodrum. Laura and I took a paddle boat out on the Marmara Sea. The students went to a discotheque and I again was surprised how late they were allowed to stay out. Then we went to Pamukkale and Ephesus. I enjoyed the history.

Today I travel again. This time to Sofia as my sister and her husband are coming with a tour group to visit Eastern Europe. Sofia was offered as a special extension tour for three days. It will be so good to see them. Then I have some medical appointments and plan to help Brandon. He is a Respond Peace Corps Volunteer and is only here for five months to help with a few special library projects in Sofia.

I'm still taking language lessons with Ivanka and also visiting and talking with her adult class and several other language teachers with their adult language classes.

If you are at all free any of the days I'm in Sofia, May 11-14, please call or text me. It would be great to talk to you again and hear about your projects

Louise

Hi Hazel,   **May 17, 2010**

Hope all is well with you. I'm sitting here waiting for news from my son and his wife about the baby. Last night we talked briefly. The baby is arriving four weeks early. So while sitting here anxiously waiting, I thought I would do some checking on fares and ideas for our summer trip. It seems that the train travel to Vienna is rather booked already; a few openings but not a lot. It seems early to me, but that could be a very popular route.

I heard from Jon, another PCV, that flying from Budapest into Burgas is much cheaper than into Sofia. I did a quick check this morning and he is right. A WIZZ air shows flights for $67 from Budapest to Burgas, compared to over $200 into Sofia. Also, I am thinking that trying four cities may be too ambitious for the time we have, so working on taking out Berlin and trying the dates with the following agenda: July 16, Fly Sofia to Prague; July 19, Train from Prague to Vienna; July 22, Train from Vienna to Budapest; July 27, Fly Budapest to Burgas (This may not be available, so perhaps July 26) WIZZ Air flies only certain days to certain cities. We could enjoy the beach in Burgas and on Tuesday you could take the express train to Sofia and I'd go back to Topolitsa.

I'd like to get flights booked, and possibly the train in May as I know summer is very popular. I would put it on my credit card and then you could pay me at our conference in Vratsa in July. After I have the flights and train booked, I'd work on lodging.

Let me know what you think, Louise

Dear Friends,   **May 26, 2010**

I'm back to Topolitsa. It took exactly 12 hours. I took the train as usual to Sofia. I caught the slow train at 7 AM to Karnobat. That is usually only about thirty minutes. Then I wait for the 8:30 train that will take me to Sofia. If it is on time it arrives at the main Sofia train station about 2:45

PM. I walked over to the bus station. There are over 25 different bus companies that have counters here. There are only two companies that have buses that go to Varshets. I bought only a one-way ticket as I wasn't sure exactly what time I'd be returning on Monday.

The bus from Sofia to Varshets takes about an hour. It's a pretty little tree-lined town, which used to be a big resort town with a famous spa. It still has a spa, and now is getting some new hotels. During Communist times it was the place where leaders were sent for their vacation. Felicia was there to meet me at the bus stop. It was rather a dinghy looking building as many are in the towns that have seen better days.

It was a long school weekend and we wanted to attend the Goat Milk festival. It really has nothing to do with goats. It's more like an arts festival. We watched an excellent documentary movie on women who have to leave their families to work abroad to earn money. It was filmed in Varschets.

We also went to Belogradchik. This is where the famous fortress is located included in the rock formations. It was up for a nomination into one of the new *7 Wonders of the World*. Sadly it didn't make it. It is very interesting and involves lots of climbing. James, another PCV, who lives about two hours from Varshets also came in for the weekend.

It was a bit complicated to make all the connections to go to Belogradchik. We – James, Felicia, and I – boarded the 6:10 AM bus to Montana, the bigger nearby town. At Montana, we took another smaller bus on the windy curvy road to Belogradchik. It reminded me of the road to Ouray in Colorado. We arrived around 9 AM. It was cloudy, but we had hopes for the sun to break through. We found an open sidewalk cafe and bought a cheese sandwich and espresso at the window. We followed the signs through town to take us to this historic spot, known as Belogradchik. We had a wonderful day climbing up the rocks and seeing the mountain views. From the top you can view Serbia. Fortunately we got some pictures just before the rain came. We made it back around 8:30 PM in time to walk around Varshets and had dinner at a lovely outdoor restaurant.

While in that region Felicia and I also went to the Klisurski Monastery which is fairly close by to Varschets. There was no public transportation. The road was narrow and windy, with no shoulder to walk on, so we called a taxi for the ride of about three kilometers.

The new group of volunteers has arrived, and six are having their language classes in Varschets. I met five of the six. I was happy to meet Naomi, an older volunteer about my age from Galveston, Texas. She was very nice. During her career she did testing in schools. As she was not a teacher, she will be placed in youth development.

This morning I went on the earliest bus available from Varschets. It took almost three hours to get to Sofia. After that I caught the train from

Sofia going to Karnobat. We sat one and a half hours on the train track somewhere between those cities waiting for a different engine. I thought I'd miss the last train from Karnobat into Topolitsa. Fortunately it waited for me, I told the conductor and she called, so that was good. I can't believe my luck; this is the second time that a conductor called another conductor and they held the train for me. Lucky American, that's me. It is very warm here. Time to see what I have to eat. Back to school tomorrow.

Love, Louise

From online newspaper – Sofia:

"The Bulgarian natural phenomenon, the Belogradchik rocks, has been placed on the New 7 Wonders of Nature Reserve List where they currently rank second. The first temporary reserve place is held by the Devil City in Serbia. The New 7 Wonders of Nature is the second campaign organized by the Swiss non-profit New 7 Wonders Foundation.

The final announcement of the New 7 Wonders of Nature is scheduled for 2011.

The Belogradchik Rocks, located near the northwest Bulgarian town of Belogradchik, are miraculous sandstone and limestone rock formations of up to 200 meters in height with various shapes resulting from erosion. They form a strip which is 30 kilometers in length and 3 kilometers in width in the northwestern part of the Stara Planina (Balkan) Mountain (translation Old Mountain).

Every single rock is named after a real object that it resembles. The rock range varies in color. The Belogradchik Rocks were declared a natural landmark in 1949. The ancient Belogradchik fortress is also located among the rocks."

LIBRARY COLLECTION DEVELOPMENT

Libraries provide a great service for all the people in a nation. The library here in Sofia is a treasure of resources for teachers of English in Bulgaria. Keeping it up-to-date and current is a valuable resource as teachers in Bulgaria reach out to teach the children of this free nation. Libraries around the world serve their communities in many different capacities. They offer to the residents in their region a variety of materials that many people otherwise would not have access to due mainly to budget restraints and storage space.

A comprehensive library offers material to teachers in the classroom, for students, residents for personal use and for professional development in a specialized field. Whether a library is for teachers in Bulgaria who are teaching English or in a scientific field the same criteria apply. Over the years libraries have acquired many different types of materials in addition to books. These include maps, games, and multi-media to name a few. Multi-media especially has proven to be a difficult acquisition to keep up-to-date. As formats changed over the years, libraries have been forced to also keep up-to-date, and acquire the same material over and over again, but in a different format. To keep a collection relevant is very expensive.

The most popular format in the multi-media is the DVD and the CD. As the DVD is geographically formatted even acquiring these from the wrong manufacturer can present a problem for the patron to use on his home or school equipment. The CD does not have the same geographic format set-up.

Also, much of the material that a library acquires is in the form of teaching or documentary information. Over a decade the presentation of this type of information often changes. Thus, a VHS (video tape) showing how to teach a science lesson might be presented differently in 2010, than it was presented in 2000. The producer of the original VHS has to write a new script, before it can be offered to a buying market. A producer of educational material especially needs to be aware of current eye appeal for the material that is offered for classroom use.

With popular media, such as cinema movies, the same requirements do not apply. A movie such as *Journey to the Center of the Earth* made in 1998 just needs to be converted to the new format by a producer. A new edition may be made for the cinema screen, but the older edition often remains popular as part of cinema history.

However, due to copyright laws a library is not allowed to take one media and convert it with its own equipment to the new format. A new purchase must be made. Keeping old out-dated styles of media serve no practical purpose for a library. Only if the old equipment is kept and maintained so that the media can be viewed does it serve any real purpose.

If the copyright law was not the issue, the cost of conversion for materials and labor would be prohibitive for most libraries. Also, in a conversion, many of the old formats have scratches and other worn marks so that a copy is often defective. It is far better to purchase new materials in the new format.

Materials held by a library need to be presented in a modern format. With the spread of technology libraries come under more and more scrutiny and need to showcase their materials in much of the same way as a bookstore or a pharmacy. People who visit a library are not often acquainted with the material that a library owns, so displaying some of the material to the patron in a user-friendly way helps the patron become acquainted with the various items that a library has to offer.

Libraries have a unique method for cataloging their material. It is arranged by subject. Unless a patron knows of this arrangement, it can be difficult for a patron to find the needed material. Having some of the items "face out" or on a special display rack can help a patron more easily locate the type of material he/she is looking for.

Magazines are often popular materials for libraries to have. To have a few of the magazine titles face out like at a newsstand helps the patron become acquainted with the titles that a library has on hand. Multiple copies, or back issues can be placed in canisters for easier retrieval.

Weeding / keeping relevant material. A modern library needs to stay relevant to serve its patrons. In order to stay relevant an annual or bi-annual review of the materials on the shelf is necessary.

The following criteria can be used as material is reviewed: Is the information still accurate? What is the date of the material? Has the material been used by a patron in the last 5years? Are newer editions of the material available? How many multiple copies are needed for patrons to use? Is the material damaged in some way? Underlined? Hand written marks? Does the library have many other similar materials that are newer? Is the material worn so that repairing it is more costly than a new copy?

Libraries around the world provide a resource to help citizens stay informed on past and current events. It is a treasure for free people everywhere.

PEACE CORPS LEGACY PROJECT

18 May 2010

I was accepted as a PC Volunteer about the same time I was retiring from a 40 plus year career in education as a teacher, public library director and college library director. Within a span of a month I retired from San Juan College where I had served for over ten years as the college library director, rented out my home in New Mexico, drove over 1,000 miles to California in my van to visit my son and his wife and then flew to D.C. to join the B-25 group of Peace Corps Volunteers to serve in Bulgaria. Earlier in the spring I had driven over 400 miles to visit my youngest son in Boulder, Colorado, where he helped me shop for a sleeping bag and other essential Peace Corps necessities. My daughter came down from Boston to join me in D.C. and met me along with the other volunteers gathering at the Holiday Inn the night before we were flying to Sofia.

There are many stories I have to tell, but I will settle on three to show some of the activities and events that made Bulgaria such an amazing experience for me.

After our ten weeks of language immersion, we were given our assignment: my contract said teaching English in Topolitsa, a village school of about 120 students and a village population of about 1,000. I found it on the map and saw that it was about 40 miles from the Black Sea.

I arrived there the end of July. There were not many folks around at that time.

Many of the people were either working in their big vegetable gardens or on a holiday. The school director and all the other teachers lived in the neighboring town of Aitos. No one seemed to speak any English and my Bulgarian was not very good. I made it a point to walk around the village every day and get acquainted and practice my Bulgarian.

The school director, Dora came to the school almost every day and together we practiced. She wanted to learn English better and I needed to be more fluent in Bulgarian.

Dora mentioned that the students would be going to camp. Where was this camp? How long? I was filled with questions. Now I realize the details were still getting worked out, but I did not understand this "last minute" style of preparation. I did learn that it was to be on the Black Sea, we would go via bus and about 30 students were going and it was for six nights.

The bus arrived about 8 AM on the morning of our departure. I had met some of the students in late June on my initial visit to Topolitsa, but most of them were new faces to me. The students were around 12 – 14 years old. I was welcomed as I got on the bus, but conversation was limited. I thought my director was going, but she announced that if possible, she would come later in the week. I was so surprised. I had not talked to any of the regular teachers except on the day of my site visit in June. I was aware that most of them could not speak to me in English. My counterpart was a sweet woman, but was more comfortable speaking Russian than English. Oh my! This would be quite a camping experience.

We stayed at a small family hotel up in the mountain overlooking the Black Sea. There were several students who knew a little English and somehow I managed. The teachers invited me to join them in the evening around the pool as the students danced. I introduced UNO to them and it became a card game we played back in Topolitsa whenever we had some free time.

The second day I was very happy to meet Sveta. She was the daughter of a colleague and a student at the University in Sofia. She spoke English very well. She explained to me a number of the logistics of camp life, including the walk down each mid-day to the town center. This gave the students of the village a chance to dress up, do some shopping and explore a world outside of village life. I had not brought a dress along as I didn't think of dressing up as part of camp life.

I found out how important "dressing up" was to Bulgarians. A bit of jewelry, fancy shoes, new hairdo and a nice dress made them all feel good about themselves. While the camping experience was unlike what I had experienced in the states, it was a chance for me to get to know the students outside the classroom, experience Bulgarian culture and to top it off, have a chance to enjoy the beach and swim in the Black Sea. Life was certainly going to be different for me in the next two years.

Another memorable weekend was the Weaving Workshop in Chiprovtsi. This is a town renowned for its finely woven rugs. This interested me as I was coming from New Mexico and the Navajo rug traditions. This was arranged by the PCV in Chiprovtsi. We stayed with a woman who ran a guest house and also was an excellent weaver. She showed us the basics of how a loom is set up and we all tried our hand at making a woven bookmark. She had exquisite rugs all around her house. She served us traditional Bulgarian meals and was willing to show us how to make them ourselves.

Weaving rugs was a cottage industry throughout the village. I had always hoped to return to visit it again, but transportation was quite involved. I had to travel on the slow train to Yambol, then the fast train to Sofia (already seven hours) then catch a bus to Montana and then another bus to Chiprovtsi. Using public transportation at the beginning of my Peace Corps time was a challenge to me. I had heard stories of going to the wrong town, finding your bus just left and other mis-adventures. I generally asked a lot of questions, and tried to find a person who could speak some English to make sure that I was going on the right bus headed in the right direction.

One more special day I want to share with you is the Rose Festival Parade in Kazanluk. My language teacher Ivanka taught English at the technical high school in Aitos and a colleague of hers was planning on taking her students in agriculture to the festival.

The group was leaving on the 6 AM fast train from Aitos on the Saturday morning, I stayed overnight in Aitos as the fast train did not stop in Topolitsa. We arrived in Kazanluk before 9 AM. They wanted to take the students out to the fields where the rose pedals were being picked. This was about a thirty minute trek outside of town. It was a lovely day in early June.

There were many folks out in the fields picking roses. Many were dressed in Bulgarian traditional costumes. The horses and donkeys were also decorated. Dances were performed in the big parking lot. Several bus loads of tourists from Japan were also there. Georgi Pervanov, the President of Bulgaria spoke briefly and Miss Bulgaria was formally introduced to the crowd.

Many photos were taken. After the festivities out in the fields, we walked back into town and stopped at the Rose Museum to learn how the pedals are converted into oil. Then it was time for the parade. There were many folks here to watch the festivities and artisans and other vendors were set up in the center of the town. It was the biggest crowd I had been in since coming to Bulgaria.

We agreed to split up and meet at the train station as there were many events to see including the Thracian Ruins on the other side of town. The Bulgarians had built an exact replica of a Thracian Tomb that was discovered near the end of World War II. It was amazing. While I was reading about it, Ivanka called to me to "come quickly."

Her friend, an artist and teacher worked at the Museum on special occasions. They were going to give a special tour to some visitors from Japan to go inside the "real" Thracian tomb. If we hurried, she could arrange for us to also see it.

We indeed hurried. We had to go in a secure gated area, and take off our shoes, leave our camera and backpack and put on a white gown. Only five people at a time were permitted to enter this special area. While the duplicate tomb was done very well, the experience of being in a tomb 5,000 years old was breathtaking to me. The colored paintings on the wall were so accurately drawn. There were paintings of horses, paintings of servants and the king and his chariot. It took my breath away. I was fortunate to have traveled to many historic places in Bulgaria, but to be able to stand in this room with these ancient paintings stands out as one of the highlights of my time in Bulgaria.

After we came out of the tomb we realized that we still had two hours before the train was to leave. Ivanka mentioned that it had been a long time since she had been to the Shipka Monastery. We checked the bus schedule and found out that we had just missed the last bus. What to do? As there were several of us, a taxi was suggested and we could share the cost. We found a taxi in the center of town and within twenty minutes he had driven us up the road to the big parking lot next to the Monastery. It is a beautiful monastery set on the top of the mountain. As it was nearing 5 PM we were in time to hear the bells chime.

The taxi took us back to Kazanluk. We bought a "duner" for a quick bite to eat as we headed back to the train station. A "duner" is a favorite Bulgarian fast food for lunch or dinner. They are found in most Bulgarian towns usually as a "pick-up" food, rather than a sit down diner. They have a big slab of meat, usually pork or beef hanging on a big hook. The cook slices three or four thin pieces. It is put into a thin piece of bread, similar to a tortilla. Then there is a variety of other fillings you can choose depending on how much you want to spend. French fries are usually put on the top with white cheese. The cost generally is 3 lev for a small *duner* and generally 5 lev for a big one.

One more notation about the day, everyone met at the station around 6:45 PM to catch the train back to Aitos. We waited and waited. Most of the time trains in Bulgaria were on time, but for some reason this train was very late. Eventually we found out that it would not come until after 9 PM. The copper wire somewhere between Kazanluk and Sofia had been cut; the line needed to be repaired before the train could continue on the track. It was nearly midnight before we made it back to Aitos. It was truly a memorable day.

POLICIES

Hi LeAnne,   **May 30, 2010**

I am sometimes so frustrated, but not sure what to do about it. Some of the Peace Corps policies seem quite ridiculous as several of us discussed it last weekend. It's hard to understand how they handle their placement and why all the adjustments seem to be put on the side of the PCV, rather than have a discussion with the site person. I think it's harder on us older volunteers with experience, as often we don't seem to be placed where our skills are put to their best use. A few of us wonder, is it more of a problem here in Bulgaria or is this a PC problem generally? For now, I will just try to manage and see what this week brings.

I spent a good part of yesterday with Vesala. She is the bilingual high school teacher from Aitos. Most weekends Vesala teaches English to groups of adults in the community. Several times now I've visited her classes and spoke to the students and answered their questions.

This coming week I'll visit another adult class in Aitos. More people there seem interested in learning English than in the village. I took the train into Aitos in the morning. Vesala has a car and she offered to take me into Burgas. We only had the morning in Burgas, but she knew I was interested in getting a keyboard. I had never bought one before. I thought it would help me through some of the long dry spells here. It was just luck that we arrived at the second music store in Burgas just as the owner was arriving. We were about ready to leave. The store was supposed to open at 10, but it was almost 11 before he came. I bought a Yamaha. I have to learn out how to use it. He had one model that played more like a piano, but it costs way too much money. Having this one at least will give my fingers some exercise and I can twiddle away in the evenings.

Milka, my landlady is often gone, but last weekend when I came back from Varchests she was worried that I had gone back to the U.S. I always tell her when I'm going and when I'll return, but due to the school holiday and the bus schedule I came back a day later than first planned. She even had asked some of the school kids. They were asking me if I had gone back to the U.S. over the weekend I don't understand such perception of time and distance. Milka left again the next day

This morning I attempted to tack up some screening. I bought part of a roll of screening and scissors in a hardware store in Aitos. I had to buy the screening by the foot and cut it to fit my small windows that open up on the top. They are about twenty inches wide and fifteen inches long and open by tilting inward. I can't seem to get very many of the tacks into the plastic that's around my windows. I also used some 3M tape but that doesn't seem to stick to the screen very well. Hopefully it will stay up and help keep some flies out.

I wore the short denim skirt that you gave me yesterday. It looked really nice on me. It's in the high 70s today. Last night it rained and it is still quite humid. Tomorrow I'll work on some Peace Corps reports.

Love, Louise

Hi Laura,   **May 30, 2010**

Just wondering if you could make it over here today? I had a chance to do some shopping yesterday morning. Vesala took me to Burgas and guess what? I found a keyboard I would love you to see it and try it out. If you can't make today, tomorrow would be fine too.

Our money is in our account.

I also bought some hot dogs and we could celebrate Memorial Day How are the kittens? I've been trying to hang some screening in my windows. I'm not sure how long the tacks will hold as there is nothing much to tack into, but I need my windows open.

Big hug, Louise

Each month the PC office put money in our account. We often emailed each other when it arrived, so that we knew we could go to the bank machine and withdraw our funds. This was also how we got reimbursed for our medical, travel to meetings, and Peace Corps related events. Sometimes it took several months to get reimbursed and made it difficult at times to handle our other expenses.

Dear Ginny,   **June 1, 2010**

It was so good to get your letter today. It seemed like a long time since I had heard from you. I was thinking of writing you yesterday – actually all week – and just didn't have the time or energy to do it.

Even though I'm not terribly busy, I get mentally exhausted. It is very difficult for me at times to stay positive, and not get discouraged about what it is I'm doing here. Some days are especially frustrating as I don't know what's expected of me. Also, sometimes when I am teaching I realize I get just plain tired. I will be very ready to retire next year.

Every day at school my schedule seems different. Now the students are having lots of tests. Generally the regular teachers give the tests; they see that as their job so then I have free time. What do I do? Well, it depends. I do a lot of reading. I have quite a few books to read, some history, mystery and some magazines. I ordered a news magazine to come, but so far I've had only one delivery. Four magazines came at once, but now I haven't received any for a month. Mail service over here is erratic.

I also have been knitting. I made a patchwork baby blanket (36 squares of 3 different colors) for the new baby. Marcus and Stacey's baby arrived May 17. They named him Milo. They are both very excited. Stacey is taking a six month unpaid leave from her job.

I am thinking of flying back over Christmas to see the new baby. I even thought of going this summer, but that would be difficult to arrange with the Peace Corps. Christmas is over the halfway point. I probably would not make it to Pittsburgh as I will only have a week total in the U.S. Next summer when I'm finished with my Peace Corps commitment I will be sure to come to Pittsburgh.

Today I have to go into Aitos. Yesterday we had a big electrical storm and a part on my computer shorted out. I had it on a special surge protector but it was a very big surge of electricity. I can still use Word, but I cannot connect to the Internet. I know it could have been worse. Whenever I can't connect online I feel very isolated here. I get lonesome and am counting the months until I return to the U.S. I do some writing in a journal and hopefully this winter I will do more.

Sometimes, I find it frustrating just to figure out what to eat on a daily basis. I eat a lot of bread and yogurt. I don't care for the processed meat. I buy fresh chicken pieces and pork once in a while. It is difficult to bring fresh meat back on the train especially as the weather is getting warmer again. I have found cans of tuna fish at the one market in Aitos. I wish I liked rice more. I do fix potatoes sometimes, and often have a salad.

The weather has become much warmer. Today it is hot and humid. My hair goes completely straight five minutes after I use a curling iron on it. School goes here until June 15. I will help with a summer program, but I think much of July I will be free. I can't travel overnight as it counts as a vacation day. Hopefully the weather will be warm and I will be able to take some day trips and enjoy the beach in Burgas.

I will print this out now and get it ready to mail. Then I will walk to my school and drive with my director into Aitos. All the teachers live there. Sometimes I wish I did also. I have a nice apartment here, but there is little to do in this village. Now that I have the baby blanket knitted, I will go back and work on the ABC quilt. That is hard on my eyes as the stitches are very small. It will take me a long time to finish.

I hope this finds you well dear friend. Even with your bumpy handwriting it is always good to hear from you. May the good Lord bless and keep you always in His loving care,

Louise

Ginny has Parkinson's

TRADITIONS

I had the wonderful opportunity to attend the Rose Festival in Kazanluk. I went with Ivanka and her colleague Tania and some students from the vocational high school in Aitos. We left on the 6 AM train from Aitos and arrived at 8:15. They were a very polite group of students.

From the train station we walked over a mile out of town to see the fields of roses. Dancers were there in picturesque Bulgarian costumes. Lots of picture-taking was done and the weather was great, not too hot, but certainly not cold. Then we walked back to the center of town where a parade was held and saw many vendors selling crafts.

Ivanka's friend, Tricia, lives there and she met us, along with Tricia's young son. We walked all around the center to find a restaurant that had room to seat us. We finally ended up at a lovely outdoor spot away from the center, but closer to the famous Thracian Museum. Tricia's husband and his colleague, who lives in London, joined us. Radostein, Ivanka's boyfriend, was also there. We made a big group. After lunch Tricia's husband and colleague left, and the rest of us went to the Thracian Museum.

There is a copy of the tomb from 5000 BC there for everyone to see. And then lucky us, a friend of Tricia's works at the Museum. She was asked to give a small group a special tour of the original Thracian tomb, which is right next door to the replicate. Lucky us. We were invited to see it also as special guests. It was indeed an honor to go inside this ancient tomb.

The big Iron Gate had to be unlocked, as other tourists looked on. We walked a short distance to a heavy metal door. It was carefully unlocked and pushed open. We entered an empty chamber. The guidelines for entering were explained to us. We had to leave our shoes, purses, back packs, cameras in this chamber. We were given white surgical robes to wear and we had to take off our shoes. We were given booties to slip over our socks or bare feet. We were told that under no circumstances were pictures to be taken. Then we were led down a narrow passageway. After about fifteen feet it opened up into another smaller chamber. It was incredible. There was room for the five of us to stand. We looked at the walls and the dome ceiling. There were horses pulling chariots. Some horses were decorated with garlands. Servants were walking along side the horses. The colors were a mixture of rose, yellow, blue and green. It was the full spectrum of colors. It appeared like a procession of a King, his Queen and his servants.

It was truly amazing to see something over 5,000 years old in such excellent condition. The colors were still vibrant. This tomb had been buried under mounds of dirt for thousands of years. It was discovered during World War II when a bomb exploded nearby. We were in the tomb for about ten minutes. It certainly is the most breathtaking artifact that I've ever seen.

The replica is also very well done. Horses, chariots, animals, servants, king and queen all in color are drawn on the dome ceiling exactly as is found in the original tomb. The area is a circular wall. There are plaques with lots of explanation of the discovery of the tomb and you are allowed to take photos. Someday I hope that I can go back and visit again.

It was already after 4 PM. Ivanka wanted to see Shipka Monastery. It could be seen at a distance from the rose fields. It was too late to catch the bus; I suggested a taxi. With the four of us it would not be too expensive. Seven lev is what I contributed.

We arrived to hear the special five o'clock ringing of the bells. I managed to record it and now have it on my computer. The only down side of the day, the train was two hours late. This was due to someone cutting the copper tubing line somewhere between Kazanluk and Sofia. I didn't know that was the problem at the time, but found this out later.

I was going to take a taxi back to Topolitsa. As it was nearly midnight when we finally returned to Aitos, I decided instead to call Vesala and see if I could stay at her place for the night. I already had stayed there the night before in order to catch the early train. She said she would come and pick me up from the train and I could certainly spend the night at her place. I would take the train back in the morning to Topolitsa. She has become such a wonderful friend.

THIS, THAT AND THE OTHER

June 29 marks the halfway point of PC; from then on it's counting down, fourteen months here, and fourteen months to go.

Today, Dora told me that the Topolitsa teachers were going on an excursion the end of June. She said it would be for two or three days. That would be great. She mentioned something about exploring caves.

An item I have on the calendar is getting my ID renewed. Hopefully, Dora will come with me to do that next Monday to help with translation. Sometimes there is a woman who works there who speaks English, but not always. Our Identity Card needs to be renewed each year that we work here as Peace Corps volunteers. Hopefully it is not as involved to have it renewed as it was to apply last year. It was similar to getting your passport for the first time as you need a lot of family records. This is something you take with you whenever you travel, even for a short distance. It reminds me too of how officials now in the U.S. rely on your car driver's license for identification purposes.

Monday, the music students are going into Burgas to perform traditional dances for a regional competition. It sounds like a very big affair as singers and dancers come not only from Bulgaria but from other European countries, including Russia. Also, I still don't know about the Peace Corps special project. This needs to be written up yet this month, but first I must meet with Dora and get her suggestions on how we make this a successful project for the school.

It is to be a collaborative project with myself, the Peace Corps administration in Sofia and the school here in Topolitsa. I have wanted to meet with her but she is always busy. This past month I worked with her on the school website. She had done much of it and asked for my help with the information provided in English. It is a good website and contains lots of history of the school, the curriculum of all the classes and names of teachers and the other staff. I found it very interesting.

I would like to review it again as I see some errors in the translation. It is on her computer so I need to work in her office for the review. I spent time on the translation of the web page of the history of the school into English. Another time I stayed until after 6 PM doing some editing. I had to hurry because that night I was going into Aitos. I've worked on it several times, but I would like to go over one more time and do some editing. It can be found on the school web site, *www. ousvetlina.com*

One more thing about today, as I was walking home from school, Milka and her daughter Trinea saw me. They were in Trinea's new van and wanted me to get in. I mentioned I had yogurt in my bag, but they said it was just a short while, so not to worry about my food. I hopped in the front seat. We were going out to the cherry fields. Milka has three acres outside of Topolitsa that is planted with assorted fruit trees and vegetable crops. The cherries hung low on the trees. I could have picked buckets full. I picked one bucket full, plus I picked some apricots. They grow apricots and peaches to make *Rakia*.

On the way back to the house, they started talking about Skype. Milka's grandson, Dimeter lives in Spain, with his father. The father is Milka's son. The grandson, Dimiter speaks English. We managed to get hold of him in Spain with Milka's telephone. However, he didn't have a microphone with his Skype so we could not connect through my computer to use Skype. That would be less expensive than through the telephone connection. We agreed to try and connect via Skype chat next Wednesday morning. He was very polite and interesting to talk to on the phone. Dimiter mentioned that he was 27 years old. In Bulgaria, it is the custom to give your age right after you are introduced to someone. I have found this tradition awkward at times. Nikolai and I joked about it, as I said I did not want people to find out that I was this old woman. That is why I started telling people around me that I was 55 years old, not 65 years old. This tradition is found more in the villages than in the cities these days.

Oh, I have not mentioned that Marcus and Stacey have arranged for me to visit them over Christmas to see Milo. They will buy my plane ticket. I am so lucky with my children. They are special and are certainly thinking of me. I will fly Sofia to Frankfurt to San Francisco and then on my return have two days in Boston to visit Gretchen. I will fly from Boston to Frankfurt and back to Sofia. Then it'll be seven months more to the finish of the term. I wonder if any of our group will extend another year. The weather has turned beastly hot. There doesn't seem to be a happy medium. It is over 80 degrees in my apartment today.

GRADUATION

Hi Ivanka,   **June 16, 2010**

Last night was a big party in Aitos for the 8th grade class graduation. It was very nice. It ended very late. On Friday I am going with Vesala and her students on an outing.

I will be happy to visit your class again, perhaps next week (23 or 25) or the following Wednesday. If you have the equipment I could show my photo CD. But I could do that also later in the summer. In the summer I hope to have lessons June 23, 25 and 30 and then we can review the schedule for July.

Stay cool. It is very hot here in Topolitsa, Louise

Dear Siblings,   **June 16, 2010**

The weather is starting to feel better. There was thunder again today and rain. It's been so very hot. Last night was the big 8th grade class celebration dinner and dance. The students were all very dressed up. I'll send photos. It was like prom night back in the States. The students are fifteen years old as they start school when they are seven years old. They looked really nice and all were very polite. The boys all wore shirts and ties. The girls were in long formal dresses and had their hair fixed in very stunning styles.

Before we left for the restaurant there were many pictures taken at the school. Parents and friends came from all around the area. This was by far the most people I've seen gathered in one spot in the village. Then the parents took their 8th grader to Aitos. A small van was there to bring the teachers to the restaurant in Aitos. The dinner and dance was at the Old House restaurant. It was the restaurant I had taken David and guests over Christmas and Belinda in spring. It is a very attractive old historic house that the Communists used as their headquarters in this area. The original Bulgarian family now has it back and they restored it into this very distinct restaurant. I had not realized what a big event this was going to be. It was a very nice affair and I'm glad that I had dressed up for it.

We were served a special *shopska salada*; it had tasty small pieces of ham and other assorted vegetables in it. *Rakia* was there for the teachers to drink. We could order our dinner off the menu. I'm not sure who picked up the restaurant tab. I think it was the parents as a thank you gift to the teachers. The parents didn't stay. The tradition is that this affair is for the students and teachers. I appreciated being included in this very special affair.

The music started at 8 PM and went until 1:15 AM. The students are great dancers. It was all very loud music which they love. There is a special Bulgarian rhythm which is hard to describe. You move around on the floor a lot. It's called *chalga* or pop folk music. It's probably good I don't understand too many of the lyrics. There was a small AC unit in the room where we ate, but not quite strong enough to really stay comfortably cool with all those gyrating bodies. Luckily I was sitting pretty close to the AC. I stepped outside for a few minutes to get some night air. I came back to Topolitsa with a set of 8th-grade parents. They were there to pick me up and their son at 1:15 AM.

Now we'll see how the summer unfolds. The teachers have some meetings, but don't think I have to go. My director will tell me the information. I think she feels it's just too complicated to do all that translating at the meeting and will inform me separately of the items that directly affect me.

This weekend I am going to Verara, a village on the Black Sea with an English class from Aitos. This is Vesala's Saturday adult class that has finished a full year of weekend English classes. It includes Standi, who co-owns the Internet shop that I use. Leko, his main technician on the road also was in the class. I stop at their shop each month to pay my Internet bill and have brought over my laptop several times for them to service. They both know how much I depend on it. The other owner, Jorge is also very nice, but usually not there. They seem very up-to-date with all the latest technical devices.

I am not sure if I will pick any more cherries. I still have an abundance of cherries in my small refrigerator, and I'm out of canning jars. I canned around 20 jars, all assorted sizes. I froze one small bag. If I had a bigger freezer I could freeze some. These cherries are very tasty.

That's all for now. Stay cool, Louise

CAVES

Hi Louise,   **June 25, 2010**

On Monday the van will leave about 7:00 from Aitos and then come to Topolitsa. We will be there around 7:20. Please wait for the bus at school. Bring comfortable shoes and warm clothes. We will visit some of the most beautiful caves – Devil's Throat and Yagodinacave.

We will also visit Asenovgrad Fortress and Bachkovski monastery. Excursion will cost around BGN 50.

Dora

Musings from my Journal:

Dora had arranged a van for this special end of the school year excursion for the teachers from Topolitsa. A few teachers who taught in Aitos also came with us. They stopped to pick me up in Topolitsa about 7:30 in the morning.

First we drove to Plovdiv and then on to Asenograd and Asen's Fortress. It is a famous fortress dating back to medieval times set up high in the Rhodope Mountains. Some researchers identified it as Petrich. The road to the fortress wound up and around, higher and higher on hairpin curves. We parked at a small parking lot close to the top. I had not expected to have to climb up a high mountain to reach the fortress and to see the preserved chapel at the top. Thankfully I had worn my sneakers.

The path to the top was narrow and steep. The sun was now out brightly and it was getting quite warm outside. Some of the teachers had worn heels. I could not imagine climbing up the mountain top in heels. You could see the fortress at the top. It was a beautiful view. It is on a high rocky ridge of the Rhodope Mountains. It was conquered by the armies of the Third Crusade. The Church of the Holy Mother of God is from the 12th century. It has been recently restored and icons can be seen painted on the walls, like frescoes.

After Asen's Fortress we drove to the beautiful nearby Bachkovo Monastery which is one of the largest and oldest Eastern Orthodox monasteries in Europe founded in 1083 by Prince Gregory Pakourianos. It is on the right bank of the Chepelare River. After walking around the beautiful grounds and courtyard we stopped at vendors for a light lunch as it was time to head on to our next adventure.

The trip to the Devil's Throat Cave was amazing. After the entrance and walking along inside the cave it starts descending. I had a flashlight with me. We walked and walked, further and further down the narrow, sometimes slippery slope. I tried not to think about how far we were descending. There were a few bigger chambers and echoes of voices could be heard. At times I found it hard to keep up with the group. Thankfully, Dora was always behind me. I think she and I brought up the rear. At places you can look down a deep crevice and at other places look up. But when you are really far down, you do not see the light of the outside. Thank goodness for my flashlight. And then when we reached the bottom we walked and walked. We ascended for a short distance and saw a very steep ladder. It went up and up. Oh my. Could I make it to the top?

There was nothing for me to do, but start up the ladder. Up, up, up I went. At the top of this first ladder there was a landing of sorts and a wooden platform to cross over. At that point Dora went ahead of me. I needed to pause and look around. There was one more very high ladder to climb up. I had not realized we had gone down so deep into the cave. That is why it is called Devil's Throat. This cave has a very appropriate name.

I started up the second ladder. Up, up and up until I could see the light come into the cave. It was great to feel the daylight. And when I got to the top and stepped outside there was a small parking lot, but I didn't see anyone around. This was not where we entered the cave. Where was I?

I looked around trying to get my bearings. Then I saw a woman on the nearby road with a basket of food items. I asked her in my broken Bulgarian where the entrance to the cave could be found. I knew the van that we had arrived in was parked at the entrance. She pointed down the road. It really wasn't a long walk, but I didn't know that at the time. After about five minutes I heard voices and saw some familiar faces. The group of teachers who included me in this fantastic adventure were sitting on some benches having a cool drink. It was an experience to remember.

That evening we had a fantastic dinner with chicken roasted on an outdoor spit. We sat outside near the fire and sang songs. After we had finished eating and drinking folks started singing. Someone had a CD player and put on Bulgarian folk music. People stood up and started dancing variations of the *hora* on the grass. It was a great way to end the evening.

The next day would be another adventure, with another cave and then we would be driving back to Topolitsa and Aitos ready to start the summer break from school. What a difference a year makes. I can't believe all the places that I've had an opportunity to travel to here in Bulgaria. I decided to make a list of the towns where meetings or workshops have been held by the Peace Corps that we were required to attend besides Sofia:

Sliven, Kazanluk, Plovdiv, Vratsa, Burgas, Chiprovtsi, Borovan.

Other towns that I've had a chance to visit on excursions with teachers from Bulgaria include:

Arbanasi, Asenograd, Melnik, Sandanski, Bansko, Razlog, Stara Zagora, Shipka, Nova Zagora, Tryavna, Pliska, Veliki Presslav, Nesebar, Balchik, Pomorie, Chernomorets, Sozopol, Varara, Malko Tarnovo, Antopol, Kotel, Sveti Vilas, Varshets, Dragamond, and Koprivshtitsa.

Exploring caves, and seeing beautiful waterfalls, historic monasteries, and gardens, ruins of ancient capitals, mountain towns, beach towns, old industrial towns, new resort towns, and then noted historic towns across the country have all widened my understanding of Bulgaria.

GARDENS

Hello Diana,   **August 7, 2009**

I really enjoyed receiving your letter and all your news. It sounds like you are adapting well.

I think our areas are quite different, and I so do wish that we were closer. I really appreciate your descriptions. You can paint such good pictures with words and drawings. I have the card you gave me in Banitsa decorating my bedroom shelf.

The weather has been very hot here too. Last night it appeared we might get some rain but we did not. There was some lightning and thunder in the distance plus wind.

I can't believe how much fruit I am getting to eat. My landlady loves it. Yesterday when I took my trash downstairs she was working in her garden which is quite a good size as are many gardens here in the village. She also has another garden located outside the village and her daughter has a villa somewhere. When she is outside and sees me she always wants to feed me. So I sat down with her and shared a watermelon. She insisted I eat three big pieces. Oh my, I was full. She also brought me several, two days ago, that I still have to eat. Zucchini has also appeared at my doorstep, along with tomatoes and peppers.

There are also many greenhouses in the village especially on the walk to the train. They look like big entertainment tents. They are white and you can see them on the train as you approach the village from the south. They are filled with peppers, tomatoes, cabbages, and onions . . . vegetables that are harvested by the local villagers and Romani who are hired to come in for the season. Many of them set up tents in a big field near the train station. The vegetables are bagged and then driven to markets in the country and may be taken also to Turkey and Greece, countries which are not that faraway.

Another way for me to tell that I'm approaching Topolitsa on the train is seeing the long row of narrow trees. They look like poplar trees to me, and are called Topol. They are very pretty and very tall trees.

Now the cows are walking down the street pass my house so I know I am in the country. They walk past every night about this time, just like the goats in Banitsa. I haven't yet explored the entire village, but today my director took me to the lone restaurant in the village. It was very nice and not far from the school. Today there was a woman who had just come back from Colorado where her sister lives. She lives in Prague and I don't think speaks Bulgarian, but was visiting a friend in Topolitsa. It always amazes me how small the world is.

Please keep in touch and continue to tell me about your life in Lom. Best, Louise

(Lom is a city located on the Danube River in the north central area of Bulgaria.)

Dear Siblings,   **June 17, 2010**

Today I'm going to try and make some cherry jam. First I have to pit the cherries, not my favorite job, but I sure like the cherries. I had not thought of drying the cherries. Maybe I'll give it a try. I'd still have to pit them, but maybe I can start with one pan. Milka wants me to pick more from the trees in her garden, but the last batch had many bugs (larvae). While I guess it doesn't hurt to eat the larvae, it doesn't excite me too much to get my protein that way. I noticed the ones I picked out in her big gardens outside of Topolitsa seemed better. I know cherries are out there, but it's too far for me to walk in this heat.

She is gone again to Serbia to get more cigarettes. The tax on cigarettes went up here this spring, and so she is doing a booming business. People come here early in the morning, and late in the evening. When they see my lights on they holler up and want cigarettes. I often don't reply, but if they're persistent I holler back, *"nay, yama"* which means something like "she's not here."

I think it takes her almost ten hours one way to travel, but must be worth it to her for the money. It's mainly the Romani who come to the window to buy cigarettes. Besides the Romani who live on the outskirts of this village, many more are now camped outside the village in a big random tent village on the way to the train station.

They're here mainly for the many garden crops. They are probably hired as day help. Horses are tethered to the trees and some of the folks have cows. Children run around, but generally stay in the tent area. They make small camp fires both for heat and for cooking. It is interesting to say the least.

Many of the Romani who live in the village speak their own language. Some know Bulgarian, but not well and that's what makes it difficult for their children in school as the law now requires that schools must enroll them. Also, these students don't have the money to buy the necessary school supplies. My impression is that most of them, while not accepted directly into their homes as family members are seen as important to Bulgaria's economy. As a result the government also has taken the responsibility to see that they are educated and receive healthcare.

I will give you an example: there's one woman who is here a lot helping Milka. She was in Milka's kitchen one cold day and sitting on her kitchen sofa. But when I came in Milka distinctly had her move to a stool, and I was to sit on the sofa

The weather is still warm today, but there is less humidity. I guess the rain helped.

I want to walk over to see if the Post Office is open. My mail is never delivered to my apartment. Sometimes it goes to the school and I can get it there. The Post Office is almost directly across the street from the school so really no problem. Maybe I have some mail. Marcus said he sent me a package.

Love, Louise

July 29, 2010, Summer time in Bulgaria, note to friends.

Today is a bright sunny day. It sure feels good. It is hard now to imagine how cold winter was. The tomatoes are ripe in the garden and lots of green peppers.

Hope that you're all having a good summer. It is always good to hear from you. Please send some photos.

With warm regards, Louise

ENGLISH FOR ADULTS

Letters to siblings, June 20, 2010

I really had a wonderful trip with Vesala and her adult class and their families to the small coastal town, Varvara on the Black Sea. We traveled in her car with another family. On the way we stopped at the big market in Burgas to buy some food for the weekend. All the families had chipped in money. We stayed in a small family hotel, where we could cook meals outside and all eat together. The first night though we went to a restaurant. We waited for all to arrive to go out for dinner that first night. We walked along the path to a big family restaurant. It was about 9 PM before we ordered our food and we were there until after midnight.

Bulgarians love to talk and visit over dinner, so this was not unusual. Last night was cooking on the grill at our family hotel. We had tons of food. Many folks brought food that they had prepared. The celebration went until 2 AM. It seemed almost everyone brought *Rakia* along, or whiskey, or beer. They don't do mixed drinks like Americans. Standi, the Internet businessman loves to spear fish in the Black Sea. He caught a number of fish earlier in the day and was happy to share them. They were grilled and very tasty.

Parents brought their children along to join us for the weekends' activities. In all there were eight children ranging in age from five to fifteen.

All were very well behaved. The group consisted of business associates, some nurses, a doctor, a few secretaries and spouses. There was a wide range of ages. I would estimate from early 20s to an older couple around 60. Thirty people in all came for this weekend celebration. One youngster brought a beautiful Persian Himalayan cat along. It's good to know that there are families with cats as pets as there are many stray cats and dogs roaming around in every village. They are usually hungry and in need of medical attention.

During the day we went to a lovely inlet beach. It was not too crowded and the waves were rolling in so it made for great fun to jump in the waves. Today we went to another beach, not quite as remote so it was more crowded and there was more debris lying around.

I can't believe all the hotels along these coastal towns. The town where we stayed still hasn't been inundated by all these hotels. It has just smaller family hotels.

We also drove down to the border town of Rezovo. The Rezovo River forms the southeastern border here with Turkey and is really a lovely spot. During the Communist era Bulgarians were not allowed to go there as it was all under a border patrol. There is a marker on the side of the road where Bulgarians had to stop. It was rather unsettling as it again was a reminder of the restrictions that the Bulgarians lived under when they were apart of the Eastern Soviet Bloc.

The first day I left my camera in the room, but have I have some pictures from today that I'll download later. I think one of the students will make a CD of photos for me. A few knew enough English so I managed, and tried to follow conversations.

I'm really tired and another big storm arrived just as I got back tonight.
Love, Louise

June 21, 2010
After the big storm last night the weather is very nice here this morning. I did a small load of laundry. Actually given the size of my wash machine I can only do small loads. I am lucky to have a wash machine. A few volunteers still have to do all their laundry by hand. I hang it out on my balcony.

I think I'm going to Burgas today with the students, but I haven't heard from my director. I'll call her in a little while and see if I can figure it out. I need to get my ID card renewed, but it may be too early. It's tricky, as it's only good for a year so has to be good until the end of next July. I heard from one volunteer who tried to renew it last week found out that she was too early. Instead of adding it on to your current expiration date, it's like from the day you renew. Paperwork and forms here seem very convoluted and complicated, but maybe it's because of the language difficulty. Our close of service is scheduled for July 29, 2011. After my trip with Hazel, I will have to go back to Burgas and pick it up and pay for my Lichna Karta. It will allow me to live and work here another year.

Friday I'm going to talk to another English class of adults and show them some of my photos. I wish that I had more of America. When I come back at Christmas I will have to take lots of photos and buy some post cards.

Enjoy your golf games LaVerne and Otto. That is not a real big sport here. Everyone is following the World Cup. Soccer is the big sport here. They know the other sports, but soccer is the passion.

I hope the Post Office is open this morning. Several people mentioned mailing items to me and also now I get *The Week* magazine. So far even though it's a weekly it has come in batches of three at a time. Few people here use the Post Office in the village for mail, but it is where they pay their electric bill, phone bill and I think it's also where the pensioners get their money.

That's good news about Ozge and her citizenship. (Ozge was born in Istanbul and married my nephew.) It should help her with her Visa. Many Bulgarians have trouble getting Visas from the U.S. government to travel to the U.S. I heard of many cases where parents have wanted to come and visit their grown children who now live in the U.S., but the U.S. embassy won't give them a Visa. I think it must be because they think they will then stay in the U.S.

Not everyone wants to live in the U.S., but parents do want to visit their children. One woman I talked to wanted to attend her daughter's wedding, but couldn't because they wouldn't give her a Visa. That has to be very difficult; I feel so bad when I hear these stories and I can't help them.

I heard that the train had problems going into Burgas, due to all the recent rains. Some of the tracks were flooded out.

Love, Louise

ONE-YEAR CONFERENCE

Hi everyone,   **July 3, 2010**

I was going to wait until morning to write, but as it turns out I may be traveling to Sofia tomorrow already. Our Peace Corps conference starts Tuesday late afternoon. It is in Vratsa. I was going to travel on Tuesday morning. Vratsa is nearly three hours north of Sofia so it is a long journey via train and then bus.

Tonight while eating a soft piece of bread with white cheese I felt something hard in my mouth and surprise; it was a piece of my front tooth I can't remember having a crown chip before. This is my front tooth. I've may have had this crown since Pittsburgh days. I've had a crown come off once, or twice, and now this, a broken crown. I'm always concerned about my crowns and can't remember the last time I bit into something remotely hard. I peel apples super thin, slice my carrots, and anything else that seems too hard or chewy I avoid. I'm not sure what caused it. After talking to another volunteer I decided to call Peace Corps 24 Duty Office. It being the holiday weekend thought I might be lucky to get a guard, but as it turns out, the Peace Corps Country Director was there on duty. She listened sympathetically to my account.

Within a half hour the emergency doctor on duty called me back. He is going to try to get me a dentist appointment Monday or Tuesday. This means I would have to travel tomorrow or Monday to Sofia. I would be very surprised to get an appointment by Monday, but Tuesday sounds possible. If I should be able to get in by Tuesday, I travel on Monday. That means, I'll be gone a week from the village, as we have meetings Wednesday through Saturday afternoon. I will come back into Topolitsa next Sunday, July 11.

Some event is going on here tonight as I hear music outside which is very unusual. Usually everything is very quiet in the village when it gets dark outside.

I had a very interesting and worthwhile excursion with the Topolitsa teachers, and a few from Aitos. I'm constantly amazed and impressed with the rich Bulgarian heritage and its beautiful natural beauty. The caves were amazing. A group of them sang songs when we were way down deep into the cave. I will have to look up the caves on Wikipedia. They were amazing.

The day after my excursion with Dora and the Topolitsa teachers I had a trip with Vesala. She drove her car. The first main road, once we left Topolitsa, we were on was awful. I couldn't believe it and neither could she believe how bad the road was. The Topolitsa road is quite bad but this road up the mountain was worse. She had not been on it for a number of years.

She explained that this region gets lots of snow in the winter and probably had not been repaired for several years. It was filled with deep potholes and cars had to zigzag back and forth to manage not to wreck their cars. She told me that insurance companies now have stated that any tire damage or axle damage due to bad roads will not be covered by insurance. Only car wrecks are covered by insurance. The road she took was supposed to be one of the better roads across the mountains, but for 45 kilometers it was covered with huge potholes.

Cars and trucks were all zigzagging around the deep holes. Several cars and trucks were parked on the side of the road, with either damaged tires or maybe even a broken axle.

Finally, after almost two hours of driving on this very rugged road, we were in another district and the road became better. We stopped at two of the ancient Bulgarian capitols, which date back to about 600 to 700 AD. The first one is called Preslav Pliska. We were walking around ruins similar to Ephesus. It was amazing.

We also went to several museums with ceramics, glass and jewelry that were found in excavations. Then Vesala drove us to Balchik where the historic summer palace of the Romanian Queen Marie is located. It has beautiful gardens right on the Black Sea including a desert garden. This is about thirty miles from the Romania border on the Black Sea.

Today we stopped and climbed up to the Aladzha Monastery. It was built in the limestone caves. This was a secret monastery under the Ottoman Empire that helped preserve the Orthodox Church during the 400 plus years of the Ottoman Empire. It reminded me of some of the Indian cave dwellings.

On the drive back Vesala drove along the Black Sea Coast. There are lots of hotels and lovely beaches. It was almost dark when we arrived back in Topolitsa. And now I chipped my tooth. I'm not sure if you'll hear from me for awhile. On Wednesday hopefully I'll be able to use a Peace Corps computer and check email.

Hope that you're all having a great 4th of July, Louise

Hi Louise,

It was good to hear from you. Sorry about your chipped tooth; not a nice thing to happen when you are in a strange country. Hopefully it'll be good as new soon. You seem to be enjoying your travels, although getting around doesn't seem to be very easy. Don and I went to Prague and Budapest in 1994, shortly after the Communist control ended. Some of the people we talked to were not happy about the change. I wonder how they feel now.

Love, Joanne

Letter to my children, July 11, 2010

Well, I'm back in Topolitsa from the Peace Corps conference in Vratsa. It was interesting going back. It seems like ages ago since I was there, and it is just less than a year. The town now appears bigger than what I remembered, but then again we really only went to meetings there and then back to our village. Everything then was so new and strange. It's a pretty train ride from Sofia up to Vratsa. At places there are mountains in the background and then some tunnels through the mountains. For some distance a river follows the train tracks and we went through a few small towns.

I had quite a surprise as when I was on the platform in Sofia. I heard my name called. There was Milka. She is always traveling going to Serbia, but this time I guess she was going to visit a friend who lived in a town north of Sofia. She got on the train with me.

I had bought a 1st class ticket and she had not. She came in my car and sat down next to me. We both knew that when the conductor came to check our tickets that she would have to move. She tried to convince him that she should stay with me. She is quite persuasive. She left. Then she found out that this was an express train and did not stop where she thought it did. Next she talked to a policeman who told her she could stay with me.

It was very hot on the train, and I find it difficult to carry on a long conversation. She got off the train with me in Vratsa. I saw a few of the other volunteers who were also on the train and I walked over to them. Milka went to Information to find out what to do. She was here back in Topolitsa when I came back this morning Sometimes I wonder what it'd be like if I knew what was going on I think she went to a Bulgarian town to see a friend who had a birthday

One late afternoon after our session, Diana, one of my site mates from Banitsa, and I took a bus from Vratsa over to Banitsa. We visited both of our host families. Dora, the widow woman I stayed with last summer was so happy to see us. She's had hip surgery and can't get around very well. Boris, her older married son was also there and seemed mellower than what I remember. It was fun being in the village again.

A few volunteers might come over for my birthday. Not too many of the volunteers have made it to the Black Sea. It's a long way to come for a weekend but hopefully they will make it.

With the new group of volunteers there will be two new women in my region. My first impression is that one is more out-going and the other more reserved. It will be great to have more PCVs in my area.

Laura, in Karnobat is the volunteer I see fairly often. We always find lots to talk about. It was Laura and her students that I traveled six days together on the school excursion through Turkey. Her Bulgarian is very good, which is also a big help to me. I'm going with her this week to get my ID card renewed. It must be done every year before it expires. The date is set from when you renew, so if we do ours July 13 then that could mean that will be our date out of country next year; otherwise we'd have to apply again next July.

Apparently, your close of service date can be anytime within 30 days prior to the official date (COS), which is July 29. The Peace Corps office doesn't want everyone leaving at once. Unless something unforeseen happens that will be my COS date, nearly a year from this week.

I'm getting the itinerary all set with my trip with Hazel. We both see this as our chance to explore some capital cities that we may never see again.

Well, I think the sun is coming back out and so I need to hang up my laundry. I hope this finds everyone well and enjoying your summer.

Big hug to you all, Love, Mom

SUMMER

Note to myself, July 14, 2010

What a week this has been and it's only Wednesday. And now I realize I better write quickly or the storm will appear and I again will lose the Internet and electric.

A brief summary of my exciting week so far:

Sunday: Return home from conference in Vratsa. I did get to go to Banitsa and visit with my *baba* and her son Boris. They were both so happy to see me.

Perhaps, when my brother comes we can go there and see that part of Bulgaria. The mountains in that region are quite different from those where I am now. And I know Todora wants me to stop in again, and spend the night. So if my brother is up to an "old house" adventure, we could try and work that in the schedule. From there we could go to Belogradchik which is also in that region of Bulgaria, only further north and west.

I was barely home on Sunday when I got a text message from one of my 8th grade students. I thought she wanted language lessons, but she wanted me to go to the beach in Burgas with her and her sister. I said okay. We could practice speaking Bulgarian and English on the way and I do like to lay out in the sun. They wanted to leave at 8 AM, but I managed to convince them that 10 AM would be better. It would have been a very long day as we have to consider the train schedule. It takes an hour each way for the trip.

I first had to go into school and talk to my director, and I wanted to check the mail. As it turns out the Post Office is only open now in the afternoon from 2 - 3:30. I find that frustrating, but there in my director's office was the package from my brother. Yipee. My director is always so impressed about how much mail I receive. She also would love to come and visit America and talks about coming back with me next year.

The beach went fine, but it is different going with two teenagers. They turn 15 in October I think. Both are very nice girls; I was basically going along as a chaperon. We ate at MacDonald's, a big treat for them and rather expensive compared to a regular Bulgarian restaurant. I paid almost 6 lev for a hamburger. They ordered Happy Meals and paid 5 lev. One girl did not like the shake though.

They were worried about missing the train back. They travel to Aitos a lot, but not to Burgas. We also had a *duner*. This is like a sandwich wrap filled with chopped cabbage, rice, French fries, chicken, onions and some sauces. It is really quite tasty. For comparison to the MacDonald's a extra large *duner* costs only 4 lev, some places 5 lev. A small *duner* is usually about 2 lev.

At the beach we bought soft drinks. The vendors charged 3 lev for a bottle of Lipton ice tea. That is the only way that you can buy tea in a restaurant here. And you have to ask for ice separately, and hopefully they will not charge you for it.

We did a little clothes shopping as well. There are many boutiques in Burgas as well as larger clothing stores and other specialty shops. They, like many young Bulgarian women are very petite and fit in a size two or four. I on the other hand, have a hard time finding a store that has clothes in my size fourteen.

On the way back to the train I could see a storm was coming. The sky was getting very dark. They were also worried about putting on their long pants. There father does not want them out in public in their shorts so before they walked home, they came into my apartment hallway and changed into long pants. The rain was already coming and it was going to be fierce. There were very strong winds. And then thunder and lightening struck. Luckily I had my PC unplugged from the morning. Generally when I leave my apartment for any length of time I unplug my computer, my stove and my hot water heater. This is the recommended practice from the Peace Corps.

Another big clap of thunder roared and I was out of power. Milka, my landlady had decided to wash my carpets that morning. She had come up stairs on Sunday night to gather them up. These are full-size carpets for a room. Everyone seems to do that here. They take them to the community water spout, lay them out, scrub and hang them out to dry. Sitting outside my apartment door when I came up the steps were two carpets rolled up. I was just laying the one out when Ca-boom! Lightening struck. The rain came in buckets and there was a flash flood. I took pictures with my camera. It ran down the street in torrents.

Milka wanted me to stay downstairs and I did and then she also wanted me to sleep down there too. She fed me and fed me and today I have diarrhea. It is the worst case since I've come. It could be from the soft ice cream I had yesterday in Burgas. I don't know. Talking to other PCVs it seems that ice cream sold by different vendors out in the warm summer air may be a culprit for diarrhea. Ice cream generally is not found in the winter months and it is so tempting to buy it on a warm summer day.

The worst things though are my bug bites. I have them everywhere. It is like having the chickenpox. My back, arms, legs are all covered with bites. I know there were bugs in my bed last night when I slept down in Milka's apartment. I could feel them, but thought it was maybe the scratchy sheets. Wrong. In the morning I saw one bug that looked very full of my blood

As I couldn't do anything about the electricity, and my landlady was going to be home to wait for the electrician I met up with Laura, the PCV from Karnobat to start the process of renewing our *Lechna Karta*. It meant another trip to Burgas. It was hot. The storm did not bring in cooler weather. I have to close this as I want to beat the next storm.

I'm not sure how much Internet I'll have in the next days. The plans are to fly out from Sofia to Prague on the 17th and back on the 27th via airplane from Venice.

Louise

June 17, 2010

I'll be leaving for Sofia this weekend and be back Monday afternoon some time. When should we send our leave requests in to the Peace Corps? We probably need to get them in soon.

Wow, it was so nice and cool this morning. I was up at 5 AM and had all the doors and windows opened. It's around 10 now and I'm just now closing up the flat to try and keep it cool, but already it feels like another hot day.

I'll be busy these next couple weeks on excursions with Ann, and if I don't respond to emails, you can always reach me on my cell. When I'm home, I'll check in with you and check email.

Hope you got a fan OK. It really does help. Hazel

Hi Hazel,   **June 17, 2010**

I'm thinking that next Monday or Tuesday I'll send in my paperwork. That still gives Peace Corps more than three weeks which should be OK.

Yes, the weather does feel better today. I opened the door off my living room balcony this morning, and while I'm at my computer I hear these birds. What do you know? There were two birds in my apartment. Somehow I managed to get them to fly back out that same door. Now I have it closed. Not sure why the creatures all like that balcony; maybe as it's right off the garden. I'm not too fond of birds in my apartment

I'll work more later today on some excursions and then send you an itinerary. I'm thinking the excursions might total around $350 to $400 for the two of us together. I'll try and give you more exact figures soon.

Stay cool, Louise

Hi Hazel,   **June 20, 2010**

Well, let's send in the paperwork tomorrow or in the next day or two. I think we send it to Dora.

I'm working on the Hungary tours now. I have found a concert in both Prague and Vienna that I think we both would enjoy.

Hope that you're having a good visit with Anne. Louise

Hi,

Storms yesterday and no Internet at my house, hopefully it will be back on by tomorrow. When I get connectivity again I will make the WIZZ reservations And then I will look at tours. Hopefully we can reserve tours and hotels and then pay when we arrive.

One idea I had that could work: I will figure out the total for the air fare and train and get them reserved and paid for the two of us. If you agree, then you can cover hotel expenses. At the end we can see who owes who. Hopefully it will be fairly even. This is how I did it with my friend from Japan on the trip to Poland and it worked out well.

Have a good week. I think another storm is coming.

There was lots of rain and thunder yesterday. Louise

To the Proprietor at a house in Sofia; I stayed there during medical trips.
Hi Evanka,   **July 28, 2010**

Thank you for the late night arrival. It all went smoothly. The "House" now feels like my home away from home here in Bulgaria. I will be there again on August 11th and 12th and also August 20th and 21st. I believe that you have those dates. I was also able to arrange my dentist appointment, so now would like to add August 22nd and the 23rd.

I left a hardback novel by Scott Turow with Evan last week and forgot to ask for it this morning before I left. Please let Evan know that I will pick it up when I come on August 11th.

Thank you again. Louise

Hi from Prague,

The trip is going well. This is a beautiful city. I can't get over all the shops and people. I love all the amazing architecture.

Rain this morning, but it cooled off and tonight the weather and scenery is just amazing with lots of people and everyone very friendly.

Tomorrow we take the train to Vienna.

Louise

Hi Louise

Thanks for your summertime newsletter. Here in Farmington it's been mostly in the 90s and, after a very dry June and July, we're starting to get more humidity, rain and thunderstorms.

I especially enjoyed the part of your email about your European sojourn. I looked in a couple of my books on synagogues, and found pictures of the beautiful one in Prague. There is also an old Jewish cemetery there. And the music was probably great too

I'm glad your Peace Corps experience is working out well.

Best wishes, Harris

Email to my children, July 25, 2010

Just a quick note, I'm now in Budapest with Hazel. It was raining today for the walking tour. I'll write more on my return. I should be back in Topolitsa on Wednesday.

Tonight we will fly to Venice on WIZZ Air.

Love, Mom

Hi Ruth,   **August 2, 2010**

So nice to hear from you, I was thinking of Bob the other day when I was in Venice and got to watch a glass blower. Is he still busy blowing glass and going to craft shows? I still have some of the beautiful Christmas ornaments that he made when the children were young.

Please greet him and your family for me.

All the best, Louise

Dear Family and Friends,   **29 July 2010**

I now have officially passed the one-year mark of my Peace Corps Service. This has been a year filled with many new learning experiences. There is hardly a day that goes by that I am not still amazed about having this PC opportunity along with the experience of living in another country amongst new cultures and traditions as a Peace Corps Volunteer. Even though this is the year anniversary, I've actually been here since May 21. The anniversary is based on our "swearing in" date July 24.

I must say it is very hard for me to believe that my 66th birthday is fast approaching. It just doesn't seem possible. I used to think that people in their sixties were old, but nay. I don't bounce back as quickly when I have less sleep some evenings, and at times these old bones creak a bit, but for the most part I am so fortunate and thankful for my health and good fortune to be able to be in the Peace Corps program.

Tonight as I write this I'm coming back from a ten-day holiday. I was so grateful that it all went smoothly. The only hitch happened at the Venice airport, when "something beeped." I don't even think it was me but the scanners at security decided to check my carry-on bag. They decided that the lovely Murano glass letter opener that I had bought for David was a weapon. It didn't even have a blunt point, but the woman was not to be argued with. Sorry David. Some airports allow you to mail such items, but not here I had to just let the security folks have it. So, I guess that means I will have to make another trip to Venice some day

Some of you have asked about our vacation time here in the Peace Corps. Basically it works like this; we earn two days off a month. We are considered working 24/7. If it is Peace Corps related it does not count against our vacation days, e.g., meetings with PC staff, workshops or medical appointments. Also, we are allowed an overnight visit twice a month to stay with another volunteer or see sights in another town in Bulgaria. Any travel out-of-country though is seen as vacation time, even if it falls on a national holiday.

As volunteers here in Bulgaria we only are given Bulgarian holidays off, not United States holidays. Easter, Christmas, and New Year's Day are the only three holidays that are observed by both countries.

As Bulgaria is in the middle of Eastern Europe this seemed like the perfect opportunity to take advantage of traveling to see some of the historical sights of nearby countries with another older volunteer. We managed to schedule four cities into ten days, with a combination of airplane, bus and train: Prague, Budapest, Vienna and Venice.

Venice just happened as a new small airline company was offering service into Sofia. Otherwise it was going to be a very long plane layover from Budapest or a very long train ride. As neither of us had ever been there it seemed a great opportunity to explore Venice for 48 hours.

Today, on the nine hour train ride back to Topolitsa, I saw many flooded fields along the way, with the poor sunflowers all bent down due to the heavy rains. We had rain several days, but did not have to cancel any of our plans. A storm that came just before I left tore up many roads making car travel on the secondary roads quite hazardous.

Prague is a beautiful city and quite easy to walk around in with a great subway system. Our small hotel was just off the Charles Bridge. To be there walking on a bridge that was built before Columbus discovered America made my knees tremble. The city is rebuilt much like it was before the war. Thankfully in the historic part of the city there is not much evidence of the block buildings that are seen so much in the construction done during the Communist era.

Another very enjoyable part of our visit to Prague was a chamber concert of American composers (Gershwin, Bernstein and Kern) in the beautiful Jewish Synagogue located near the heart of the Jewish ghetto dating back to the medieval era. This "new" synagogue was built in 1868.

After Prague we took the train to Vienna. A very different city, but it's marvelous to behold. And with the public transportation system it was relatively easy to get around. We were able to take public transport from the train to our hotel, and then back out again to the airport.

In Vienna we again went to a concert, this time all Mozart. The musicians were all dressed in 18th century costumes, so that made the evening really seem like we had gone back in time. The walk through the famous Opera House, Schonbrunn Palace and the Albertina Museum only whetted my appetite to come back for a much longer stay.

Then it was on to Budapest. Each city has its own appeal and it is hard for me to say, which city I liked the best. They all have been on my list to see for a very long time, and I feel so lucky that I was able to manage each of them in about forty-eight hours.

All these cities are on major waterways. In each we managed a boat ride to some historic spot. We also visited many churches and cathedrals, as well as museums and ate the traditional dishes of each culture. In each city I had lined up a four to six hour guided walking tour and that gave us a good overview of the city. Each group was small enough so that we could visit and share with the other travelers. We talked to a number of Americans, but also Australians, Japanese, Canadians and of course other Europeans.

It surprises me how universal English has become as a language, but it certainly helps knowing two or three languages to more easily converse.

This weekend a few volunteers are stopping in to help me celebrate my birthday. My niece Debbie will be visiting me mid-August. If the weather cooperates we'll head to the beach in Burgas, or Nesebar, both on the Black Sea.

Monday, August 2 I start an "English for Fun" program with the children in the village. Before the school year starts back again on September 15, I hope to have about 150 English books set up in a part of a refurbished classroom library for the children. Thank you all for helping to make this happen. Another project on refurbishing the school play area is still in the developmental stage.

Milo is now ten weeks old. I am now saving my vacation days so that I will be able to travel to California over Christmas. Marcus and Stacey have generously given me this gift so that I can see my new grandson over the holidays.

Refreshed with this vacation, I will go back to my Bulgarian language lessons and see what the second year brings. I must say, coming back into Bulgaria the language sounded more familiar than the languages did in Hungary, Czech Republic or Italy. I think that is a good sign. I'm certainly not fluent, but saying "*dober den*" or "*blagodarya*" seems pretty natural.

With that I'll close. Please continue to keep in touch. I appreciate hearing from each of you via snail mail or long or short emails. Thank you all for your gifts of friendship, love and prayers.

Louise

Hi Loren,   **August 6, 2010**

I'm sure we can make those dates work for you to come and visit. I'll continue to think through ideas for an itinerary. That is a good idea about coming in on the 31st and adjusting to time change. I have a great place to stay in Sofia and a taxi is easy to arrange from the airport. It's a small hotel, they know me, and most of the staff speak English. You could manage yourself without any problems I am sure.

I can't believe the heat we've been having, around 100 degrees and humidity about the same. YUK! Two girls from my 8th grade class want me to go to the beach with them today in Burgas. Nope, not today. I just got a text message and the weather is threatening so the trip is postponed. The train travel is so hot I can't believe it. All the windows don't open and even if they do open some people don't like them opened. Many people here have a "thing" about drafts. It's really something. I can't believe it. Often at school they worry about me catching a draft if they think I'm not dressed warm enough.

Also, another custom, don't put your bag on the floor. NEVER. They will pick it up for you or find a chair or give it to you to hold it on your lap. This is shopping bag, purse, anything, not on floor anywhere.

Felicia's brother visited her last year and he rented a car. I was thinking of just managing by train, but I did want to throw this idea out to you. It's not that drivers are much crazier here than anywhere else, but the roads are generally poor especially the country roads, and there are not many road signs. If we thought Italy was difficult this would be more so. (My brother was planning to visit during the school spring break the following April.) It does make time more flexible though with your own transportation. So I did want to mention it to you. I couldn't drive (PC rules) and you would have to buy the super inclusive insurance. I think we could manage with the train and maybe some bus.

I'm looking at one circular trip to some historic and interesting cities I was told. I'll map it out and send it to you. These would all be in Bulgaria. I'm happy to stay in Bulgaria, but did want to mention the option of Macedonia to you.

Stay cool. Thanks for sending the garden pictures. It looks great.

Love, Louise

(A few years prior we rented a car and toured Italy together.)

Hi Debbie,   **June 12, 2010**

I'm checking on a tour via air conditioned car to Koprivshtitsa. I haven't quite mastered how to pronounce it. It would make it a pleasant ride into the mountains of Bulgaria. If you have a Bulgarian guidebook you'll see this town written up. It is especially noted for its many decorative houses called National Revival. The town is also remembered for being involved in the April Uprising, similar to Lexington and Concord in the American Revolution. Like Concord, it also has a bridge to walk over. It appears like a very interesting town. It is more difficult to travel to it on public transportation.

Today I went into Burgas to enjoy the Black Sea. The beach there is really very nice. Lots of cafes are set up on the beach. You see many families and young people, all ages and sizes. Here in Bulgaria as in other European beach areas, there is some topless bathing. No big deal is made of it. It seems to be ignored by the other bathers, but for some Americans when they first come here they are surprised. Burgas also has lots of shops carrying everything from knick knacks to perfumes to very expensive clothing and art stores. It also has a library with a section of English books. This is on the street as you walk to the beach.

I'll keep you posted. Louise

Dear Louise   **August 17, 2010**

I hope you are doing great and I would like you to reconfirm your trip to Koprivchtitza on the 21st of August, because I have to call the driver

Louise, as I have told you, I reserved a nice mini car with air conditioner. The trip is about 8 hours. The price is 160euros. Museums, lunch and tips are not included.

If you could tell me when you plan on doing the trip and how many of you are going, I will be very grateful. Please, tell me also at what time and where the departure will take place?

As I have to pay the driver before the departure, I would like you to pay me in euros before we depart to Koprivshtitza.

Looking forward seeing you, Rumi

A letter sent to me and my siblings, August 30, 2010

After my trip to Germany, I came back to Arizona and a month later repacked my bags and flew to Sofia. I surprised Louise with a suitcase weighing 40 pounds filled with goodies for her: books and supplies for her school, jello pudding mixes, cookie mixes, make-up, and DVDs. It was hard getting my suitcases on or off the trains. It was very hot and humid the entire time I was in Bulgaria. Louise said the people there were talking about how many days in a row that it was so hot, so it was hot. You would have thought I would be used to it being hot, living in Arizona for 50 years, but when I get hot here, I can go into my air conditioned house or into an air conditioned building. The only air conditioning we had in Bulgaria was while we traveled and stayed in hotels. We also traveled by train, but, again, no air conditioning. Some of our trips on the train were 2 to 6 hours. Louise has a table fan at her apartment, but that's it. She gave that to me so I could sleep at night while we were at her apartment. Then, one night, the electricity in their entire village went out. It was out all night Therefore, no fan. Yuck!

Some of the highlights of my visit were:

Sofia: Walked around capital city of Bulgaria

Plovdiv: Walked around this old town. Saw the Amphitheater (a smaller version of the Coliseum in Rome)

Topolitsa: This is where Louise lives . . . her village. We walked around some, but it was so hot. We saw her school with the outdoor toilets (Louise just wrote me and told me that they are now constructing bathrooms inside of their school, which will be great). We also walked to her "grocery store" (called a magazine store). It's like a very small Circle K store. I met her landlady, Milka, who only speaks Bulgarian. Nice lady.

Sozopol: Took the bus (no a / c) and walked around this old historic town. I had lunch at a restaurant overlooking the Black Sea, lots of shops and restaurants.

Burgas: We stayed two nights in Burgas by the Black Sea. This was one of my favorite spots. There were lots of street vendors, shops and restaurants. A pretty garden and what Louise would call a short walk to the Black Sea. It was probably a 15 minute walk . . . not too bad. The water was warm because it was so hot there I also met Laura, another Peace Corps volunteer. She was in town needing to take care of some Peace Corps paperwork and had a craving for a piece of America . . . so we had lunch at McDonald's. Yes, there are McDonald's in Bulgaria

Aitos: Took the slow train to a "larger village" where we had lunch with Louise's language teacher. She had a car, so it was nice getting around in a car. She took us to a very pretty mountainous area. I also purchased a small ceramic bowl there.

Koprivshtitsa: I paid for a guided tour of this small charming city . . . believed to be one of the prettiest areas in Bulgaria. We were driven in a Mercedes Benz van from Sophia to Koprivshtitsa, which was about 1 1/2 hours away. We had lunch there and walked around the area. It was a very pretty area.

All in all, it was a nice visit. And I think Louise appreciated seeing an American.

I have to give Louise credit for taking on a new job, moving to a new country, trying to learn a new and difficult language, and learning a new way of life/culture. Just the logistics of getting around, i.e., learning the train schedules, the bus schedules, etc., in a different language is hard enough. But when you have to learn their customs and try to communicate with the people, it's really hard. Congratulations, Louise

Love, Debbie

Dear Ginny,   **August 29, 2010**

I hope that you have received some of the postcards I've sent your way. I think the last one I mailed around the middle of this month. I was at the Sofia airport waiting for my niece Debbie to arrive.

Debbie lives in Arizona. I was still in grade school when she was born. My brother and his wife moved out to Arizona when she was 4 years old, so I really didn't see her much. Usually every two years my brother drove back with his family to Wisconsin. And I would see her when I visited my mom in Arizona. This visit was the longest time that I spent with her ever. She really is nice.

She loves to shop like I do and so we spent some time checking out the stores in Burgas and Nesebar, Plovdiv and Sofia. We walked around old historic towns and had some time at the beach in Burgas. As we were traveling around Bulgaria a lot, we mainly ate out in restaurants, a real treat for me rather than planning meals in this warm weather.

As the weather was so very hot I planned that we would stay in hotels that had AC at least half the time she was here. We also did a one day excursion to an interesting historic village, Koprivshtitsa. She paid for the special tour which included the four hour round trip drive into the mountains in an air conditioned car, along with a driver and a guide. So that was really living it up for me. She is very generous that way.

We did travel by train for the most part and the trains are not air-conditioned. They don't even sell water or food, even for the six to eight hour train rides, so a person has to be prepared. At the end of the trip, your water is warm and you are very hot and sweaty. Soon the weather will be cooler and the heat will be but a memory. Tonight it is raining which is the first time this month I think. It just has been hot and sticky. I'm lucky to live near the Black Sea. I think I've been there at least six or seven times this summer.

Debbie and I stayed at a hotel near the sea, so that was a special treat. In less than fifteen minutes we could just walk back to the hotel, shower and change clothes. All along the nearby streets we could walk to any number of very nice restaurants. Generally we sat outside to eat and there was a breeze. One restaurant had AC on the second floor so we had lunch up there one day.

Now I'm back in my apartment, and soon my regular class schedule will begin. I am getting anxious to come back to the U.S. Did I tell you that I'm coming back for Christmas now? Marcus and Stacey bought me the ticket. I'm so glad that I'll get to see the baby; he's already 3 months old. David will also come to California for Christmas. After a week in California I'll fly to Boston and see Gretchen for two days and then back to Bulgaria. It'll be hard to come back I know. Hopefully this year will go fast. As it looks now I'm planning to be finished here by the end of June 2011.

The teaching is fine. I still get lonesome. It's still difficult living in a village where it's hard for me to communicate. But everyone knows what I'm up to as I'm the only American and they keep an eye out for me. I ask a lot of questions It is small town life, just like in the USA.

I can feel the difference in the air tonight; fall is coming. Perhaps next week I'll have to get out my long johns again I have to take the train into Sofia again this week. I need to get a new crown for my front tooth. My old crown chipped and needs to be replaced. I was there last week after Debbie left and he took the impression for the new tooth. Hopefully the train ride will be cooler than it was in the summer. I always have to stay overnight in Sofia when I go in for any kind of medical appointment as it takes me over seven hours one way. By the time I come back to Topolitsa I'm exhausted.

I have one more piece of exciting news. The Topolitsa School is getting indoor toilets. Thank goodness I really disliked the outdoor ones they had. They kept them as clean as possible, but there were no hooks to put your jacket, no paper around to use (everybody brought their own) and of course no seat. The school had what is called the "Turkish toilet." It's shaped like a triangle cut in the floor and you just have to stoop carefully and aim right. Of course you must hold up your skirt and pants just right. A number of places, especially the older restaurants and schools, also have this style, but with a flushing mechanism, so not quite so primitive. It indeed is a challenge, and reminds a person of things that are often taken for granted. Here at the village school, there was a separate building way out in back of the property. I was so happy last week when I saw the workmen and learned the school was getting indoor toilets. Yippee! Well, that's the news from the village.

Hope all is well in Pittsburgh and you are doing well my friend. It is always a treat when I hear from you. A big hug sent with love, and with special prayers for your health and happiness,

Louise

Journal entry, August 2010

It has been very hot. Was it really this hot last summer? Yesterday I thought I would pass out. I have bought a fan. First I put it together "not quite right" so had trouble with it, but now think I have it figured out.

Yesterday it was just blowing hot air. Milka decided to paint my "computer room." I guess I should call it my great room. It's the room where I eat, have my computer and printer set up, where my wood stove is and also has a bed. I slept here when it was so terribly cold in the winter. This great room has windows facing on the street and unless I keep the drapes pulled shut it's easy to look inside. It looks out over part of the garden and the street coming up from the train station. But because of the wood stove, the room really needed painting, but to take everything out is a lot of work. Before 7 AM Sunday Milka was ready to start. She did all the painting, thank goodness.

I washed the drapes. I put them in the bathtub. I used a bowl over the drainer and then filled the tub. They were really dirty. I hung them out on my balcony to dry. Then of course I had to hang them up again, which again was a challenge with the ceiling being so high. In the end though, the room did feel and look much cleaner. Oh, it is so very hot.

I could take two showers a day and still be warm. Usually I lock my door, but I think with Milka going up and down I forgot. I really like my bedroom space better as it faces out to the garden and has a small closet and some shelves to hold my personal items. I took a shower, and didn't lock my hall door. I was laying down in the living room. I thought it was a bit cooler there, lo and behold; all of a sudden Milka was at the door with Rosa to show her the newly painted room. No knocking, just called out, "Louisa, Louisa."

I quickly ran into my bedroom and shut the door. I was so disappointed with Milka.

I know she means well. She wants me down in her house every day. She does have an AC there, but still, there is so little I can talk to her about. And people come every ten minutes to buy cigarettes from her. She goes into Serbia to get them which is really illegal.

It seems to be mainly the Romani who are coming to the door. They come at dawn, and until dusk. They call her name until she comes to the door.

Now I think she's about out of cigarettes and indicated problems at the border so maybe it will stop. There's a new tax on cigarettes in Bulgaria with guidelines from the EU. They are trying to get people to stop smoking. So many people here smoke: teachers, everyone it seems to me.

I don't know how they can afford it. Not sure what the new price is, but I think the old price was around 4 to 5 lev a pack. So when I do my math, even a pack a day that's 35 lev a week, or 150 lev a month. For a teacher that's 35 percent of their salary. Some volunteers also smoke. I know it's an addiction and thankfully I don't have it. I never really had the urge and just knew I could never afford it.

Later:
Today Marianne and Rachel came over and we walked up the mountain. They are two of the three new volunteers in this area.

It was great. I needed some outside activity. It took us about two hours to go up and about 75 minutes to come down.

Back at my apartment I fixed us grilled cheese sandwiches. I gave both women a jar of my canned cherries. They enjoyed looking at my books and I gave them a few to take along with them: *The Mire* by Krassin Krastev; *By the River I Sat Down and Wept,* Paulo Coelho, and some lighter fiction paperbacks that they could pass on.

We mentioned about doing the hike again in a month. Hopefully, by then, the leaves will be turning bright fall colors.

I don't use my living room very much. It has a pretty sofa in it with a matching love seat. It also has a coffee table and some built in book cases. It is pleasant to sit in when I need to do needlework as it gets the afternoon sun. After I bought the drapes for my "great" room, Milka found some lovely drapes for the living room. My guest bedroom is handy for storing my suitcases and boxes where I collect paper to burn in the winter. It has a ceiling light, but no curtains and a linoleum floor over cement.

Hi Vesela,   **September 2, 2010**

I looked up Zheravna village on google. It described this very attractive village.

Then it had a link to guest houses. The one I looked at was Hadjigergy's House. It sounded very nice. It only had phone numbers as contact information. It mentioned being located in the "Gorny Kray" part of the village. I will wait to hear from you if your friend will be coming also.

I am looking forward to visiting this village with you, Louise

Vesala and I had a wonderful two days visiting Zheravna, going also to Kotel and visiting the museum there and the seeing beautiful woven rugs that made the town famous.

Hi Stacey & Marcus,   **September 20, 2010**

I had my computer checked out today in Aitos. The problem could have been related to the radio station not being shut down although I thought it was, but thankfully, no virus. They also reinstalled Skype as I told him about the ongoing camera problem. If this doesn't help, he mentioned something about needing new "drivers." I'm to try it out a few times in the next few days.

Email is working. I'd love to do a video chat if you have any free time in the next day or two. These two guys run one of the local Internet companies and are really nice. They speak a little English, so we manage. They were both in the English class that Vesala taught and came to the camp celebration in Varvara back in June. Vesala lives and teaches in Aitos. Her school is not too far from their shop so she came over in between one of her classes to help answer any questions I might have. Without her I really would have a tough time here.

Love, Mom

Hi Louise,   **June 18, 2010**

I arranged your visit to the hairdresser on Wednesday, the 23rd at 1 PM. I explained to her that you want coloring and a little cutting of the edges of your hair.

Ivanka

Hi Ivanka,   **September 21, 2010**

I hope that the new school year started well for you.

If you have an afternoon open, I would like to take lessons again this fall. It doesn't matter what day, perhaps Wednesday again, but it could be Tuesday or Thursday. I think Monday and Friday are not so good. I could start next week if it would suit you. I am thinking of 2 hours, one day a week. Or I could come this week on Thursday if you are free.

All the best, Louise

FALL JOURNAL, 2010

Three months to Christmas. That is a wonderful feeling. I will be spending it in California. Have I written that Stacey and Marcus have bought me a round trip ticket to visit them and Milo at Christmas? David also plans to come to their home for Christmas. It will be so good to see them all.

Now I am pondering the idea of making February my last month. I am getting anxious. It is getting so frustrating with the house. The tenants have not paid again in September. I have been doing my figures and with using my insurance money it looks like I could manage expenses until about August 2011. So that will be my goal for when I would like the house sold. Is that possible? I certainly hope so. If I return back to U.S.A. in winter months, then hopefully I could have the house on the market by May or even April. There will lots to do: paint all the interior walls, clean the carpets, yard work and all the necessary repairs. I am thinking of selling most of my furniture. That will be difficult for me to do, but if I sell my house I can't afford to move all my belongings nor would there be room in a small apartment. How will I manage? I don't know, but it will be time to start afresh.

How fortunate I have been this summer to be able to travel both in Bulgaria and in other parts of Europe. My trips with Vesala were so interesting. She drove me to the ruins of the first capital city, Pliska and then on to see the ruins of the first Bulgarian capital, Veliki Preslalv and to Balchik. And early this fall we took a weekend trip to Zherana and Kotel.

Another unique trip was with the Topolitsa teachers hiking in caves. Arrangements were made as the school year closed to hire a van and explore Devil's Throat cave and Yagodina Cave, the fourth longest cave in Bulgaria near the Buynovo Gorge. It was beautiful. We also hiked up the mountain to Asen's Fortress. This historic area is not far from Plovdiv.

My 66th birthday was celebrated with Peace Corps friends coming to spend the weekend: Felicia, James, Tricia and Diana all made the trek across the country for my birthday. We went to Sozopol and Nesebar as well as Burgas. (In Burgas I found a colorful painted set of wooden Cyrillic alphabets. I bought them for my new grandson.) Milka made a huge Banitsa to help us celebrate this time together for my birthday.

This summer I also had a wonderful visit with my niece Debbie. Even though the days were very warm, it did not dampen our spirits. We stayed several nights in a small hotel in the center of Burgas and enjoyed the waters of the Black Sea. We visited Sozopol and Burgas, and then took the train to Plovdiv. There we stayed at a very modern boutique hotel** in old town Plovdiv with cobblestone streets and a mixture of Balkan architecture and Roman ruins.

(This hotel was recently restored, keeping the outside ancient facade. Breakfast was served on the enclosed rooftop. The owner had put in an elevator to the top and we noticed the elevator had a sign for a swimming pool. He had not mentioned a pool to us. We hit the down button with the sign to the pool. Luckily, we were cautious as the door opened. The pool area was dug out, but as the door opened on the bottom floor right in front of us was the excavation for the pool. Hopefully, now it is finished and no one has fallen into the abyss.)

Also in Plovdiv is the Jumaya Mosque. This is from the Ottoman reign. They conquered Plovdiv in 1371. It is one of the oldest mosques in the Balkans and sits near the recently discovered stadium of Philippopolis under the busy modern shopping street where this past Christmas I had my picture taken with Marcus and David. While in Plovdiv with Debbie and exploring the ruins of the Antique Theatre of Philippopolis — the design by the Romans looks like the Coliseum in Rome. It was built in the 2nd century and has been partially restored. It seats 5,000 persons and concerts are still held there — we heard a voice from above calling out, "I'll take your picture." Here was Nikolas, a Peace Corps Volunteer who recently completely his service in Kyrgyzstan.

Nikolas was hiking his way across Europe. We spent some time getting acquainted and taking photos. He had joined up with the WWOOF organization. This is a new organization where a person can volunteer their services in exchange for helping out on a farm, garden, child care or whatever else needs to be done in exchange for room and board. I invited Nikolas to visit the Black Sea region and offered my extra room for his lodging. He arrived on my doorstep in mid-September and stayed for about a week.

When my front crown broke, Peace Corps covered the costs to have it replaced. And now I will get the other front crown redone as it appears there is decay behind it. From the dental visit I went on to Vratsa for the One-Year conference. It was so good to see everyone again. Felicia changed sites in early summer and now is in Dragamond, the last town before the Serbia border. I hope to visit her when I go back to the dentist in October. School started September 15. I will start language lessons with Ivanka again next week.

I got my ID card renewed. Laura and I managed together. I picked it up by myself. I had to make an extra trip as I had forgotten to take in my Passport. I also got a new train card. So I think all my paperwork is done now. I still have some minor reports for Peace Corps to do, maybe tomorrow or Monday afternoon. I'll stop for now; I have so much more to writeup.

Dear Family and Friends,   **October 2010**

It has been several months or more that I have written to many of you. Sometimes I find it hard to believe that I have lived here in Bulgaria 17 months. Other times it feels like I have been here years and years.

In many ways the second year is easier. I know what to expect. While the language can still be a stumbling block to smooth communication, I am managing. I understand the school calendar better and the pattern of the school year. Working with most of the same students as last year, also makes it easier. On the other hand, with the second year comes the expectation and longing to come back to the U.S.A. It seems a long time since I've had central heating, a clothes dryer or just driven a car to a supermarket or a mall. Cooking on my two-burner stove is easier now for me, but I do miss having a big oven and being able to bake several pans of cookies at once without constantly watching them and hoping that I have the temperature right so that they don't burn.

This year, thanks to care packages from family and friends, I have a bigger variety of food in my kitchen and clothes in my closet. Several times now I've baked chocolate chip cookies and even an apple pie and a plum pie. I've also canned ten quarts of cherries. I would have canned some tomatoes, but I didn't have any more jars. For several months in the summer I enjoyed fresh produce from my landlady's garden, mainly tomatoes, peppers, a little corn and some squash. In addition to clothes mailed to me or brought over on trips I've discovered second-hand stores. They are very popular here. The items in the store are from all over Europe, mainly UK and Germany so a big variety of styles can be found. There are more selections for the petite, size four figure, but I've managed to put together an eclectic wardrobe that give me a variety besides the same pair of black pants and turtle neck everyday.

This summer another group of volunteers from the U.S. arrived and three were placed in nearby towns. Several weeks ago two of them came over and we walked up the mountain here in Topolitsa. It was a fun hike. Along the way are *heishas* or huts for hikers to stop and rest. They are like a big summer cottage. Some are owned by companies and they rent them out to hikers for overnight or a week or two stay. There is also a river on one part of the mountain top, but on our hike we didn't locate it. I hope to make another excursion up there before the snow flies. I have been very fortunate to have family and friends visit.

This past August my niece was here for ten days. She came with a suitcase laden down with food, books and games for the school children and some sundry items. We were in the midst of one of the longest heat waves on record, reaching over 100 degrees most days she was here. Without air conditioning, living on the second floor I can say unequivocally it was hot. I have to commend her for being such a good sport through it all, from the hot sticky train ride, to my very warm apartment and traipsing back and forth to the train station with our luggage. We stayed overnight in Burgas, Sofia, Plovdiv and Topolitsa.

This week I hope to get the school library up and running. I have over 150 books to put in the school library. Thank you all so very much for sending books over to me for the school. The teachers have been helping to clean out the room that had been a library years ago, but had been neglected the last number of years. The past year already I've been taking books to classes to share with the children that they enjoy, but now I also hope that the system can be arranged for the students to take books home to read and share with their parents. I hope to have regular library hours in the afternoon. I also have some games and puzzles for the students. Many of the students can read some English, but still have a difficult time in speaking it, or understanding questions that I put to them. This fall I am working with students from grades 2 through 8. The younger children particularly are eager to learn. In all there are about 120 students in the school. They love to play word games and to sing American action songs.

Another big improvement for the school this year is indoor toilets. I was so happy to see this project develop in late August. What an improvement it is and much appreciated. No one liked having to go outside in the cold weather. While most students here have indoor toilets in their home for some this is also a new novelty and some new guidelines needed to be laid down.

Many of you know that this summer I was able to take a trip with another older volunteer to several of the European capital cities. She was a teacher in the Phoenix area for many years. We both enjoy history, art, music and water so in addition to tours of castles, churches and historic old towns; we enjoyed an all American composer concert in the beautiful Spanish Synagogue in Prague. In Vienna we had another delightful evening, attending an all Mozart concert with the musicians dressed in the costume of the time period. In each city we took a boat ride to historic sites. We flew first to Prague, then by train to Vienna, bus to Budapest and then flew to Venice and back to Sofia. While the cities were quite different in appearance, all had a great appeal to me and I hope after Peace Corps I will have a chance to go back and have a longer stay at each of them.

The highlight of the year is of course the birth of my first grandson, Milo. He arrived in May, almost four weeks early, but is doing fine. What can I say? He is a cutie. I understand he doesn't especially take long naps, but I have known of that happening with babies. I am so excited that I will be able to go back at Christmas time and meet him and hold him.

Bulgaria continues to be a land of contrasts to me. On the one hand I see the tents outside my village where some families live most of the year. On the other hand, I have students in my classes who have the latest phone, cable television and live in three or four story houses. One student spent the summer with his dad in Greece, while another student has her mom working in Spain as a domestic most of the year to help support the family.

Bulgaria is emerging and I feel in another ten years there will be many more changes. It is meeting many challenges from its years of being a puppet state in the Soviet Bloc. It is difficult for the culture to emerge from nearly fifty years of Communist suppression to becoming independent not just on paper, but in the thoughts and ideas of the people. For people to understand about making decisions and learning that it is up to them to encourage their leaders to perform is a big step towards democracy. It is hard work to get involved in messy local politics. It is hard work to help PC change local laws and to improve the education of their children. This is all new territory to them. The idea of committee work, while at times cumbersome, is also democracy in action. This is a new concept for citizens who live here. In the past it was all top down control and free thought and free initiatives were not only frowned upon, but punished. As one teacher told me, it will take until the generation that lived under Communism to die off before the generation, now in their early twenties, fully understands the mantle handed to them in a free country.

Hopefully I can instill a bit of the American dream of working towards the common good in the children that I teach by my example and sharing with them stories of America. The U.S. is seen as a beacon of hope and I have never been so proud to be an American.

Thank you all for your support with emails, gifts, and prayers. It means more to me than I can say in mere words. Thank you.

With warm regards, Louise

Dear Evelyn,   October 9, 2010

Barbara wrote me via email telling me that you are now living in a nursing home. I assume it is in Waupaca (Wisconsin). How I wish that I could come and visit you. Now I am serving in the Peace Corps. This is the program started 50 years ago by President John Kennedy. There are volunteers all over the world. Bulgaria was part of the greater Soviet Union after World War II, but since 1989 has been independent. But those years under Communist left the country in very bad condition. People did not starve, but many things were neglected.

Factories were only built for industry and it was to serve Russia, not every day items for the people. Slowly the country is recovering. Roads are being repaved and the clothing industry revived, and children are being taught English in the schools along with Bulgarian. In the bigger cities, like Sofia and Plovdiv English has been taught for many years, but in the small villages, like Topolitsa where I live it has only been the last few years. There is a shortage of English teachers. So that is what I do. I teach English here in the village school to grades two through eight. I have about 120 students. Not every grade has English every day. It is a nice school for a village, and this year I was so happy that they were able to install indoor plumbing for the toilets. Last year it was an "outhouse" much like we had in Fremont those many years ago.

We are not allowed to drive a car while in Peace Corps so I have to depend on public transportation. Luckily a train stops just outside the village six times a day, so when I need to go into the bigger town for some shopping I go on the train. This afternoon I plan to go into the town of Aitos. It is there where I can buy meat, fresh produce, and household items. We do have several little stores in the village, but I can't buy meat or produce there. Many people here have gardens and this summer my landlady shared some of her produce with me. I had fresh tomatoes, peppers and squash. Now most of it is finished for the winter. Luckily I was able to can a few cherries from her cherry tree so I will enjoy those this winter.

For Christmas this year I am coming back to the U.S. My son Marcus and his wife Stacey had a baby boy in May. I am excited to see my first grandchild. They live in California. My son David who lives in Boulder, Colorado, will also be there. Both Marcus and David work on energy-related jobs.

My daughter Gretchen lives in Boston and is an architect. I will also stop in Boston to see her for a few days before I fly back to Bulgaria. It will be so good to see them. Last Christmas Marcus and David were able to visit me for a few days here in Bulgaria which was wonderful. Gretchen has not been able to come, so it is now nearly two years since I've seen her.

I saw LeAnne and Willard for a few days in May. They were on a tour with a group that came to Sofia. That is the capital city of Bulgaria. I traveled by train there. As it is completely across the country, it takes over seven hours by train to get there. It was so good to visit with them.

This past August my niece Debbie, Lyle's oldest daughter, came to visit me. It was a week that the weather was very hot. It was over 100 degrees on a few of the days, and I do not have any air conditioning in my apartment. And the trains are not air conditioned. Debbie lives in Arizona where it is hot, but of course she is used to AC. And it is very humid here in Bulgaria. But she was a good sport. Thankfully Bulgaria has good water and Coca-Cola is found in most stores.

Now the weather has turned cold. In fact, this morning I started a fire in my small wood burning stove. This village is on the side of a mountain and it gets very strong winds. Yesterday the wind blew and blew for over three hours. I was without Internet or electric. That is when I feel most isolated as I have no way to get in touch with anyone.

With much love, Louise

Dear Evelyn,

I have so many fond memories of coming over to see you as a little girl. You were such a good friend to me. I loved playing with your jewelry and high heels. I don't think any little girl could ask for a better neighbor. And to become your flower girl was the highlight of my childhood. Thank you again for allowing me this special honor.

If I come back to Wisconsin next summer, I will for sure come and visit you. In the meantime, I will send you a note now and then via Barbara. What a special friend you are and always have been.

With much love, Louise

Evelyn was my neighbor when I was a child growing up in rural Wisconsin. The summer I turned five she got married and asked me to be her flower girl. She has always held a special place in my heart. Barbara was her niece and went to Zion School where my dad was a teacher.

FUNDING

Hi Gretchen,   **March 29, 2010**

I'm happy to hear that you have Skype and Google chat set up. Could we try it Tuesday noon Boston and 7 PM for me?

Wednesday I travel to Sofia and I won't have my computer with me and it would be nice to talk. I have about thirty minutes on my phone yet, and if Tuesday doesn't work, I could take my phone with me and call you Wednesday night. On Skype I won't have to worry about minutes. What is your Skype name or address? I see a new business email for you. How are things going?

This afternoon I spent three hours with my school director. I am going to work on a special PC grant project for the school. I will probably be asking for $5,000 to repair the school sports playground. I can ask U.S.A. friends to help and foundations. Maybe you will have some ideas for me of where to ask for money. It's been awhile since I've had to raise money.

The school director is very assertive about getting funds for her school. Catholic Relief funded their new radiator project. And apparently another non-profit group purchased new windows for the school. Now she is looking for money to get indoor plumbing.

It is still somewhat difficult communicating on these types of projects as we have the language barrier. She used a Google translation site and that helps, but doesn't always get the correct translation.

Generally speaking, I am fine. I have more bug bites and I am not sure where they're coming from. The next days will be quite busy for me: classes tomorrow, then the train to Sofia, medical annual physical. Belinda arrives from Japan. We'll travel by train back to Topolitsa for two days, back to Sofia and off to Poland. It is good to be busy. I manage with the language, but will take another year I think to do more than just basic survival with it.

David mentioned you sending me a package. Have you mailed it? Do you have the date? As mail is so erratic here, it helps me to know when to find the Post Office open. The Post Mistress keeps rather erratic hours.

Big hug and loads of love, Mom

Dear Sisters,   **October 4, 2010**

Today I had a rather difficult day, emotionally anyway. There was a special celebration at the Hristo Botev high school in Aitos. The America for Bulgaria Foundation gave money to renovate the classroom to have a state of the art language lab. It was called One World Classroom. I was involved only as a consultant. Vesala, a Bulgarian friend and language teacher I've helped in adult English classes wrote the initial proposal with her Bulgarian colleagues. A quote from the program: "A different language is a different vision of life." —Federico Fellini. Sometime late last spring she asked me to review and correct any grammatical errors she might have made in the translation and also to clarify the assorted points of the document, especially terminology and phrases used in grant writing. Local dignitaries were invited, and local school directors.

My director was asked to bring me. I was happy to see other Peace

Corps Volunteers from the area also present with their language teacher or director. It was a well presented program. It appeared that my director was perhaps jealous of this funding that this school received. Budgets for special programs are limited and I can often feel the competition between the schools. It is especially difficult for the Peace Corps Volunteers who have been placed at two different schools in the same town.

It felt to me that all my director was interested in was to make sure that I spoke to the Foundation folks to get information about grant ideas.

It was great having a chance to speak to the people from the Bulgaria for America Foundation as the President is an American. He splits his time between Bulgaria and Chicago. They do a lot of projects with libraries. At the reception, my school director detained the assistant director of the program, and subsequently me for most of the reception time. I'm sure sometimes that is a way to connect with foundations. Living overseas now for over a year, I was interested more in speaking to them just as an American. On the way back she kept asking me if I had ideas for a grant for Svetlina School. However, I don't feel I know Bulgaria and the school system well enough to come up with new projects on my own. The library project and even the playground project are on a much smaller scale of what she was thinking.

Several people came and said hello to me. It was nice to see folks outside of the teachers that I see on a regular basis. One teacher stopped by who had been on a bus trip I was on last year and spoke to me. I was introduced to the musician who played for the event. It was fun talking about music with him. He knew of Topolitsa and obviously felt sorry for me living here in the small village. He thought maybe he could handle it for two hours, at most. This is generally the impression I get from many people who live in even not much bigger cities. They realize that very little happens in the village. Most Bulgarians outside of the village have a hard time understanding why Peace Corps would have us live on our own in these very small villages.

We rushed away in the middle of the reception as she misunderstood the train time. She drives her car everywhere and generally doesn't use the train or the school bus. I had hoped to stay and visit some more and wanted to eat a little of the very delicious appetizers that were spread out, but it was "hurry Louise."

She had a hard time walking. She usually drives everywhere, but her hand and foot have been bothering her since she had an accident with her car. Coming around the corner in Aitos the other morning, a horse-drawn cart pulled out in front of her and she had to slam on her brakes. No one was injured, but her car sustained damage as did the cart and her foot.

I managed to stop in the food bazaar that we walked through on our way to the train and bought a head of cauliflower. It was the first time I've seen it here in Bulgaria. I also bought some fresh lettuce. We then hailed a taxi to take us to the train station, but as the schedule was misread we still had thirty minutes to wait for the train back to Topolitsa.

I don't know why I wasn't given a library assignment which is what I had originally been told I would be given, or else work with training teachers. Oh my. Who is to say? It would have been a very different experience if I had been assigned to work in Sofia. I like village life, but at times I miss the interaction of the city and all the activities that come with living in a metropolitan area.

The children and teachers are fine at school. Hopefully I will get this library set up yet, but there still is much to do to get the room all cleaned out and then painted. It is filled with old textbooks as it has not been used as a library for a number of years. Most of the books I have been sent by friends and colleagues are in my apartment until I have a bigger space for them. I usually have been bringing over ten to fifteen books at a time to share with different classes.

The weather has turned quite a bit cooler. I actually just got out my little heater. I did mention to my director that I need wood. I asked her also about a bigger electric heater, to use maybe an hour or two a day to take the chill off in the mornings. Luckily I have lots of wool sweaters here. It seems I have gone from shorts to long pants, to turtlenecks and vests in just this past week. It was about 60 degrees F. here now in this little room, when I decided to find my little heater. I try to be a happy camper, but sometimes it is difficult. Love, Louise

Hello from Bulgaria (Letter to siblings)   October 9, 2010

It's just past 6 PM here. The wind has finally died down. It turned so cold yesterday and the wind was blowing all day long. There is a breeze in the air, but not the strong wind.

I took the train into Aitos this afternoon and walked over to Vesala's house. She's has taken me on several excursions in her car. She is also a good seamstress, so I thought I would ask her to alter a couple of my outfits. One is a dress that I bought in Arizona I think or New Mexico and I like it, but it is too long for today's styles. The sleeves are too long also. She will cut off about ten inches from the hemline. The other outfit I brought to her for fitting is a lovely beige linen pantsuit I bought when I was NMLA President. I've lost some weight, plus with all my walking it is now really baggy on me. So she will take that in also.

Tomorrow she's going to Turkey. She wrote three special grants last year for her school. One of the grants is to take her students on five different field trips over the course of the next two years. They will visit certain schools. I think they stay in homes and sight see. It's a great opportunity for her students to see the world outside of Bulgaria. Another project was to get the new language lab, called *OneWorld Classroom.* This is the one I helped her with clarifying her English.

It looks like my library room is finally coming together. I will bring the rest of the books over this week, and hopefully can start working with the students in the library after their regular afternoon classes.

Some people do have apple trees here, but not my landlady. I can buy them in Aitos at the market. Last week I bought some and then made an apple pie. It was so good. I also did some laundry this morning. I hung it outside, and it didn't really dry, so now I brought it inside to hang. This is when I miss a dryer. It feels a bit warmer tonight without the wind, so not sure if I'll start a fire or not. It's about 60 degrees F. in my apartment, which isn't too bad.

Hope to talk to Marcus and Stacey tomorrow and see Milo on Skype. Soon he'll be five months old; that is hard to believe. It seems everything is going well. I also hope to talk to my brother, and maybe my friend Donna. These are free calls through the gmail program – a promotion until the end of the year I think.

I was offered a ride up to my apartment from the train station earlier today. I was so surprised. It turns out these people are my neighbors up the street. It was a young couple who I've seen around. This is only my second time I've been offered a ride. Many people walk, like I do, but some have a car that they park in the area by the tracks, and others are picked up I'm assuming by family members.

Another lady on the train offered me her magazine. It's in Bulgarian, but apparently she's studying English. I've seen her on the train a number of times. She lives in a neighboring town.

Many of the conductors know me and some even give me the special senior discount, even though I technically don't qualify for it as I'm not Bulgarian. I do get the regular train tickets at a discount because I bought the special train discount card. Even though that cost me 45 lev, it is a big help for me as I have to use the train so often. Have a good weekend, Louise

ROSES, ROSES, ROSES

Earlier this year I had a chance to attend the annual Rose Festival in Kazanluk with my language teacher and a colleague from her school and a group of students. It was a wonderful festival and I saw the Rose Queen being crowned by the Bulgarian President, Georgi Parvanov and watched the parade. There were many floats, persons in costumes, folk music and modern music with people everywhere lining the streets. Artisans were showing their many different types of endeavors. I even talked to several Native Americans from New Mexico who had come all this way to show their crafts. It had been a great day.

This region started growing roses back in the 18th century. At that time the Ottomans controlled Bulgaria and brought rose bushes from Damascus. They found that the climate and soil was perfect for growing this very fragrant rose. This valley is situated between two mountain ranges, the Balkan and Sredna Gora Mountains. These ranges help stop the cold winds during winter time and give this area its specific climate ideal for growing roses. On my earlier visit to Kazanluk I had a chance to visit the Rose Museum to see how the process works of extracting the rose oil from the pedals. Bulgaria ships rose oil all over the world to make the beautiful and fragrant perfumes and soaps.

In Kazanluk especially, but now all over Bulgaria bottles of rose perfume, rose water, soap and other rose products can be purchased at a very reasonable price. I have been buying them and I hope to take a few items back with me to the U.S. They are really nice products and reasonably priced.

And now I had another reason to visit Kazanluk as a new volunteer was placed there to work in the education field. She too was an older volunteer. Now I was no longer the oldest volunteer, as Naomi was a few months older than me. I had first met her when she first came to Bulgaria with the B-26 group back in May training in Varschets. I was so glad that her placement was relatively close to me. It meant going first to Aitos (opposite direction) and catching the early fast train to Kazanluk. The alternative takes about the same amount of time was waiting for the fast train in Karnobat for about a half hour and then getting off in Kazanluk.

As older volunteers we faced issues different from the younger set. Most of us had a house that we had to take into consideration if we were going to serve in Peace Corps for over two years. Some of us had children who were still in college, or getting married or having their own children. It would mean saying good-bye to them for over two years. And some of us had an elderly parent that we were afraid to leave at this stage of their life. Most of us were independent and leading our own lives, or in charge of libraries, companies, staff. Now we were considered just another volunteer. Studies have also shown that it is harder to learn a language when you are older, certainly when you are in your forties or older.

All in all being an older volunteer presents different challenges to us than for the younger set. It is great seeing the enthusiasm of the younger volunteers. We bring years of experience and a perspective on different cultures around the world. All in all we made a good balance for each other.

Hi Louise,   **October 12, 2010**

What a beautiful picture. He is adorable, and so is the blanket that you made. I can sew, but never learned to knit or crochet. My mother would always make the most beautiful things for me and my children. She taught my daughter to crochet, but I could never teach her to sew.

Are you going home for Christmas? I am too.

Deborah is coming here for Thanksgiving. We have a meeting starting the next week so we will leave from here. We don't know where it is right now Just the date.

It sounds like you will have a wonderful time there. Work has been so slow to start up I have been very discouraged, but it is getting better now. You have an open invitation to visit me here. Take care and if I don't see you have a fantastic time Thanksgiving and Christmas.

Naomi

Hi Naomi,

It is great to hear from you. I can empathize with the beginning. To me it is a constant up and down of emotions regarding the work and life here. While there are many similarities in the American and Bulgarian cultures, there certainly are differences. And I think for those of us who are older, living overseas for this length of time, is indeed a different experience than for those younger volunteers.

I would love to visit you. Are you going to the Halloween bash in Veilko Turnovo? While I'm sure it's a great get-together, I'm not so comfortable attending these bigger affairs. I do want to get to Veliko Turnovo and have been discussing the idea with Felicia.

Perhaps if you are not going that is a weekend I could make it out your way. Do you live right in Kazanluk? If not that weekend, perhaps another one in November. Let me know what might work for you.

I'd rather do it before Thanksgiving if possible. Yes I'm going back to California for Christmas to be introduced to my new grandson.

All the best to you, please keep in touch. Louise

Hi Diana,

Sounds like you're really getting things going at your school. Great! It looks like I may finally get the library open for the students to use this week, but other than that no other special projects at this time.

I hope you can consider coming for Thanksgiving. I sure would love to see you.

Big hug, Louise

Hi again.   **October 12, 2010**

I am not going anywhere because I'm saving my days. I will have eight and will have to borrow six in order to be able to stay about two weeks in the States.

I had not planned to do this when I left, but it has been much more difficult than I thought. I would love for you to come on the last weekend of October or any in November.

I live close to the bus and train station and to the center of town. I have a great location. My apartment is old, but the woman who owns it was going to be a counterpart to one of our group who went back home. So, she knows about PC and she left almost everything I need here.

This was her family home. Her parents died about three years ago. The couch makes a bed. So, just let me know when you can come. I will walk to the train or bus station to meet you. They are about three blocks away.

We will find something to do that is fun or just visit. I'm sure the weather will dictate much of that. It would be great if Felicia could be here too.

I will be excited to hear from you, Naomi

Hi Naomi,   **October 12, 2010**

That is great that you are planning to go to the U.S. over Christmas. I am sure that you miss your family, especially the grandchildren.

There are so many aspects to living in a foreign country that unless someone has done it, they don't have any idea what it's all about. Also, as we are for the most part by ourselves, I think it makes it two or even three times harder than if we were in a community with other Americans, or other foreigners. Even when we have colleagues who may speak English, the culture is different. For now I'll plan on coming the weekend of the 30th. I looked at the train schedule.

I would have to stay in Aitos Friday night, as the fast train to Kazanlak leaves at 6:03 AM (and doesn't stop here in Topolitsa). I will see if Rachel is there, or if not there is a Bulgarian teacher who has let me stay at her place a number of times. The 6:03 AM seems like the best possibility. It arrives at 8:21 AM.

I'm quite sure we have a school holiday on the 1st of November so I could stay over until Monday. The train back leaves at 11:52 AM but the connection is horrible, (4 hour wait in Karnobat) but I will see if Laura will be there and I could spend a few hours at her place or else take a taxi to Topolitsa. Having a car would make transportation a whole lot easier.

And don't worry about what to do. Just having time to visit will be great. We can walk around the center if you like. I always like checking out the second hand shops, but mainly just to visit, eat a good pizza maybe or other Italian food. I seem to remember from a meeting there was a good Italian restaurant close by the center. I'm mainly coming to see you.

Another thing to think about – next weekend I'm going in to Sofia for the dentist. My appointment is on Friday. Felicia and I are thinking of shopping. We mainly just want to look at the new mall and a store called Jumbo. It is like Walmart I understand. This would be on Saturday. Perhaps you could join us for the day. I think by now you are allowed one overnight a month, so you could stay overnight Saturday night and we could catch the same train back on Sunday.

I have to check, but I know one goes through Kazanlak and one goes through Plovdiv. Give it some thought. It would be fun for you to join us. Felicia has room in her apartment for you to stay. She's in a new place, Dragamond which is about an hour by train from Sofia. I haven't seen it yet, so I'm planning to stay with her and she said she'd love for you to come to. It will be good to get together and share experiences. What is your phone number? I'll mainly email you as I work out the details, as I have a phone plan and not minutes, but I think it's good to have each others number, just in case.

Take care, Louise

Dear Louise   October 12
I am so excited about a visit from you. There is a wonderful Italian restaurant directly behind my apartment. I can look down on it from my kitchen window and then the New York Pub in the Center. There are lots of places to eat here. I envy your travel skills. I am not that self assured yet. I am sorry you can't just get on a train or bus and get to Kazanluk.

I probably won't come to join you in Sofia, but it does sound like fun. I know we will talk more before you arrive, but I will be at the train station waiting for you. I'm glad you can stay until Monday. I didn't know it was a holiday.

Чао Naomi

Hi Louise   October 15, 2010
Sorry it took a bit of time to get back to you; I've been sick this past week and only now do I feel well enough to do something other than sleep. Milo is so precious on his blanket I love it. It looks very warm and cozy. He's very lucky to have a doting grandmother.

Thanks for the Thanksgiving invite. I'll let you know if I can make it. I wish we lived way closer.

The hike sounds like it would be a lot of fun. It is definitely something to consider. I hope you guys have fun on it this weekend.

How is the school year going for you? I like the 2nd year better already. It's nice to already know most of the kids and enough of the daily routine. Today my counterpart and I did a presentation for the global hand washing day. It was pretty successful I think. Well the kids were interested at least. Hopefully they will wash their hands way more often. I must run now, but I will talk to you soon. Stay warm!

Have happy Halloween lesson planning.

Heart, Diana

Louise, **November 5, 2010**

I do know about the play on Tuesday. It's a performance of Dostoevsky's *The Idiot* and a lot of teachers in my school are going.

There was some kind of group ticket and I bought in. I'd love to see it with you as well and you're more than welcome to stay over on Tuesday night. Mary might be interested too; you can send her an email if you want. She's also welcome to stay over, but she would have to sleep on the floor. I have a sleeping bag that she can use.

The medical office responded and said that they would send your glasses. So you were right, it's a good thing that you didn't stay over.

Hope your day is going well. See you soon, Rachel

I had thought of staying over another day in Sofia; my glasses might be ready for me to take back with me. However, I wasn't sure they would be available for me to pick up. I decided to come back on Sunday hoping to make arrangements to have my glasses sent to Topolitsa.

Hi Rachel, **November 8, 2010**

I called Vesala and she is going to check on the ticket for me. She teaches at Christov Botev School. She will take me to the train after the play in her car. That will make it easier so I didn't have to bring my stuff to sleep over. I will be bringing things for Felicia, PC library and a book of Naomi's. (If a Peace Corps vehicle was in our region we could arrange for them to take items back to the Peace Corps headquarters in Sofia. All volunteers had a mailbox there and were encouraged to check in when they came into Sofia.) I will take a taxi to your place and then when you are free we can visit before you go to class. I really don't have any shopping I need to do, so I will bring my book to read in your apartment and perhaps do some emails if I can use your PC, but not a problem if it's not handy.

Do you need more magazines for your students? I could bring you the ones that I've finished. I have a full day of classes until 1 PM and know that I will be tired. I can tell I can't bounce back as quickly as I used to, but I do want to see the play. Theater has always been a big interest of mine, so I do enjoy having this chance to go. I bought a roasting chicken and would love to make it this weekend. I'll check with Mary and Laura and see if they can come to Topolitsa.

See you around 2:15, Louise

Many schools in Bulgaria were named either Christov Botev or Vasil

Levski; much like in the U.S. we have many schools called Washington or Lincoln. Both men were involved in helping Bulgaria gain their independence from the Ottoman Empire. Botev was a poet and a teacher and wrote poetry and short stories. He was influential in helping to organize the insurgency. He was killed for his efforts in 1876. Botev was friends with Levsky and also died for the revolution at the age of 35. He too is considered a national hero: "He, who falls while fighting to be free, can never die." —Christov Botev

Louise,   **November 8, 2010**

This all sounds good. My place is your place while you're here. You're free to use my computer, read my books, eat my food; though I don't have a whole lot of food right now.

If you have extra magazines, I'll take them. I have a stack here but I plan to cut them up for class, so the more the better.

I have three cats living in my apartment with me, two of which are very friendly. My place does smell like three cats though, so FYI.

I also love to see theater, so I'm really happy to see this one. I need to look up the plot of *The Idiot,* so I can have some inkling of what's gong on.

I'll be in my apartment at around 2 so give me a call when you get there or if the taxi driver can't find my apartment. If that's the case, just tell him the bus station and I can meet you there. It's less than five minutes from my place.

Looking forward to seeing you, Rachel

Hi Donna,   **November 2010**

I'm here in Kazanluk, a city of about 60,000. I was here for the Rose Festival in June. Today is a very nice fall day, and I'm here visiting with another PCV Enjoying the fall day, we went walking around the town center and saw some oak trees with bright yellow leaves. Tonight we're going to meet with Anne and Josh, a married Peace Corps couple who also teach and live here, but at a different school than Naomi. There is also another woman coming who works in an orphanage nearby. Those are the really difficult assignments, as there is so much need and so few resources available.

Interesting, she and I have some of the same concerns regarding our work places. She worked for years in assessment, not direct teaching, and is having a hard time relating to her director and the needs of the students. Naomi came over earlier this year and we are about the same age. It's nice to be here and have this time together.

She's also planning to go back and visit her family in the states for Christmas. She has two grandchildren in college and four younger grandsons still in grade school. Her dad is still living and doing poorly. They all live in Texas.

I had to be at the train station at 6 AM this morning so a long day. I'll sleep good tonight.

Love, Louise

Kazanluk is home to the Rose Valley. Last summer I had to visit the special Rose Festival with my language teacher and another colleague from Aitos and her class. We walked out to the fields of rose bushes and picked the special rose pedals. We visited the "Rose" museum and watched the parade led by the Queen. The President of Bulgaria was also there and gave the welcome. Kazanluk is located in the center of the country. It supplies rose oil for perfumes around the world and is mainly exported to European countries.

Soap, hand cream and many other toiletries are made from the precious rose oil and can be bought in towns throughout Bulgaria. In addition to the roses, all around Kazanluk are Thraician Ruins, which are truly amazing. I was fortunate to not only go in the replicate of a ruin from around 5000 BC, but with a special invite to Ivanka we were able to enter the original ruin. We wore special clothing to cover our street clothes and our shoes.

BITTERSWEET THANKSGIVING

Letter to my sisters, November 1, 2010
Bulgaria went off DST this weekend so now there is only six hours difference between here and the East Coast, but I know this coming weekend the U.S. changes the clock back. Tonight coming back on the 5:30 train it was already dark outside. I had a nice weekend visiting with another older volunteer.

She is really a neat person. We had a great visit. She came to Bulgaria this past May. I had meet her briefly earlier in the summer. She was a school counselor for many years, and is now a widow. She lives in the town where the Rose Festival is held. Kazanluk has about 60,000 people, so quite a different living experience from Topolitsa and yet she's facing some of the same issues that I do. She was all set to put a special breakfast casserole in the oven to serve me when I got there, and oops, she made the mistake of also turning on her heater, and a fuse blew. These are different fuses than we use in the U.S.

A man came to fix it, but at night, it broke down again, I don't know why. Finally she was able to bake last night, and we had casserole with beans. It was tasty. We finished it up today at breakfast.

If there was a direct train from Topolitsa I could visit her more often, but I have to catch the fast train, and that only stops in either Aitos or

Karnobat and it is not always easy to get the connection. Today I had to wait three hours for the train to my village. The distance is only ten miles, but I can't walk it. It is not safe, even if I wanted to do it. Last night we watched the new Sherlock movie, another Bulgarian had downloaded on her computer. It was really good. The setting is modern London, and Doctor Watson has served as an army doctor in Afghanistan and Sherlock uses a computer I think it was either done for PBS or BBC.

Saturday night we had dinner at a nice Italian restaurant, and the young PCV couple who is there joined us. They're from Colorado. It was a nice weekend. Today is a special education holiday called National Enlighteners Day or sometimes called National Revival Day. It pays tributes to those committed to help bring about Bulgarian independence.

Tomorrow I have a full load of classes, but Wednesday I again travel to Sofia to get my new crown. I'm happy about that. I also hope that my new glasses are ready to be picked up. The weather is nice here today too. I decided to make a fire tonight though as it is rather cool in my apartment, thankfully no rain. But, I'm almost out of wood. It is so frustrating to always have to request wood. I wish the school would bring a month supply.

Time for bed. I can't get the light bulb out of the socket in my bathroom to change it. I will have to plan my showers for daylight hours. Good thing I'm going to Sofia. I will be able to have a warm shower at the hotel, simple pleasures.

I haven't missed hearing about the election. I read about a woman not even knowing that the 1st Amendment was about the separation of church and state. What a sad state of affairs.

Have a good time at the polls tomorrow.

Love, Louise

My sister and brother-in-law worked many years at the polls for elections.

Hi Louise, **November 16, 2010**

Great idea for coffee tomorrow, I am free on Wednesday from 12:15 till 1:45 PM. If this time is convenient for you I can bring with me the small whiteboard which I promised to you.

By the way there will be a trip to Veliko Tarnovo city, Arbanasi, Dryanovski monastery, Lyaskovski monastery, the gold dome of the church of Shipka village, and the cave Bacho Kiro on 27th and 28th this month, Saturday and Sunday.

The fee is 50 lev and includes traveling expenses, lodging overnight in Tryavna city and one breakfast.

Ivanka

Hi Ivanka,   **November 16, 2010**

I am so happy that we can meet for coffee tomorrow. 12:15 is a good time. Can we meet inside the Boulevard Restaurant in the Center? The trip sounds great too. I would love to join the group. When would I have to decide? Louise

Hi Louise,   **November 23, 2010**

Just right now I received all answers you need:

First, I arranged to have your hair trimmed and dyed on Friday at 3 PM. The number of the color for your hair is 7 not 8 what you have written on the note because number 8 is brighter. Number 7 is the color which the hairdresser uses every time to dye your hair.

Second, about the trip: we are leaving at 4:45 in the morning on Saturday. You can wait for us in front of Rachel's apartment at 4:20 AM.

The bus is going to wait for us on a place close to Bulbank. We will come back to Aitos not earlier than 7 PM on Sunday. Prepare some food – maybe sandwiches – for yourself because we have only breakfast in the hotel.

Don't forget your ID card, Ivanka

Hi Tatyana,   **November 22, 2010**

It is so good to hear from you. And thank you for the Thanksgiving wishes. It will be school as usual for me next year back in the U.S. I will have a big celebration. I wish that you and Peter could come and visit me when I return to the U.S. Generally I've just been busy with school.

I've worked with Rachel, the PCV in Aitos and we've held another teacher training session, this time on Classroom Management. It was this past Saturday and we held it in the Park Museum in a room set aside for meetings held there. We were happy to have 15 teachers from her school come, and my school director. I did make it to Kazanluk to visit Naomi, the other older volunteer. It was good to share notes with her. She is not in the TEFL program, but works with students in testing and an orphanage.

I'll send you separately a video my son sent this morning of Milo. He is now six months old. I am getting very anxious to see him. I'm still working on the quilt for him, but I don't think that I'll have it finished for Christmas. I'll send you several photos that I took of it this evening.

This weekend I plan to go with my language teacher and some of her friends on an excursion to Veliko Turnovo. She mentioned it to me last week. I remember discussing it with you and telling you how much I wanted to go there, so I was so happy to get invited to come along. We will also go to the Dryanovo Monastery, St. Michael the Archangel, and Petropavlovski Monastery, Saints Peter and Paul, are nearby and the Bacho

Kiro Cave. Thank you again for keeping in touch. It is always good to hear from you.

Please greet Peter for me. Louise

There are over 120 monasteries in Bulgaria. Many were destroyed when the country was ruled by the USSR. Some were destroyed during the Ottoman reign which lasted over 450 years. Some have been rebuilt. Many of the monasteries date back to the 9th and 10th centuries, the earliest date back to the year 344. They vary greatly in size, and may have as few as three monks or as many as fifty. They are overseen by the Patriarchate and the Bulgarian Orthodox Church. The Bulgarian Orthodox Church has been its own entity since 927 AD. It is believed that Christianity was brought to the Bulgarian lands by the apostles Paul and Andrew in the 1st century AD and by the 4th century was the dominant religion in the region. Veliko Tarnovo was the capital of the Second Bulgarian Empire (1185-1393) and has many historic sites to see and explore.

Email to Hazel and Naomi, November 25, 2010
Happy Thanksgiving

It sure doesn't seem the same without the turkey, does it? Next year I think I will plan a very big celebration on this very American holiday.

I wanted to update you with my news; I've discussed my situation with only a few others, trying to figure things out and what course of action I should take. I think it's harder for the younger group to understand all the different pieces that an older volunteer has to consider when she makes this commitment for two years. I thought I had it all in place, but it reached a point with the tenants staying in my house, that I realized they were taking advantage of the situation in a big way.

I plan to tell Dora, my school director in Topolitsa on Monday. I leave with many mixed emotions. October and November were like a roller coaster ride dealing with the problems of my renters in New Mexico. PC is offering me an "interrupted plan" which I still need to get more details on. I might get them tomorrow, or else next Wednesday when I go to Sofia. Perhaps it will be my last train ride across Bulgaria. Coming back in March may be an option if I can get it sorted out by then. Otherwise, sometime I think I would consider a six-month commitment, if that would be open to me.

I really don't know how the school will react. I know they will do fine without me, but I sure hate leaving the children, even though at times they can certainly be difficult and seem to have little interest in learning English. I'm going with my language teacher to Veilko Turnovo Saturday. The trip just happened to come up last week, and I was glad for the diversion. But for now, I'm sitting here looking at my three suitcases and trying to figure how to manage it all. Hope this finds you both well, and that when we're all back in the States we can get together and reminiscence about Bulgaria and our Peace Corps days. If by chance you're in Sofia next week, please let me know. I'd love to have a cup of coffee, or a beer and just be together.

All the best, Louise

Happy Thanksgiving. I hope that today you are all having a wonderful celebration with your family and friends.

I will miss having turkey today and all the trimmings, but to help the lonesomeness I had a few volunteers over several weeks ago and roasted a small chicken and made stuffing and mashed potatoes. It tasted so "American" and they loved it. To top off the meal I made an apple pie. It was a wonderful celebration.

Today is a regular kind of day here. Some volunteers are getting together in various places over the weekend to celebrate this American holiday.

I want to share with you the news that I have talked to Peace Corps as I have to consider returning to the U.S. earlier than originally planned. I may come back to Bulgaria later in the spring if the situation with my house in Farmington can get resolved. Next week Wednesday I will travel to Sofia and fill out all the necessary paperwork and most likely fly to California early in December. The next few days I will be busy packing, sorting through all the things in my apartment to be given away, packed, or thrown away. Monday most likely will be my last day teaching and I will have to tell the staff the news of my departure which I know will be difficult to do – especially with children whom I have grown very close to.

On my return, I will stay with Stacey and Marcus and Milo for about ten days and then fly to Albuquerque and rent a car to drive up to Farmington. I have had to ask my tenants to vacate my house and I plan to put it on the market to sell. A friend from Farmington has helped coordinate the logistics of dealing with my house. Needles to say, it is upsetting that the tenants have not taken the responsibility of renting and caring for the house.

I am thankful that I have good friends to call on. I feel very lucky that way.

While over here in Bulgaria all of you have been so wonderful keeping in touch with me, sending me care packages, sending gifts, books and school supplies. I couldn't have done it without all of your help. Thank you very much. The children have been reading the books that have been set up in the library at the school. After I return I will write more about my adventures here in Bulgaria. It certainly has been a learning experience. Working with the children, meeting new people, living in a different cultural all has added to the richness of my life and I am very grateful to have had this opportunity to be in the Peace Corps.

Happy Thanksgiving! May the days and weeks ahead continue to be filled with rich blessings, joy, peace and love.

With love and prayers, Louise

TIME TO LEAVE

Dear Sis,   **November 9, 2010**

It was very difficult tonight meeting with Vesala and telling her that I might have to terminate early. She was telling me places that she wanted to take me to visit. Just knowing more people makes it all that much harder. I talked to a very nice woman on the train; it hits me like "darn it all anyway" that I have to think of leaving my Peace Corps position earlier than first planned.

I want to get a few more answers from my friend in Farmington and the realtor about the situation there, before I tell Peace Corps.

Hopefully I will get some answers yet this week and then need to talk to PC which I'm dreading. I expect to call after Thanksgiving. After that specific dates are discussed as I understand the guidelines.

Mailing a few more things back; they are still worth more than the postage in the long run I think so hope to get the boxes to Burgas either Thursday or Friday. If I didn't have to carry them all the way to the train, I wouldn't have to make so many trips but that's how it is. I'm just frustrated with the whole situation tonight.

Love, Louise

Hi Sis,   **November 11, 2010**

I'm sorting and packing. Today after classes I walked to the train with five boxes; two weighed about five kilos each, and the other three were smaller, about two kilos. I had sealed the small ones, thinking they didn't need to be inspected. Wrong I had to open them up, (this was at a different window than where I take the big boxes) but eventually got them open and resealed and filled out the forms and the postal clerk took my money.

Then I went to the Customs regular window and filled out more forms and got it inspected by the woman who remembered me from my previous visits.

Then I went back to the post office area where they were weighed again and more forms are filled out. I made it back to the train just in time so that I wouldn't have a three hour wait for the last train back for the night. Tomorrow I'll repeat this procedure and then I think everything is mailed that I can for now. The rest of my things will have to fit in my three suitcases.

Yes, this has been a tough teaching week and tomorrow again I will have 6th, 7th and 8th grade. The children are certainly keeping me on my toes.

Well, I have to get back to tasks. I have a feeling that I might be teaching on Thanksgiving Day as well. Oh by the way, when I came back from the train four big gunny sacks of wood were sitting in my downstairs doorway. I managed to cart it all upstairs. It's been warm here too, but I'm sure it'll be cooler soon.

Love, Louise

Hi Louise,   **November 11, 2010**

Hope your day is going well. I can imagine teaching is wearing; always keeping one step ahead of the kids isn't easy and I don't imagine the language barrier helps. Hopefully you'll get the house situation straightened out, but it doesn't sound like fun.

Love, LeAnne

Dear Sisters,   **November 14, 2010**

My Thanksgiving dinner with the two Peace Corps Volunteers went well. They seem so young to me. Both are around 24. Another volunteer who was going to come has been sick. She has an ear infection and has been running a temperature all week. She did come over for a while yesterday as she's taking some of my things that she could use in her apartment.

Her boyfriend was here to help also. He's PCV, in the B-26 group. He came over in the spring. He is further north, about four hours away by bus. He seems a very nice young man. Did I write about telling the Bulgarian friend that I might have to return to the United States? She was very upset. She couldn't understand why Peace Corps just couldn't give me some extra time off. I know that they won't change their policy just for me. But for now, I let the question remain open and am not going to discuss it with anyone else until I have exact dates lined up.

My apple pies really turned out well. Rachel enjoyed watching me make the stuffing. I forget how little experience most of them have had in cooking, so that in itself is a much bigger deal. Mary offered to peel potatoes and though willing, I could see that she had not done it much. Funny the little things I take for granted.

I had the chance to talk with all three of my children last night which was fun. All seem to be doing well. I am so thankful for that. I really shouldn't refer to them as children, as they are all grown adults each with several college degrees and living on their own with responsible jobs. The weather has really been nice this week. I am extremely thankful for that. Well, I need to get ready for bed. I have another week of teaching coming up.

Love, Louise

Hi LeAnne,   **November 16, 2010**

It would be much easier in the planning if I could discuss options with Peace Corps ahead of time, but that is not how the system works. I'm trying to figure out what I think will happen once I discuss it with them. I may be back in the states by the first weekend in December. We will see.

Actually today I found out about a small two-day excursion from my language teacher to several historic towns that I'd love to visit, so I'm wondering now if I can manage to work that in the schedule. It is the 27th and 28th of November. I talked to my realtor who is working with the lawyer in Farmington. He thought the people were out of the house. I know sometimes they have stayed at her mother's for some reason or another, and didn't really move out. Once it was waiting for a part to the refrigerator.

The woman, who co-owns the realty company with her brother, was killed in a car crash last Wednesday. I'm sad to hear of her death. She was a very nice woman. Besides her sad and sudden death, her death complicates my situation as my realtor is one of her main agents.

Thursday Peace Corps is coming for a site visit. This is done about every six months just to see how everything is going. Tomorrow I'm going in to Aitos to have coffee with Vesala. She was here Saturday and got very upset when I told her what might happen. I also have my regular lesson with my language teacher.

Today I was down stairs eating: lamb, salads, and deserts, all good, but too much. The lamb was very good; fixed in a stew rather than grilled. Milka, my landlady, gave me another big bowl to take upstairs for tomorrow. *Rakia*, of course was served. Milka told me they made 1,000 liters of *Rakia*. Her daughter and husband made it I think. I believe they sell to people all over Bulgaria. Many villagers still come to buy cigarettes, all in all another story for sure.

Time for a cup of tea, and then maybe I'll try and watch a DVD just for something different. What a mixture of emotions I'm going through this week.

Love, Louise

Dear Felicia,   **November 18, 2010**

The Bulgarian Inspector of Education was at school today. I even had a meeting with her. It was mainly in Bulgarian. I did not understand all of the discussion parts.

Yesterday worked out okay. I called Vesala again when it appeared she was running late, so I just asked her when she would be returning to Aitos. I'm quite sure she said the 26th I mentioned about the possibility of going to Veliko Turnovo with Ivanka. She was happy to hear that and

I just told her I'd talk to her when she was back in town.

Then I met with Ivanka for my language lesson. We discussed literature and the Bulgarian education system. You would have enjoyed her insight. I also gave her a copy of my book *Goulash and Picking Pickles: an almost boomer growing up in rural Wisconsin with recipes from Grandma, and other relatives*. She gave me a large white magnetic board that she had. I had told her previous about the letters that I had bought in Jumbo. We had a nice lunch.

I paid my internet bill, but no phone bill due yet. It sure is a mystery to me why it's not ready yet. We'll see what this afternoon brings. Chavdar (Peace Corps administrator) is coming.

The news from New Mexico is much the same. Because of the death of the realtor things are not moving as fast as I hoped. Hopefully by this weekend the papers will be drawn up to evict my tenants. They now owe me thousands of dollars, and I understand from my realtor who stopped at the house, that it is a total disaster. He said it will take thousands of dollars to clean it up. They even had two dogs in the house, and the neighbor had to call the Humane Society as they were not being fed. The utility bills have not been paid as well. I never expected it to come to this.

Any plans for the weekend? I'll try and call you. The Veilko Turnovo excursion is a maybe as the first bus is already filled. Ivanka is hoping that they will add a second bus.

Wish you could come too, Louise

Hi Mary,

If you could come over Monday afternoon, perhaps via taxi, that would be great. I'm talking to PC about having an extended time back in the states to deal with my house situation there and that may happen as soon as next week.

I'd love for you to use the printer while I'm in the States, as long as three months perhaps. Then when I return I'd like to borrow it back until I COS and then you could have it permanently. I have the box for the printer and the warranty which is good for two years.

This weekend I'm going with my language teacher to Veilko Turnavo, but I'll be back Sunday night. I'm staying at Rachel's tonight as leaving early tomorrow morning from Aitos.

Please let me know if Monday will work for you.

Call me tonight or I'll try to reach you, Louise

Email to my children
Hello dear ones,

Some of the volunteers know that I have made the difficult decision to return to the U.S. due to the house situation back in New Mexico.

Tomorrow I will tell Dora and the school faculty and the students. It will be difficult.

Also tomorrow a Peace Corp van will come and take my big luggage to Sofia. They are at a meeting in Plovdiv and agreed to help me out. This usually is not done, but I know they have done it a few times before. That will certainly be a big help. It is difficult to board the train with numerous items and then store them on the train, especially as its a seven hour train ride. I have lots of things that need to be returned to the PC office. I need to return the fire extinguisher, the medical kit, bike helmet (I always was going to get a bicycle), smoke alarms . . . many things. I've asked Laura to come and take clothes to the orphanage and some of my household items.

I will be able to leave a few things for the next volunteer like my printer, toaster, and Christmas tree. All my school supplies I will take over to the school office for the teachers to share amongst themselves. I just came back from a nice weekend with my language teacher and visited a few more monasteries and other historic towns. Now I have to finish packing my suitcases.

I'll be relieved when the heat is turned on at 2907. Do you know if the people have moved out? I've not heard from the realtor and now I can't call him via gmail. That telephone service maybe is done, or just for this holiday weekend. I don't know. If all goes as planned I come back by United on Saturday around 12:30 PM. There is a direct flight from Frankfurt.

Please hold off on canceling the Christmas ticket. Peace Corps doesn't issue my ticket until all the paperwork is approved; if you can wait for a few more days that would relieve me. It doesn't feel real.

Love, Mom

What a surprise I had Tuesday morning when I went into school. All the children were there to greet me. I received many many hugs. They had flowers for me. There was a Banitsa and other tasty food. The children sang some traditional songs. Lots of pictures were taken. We were all crying.

Dora asked me to come back later in the afternoon. It turns out she prepared a special CD for me with pictures of our summer excursion on it. That was so very kind of her. Also she gave me a lovely framed picture of all of the teachers. I am on it as well. It was taken for the 125th Anniversary Celebration of the school.

Later, some of the young female students came over to my apartment. They had presents for me and I found some gifts for them. It was very hard to say goodbye. I hope I will have a chance to return while they are students. Many students gave me gifts, handwritten notes, or pictures.

Good-bye Mrs. Hoffmann. Stay with me . . . don't let me go. Cause I can't make it without you. Just stay with me, and hold me close, because I've built my world around you. We love Mrs. Hoffmann! Aeize Valentine Eleonora Eshiret Gigz Krasimir Radostin Seid Fabregul Chavdaar Shetuet Mrs. Zlateva.

Lots of hearts and signed by all the students in grade 7. It still brings tears to my eyes. This has been an amazing adventure. I really don't want it to end.

Hello Dora,   **November 30, 2010**

Thank you again for your understanding of why I must leave Topolitsa and go back to the U.S. It means very much to me that you have been so supportive of my time here working with you and your staff and the students. Thank you, thank you. I was overwhelmed today with the gifts and the love shown to me by everyone at the school. When I return to America I will share the photos, the gifts and the stories of Topolitsa, the students, the staff and the dedication that you have for your students here in Bulgaria.

It is important I feel for Americans to learn about Bulgaria and the life and culture here. I was happy to share stories about life and my family in America. I will stay in touch with you, and I hope that some of the students also will write me emails or "old-fashioned" letters via the post office. It would be wonderful to get letters in America from the students.

I have emailed Laura and asked her to be in touch with you before she returns to America in the summer and to bring the keyboard to the Topolitsa school for the students to learn music.

I know we will stay in touch – and I will let you know my plans. If I cannot return to teach as a PC volunteer, I for sure will come back to visit you and the students as soon as I can arrange such a trip.

And thank you for the arrangement for me to go to the train tomorrow. It will help me very much. I will wait outside my door at 6:20 AM for the ride into Aitos.

Also, please remember that you, your family and the staff are always welcome in my home in America.

All the best to you, Louise

Hello Louise,   **November 30, 2010**

Thank you for the nice words. For me also it was a pleasure to support and care for your comfort. I appreciate your warm feelings towards Bulgaria and the great interest in our culture. With sorrow I heard your news about your departure. I hope you can stop the problem with your house. It will be good to be near your family. I believe in you. You're a good person and deserve better.

Someday I may indeed be able to visit America. This is my dream.

Hopefully this is a short separation and will be a step to new opportunities. I wish you success and faith.

Thank you for your support for the project in music. I'm sorry you did not have the opportunity to teach the children piano.

Dora

Email to my family

I'm in Sofia. I arrived around 2:30 yesterday via train. The custodian gave me a ride in his car, picking me up at 6 AM to Aitos, but unfortunately his car broke down halfway there. Milka had come along and she did manage to reach her son-in-law and so he came in his car. It was still dark outside and all my bags had to get transferred to another car. But I made it to the train with a few minutes to spare. Fortunately a young woman who had been at the Topolitsa village the day before giving the students yoga lessons was also boarding the train and could speak English and she helped me with my bags.

Now I'm at the Peace Corps office doing lots of paperwork. I need to visit the medical, the dentist, the bank and hopefully finish by five tomorrow. Then they give me my plane ticket for my Saturday 6 AM United flight back to the U.S. It all seems rather unreal that it is happening.

Today I heard that there is snow in Europe and some airports were closed. The weather is changing here, from being very warm and now rain, cold weather, but hopefully no blinding snowstorms preventing flights. I should be in San Francisco by 12:30 PM California time. Safe travels to all.

Love, Louise *aka* Mom

Good morning —

Yes, it's been quite a week. There is so much to absorb and think about. Thanks for the photos. It's hard for me to believe that so soon I will be back.

And to help ease this last day, Felicia came in last night and stayed at The House with me. She said that she would stay over night and go to the airport with me in the morning. That is such a relief.

I have three bags to check and hopefully they will allow me my smaller gray carry-on and red bag that attaches to it, plus my purse. It's Lufthansa out of Sofia to Frankfurt. I am arranging the taxi for 4 AM.

Today it's more forms. I had lunch and a good meeting with Leslie, the Peace Corps country director. Tomorrow I go to the bank and have a final medical review and then I get my airline ticket.

It is considered interrupted service. This will allow me to return in 90 days. It also seems a possibility of keeping the window open for up to a year. We will see, what will be, will be.

I just found out from the Peace Corps woman working on all these final arrangements, that my third bag will be 215 euros But I don't think I can give away all this stuff; so I will just put it on my credit card.

Maybe I will have a friendly agent at the counter and be given a break. I noticed military personnel are allowed 70 pounds, but I guess Peace Corps workers are not. Oh my, thanks again for the photos. Milo is sure a cutie. Soon I will be there and give him and all of you a big hug.

Love, Mom

Letter to teachers and students in Topolitsa
Greetings from New Mexico,   **December 21, 2010**

I want to send you and the teachers and students special holidays greetings. I miss you all very much. I have been very busy dealing with my house here in Farmington. The people who lived in my house left it in a complete mess. Gradually I am getting it cleaned up.

Thursday I will be flying back to California and spend Christmas with my son, his wife and Milo. My son David, who lives in Colorado, will also be there. Then I will fly to Boston to spend some time with my daughter.

Perhaps later in January we can Skype chat. It would be fun to see you and all the students and chat for awhile. I could use my son's computer. Today I am using my friend's computer. My house is such a mess that I have not been able to stay in it. The weather has been overcast, but we have not had snow. Has Topolitsa had snow?

Last Friday I gave two special programs to people here in Farmington telling them about Topolitsa and my wonderful friends back in Bulgaria. They all enjoyed it very much. I want to wish you all the best and thank you again for allowing me to be a part of your school program. I am looking forward to hanging up the photo and the special gifts that you gave me in my house. And I know that I will return to Bulgaria, I just do not know when it will be.

Please also greet Milka for me when you see her.

Merry Christmas and a Healthy and Happy New Year, Louise

BACK IN THE USA

Letter sent to friends, December 6, 2010

This has been a very traumatic last several weeks for me. As some of you may already know, I felt compelled to ask PC to let me return earlier than originally planned so that I could deal with my house problems back in New Mexico. To make a long story short – my tenants took complete advantage of my absence and not only decided not to keep up financially with the payments due, but also to not take care of the property. As a result I had to hire a lawyer and pursue eviction procedures against them.

The Peace Corps staff in Bulgaria was most cooperative, and there is a possibility that I will return to PC service. I'm just not sure when. As a returned PC volunteer there are some options open to me. For now, I have to deal with things here. I formally resigned December 4 and flew back to California.

I left Sofia at 6 AM for the two-and-a-half hour flight to Frankfurt. My son and grandson met me at the San Francisco airport after the 12 hour flight from Frankfort. It was very difficult and sad to leave Bulgaria. The school staff and the students were very understanding and gave me a warm send-off. Prior to leaving I had three intense days dealing with paperwork, including a complete physical. I'm in good shape, except having several toe nails coming off, probably due to all the walking and assorted types of shoes I was wearing. I don't remember dropping anything heavy on them.

Friday I will fly to Albuquerque and drive up to Farmington. The tenants are now out. They had not paid any utility bills recently so the house was cold, and some pipes froze. The lawyer will be assessing all the damages, including cleaning. They had two dogs, clearly against the contract. One step at a time.

I do hope to put the house on the market at the beginning of the year. I will be spending my time going back and forth from California. I also want to take a trip to New England to see Gretchen. At some point I'll have to get a car. One step at a time. David will also be here for Christmas. Milo is a real sweetie and smiles a lot.

Please keep in touch, Louise

Hi Louise,

Your message was quite a shocker! Too bad you had to end your assignment because of the house. How did you get all of your Bulgarian treasures back by yourself? I'm sure Laura and all the volunteers and Milka are going to miss you

Hope there isn't a lot of damage to the house. I guess you'll see how bad it is in a few days.

Take care, Debbie

Hi Debbie,   **December 8, 2010**

Yes, it was a very big disappointment to come back early especially as I had put in a year and a half. It is still considered as a fulfilled commitment to Peace Corps service. I do have the possibility of reinstatement in Bulgaria, or I could apply at a new service that they're offering to former PCVs for short term contracts, six to ten months. It all depends on my house.

I gave lots of my stuff away to nearby volunteers and some I took into Sofia for a general box. They have a room there for volunteers to go through teaching materials, clothes, and miscellaneous items. Fortunately,

Peace Corps helped me out with transportation. They had a meeting in Plovdiv last week and drove a van to Topolitsa and picked up my two big suitcases and things like the fire extinguisher and medical kit. I ended up with seven assorted bags for the train. I'll write up that story and send it out to you and a few others. Even my last morning there had its excitement.

Milka was quite upset on my leaving. I'll be sending her postcards and photos. I'm so glad that you could come this summer and that we explored some of Bulgaria together. Hope to see you soon. Louise

Dear Family and Friends,   **President's Weekend 2011**

As many of you know I have returned to the U.S. This was due to my house situation in Farmington. The tenants were asked to leave and I am working with a lawyer to get the situation resolved. I still hope to put the house on the market this spring. Hopefully the housing market will be such that a buyer will come through and be approved. I know many people are in the same situation that I am in.

In the meantime, I will try to use this transition year to visit family and friends, see a bit of the U.S. go through my many boxes that have been stored and hold one more garage sale so that when the time comes to move it will be more manageable.

I miss Bulgaria. I did not have time to say farewell to many of my colleagues in the Peace Corps or Bulgarians whom I had met. Peace Corps has a new program for returned volunteers where you can sign up for a specific job in a specific area. The time frame is usually anywhere from 6 months to a year. Hopefully in the not too distant future I may be able to go back to Bulgaria or a nearby country and serve for this shorter time commitment.

Peace Corps offers a unique program for Americans. It is a one-to-one opportunity for many people in foreign countries to meet an American for the first time. Prior to meeting a PC volunteer their only impression of Americans is probably through some B-rated movie or television show or American pop music. One Bulgarian I met where over there and now lives in Florida told me how he loved American music as a teenager, but had no idea of what the words meant. Now he has learned more English, and realizes that how "insulting"many of the lyrics actually were. In the bigger cities English has been taught at the universities for many years, even under Communism. But in the smaller towns and villages, most do not know English and have had little or no contact with an American.

This is the 50th anniversary of the PC and celebrations are being held as well as various news shows and surveys as to PC effectiveness. While it is not perfect, it is still in my opinion a wonderful way to show people around the world a face of America that is not always seen in the news, in television and in the movies. I felt honored to be invited to sit down with Bulgarians and enjoy everyday conversation. To celebrate with them their birthday and to learn about their traditions was a privilege.

Teaching in a Bulgarian classroom was a wonderful opportunity to share with them American traditions. The children were very interested to hear about my family, what we did on vacations, how we celebrated birthdays and weddings. America is a magical land to many of them and so to meet and talk to an average American was a treat for them.

At the same time I hoped that I helped the students see that their country also was a very special place and one that they should be proud of. I think it is hard for some of them to see that. When they see and hear on the news all the things that Americans have, it is hard for them to see that no matter the size of their country or their world ranking, each country is unique and special. Bulgaria has a rich history and one to be proud of and I felt it was important to try and instill a sense of pride in their country. Bulgaria's history goes back thousands of years and now is making a big leap into the modern era. Twenty years free from Communism is a relatively short time for a country to transition to implement democracy, freedom of speech, free enterprise – all the freedoms that we so easily take for granted. Bulgaria is in the early stages of being part of the European Union.

I was also very happy to have the opportunity to talk to a class of students at the University of California, Berkeley. For many years UC has had many of its students sign up for a Peace Corps assignment. I told them about my experience in Topolitsa, learning the language and sharing with them some of my stories of heating my apartment, going seven hours on the train for medical appointments and general life especially as an older volunteer. They asked many questions. It was a very interesting experience for me and I hope worthwhile for them to speak to a volunteer who had returned after living over 19 months in a former Soviet Bloc country. I hope to do the same at San Juan College and I am thinking of doing some classes in the Adult Ed program on the history of Bulgaria.

This year Lonely Planet listed it as one of the top ten places to visit. I hope that I will have a chance to go back soon and I hope that you too consider it. I have thousands of pictures that I took while there and in the next months I hope to make several power point presentations with them and some special photographic books about Bulgaria.

This past month I have been kept busy taking care of my new grandson while mom and dad work. Babies are indeed a delight, but I think I had forgotten how much time and energy they absorb. I'm traveling back to New Mexico next week to hopefully resolve some of my house issues. I bought a car so this summer I hope to make a road trip via Canada to

Pennsylvania and Wisconsin. While flying is faster, I am looking forward to seeing some of the small towns and countryside of Canada and the U.S. that is missed when a person is at 20,000 feet.

Before I close I want to take this opportunity to thank each and every one of you for your special support while I served as a PC volunteer. There are thousands of volunteers all over the world and if you want to learn more about PC please go to the official PC site, *www.peacecorps. gov*. They have a section that shows some of the special projects that PCVs are working on. I feel very honored to be a part of this wonderful group. I hope that I will continue to hear from you and that our lives will continue to cross.

With warm regards, Louise

Hi Rachel,   **April 3, 2011**

That sounds like a wonderful trip with the other volunteers: Vienna and Prague are two of my favorite cities. I went with Hazel last summer, but we only had two days in each as we added Budapest and Venice to our menu. The trip gave us a good taste of beautiful European cities.

I'm excited to hear that you'll be teaching journalism at the American University in Blagoevgrad this summer. That is indeed an honor. Do you have any idea of how many students you will have? What ages? That is great news that your parents can come to Bulgaria as well. I know that you will be a very good tour guide. I know how important it is to get away and to talk to someone else.

Getting another perspective on how to look at things can help. It doesn't necessarily change things, but helps us view it from another point of view. Teaching is tough and I think particularly so in a foreign country and in a school where learning a second language is not seen as necessarily helpful or needed. It's a shame, but true. Just do the best you can every day, and even though you may feel that some days are a complete loss I am sure that your presence saids a lot. This year's almost over and it's spring, which is a good thing. You will make it.

Yes, I had my garage sale and did okay. It covered about half the lawyer's fees and the family's stuff is gone. I donated the left over items to charity (per the court agreement). Lots and lots of people came from about 8 AM to 2 PM. Thankfully my sister and her husband were able to drive up from Mesa, Arizona, to help me and also a few friends from Farmington.

Now I am beginning to feel that it's my house again, but I still need to do lots of repairs and get all the rooms painted. In the summer I will tackle the yard and patio. What a disaster they are, mainly because of their dogs, the couple drank and he smoked. I didn't count how many bags of garbage got hauled away but they filled up a pickup truck twice.

With all that has been going on in my life, I realized I needed to stop setting deadlines for myself. I decided I could not mentally or physically just turn around and put the house on the market. I need time to just "be." Also, I didn't care for my current realtor. He kept telling me all the things wrong with my house and wanted me to do even more major renovations. So I decided to take it off the market. In due time, I will list it. In the meantime, I'm making it my home.

This week I'll travel to Boston for my daughter's wedding. Then back to New Mexico for a few days, before I drive back to California for 6 weeks where I'll again take care of my grandson who turns 1 in May.

I do want to come back to Bulgaria. It will probably be just for a long visit, and am hoping that maybe it could be next spring or early summer. I'd like to come when you are still there. Hopefully Felicia and Laura are extending. I'd also like to see Naomi. At some point, I'd like to consider a Returned Peace Corps Volunteer position.

If you see or talk to Laura please tell her to email me and let me know what's going on in her life. I did get a chance to talk to Felicia the other day which was great. She is very busy with the spelling bee. Any news of Topolitsa?

Have you had a chance to meet up with Ivanka? She is very interested in planning trips around Bulgaria and just a good listener and friend. Did *The Week* magazines arrive?

Do take care of yourself. I always enjoy hearing from you. I hope that you are able to plan some special trips over the summer besides the teaching in Blagoevrad. I found that it really helped to have something special to look forward to. How I'd love to meet up with you, maybe next spring.

Big hug,

With warm wishes and much love, Louise

Hi Louise,   **April 27, 2011**

Happy Easter to you too, I wish you to be a cheerful person to save your inner light, and be blessed.

On Easter Sunday my friends and I went to Topolitsa and had a barbecue up in the hills near the White River. And being in Topolitsa reminded me of you. I remembered that we had a fantastic time when you were here in Bulgaria. I realized how I miss the conversations with you.

On Saturday night I attended the whole Easter church worship for first time. First, at midnight all the people including me circled round the church with our candles lit up by the blessed light from Jerusalem. I had to mind the light of my candle. The feeling was astonishing and it was beautiful to see the many lights that people were carrying in the darkness as little shining stars or fireflies. Then we brought the lit candles in the church. I decided to stay till the end of the church worship, 3 AM. The experience was wonderful.

I finished my driving course. I passed my theoretical and practical exam successfully. Now I am waiting for my driving license. It will be very nice to arrange a tour when you come to Bulgaria if you can trust my driving.

I continue to teach my private students and have an offer to lead some English courses in Burgas in a private language company in July. I am so glad that I have more free time. I use it to read books and develop myself. I also do yoga courses three times a week and the results are amazing. Now I am feeling full of energy and in a good mood. The group is very nice and I enjoy doing yoga.

I am greatly impressed by your book. It is very readable and I enjoyed it a lot. Thank you very much for this precious present. I appreciate the book because it gave me a lot of moments of fun, laughter, and deep thoughts.

Best, Ivanka

Hi Louise,   **May 10, 2011**

I've been meaning to write a letter to you for the entire year now but every time I sit down to write I get distracted by something else. This year has been quite difficult. Ever since January 1st I've had problem after problem after problem. Back in January I got the bed bug infestation, which was a total disaster, Louise. Everything was so out of control. You wouldn't think a tiny bug would interfere with your life so much, but it did.

I got the bed bugs because I was collecting clothes for an orphanage and someone gave me an infested bag. (These were not the clothes from you Louise.)

The landlord blamed it on the cats. The cats had to leave and luckily Rachel pulled through and watched them for almost two months. But this meant she had four cats in her apartment and I could tell the stress was getting to her.

After Rachel, I took the cats to a guy named Tim who lives outside of Razgrad. Rachel offered to go with me which was fine. But I was so exhausted that I didn't even realize that I switched the names of the town. I thought we were going to Zdravets when we were actually going to Zavets. It's a little village outside of Razgrad and you have to take a bus to get to it.

We had missed the bus so I would have just stayed at a volunteer's house in Razgrad but Rachel wanted to get to the village so we took a taxi. That was fine with me and I could understand her viewpoint. Well, off we went to the wrong village and almost two hours and 40 lev later, we wound up back where we started and very stressed. Finally the next day, Tim came to pick up the cats for me and about a month later he said he couldn't keep them anymore.

When I saw them again they looked awful, Chavdar had cuts on his face. That really upset me. Luckily I had someone else who offered to foster them and that's where they are now. He's a B-26 volunteer and he lives in Gabrovo. Chavdar and Pepa both seem fine with him for now. In the meantime, Phil (Peace Corp assistant director) is helping me find a family with the American Embassy. We'll see how that goes. So that's this year in a nutshell. It's been a mess.

I'm tired and I'm really ready to go home. I was seriously contemplating extending for a year, but in the end I found myself trying to convince myself to stay. We had our COS conference last week and you were missed. I have missed you a lot, actually, and I often wish I could just retreat to your apartment and have tea, or pie and coffee. You helped me pass the days, Louise, and I miss your laughter. How are things going there? How's the house situation? Felicia told me your daughter got married. That's exciting, How was the wedding? How is your grandson? Please fill me in. I also hope that you had a really great Mother's Day. Tell me what you did. I'm sorry this is so long.

I love you, Louise. Laura

Hi Laura,   **May 11, 2011**

Wow – I don't know what to say . . . what a year you have had. You sure have tales to tell and I know that it is all too real.

I feel especially bad about the cats. I sure hope Rudy finds a permanent home for them. Poor cats. What an ordeal they have gone through and none of it is their fault. I thought you might extend your time, but sounds like you're ready to come back to the U.S. and start the next phase of your life.

I've been thinking about our trip to Turkey many times. I'm so glad we got to do that together. It was fun, it spite of all the loud music and noisy passengers, not to mention the long hours on the bus. And I thought we would never stop for the bathroom. I thought my bladder was going to burst. And not being trusted to walk down the street from the hotel, the first night in Istanbul made me feel like I was fifteen, rather than 65.

And to have to deal with bedbugs in your apartment! That certainly had to be very frustrating. As many Bulgarians are not used to pets staying in the house I can see how they would blame your cats. But you've had the cats since you came there and have always kept them indoors.

I must ask, do you still have my keyboard? I know Dora in Topolitsa still would like it for the school. Maybe she could pick it up from your apartment? Do you need me to get in touch with her? I have had a few Skype chats with her. It is a bit difficult for me to remember my Bulgarian, but I could also send her an email about it in English. She knows that you have it.

Your trip to Greece sounds great. Maybe we could talk via Skype. I want to mention quickly, that if you need a place to stay anytime in the U.S. my house is always open to you. I'm working on refinancing my house now. Hopefully I will qualify for a new loan; my finances are okay, but not great. There was lots of damage to my house while I was in Bulgaria. The young couple who stayed here brought in two dogs, appears they had drugs and generally left a very big mess for me to clean up. I ended up hiring a lawyer to serve formal papers on them and that alone ended up costing me over $4,000.

Take care of yourself dear friend, and please write soon again or Skype me soon. Stay safe and well.

I love you, Louise

Hi Laura,   **May 26, 2011**

I hope that things are working out for you. It will be a tremendous culture shock when you get back to the U.S. It's hard to define exactly. For now you're living in a different world. I know it's a different country, but here in the U.S. most people I run into have no idea of the Peace Corps and what it means or what it stands for. If you need a place to chill out, or whatever the word that's used these days, please know you can come to New Mexico and stay with me.

I'm still in California, but plan to drive back to New Mexico in about a month. I wish that you could take the ride with me. I hope to stop in some of the National Parks along the way. If you want to come to New Mexico and spend some time, you're most welcome.

Before I turn in tonight I've been working on trying to refinance my house, but not sure I'll be able to do it. I ran into a stumbling block today and guess what? Because I had this couple live in my house and I have not lived it in over a year since I returned from Bulgaria, this company I contacted said that I don't qualify for a FHA loan. I am discouraged. I'm going to try another company. This house dilemma is really getting to me.

Oh, I must ask you about the key board again. Dora from Topolitsa called me via Skype and wants to know when she can have the keyboard? A new volunteer has been assigned to Topolitsa and she is counting on him doing some music with the kids. Could she call you and make arrangements to pick it up? What is your phone number? Any news about your cats?

Big hug and LOL, Louise

Hi Louise,   **May 26, 2011**

I sent you an e-mail about the keyboard; please let me know if that plan is okay. I should also mention that the reason another volunteer has it is because I had to move to a different apartment because of the bed bugs and he offered to look after it while I figured everything out. It just happened to be the case that he could use it for his job as well.

I miss you too. I made an apple pie the other day, and the smell reminded me of our afternoons together in Topolitsa.

It's funny you suggested I was welcome in New Mexico because I've been looking at a program with Western New Mexico University Gallup Studies Center. It's a two-year Peace Corps fellows program and at the end of it I'd get my MA in education nearly free, if not totally free.

The catch is I'd teach in rural schools on or near the Navajo Nation and schools with a high number of Navajo and Hispanic students. So, I'd be employed by the school district and I'd study at the university on evenings and weekends. It's with the Gallup McKinley County School District, and like I said schools in or near the Navajo Nation. I'd have the option to live in Gallup or on the reservation.

I have no idea if I'd even want to do this. It would certainly give me a new perspective, and I'd have an MA for nearly free. What do you think? I'm still thinking, but leaning towards applying.

Your road trip sounds like fun. Wish I could join you too. Be sure to take lots of pictures. That's terrible about the house. I thought you were going to put it up for sale? Let me know what happens.

Love you, Laura

Hi,   **May 26, 2011**

It sounds like the keyboard logistics will be worked out. Many many thanks. I had told Peace Corps that I would have it passed back to Topolitsa upon your return. I sure didn't realize when I bought it how important having a keyboard at the school would be. It is a nice keyboard. There are times I wish I had it in the United States, but I do have a piano at my house.

How great that would be if you came to New Mexico for graduate school. Terrific! Gallup is about 120 miles from Farmington. I think Western New Mexico University may even offer classes at San Juan College here in Farmington. I'm not sure if it's graduate level classes or just their undergraduate program. New Mexico is a draw for many Easterners who want to experience Hispanic or Native American culture. You should check to see if the classes you want are offered in Farmington or only in Gallup. You could stay with me. I have an extra bedroom with very reasonable rent.

Teaching on the Rez (reservation) would be a challenge, not unlike with the Peace Corps to a certain extent. The Navajo Nation is both in Arizona and New Mexico. Many of the students at San Juan College live on the Rez. You would need a car wherever you would live in New Mexico. In the meantime, I'd love to show you the sights. New Mexico is a combination of Hispanic, Native American and Caucasian. It is always good to hear from you and I am very excited that you might be coming to New Mexico.

Love, Louise

Hi Louise,   **May 10, 2011**

How are you? The weather is getting nice here and in two days I'll have been in Bulgaria for a year. That's amazing. Do you remember when you hit your year mark? The news that I've heard is that Topolitsa will get a B-27. My colleague who lives in Topolitsa, said that the volunteer is a young man, about 24 years old. He's having his site visit next Monday. I hope to be able to meet him then. He'll move in June. There's also a new volunteer slated for Karnobat to take Marianne's position. I'm anxious to finish the school year and move on to the summer. Did I tell you that I'm going to work at the American University in Bulgaria's summer camp this year, teaching journalism? It's for three weeks in July.

My family is visiting the day after the camp ends for about eleven days. Things are generally good. I have the normal peaks and valleys of a day and sometimes intensified emotions. I'm beginning to think a little bit more seriously about what to do after the Peace Corps, possibly because some of the other volunteers are buzzing about graduate school. I've thought of either law or social work, and thinking about that makes me realize how important knowing Spanish would be for either of those professions.

Thinking about that has led me to think about trying to find a job or volunteer position in Latin America for a few months, possibly even a year. I think working in Mexico would be fascinating especially because so many immigrants to our country come from Mexico. How are things going? What's the latest with your house? Hope things are good.

Best, Rachel

Hi Rachel   **June 5, 2011**

I'm sorry it has taken me so long to reply. I'm in California again helping out with my grandson and don't get much time to sit. Even though I've been back here now in the U.S., I must tell you I miss Bulgaria, and especially you, and the friends I made there.

When you see Pauli please tell her hello from me. I don't seem to have her email address. Could you please get it for me? Do you ever see Ruslan? I could email them, but don't have their addresses.

I'm hoping when I'm back at my house in Farmington I'll have more time and could maybe even Skype. Time is so different here. I certainly was busy in Peace Corps, but in such a different way.

Last night using my son's Mac computer I finally had a chance to work on my photos. I want to create some photo books of Bulgaria. Oh, the memories. It was such a special time for me, even though it was very difficult at times, it was still an amazing experience. I'm still hoping that I can comeback, if not in a RPCV position than for a long visit next spring.

My financial situation is still very tenuous; so much depended on my house. Now I'm hoping to refinance it. The market to sell still is not good here in the Four Corners, which is what I really want to do. If the refinancing comes through, than I'll start making more definite Peace Corps plans.

Somehow I will make it work. That is good news about Topolitsa getting a new volunteer. If you get a chance to see him, please give him my email address. I'd love to be in touch with him. I'm sure Dora (school director) is happy about it as well be the students. I've been in touch with Laura and hopefully she can work out with Andrea on how to get the keyboard to Joe.

If you see Vesala please tell her hello. She was such a good friend. Have you met up with Ivanka? I was so fortunate to have so many good friends. I'm so glad that I got to know you. I'm sure hoping I'll make it back to Aitos before your Peace Corps time is finished. Day to day can be tough, but the second year is definitely better. Your summer sounds like it will have several great adventures. I never made it to Blagoevgrad where the American University is located. That should be a great experience. I think on the one excursion with some teachers from Aitos we went through the town late at night. I always thought I'd have a chance to comeback. I'd love to see the campus.

Yes, I think working in another country would be a good transition. I think what I find hardest is that people here generally aren't all that interested in hearing about life overseas. Their lives are settled here. They might say, "Oh that was a good thing to do," but other than that their lives are filled with just their day to day events. It's hard to find someone to share the Peace Corps experience. I thought people would be more interested. It was always my dream to join Peace Corps and I guess it's a let down that it isn't everyone's dream.

I've rambled on long enough. How I'd love to hike up the mountain again with you, maybe next spring. Thanks for keeping in touch. The last weeks of the school year will be busy I know.

Big hug and LOL, Louise

RETURN TO BULGARIA

Dear Louise,   **March 2012**

I was delighted to hear from you and especially the news of a possible trip to Bulgaria. Peter and I started making plans in preparation for your visit. It'll be great if you can make it. It's been a long and cold winter and now with spring in the air I hope to have inspiration to see the bright side of things.

Have you heard of Christo? He is a Bulgarian artist famous for his projects of wrapping buildings; he is unique. He worked with his wife but she died about two years ago. I listened to an interview with him and was impressed by his hard work and devotion. I remember The Gates in Central Park New York.

Have a nice week and enjoy the freedom you have, Tatyana

Hi Tatyana,   **May 12, 2012**

I hope the school year is winding down pleasantly for you and that you are not too overworked. I have been busy working on my yard. I've planted lots of flowers and now hope to get some grass started in a small section of it. As I live in the area of New Mexico called "high desert" it is necessary to water plants and grass almost every day. I do have stone on most of my yard, but I still like to have a few flowers and some grass.

I've been doing a bit of traveling. In April I took a trip to Lexington, Massachusetts, where my daughter and husband live and my new grandson, Samuel now almost six months old. The end of June I'm going with my son Marcus and his wife and two-year-old Milo up the Inland Passage to Alaska. They asked me to come along and help with Milo. At the same time it gives me the opportunity to visit another state. I am delighted as then I will cross Alaska off my list of States. After that tour, I will have put my foot in all 50 of our United States.

The most exciting news for me is that I've booked my flight to Bulgaria I'm flying out of Denver as I can drive up from Farmington, New Mexico, and visit my youngest son there. He lives and works in Boulder, Colorado, about 40 miles from Denver.

Coincidentally, it takes me about seven hours from my home to drive up through the mountains to where David lives. I always figured that it took me a minimum of seven hours to take the train from Topolitsa to Sofia. I'm going to fly out of Denver on August 28th and will spend the entire month of September overseas. I hope to do some traveling with Felicia. We are talking about renting a car and going to Romania and Macedonia for a few days. I certainly want to visit you and Peter in Yambol. Any other suggestions that you have for sightseeing would be most appreciated.

Please look at your schedule and see what dates would suit you for my to visit. I also hope to see Vesala in Aitos and then after the school year starts mid-September spend some time in Topolitsa. They have a new Peace Corps Volunteer there, a young man named Joe.

Hopefully I also will have a chance to visit Ivanka in Aitos and some others. My friend Felicia is now living in Sophia working for the Peace Corps. Her service may finish the end of August.

I do know of Christos. He spoke at Smith College in Northampton, Massachusetts, just this spring. Smith is where my daughter earned her BA degree. I wish I could have been there to hear him. Gretchen saw his "wrapping art" in Central Park in New York City a few years ago.

Words can't convey how much I am looking forward to seeing you. I hope this finds you both well. We can be in touch as the time gets closer.

All the best, Louise

Hi Vesala,   July 12, 2012

I hope this finds you well and enjoying your summer holidays. I expect that you will again be spending August in Sofia with your daughter and her family.

Felicia is now living in Sofia working with the Peace Corps. I am really looking forward to coming back and visiting with her and you. I also hope to see Dora and the students in Topolitsa. And I am planning to visit Tatyana in Yambol.

Felicia and I had been talking about renting a car and driving around the country and maybe Romania. But now Felicia found a cruise in the Mediterranean that will allow us to visit several countries and at a big discount. Plus we won't have the worry of driving a car. The cruise is scheduled for September 6 to 18. It will take us to Naples, Greece, Israel, Egypt, and ends in Athens. If we can manage it we still might take a bus trip to Macedonia.

I am hoping that the last weekend in September will work for me to visit you. I am thinking of coming to Topolitsa around September 25 or 26. I don't have to be back in Sofia until October 2. I will visit the school children and Milka, and then if your schedule permits I could come to Aitos September 28.

If you have the time to do a small excursion that weekend with me that would be wonderful or we could just go into Burgas or somewhere in the neighborhood. It will be so good to see you. I wish my trip could be longer, but until I have my house sold I have limited time.

My daughter and her husband and their new baby were here last month with me in New Mexico. They live near Boston. They put in a new kitchen counter for me. My son Marcus was here earlier in the spring and worked on my yard. Next spring I am going to try and sell my house. I like my house now that it is getting fixed up again, but I would rather have time to travel and spend time with my children and take trips. The housing market has not been good here, but I am hoping that by next year it will improve.

I will be going to California to help take care of my grandson for a few weeks before I come to Bulgaria. Then I will drive up to Colorado where my youngest son lives. He will keep my car for me while I'm in Bulgaria. I'll fly out of Denver. It is expensive to leave your car at the airport, so this way I will be able to visit with my son and get free parking for my car. It is about an 8-hour drive up to Boulder from Farmington, just like my train trip from Topolitsa to Sofia.

Let me know if those dates work for you, I'd take the train back to Sofia on the 1st to make it back in time for the special Peace Corps Celebration of serving 22 years in Bulgaria, October 2nd. Have you met Joe, the new volunteer in Topolitsa? I hope this finds you well and that I will hear from you soon.

Your friend, Louise

Christos Vladinov Javacheff and Jeanne-Claude are married and they created environmental works of art. He is from Gabrovo, Bulgaria a town near Shipka. She is from Casablanca, Morocco. The stop in Egypt was canceled due to the turmoil that September. As a substitute the Cunard excursion stopped at Rhodes, which is also filled with much history.

At the end of August 2012 I returned to Bulgaria. It holds a special place in my heart. I decided to return in the fall for several reasons. I wanted to be able to visit my students and colleagues in Topolitsa; and the Peace Corps was having a special 22nd Anniversary Celebration of being in Bulgaria in early October; and generally flights were cheaper in the fall than the summer – three good reasons to travel in the fall.

I was very happy that I had the chance to go back and visit my friends in Bulgaria. I wanted to go back and visit Bulgaria while Felicia was still serving in the Peace Corps. She and ten others had extended their time in Bulgaria to serve another year. Felicia and I shared many experiences as Peace Corps Volunteers while I was also serving over there. She was a young career woman. She had decided to take a break from her career and serve her country by joining the Peace Corps. Lucky for me.

Even though while in the Peace Corps we did not see each other all that often as we were serving on opposite ends of the country, we emailed each other fairly often and when we had enough phone minutes we called each other on our Bulgarian telephones. We had gone together to Istanbul our first Christmas and New Year's break and visited each others sites, but usually we met in Sofia as we were there for medical reasons or a PC meeting.

Felicia was still serving as a Peace Corps Volunteer. After her first extension, she and Raf extended their stay for another year for a total service period of four years. Her big project was establishing the National Spelling Bee for the Bulgarian school children. This included funding, guidelines and a summer camp for children who won in the different regions of the country. She did have vacation time saved up, and so when she knew that I was coming for a visit we discussed possibilities of where to explore.

It was a long day's journey that involved three separate flights for me on my return. The first leg was the flight from Denver to Montreal, the second Montreal to Frankfurt and then Frankfurt to Sofia, overall about 16 hours of air time. It's a good time to catch up on some reading, watch a few movies, or catch some sleep.

At first we had thought of renting a car and driving into Romania and possibly some of the other Eastern European countries. Neither of us had a chance to do that in our first two years of service. As Peace Corps volunteer, a person is not allowed to drive a car, but as I was no longer sworn in as a volunteer I could drive and Felicia could navigate.

In July as I was planning the trip she asked me in an email if I would consider a cruise. I had recently taken a trip with my oldest son and his family up to Alaska on a cruise ship. It was fun and I found it an easy way to explore a new piece of the world. What did she have in mind? What was the cost? Would the timing work? She had found a cruise on Cunard, the Queen Elizabeth that had a special deal that would visit Italy, Israel, Egypt, Turkey and Greece called the Holy Land Explorers' Cruise. That sounded fantastic.

Could we afford it? I'm always willing to explore new places, but often the price is prohibitive. When we discussed what it would cost us to rent a car, buy our meals, lodging, and incidentals I knew that could also be more than we could really afford. Generally though, Eastern Europe is not expensive compared to the U.S. I told her I would consider it. Via email and some Skype chats the arrangements were made. I arrived in Sofia on a Tuesday. Felicia met me at the airport. We took a taxi to her apartment near the U.S. Embassy. The next day I just relaxed and caught my breath.

Then on Thursday I went to the central bus station and found the bus that would take me to Yambol. Tatyana and Peter, both very good Bulgarian friends lived there. Tatyana was a high school teacher and taught English literature and Peter was an engineer. She spoke English very well and we could have very interesting conversations about literature, movies, cultural, teaching and just life. It was wonderful for me while in Peace Corps to have met Tatyana and Peter. I was anxious to visit them again.

It was about a three hour bus ride from Sofia to the city of Yambol where she lived. I could trust that Tatyana and Peter would be at the bus stop to meet me. Felicia had managed to get a Bulgarian phone for me so that I could call Tatyana if necessary. Thankfully some of my Bulgarian language skills came back to me, but I still got nervous when I traveled.

Many Bulgarian buses did not have a toilet on the bus. It was one of the reasons I often didn't take a bus when I lived over there. Another reason was that there was no direct service into Topolitsa. I could catch the school bus into Aitos and from there transfer to the regular bus service. Generally I found it easier to just take the train from Topolitsa. And another plus, trains had toilets and online I could get the train schedule. If I followed carefully along, I knew where it was stopping. As there were so many different bus companies, there was not a complete central listing of bus services.

A person had to search different companies schedules and know who went where. At the bus station in Sofia there were over 30 different parking spots for the different companies. And some companies shared a spot. It all was quite confusing until you learned the protocol.

The main bus station in Sofia did have several places to eat and also some newsstands, plus two restrooms. You had to pay the attendant, but the toilets were kept very clean. Sometimes, even when I took the train if I had time I would walk the long block from the train to the bus terminal to use their bathrooms. The train station did have toilets, but they were all the "stoop" kind. I was used to using that kind of toilet, but if you had a lot of luggage, and were by yourself it could prove quite awkward

Within minutes of arriving in Yambol Tatyana and her friend Peter were there to greet me. The other passengers looked on in fascination as now of course we were speaking in English. It was so good to see Tatyana and Peter. It was like I had never left Bulgaria. It had been almost two years since I had seen them last. We walked down the bumpy cobblestone sidewalk to Peter's new apartment. They explained to me that he had sold his other apartment. It was on a noisy street and needed many repairs. This new apartment was on a quiet street and from his balcony you could see the Tunzha River.

His daughter had spent much of the summer there getting it painted and refurbished. It was wonderful. His daughter was married and lived near London with her husband and two children. Peter's new apartment reflected the English style in furnishings and modern appliances. It was not the typical Bulgarian apartment that I had often seen while I had served in the Peace Corps. The bathroom and all the fixtures were all very modern. I could have been in a London flat. Tatyana had prepared a very typical Bulgarian dish for me, called *mousaka.*

It was wonderful. I had missed Bulgarian food. In the summer months I had eaten a *shopska salada* (chopped cucumbers and tomatoes) almost every day. *Tarator* (cold yogurt soup sprinkled with chopped nuts and sometimes bits of cucumber) was a summer staple. *Perjunee kartofee* (French fries topped with *siranade,* white cheese) was a favorite snack or a light lunch. In Bulgaria, as in many places of Europe, the main meal often is at noon and the supper meal is lighter in fare. Desert is often fruit.

It was a warm day. I had left Felicia's apartment early in the morning and I still had jetlag. So while I had the opportunity I took a nap. It was refreshing. After the nap Tatyana and I took a walk to the park to see the new improvements that had been made. It looked wonderful. There were lots of flowers in bloom and children out playing on the new play equipment. Tatyana was greeted by many friends. There is a feeling in many European cities of community and congeniality that I do not notice in the U.S.

I have felt it in bigger urban areas of the U.S., but not in the smaller cities (100,000 and under range). Yambol is a city of about 150,000 people. In the mid afternoon folks are out and about, having a coffee, sharing French fries, walking in the park and enjoying the fresh air. This is not so typical in the United States. It is fun to people watch. It is fun to watch the interaction of parents and their children. It is fun to see children riding their bikes, shouting out to friends, teenagers having their own special communiqué and yes, texting on their phones. People are in a community. It has a special feel.

Peter grew up in Yambol and still owned his mother's flat. To give me privacy and more space I was offered the opportunity to use his mother's flat for my stay with them. It was about a fifteen minute walk away. That first night they walked over with me.

It was an older typical block apartment. There were thousands of these built during the Communist era in Bulgaria (1944-1989). From the outside they looked like a tall cement block building with no décor. Some of them had a small plot of land in the front where flowers could grow. A few apartment buildings I saw had some vegetable gardens in the front or on a side yard. There was often a bench where folks could sit and visit with each other. If you were lucky there was an elevator that worked and stopped at each floor.

The elevator in this particular block apartment worked, but not exactly. The apartment was on the 9th floor. The elevator stopped at the 8th floor and the 10th floor, but not the 9th. A person had to decide if you wanted to get off on the 8th floor and walk up one flight of steps or get off on the 10th floor and walk down one flight. Many of the apartments had a balcony and there was a lovely view of the city from this 9th floor balcony.

In the morning, Tatyana met me at the front entrance of the apartment complex and we walked to the center of the town stopping at a pastry shop for a breakfast sandwich and a coffee. The sun was out and we sat outside enjoying conversation, food and drink. One day we walked around the shops, another time we met Peter at the park and walked up the high hill that overlooked the city and saw the beautiful view of the valley below. Each day Tatayana prepared for me a favorite Bulgarian recipe.

Neither Peter nor Tatyana had a car; they asked a friend if he would have the time to take an excursion. Not too far from Yambol can be found the ruins of the ancient city of Kabyle. The town was founded by

Philip II and was under his rule and heirs until 280 BC and then it came under the control of the Thracians. Many artifacts have been unearthed by archaeologists. There are both Thracian and Roman ruins on display at the museum. It is filled with ornate pottery, glassware, coins and other artifacts.

After the Thracians the Romans came. Around 900 AD Bulgaria became a nation onto itself led by Czar Simeon. It was at this time that two monks Cyrus and Methodius developed the Cyrillic alphabet and transcribed the first Cyrillic Bible. This was the start of writing and reading in the Cyrillic language and used today by many countries in this region.

As it was a lovely fall day we enjoyed walking around the area and took many photos. Leaving there we stopped at a historic monastery built in the late 1800s, near the village of Kabile. In English the monastery is called "Staint Mother of God." From there we drove back to Yambol and enjoyed a pizza at a lovely restaurant which bordered the Tundzha River.

The next day it was time for me to head back to Sofia. That evening I did some shopping with Felicia to get ready for our cruise and sightseeing on the Mediterranean. Her apartment was near the City Center. She lived on the top floor of an older house that had been converted into flats. There were over 100 steps to her floor. This made it very important to me to remember my keys, water and tote bag as I left. I decided that if I went up and down the steps two or three times a day I would not need any further exercise. There was no elevator in the building, so this meant also that I carried my suitcases up and down the steps, both upon my arrival, and again for the cruise and on my departure. When I took the bus to Yambol I took only my small suitcase with me.

During the time Felicia finished up some projects with the Peace Corps Staff I made arrangements to meet Nikolai at the University Library. There was a lovely outdoor garden behind the library where students and faculty met and not far from Felicia's apartment. It was terrific to see him again and share stories. His book had been published. As a very special surprise he brought along a copy for me. It was the abridged version but still quite hefty to put in a suitcase. I teased him that I would have to buy an extra suitcase to take back with me in order to bring it back to the U.S. The book is filled with many photos taken all around Bulgaria of the many monuments that were constructed under the Soviet Regime. In the text he explained much of the how and why. The book is titled, *Witnesses of Stone: Monuments and Architecture in Bulgaria 1944–1989.* I feel honored to have an inscribed copy.

Felicia and I had a 7 AM flight to Rome from Sofia. This meant leaving her apartment at 5 AM. I had to allow myself an extra ten minutes to carry my two big suitcases down to the entrance door. I had brought two suitcases with me and I weighed them carefully so that neither went over the fifty-pound limit. I was bringing a number of gifts along for my friends in Bulgaria and I was counting on their weight to offset the weight of any gifts that I would buy to bring back to the U.S. I love shopping for souvenirs and gifts for friends so this fifty-pound limit often played havoc with my best intentions.

The cruise lived up to our expectations. It was a ten-day cruise leaving out of the Rome port of Civitavecchia about an hour via bus from central Rome. The flight from Sofia was less than two hours and this gave us almost a full day to explore this wonderful historic area. The next morning we had a few hours to walk around before it was time to go to the ship. The Cunard QE2 voyage was called the Holy Land Explorers' Cruise. It was an amazing trip within my visit to Bulgaria. The only disappointment was that the stopover in Cairo, Egypt got canceled due to the political climate unfolding in that area. As a substitute we stopped at Rhodes. We had a full day in Athens seeing the ancient site before it was time to head out to the airport and back to Sofia.

A highlight of this third part of my trip was going on the narrow-gauge train that runs between the Rhodopes and Pirin mountains. First Felicia and I had to catch the train from Sofia at 6 AM and got off at Septembri, which is in the south central region of Bulgaria. At the Septembri train station we saw a sign directing passengers to go down some steps. This led us on a passageway to the narrow gauge train. A bunch of bikers were already waiting to board as it is a favorite area of hiking and biking. We found seats in the front car. This train would stop at many mountain villages and traverse numerous tunnels. In all it was about a four hour trip so we could just watch and enjoy until we came to the town of Razlog.

Razlog is a mountain resort area which is popular in the winter for skiing. It now also houses a time share resort and this is where my two American friends were planning to spend a few days after their time with me in Burgas and Topolitsa. To go back the same way we came, would have meant a sleep-over as the train ran each way only once a day. We decided to take a 6 PM bus back that would get us to Sofia around 9 PM. The trees were just starting to turn fall colors and it made for a lovely day.

In Razlog we met up with Seth a Peace Corps volunteer who served there. He was in the last Peace Corps group (B-27) serving in Bulgaria. He walked us through the town and we caught up on the Peace Corps news. We only had time to get a coffee and a light snack before we had to catch the bus back to Sofia.

My friend Trish and her friend Kathleen were arriving the next day from the United States. I had recommended for them to stay at The House, my favorite small hotel in Sofia. I had given Trish directions as to how to catch a taxi at the airport and my friends at The House would see that all went well. Trish had hoped to visit me while I served in Peace Corps, but at the time she was still working so it was difficult to work in the limited timeline of her summer vacation. When she heard I was planning a return visit in the fall of 2012 she was very excited. She was retiring that June and thought perhaps we could make it work so that we could meet over in Bulgaria.

A retired teacher friend from Arizona, who also was interested in coming to see Bulgaria, came with Trish. Trish found out that her time share had a new resort in one of the ski areas in the Rila Mountains. Was that any-where near Topolitsa? Well, not really as it was located in the western part of the country and to the south. But I didn't feel that should hinder our plans. We could figure it out and make it work. And we did. I met Trish and Kathleen at The House. Felicia would come over to join us for dinner.

There was a new restaurant across the street from The House that we decided would be fun to try. It served both traditional Bulgarian dishes and Italian food. The House restaurant is also superb, but they had eaten there the night before so we decided to try this new place. Having an early, and nearby, dinner made sense after a day of touring, still on jetlag.

We reviewed our schedule for the coming week. How much could we do? How much could we see? Tricia had her Time Share reserved for the following week when I would not be with them. I knew at an International Resort, activities and excursions would be available to them. English would be spoken at this new resort owned by an American company.

In general it is much easier to find an English speaker in the bigger cities, like Sofia and Plovdiv than when a person travels to the smaller towns and further away from the bigger cities. Even finding a menu in English or the bus schedule in English becomes a challenge the further you are away from Sofia or the bigger the resort areas.

We decided we would leave on the 7 AM train to Burgas. This would give us some time to explore Burgas, a lovely University City on the Black Sea. From there we could catch the slow train to Topolitsa. Burgas has lots of hotels and this would make sleeping much less of a hassle. I knew my landlady in Topolitsa would be willing to have us sleep there, but at this time she was also housing some of the crew who were working on repairs in the village. My apartment now had Joe, the current PCV living there. And while Trish and Kathleen wanted to see Topolitsa, meals and sightseeing were certainly more limited.

We arrived in Burgas mid-afternoon. It was quite warm outside. We found the hotel. There were two hotels with similar names and first I went to the wrong one, oops, they didn't have our reservation. With a little checking I found my mistake and found that we were at the hotel less than a block away and a very short distance to the train and bus station.

It was only a fifteen minute walk to the Black Sea. After we checked in at the right hotel, we changed to some cooler clothes and went to explore Burgas. There are many shops and restaurants lining the streets to the beach. A person can purchase clothing, jewelry, shoes, souvenirs, books, visit the public library or enjoy a gelato from a street vendor.

I remember so well my first viewing of the Black Sea. I was with my school director Dora and her son George. He was a student at the University of Burgas. She drove us there on my initial visit to Topolitsa. The Black Sea is lovely. The sand stretched out for miles. In some of the towns as you drive up the coast, hotels are built almost on top of the sea, but in Burgas the sea front was saved from developers. There is a big grand garden public park, called the Sea Garden, separating the shops from the beach. In the park are lovely gardens, a stage for outside concerts, s few restaurants, benches, statuary, public bathrooms and lots of open space. It was lovely.

Work was being done to repair some of the areas neglected under the Communist regime. But generally Burgas and a few other sea towns were used as resorts by the Communist government to reward bureaucrats. As a result the Sea Garden was preserved and is now one of the high lights of any visit to Burgas. There are of course other less attractive parts to Burgas but to me it served as a special oasis of a relaxing day while serving in the Peace Corps. Since 1989, the fall of Communism in Bulgaria, many European countries, especially Germany and Great Britain, have come to Burgas and invested in vacation homes, hotels, restaurants and shops there. Many companies from those two countries, and also Japan have built many of the resorts along the Black Sea.

Trish, Kathleen and I walked down to the water. As it was already mid-September and a week day the beach area was not very crowded. In the summer months it is filled with folks soaking up the sun and enjoying the waves. As I write this now, I realize I miss Bulgaria, especially my days along the Black Sea.

It was a warm day so we decided to have our dinner at one of the restaurants that I knew had air conditioning. While most upscale hotels have AC, not many of the restaurants along this walk to the sea have AC. Many of them have outdoor tables. By tradition, Bulgarians have a late dinner. Nine o'clock is when many eat. Fresh fish is a favorite along with French fries, a cold soup and maybe some fruit for dessert. Beer, wine or *Rakia* were the favorite drinks. Coke could easily be bought, but it is a surprise to many tourists that soft drinks are usually more expensive than beer.

We would have breakfast at our hotel. Breakfast was along the European style: boiled egg, tomato, yogurt, fruit, cheese and maybe salami and espresso coffee. The next day I planned to take them to either Nesebar or Sozopol, both wonderful old GrecoRoman towns that had been well preserved. Both also had a new section but generally the tourists didn't find these near as interesting. I had planned to use the bus service that I knew could take us to either town, one is north of Burgas the other south. Via bus, it would be hard to visit both towns in the same day.

They are similar, but of course they each have their special attractions. I had been to both and sometimes got their similar historic sights confused. I knew that either of them would give them a better flavor of Bulgaria's past history and how it was part of the Roman Empire and before that the Greeks under Alexander the Great. In central Bulgaria there are many ruins dating back to Thracian times and now even some artifacts have been found in Sozopol as well.

While trying to figure out what schedule best suited our needs, a man approached who spoke some English. He was confident, he told us, we would do better having a private taxi take us rather than a general bus. I wasn't sure.

Trish and Kathleen liked the idea of a special service and that with a taxi we could manage both towns in the same day. So it was settled. For around $25 each we would have a taxi driver take us first to Nesebar and then to Sozopol with a special stop at St. George's Monastery in Pomorie where we could watch the monks make Rakia.

That evening we walked around Burgas. My friends were struck by the many people walking around the city, enjoying the many cafes, Sea Garden Park, shopping in the numerous shops or just out for a stroll. A free jazz concert was held in the evening in the Centre Plaza for all to enjoy and then a video was shown interviewing some of the Bulgarian artists who had recently immigrated to the U.S. and their experience in New York City.

The next morning we took the slow train into Topolitsa. It was great going back. The students gave me a royal welcome along with my two American friends. The students love Facebook and all the modern tech gadgets. Joe, the current Peace Corps Volunteer is now teaching English to the students and working on the library projects that I started when I was there. New book shelves were purchased and the school received a grant to buy some new Bulgarian books for the students to read as well.

It was so good to see Milka again. My friends and I were all heartily welcomed and served much food as is the Bulgarian tradition. We walked around the village and I had a chance to say hello to many of the people. Thankfully, I remembered a little Bulgarian.

Some of the train tracks are getting a much needed overhaul. But sad to say, as a result some of the slow trains run even slower and only one fast train a day from Sofia to Burgas. We took the slow train back to Burgas to spend our last night at the hotel there. Buses also go regularly between the major towns and the roads are slowly seeing improvement. The buses generally are faster and cost about $6 to $8 more a ticket. The drawback is that most buses do not have bathrooms and usually only stop once in the five- to six-hour ride across country. The price is right, about $2 via train across country. It takes about seven hours as a passenger still needs to stop at Karnobat to catch the express train, or leave early enough and go into Aitos to catch the express train around 7:10 AM and arrive in Sofia about 2:45 PM. If you wanted to go to Topolitsa from Burgas, you had to make sure that you caught the slow train, as the express train does not stop in Topolitsa. It zooms on by.

Trish and her friend left for Sofia via bus the next morning from Burgas. It was wonderful having them visit and having the opportunity to show them a bit of my Peace Corps experience. After they left I packed up my suitcase and waited for Dora, my school director from Topolitsa to pick me up. She had offered to come to the hotel in Burgas and take me back into the village so I could spend another day with the students and walk around the village and say hello to the friends I had made. In the late afternoon I took the school bus into Aitos and was able to meet up with Ivanka, my language teacher and friend and Vesala.

I visited a few of their high school classrooms yet that afternoon and answered questions. In the evening they arranged for other friends to join us for dinner at a restaurant in Aitos.

It was great joining my former language teachers and once again sharing some coffee, beer, *Rakia, pershnee kartofe sic siranade* (French fries with feta cheese on the top) fresh fish, *shopska salada* (chopped tomatoes, cucumbers, and *siranade*), *Banitsa, Baklava, tarator,* (cold yogurt soup with minced garlic and cucumber) *mycaka* (potatoes, minced meat, tomatoes) *kyopoly* (eggplant, peppers, tomato, garlic). Having a meal with friends is a wonderful way to promote good will and friendship . . . it crosses all language barriers.

The next day Vesala and her friend Deana gave me a grand tour around the historic places on the Black Sea. She drove us to the Strandzha Nature Park. We arrived in time to take the boat ride down the Ropotamo River with a few other sightseers and saw hundreds of birds. Up until 1989 this area was closed to Bulgarians as it was part of the border zone with Turkey. Mountains in the South provide the border areas with Turkey and Greece. We also visited the historic village of Brushlyan located inside the park borders. The day ended with a special dinner about 9:30 that evening with fresh fish at Deana's home. I had many wonderful dinners while in Bulgaria. It would be too long to list them all.

I had a few days in Sofia before it would be time to return back to the U.S. I went with Felicia to her office where she was working on several projects with Peace Corps Staff. Her main project was the Bulgarian Spelling Bee that she had help organize two years prior. Students all over Bulgaria now were excited about this new program. There were local, regional and national competitions.

In the evening I went with Felicia to an English discussion group that she headed. Then we went to a restaurant that reminded us both of being in Greenwich Village. We also took the Sofia subway across the city to check on a colleague's plants, and cat, while he was out of town.

In the evening was the special reception held at the American Embassy to celebrate the 22 years that Peace Corps had been serving in Bulgaria. The next day was the special Legacy Celebration in a beautiful theater setting where dignitaries from both Bulgaria and the U.S. spoke.

Living here in New Mexico a popular plaque you see is *Mi Casa es su Casa;* this is so very true in Bulgaria. It is from the Spanish, and basically means, "My home is your home." A guest is always welcome in your home. How grateful I continue to be for this very special experience I had while serving in the Peace Corps. It was well worth the wait of 49 years.

Thank you Peace Corps for giving me this opportunity, thank you Bulgaria for welcoming me in your home, your country, and allowing me to live, work, and enjoy your beautiful country.

TUESDAY WAS SALAMI

Peter was a small boy. He was small for his young age of six. His mother worried about his health as she didn't know how to get him interested in eating new and different foods. He sometimes refused to eat even if he was hungry because he did not like the food.

There were not many new foods for her to choose from so frequently she tried to make the old foods different ways in the hope that he would try to eat them and like them. She used herbs that she raised in her garden. She traded different food with her neighbors. But still there were not very many choices and Peter continued to be a very fussy eater.

Most of the food that Peter's family ate was raised in their vegetable garden. Both of Peter's parents worked hard in the garden so that the vegetables would grow. Of course it also depended on having enough rain in the spring and summer months. Too much rain could also be a problem especially if it came when the plants were small, if too much rain came, and not enough sunshine, the plants could drown or rot.

Every day after work Peter's mother and father worked in their garden. It was a small garden. In these days of Socialist Communism families were all given the same size of garden for their personal family use. It was about ten feet by ten feet.

Sometimes in the summer Peter and his parents worked in the garden before they went to work. The weather was not so hot at five in the morning and the children were still asleep. There was not very much time to work in the morning as Peter's mom had to fix breakfast for the family, make sandwiches for her and her husband's lunch and then get the baby ready for day care and make sure that Peter was ready for his kinder school. The baby was only six months old, but already the mother had to go back to work at her job in the sewing factory and place the baby, Timothy, in the day care with all the other infants. It made her sad to do this, but there was no other way.

The rules were made by the Socialist Communist government and if you disobeyed the rules a person would be severely punished. Peter's mother knew of a young mother who was sent off to a prison camp because she wanted to stay home with her baby. She had told them she was too weak to go back to work so soon. It made no difference to the government workers.

They obeyed the rules that were given to them by their bosses in Sofia. If they disobeyed then they would be punished. Punishment usually was being sent far away from your family. It meant working under very harsh condition, perhaps in a coal mine or a cement factory. Often there a person could not get in touch with his family and often families did not know what happened to their loved one.

It was better to obey the rules than try to make your boss understand why the rule was a difficult rule. Fortunately Timothy was a pleasant baby and smiled a lot. The workers at the Infant School liked to hold him as he did not cry. He drank his milk from the bottle and then would sleep. He played with his toes and rolled around his bed. The babies were all kept in a crib by themselves. They could only look at each other. They had a label on each of their beds so that the daycare workers would know what bed to put them in. On their wrists they had a name badge to help the workers remember their name.

Sometimes there were twenty-five babies for the workers to feed. If a baby was sick it was lucky if a worker had time to hold it and give it extra attention. Often the baby cried and then in exhaustion fell asleep. The workers were usually young women who did not have much education.

Education was important in the country, but not all young people liked to learn and study. This was especially true if their parents could not read well. They could not see any reason to learn mathematics or history or read stories about Old Russian Czars. Many young people did not like school and only went until they were sixteen years old. At age sixteen the government let them leave school and allowed them to start working in a factory.

The young girls hope by then to have a young man to marry them.

344

They did not think about how difficult there life would be. Even if they did get married and had children, the government would make them go to work. Without a proper education they would have to work in a factory job. They probably would not get a job in an office. Sometimes if their father or mother belonged to the Communist Party exceptions were made and they would be given an easier job. Some of them if they were not particularly strong might be lucky and get a job at the Infant School where they took care of all the young babies. Sometimes their own child was there; sometimes they had to work at an Infant School not near where they lived. They were not given a choice where they worked.

In the gardens the families grew a variety of vegetables. There were four rows of tomatoes. Each row was a different variety, small plumb tomatoes, big tomatoes for *shopska salada*, medium size tomatoes for making stew and a special variety for making sauces. Cucumbers were also in the garden. There were stakes driven in the ground and the vines were tied up on the stakes so that they did not take up too much room. Carrots, eggplant, cauliflower, cabbage, peppers and a variety of beans were also grown. Another family grew potatoes and they traded their cabbage and carrots with this family for potatoes. At the edge of the garden Peter's dad had planted some strawberry plants. They were seen as a luxury as most people did not think it was necessary to eat strawberries for a healthy diet. Peter's mom wanted her children to eat fruit and to learn about fruits that usually were not found in the shops. Another family had a peach tree and if it was a good season, they gave some of the peaches in trade for strawberries. A grape arbor was built by Peter's father for the grape vines. This gave shade to some of the garden and in the fall, fresh grapes were there for eating, for jelly and if it was a good season some wine could also be made.

It was important to grow as much food as possible as then the family did not have to buy vegetables in the store. The money could be used to buy flour, salt, rice and other foods that they could not grow in their small garden.

One of the items that Peter's family could not grow was meat. But they did have a few chickens so that they could have fresh eggs. Sometimes for special occasions a chicken was killed, but mainly the chickens were there for the fresh eggs. Peter's family did not have space to have any other animals like a sheep or a cow. Milk had to be bought at the small magazine in the village, along with bread and butter. Sometimes Peter went to the store for the family to buy the bread.

Each family was allowed to buy one loaf of bread a day. If you came too late the bread might all be sold. Often the store did not receive enough bread for every family to receive one loaf of bread a day, or another family might have been given an extra coupon because they had guests or some other special occasion so on that day the shop would not have enough bread for everyone. It was best to get in line early at the store to make sure that when it was your turn to be waited on by the shopkeeper he would have a loaf of bread for you.

It was always upsetting to Peter if he was waiting in line to buy the bread and then be told that now it was all gone. He was too late. On those days there would be no sandwiches and that meant that sometimes his parents would go to bed hungry. His mother usually saved some bread for the children, so that each day they at least had bread for breakfast and a sandwich for school.

Peter loved going to school. He loved to learn new words and practice his math. He liked to write his name and he liked to write sentences. He knew how to read since he was four years old. Every day his mother read a story to him and many of them he knew by heart. He especially loved the stories of Winnie the Pooh, that silly old bear who was a special friend to Christopher Robin. Hearing about the adventures of Pooh helped Peter imagine a world beyond his village. The village where Peter lived was not too big. It had a school for all the children to attend up until class eight. It had several shops, called magazines where the family could buy bread, flour and milk. There was another shop that sold shoes. Some shops did not have many shoes to sell. Often they had only one style of a shoe and in only one color, black or brown. It presented big problems for mothers with growing children to provide them with shoes for their children.

When Peter needed a new pair of shoes because his old ones were worn out, or had become too small Peter's mother would walk to the shoe store with her young son. Sometimes the shopkeeper did not have any shoes that fit him. He would have to wait until more shoes were sent to his shop. Sometimes he would to wait more than one month for a new pair of shoes.

Peter's mother had saved money from her job to buy the shoes, but there were no shoes to be bought in this small village. The year Peter was going to start class one his mother wanted to get him a new pair of shoes. His old ones were very worn and getting too small. But the shop in the village did not have any shoes his size. What to do? Peter's mother decided it was important that he have new shoes for school. On the next Saturday she decided that she would take Peter and the baby on the bus to the city of Sofia. This could be a special outing. It would give Peter a chance to see the big capital city.

There were many beautiful buildings in Sofia. Some of them were built centuries ago. Many were rebuilt or restored after Bulgaria became free of the Ottoman Empire and went through a period of revival. But in 1453 the Ottomans won the battle at Constantinople and took control over the

Bulgarians. Before that time Bulgaria had its own kings and made its own rules. Bulgaria as a country goes back to the 9th century.

Under the Ottoman's the changes came gradually. People just had to give their tax money to a different officer. In Ottoman times, the officer in charge was called the Sultan. The people in the villages continued on with their life. But with time, many of the people were required to change their religion. Some people had to change their jobs. In the small villages in the mountains life went on as usual as they were almost forgotten. People continued to study in Bulgarian and go to their church. For many of the people living in the cities there were changes.

They could not make the rules. They were not free to move to other cities or work at different jobs. For many of the people of Bulgaria it became a very sad time. Their traditions were being lost. The stories of their great kings were not being taught. Only by fathers telling their sons and mothers telling their daughters was the history of their country preserved. Priests in the churches kept the language alive by using it for services. In some places services were not allowed, but in the villages it usually was a gathering place for the people and the Sultan if he was wise, allowed the people to meet there. The Bulgarians were proud of their heritage, but it was difficult to keep the history alive.

Peter was excited to go into the city of Sofia. He was too young to remember the last time he was there. In order to go into the capital city of Sofia it was necessary to get up early. The first bus came at 7:50 in the morning. Peter's dad was home and would take care of his baby brother. This would be a special outing for Peter and his mother. She made sandwiches so that they would not have to buy lunch. There were not many restaurants in Sofia and it would cost extra money. The restaurants often did not have the food listed on the menu. Sometimes they only served one kind of sandwich, and some days they did not have milk for the children to drink. It was much better to bring your own lunch into the city to be sure that you would have food to eat that you liked. And then you could eat it when you were hungry and would not have to find a restaurant.

Peter and his mother were at the bus stop by 7:45 AM. They did not want to be late. The bus driver never waited for anyone. He expected everyone to be on time. The ticket was bought on the bus from the driver. It cost fifty *stotinki* for an adult and twenty-five *stotinki* for a child. If a child could sit on the mother's lap there was no charge. A young child five or six years old, a child wanted to have his own seat. The bus came right on time. Peter and his mother along with several other village people boarded the bus. It was a dull yellow color. The seats were old and worn. The people on the bus looked tired. Peter and his mother though were excited to be going into the big city of Sofia.

After about twenty minutes the bus came to the first stop. Here is where they had to get off and wait for another bus. This next bus would take them into the city. It was due to come in about twenty minutes. It was a hot day as were many of the days in August. It was only 8:15 but already the sun was out and making everyone feel quite warm. They saw a shady tree and went and stood under it to wait for the next bus. Finally after about thirty minutes the next bus came. It was already quite crowded. Many people were going to go into the city to shop. School would be starting soon and mothers wanted to get their children ready for school with some new clothes and school supplies.

The bus was crowded with shoppers. Peter and his mother had to stand. They had to buy another ticket for each of them. Soon they would be in the city. Standing up made the ride seem longer. With so many people on the bus Peter could not look out the window. All he could see were people's legs. This was not fun. Finally they were at the stop where the shops were.

This was the big store called TZUM. It actually was one big building with many small shops inside of it. There were shops that sold food, shops that sold pants, shops that sold lady's dresses, and of course shoe shops. The store did not have many shoes for children, but it had a few. The clerk found a pair that was a little big, but that was good. In this way the pair of shoes could last the entire year even if Peter's feet grew. Peter was happy to have a new pair of shoes. He had fun looking in the windows. Even thought here was not much to see, it was interesting to see all the big shops.

From The TSUM store Peter and his mother walked passed the famous round church or rotunda church called Sveta Nedelya (Blessed Sunday). It was first built on this site in the 10th century. It is known as the church of the bombs, as during a funeral service on April 14, 1925 bombs that had been planted in the attic exploded during the service. After a long investigation it was revealed that this plan was initiated by the Communist Party to kill the Bulgarian King, Boris III. However, he did not attend the funeral and so the plot to take over the government failed. Sadly though, many officials and their families were killed. In all, 150 persons were killed when the bombs exploded and around 500 people were injured. Up until 2001 it was the most people killed in a country that was not at war by an outside enemy. Ironically, under Communist rule from 1944 - 1989 it was one of the few churches allowed to remain open.

Now it was time to stop for lunch. They sat under a tree in the beautiful area by the National Theater that was built in 1904 when Bulgaria was an independent country. The theatre is next to a beautiful park with a fountain.

After lunch they continued their walk and came to what is often called the Russian Church, but is officially the Church of St. Nicholas the Miracle-

Maker. It was built in 1882 as the official church for the Russian Embassy. It is very similar in style to many of the churches in St. Petersburg and Moscow.

And not too far away is the biggest church in Sofia, known as Aleksandur Nevski Cathedral. This was built by the Russian Government to commemorate the Russian soldiers who died giving their life in the battle against the Ottoman Empire for the freedom of Bulgaria in 1878. It can hold up to 10,000 people and is the second-largest cathedral located on the Balkan Peninsula. It stayed open during the Communist reign but was considered a museum, not a church of worship. Services are held there now under the realm of the Bulgarian Orthodox Church. It was wonderful to see these sights but now it was time to catch the bus and return back to the village. They walked a few blocks and waited for the bus to take them back home.

Soon school would start. All children were treated alike and so all children had to dress alike with a uniform. In addition, all children had to bring the same lunch to school that was prescribed by the education committee. The type of sandwich, and what fruit or vegetable to bring along was all decided by the day of the week. On Tuesday it was a certain type of salami, not just any salami. Peter did not like salami, especially the flavor that was chosen. His mother had no choice. Each day she would pack his lunch in compliance with the rules.

On Tuesday Peter would not eat lunch, just looking at a salami sandwich made him feel sick. His mother was worried. It was not good for a young child not to eat all day at school. And it was a long school day, from eight in the morning until four in the afternoon. What was she to do?

After several months of not getting Peter to eat lunch on Tuesday she went to talk to the school officials. She asked if maybe, an exception could be made and Peter could have a different type of salami in his sandwich. The official agreed.

The next week at school Peter ate his lunch. The other children were so surprised. What had happened? Why did Peter eat his lunch today? Being six years old, Peter just explained that his mother had given him new salami in his sandwich. How could that be? Everyone should be treated the same.

The school year continued and Peter again went without lunch on Tuesday. The rule was the rule and a six-year-old boy could not change it. On Tuesday you ate the salami prescribed by the school officials.

This story was inspired by Nikolai's experiences as a young child. Other Bulgarian Peace Corps Staff have also shared experiences as to what life was like during the Communism Era. I'm in awe of their perseverance, tenacity in spite of the hardships they faced, and see them as a true inspiration for democracy in the spirit of friendship extended to people everywhere.

BIBLIOGRAPHY

Bai Ganyo: Incredible Tales of a Modern Bulgaria, Aleko Konstantinov
Balkan Ghosts: A Journey through History, Robert D. Kaplan
The Balkans, Mark Mazower
Belogradchik Pocket Guide, Mihail Mihaylov
Bulgaria (Lonely Planet), Richard Watkins and Tom Masters
Bulgaria (Bradt Guide), Annie Kay
Bulgaria, Marco Polo Guide
Bulgaria, DK Eyewitness Travel
Bulgaria Guide, Domino
Bulgaria Tradition & Beauty, Elizabeth I. Kwasnik, editor
Bulgarian Kingdoms, Overview
Bulgarian Rhapsody: The Best of Balkan Cuisine, Linda Joyce Forristal
Bulgariana: A British Humorist Takes a Look at Life in Bulgaria,
    Randall Baker
Bury Me Standing: The Gypsies and their Journey, Isabel Fonseca
Cold Snap, Cynthia Morrison Phoel
A Concise History of Bulgaria, R.J. Crampton
Contemporary Bulgarian Plays, Anna Karabinska & Josepha Jacobson,
    ed.s
Culture Shock Bulgaria, Agnes Sachsenroeder
Crown of Thorns: The Reign of King Boris III of Bulgaria 1918-1943,
    Stephane Groueff
Don't Eat Brown Sugar, Peace Corps Bulgaria Cookbook
Dreams and Shadows: Memories of Bulgaria, RadkaYaki
Eastern Europe Phrasebook, Lonely Planet
Forbidden Sea, Blaga Dimitrova
The Fragility of Goodness: Why Bulgaria's Jews Survived the Holocaust,
    Tzvetan Todorov
Glimpses of the History of Bulgaria, Galin Jordanov
Hristo Botev, poetry and stories, Hristo Botev
*An Introduction to Post-Communist Bulgaria: Political, Economic and
    Social Transformation*, Emil Giatzidis Kazanluk
Thracian Temples and Vaults, Evtimka Dimitrova
King's Ransom, Jan Beazely and Thom Lemmons
Koprivshtitsa History and Architecture, Viara Kandjeva and
    Antoniy Handjiyski

Last Minute Bulgarian: Phrasebook and Dictionary in One, Pons

The Mire, Krassin Krastev

Must See Bulgaria Collection: The Bulgarian Way, Julian Angelov

My Country is the Whole World, Womenin

Bulgarian and Anglo-American Literature, Vesela Katsarova Nessebur

A Town with History, Janet Miteva

Old Plovdiv, Alexander Pizhev

Regional Ethnographic Museum: Plovdiv, Katerina Popova

Pliska: The first Bulgarian Capital, Dimitar Ovcharov

The Price, Marko Semov

Solo, Rana Gasgupta

Street without a Name: Childhood and other Misadventures in Bulgaria, Kapka Kassabova

To Chicago and Back, Aleko Konstantinov

Voices from the Gulag: Lovech, the Prison, TzvetanTodorov

Waiting for Better Times in Bulgaria, Conor Ciaran

Wall-to-wall Poetry Europe: Unity in Diversity, Various authors

Witnesses of Stone: Monuments & Architecture in Bulgaria 1944-1989, Nikolai Vukov and Luca Ponchiro

FAVORITE BULGARIAN RECIPES

SHOPSKA SALADA

Traditional Bulgarian salad Ingredients

4 ripe tomatoes

2 long cucumbers

1 onion

1 green or red pepper

1/3 bunch parsley

2 tablespoons oil

2 tablespoons red wine vinegar

1 cup Bulgarian white chesse or feta cheese

Preparation:

Chop all tomatoes, cucumbers and the pepper in medium size chunks and put in a bowl. Add the finely chopped onion and parsley.

Sprinkle with oil and vinegar and stir gently. Sprinkle the cheese on the top.

About *shopska salada*

Traditional Bulgarian cold salad is very popular in the summer and fall. It is named after a group of very frugal people called *shopi* who lived in the capital city Sofia.

TARATOR
Bulgarian yogurt cold soup
Ingredients:
  1 long cucumber, chopped or grated, peeled if you prefer
  1 garlic clove, minced or smashed 4 cups yogurt
  1 cup water
  1 teaspoon salt
  1 tablespoon dill, finely chopped 4 big pecans, well crushed
  3 teaspoons olive oil
Preparation:
  Put all ingredients together and mix well. When ready garnish with olive oil.
  Serve when chilled. Hint: Try it with no dills and pecans.

BULGARIAN TRADITIONAL TRIPE SOUP
Ingredients:
  1 pound tripe (calf stomach)
  1 cup sunflower oil
  2 cups whole milk
  1 teaspoon paprika
  1 tablespoon ground black pepper
  1 tablespoon salt

SHKEMBE CHORBA
  4 garlic cloves, peeled and thinly diced
  1/3 cup red wine vinegar
  Dried hot chili pepper mix
Preparation:
  Boil the tripe for about 30 minutes: Add oil, milk, black pepper and paprika and boil for another 30 minutes, occasionally topping with water. The longer you cook it, the better it will taste.
  Combine some salt, garlic and vinegar in a separate dish and let it soak about an hour. Serve hot.
  Garnish with the garlic and vinegar mixture and the hot chili pepper mix.
  Suggestion: tastes best with *Rakia* or beer.

KEBAPCHE
Minced meat grilled sausage
2 pounds minced meat (60% pork, 40% beef)
1 tablespoon salt
1 tablespoon ground black pepper
1/2 teaspoon cumin
1 clove garlic, minced (optional)
Preparation:
Mix all ingredients together, mix well. Leave in the fridge for at least 30 minutes. Take out and roll in sausage-shaped pieces.
Makes about 30 pieces.

BANITSA
Bulgarian cheese pastry
Ingredients:
1 pack of filo dough
3 eggs
1 pound Bulgarian cheese or feta cheese
3 tablespoons butter
1 cup of whole milk or yogurt
Preparation:
Mix the crumbled cheese, milk and eggs together. Don't over mix – cheese should be lumpy.
Melt the butter in a cup.
Butter the bottom of a casserole pan.
Lay 5 – 6 sheets of filo dough, one after another (not together)
Spread some butter in between layers – use a brush for this.
Spread some of the cheese mixture on top, lay another 3–4 sheets,
Spreading butter in between Repeat until all the mixture is used.
Lay the last 3 – 4 sheets on the top with no butter in between
Spread the rest of the butter on top.
Cut in portion-sized squares and bake in the oven until golden – about 30 minutes on 400 F. Traditionally, *kismets* (lucky trinkets) are put into the pastry on some of the national holidays. They are usually small pieces of a dogwood branch with a bud, this symbolizes health and longevity. Other wishes include happiness, health and success throughout the New Year.

Banitsa is served for breakfast with plain yogurt, ayran or boza. There are several varieties, which include *banitsa* with spinach, with milk, with pumpkin.

Ayran is a cold drink mixture of yogurt and water, salt is sometimes added, very popular in the summer months.

Boza is a malt drink made of wheat or millet. It has a thick consistency, a low alcohol content (around 1%) and a slightly acidic sweet flavor. There are variations of this drink in Turkey, Romania, Albania and Kosovo. It goes back to the 8th century BC.

MOUSSAKA
Traditional Bulgarian dish with potatoes and minced meat
Ingredients:

2 pounds potatoes, cut in small cubes

1 pound ground meat

1 onion chopped

4 eggs

2 cups milk

2 tablespoons paprika

1 tablespoon salt

1 teaspoon crushed black pepper

1/2 cup oil

Preparation:

Cook the onion in 1/4 cup oil in a pan until golden brown. Add the meat, half of the salt, the pepper and the paprika. Fry until meat browns. Remove the pan from the heat. Add the potatoes

Add the rest of the salt and mix well.

In casserole pan put the rest of the oil and add the mixture.

Bake in the oven about 40 minutes at 425 F.

Mix the eggs and the milk separately and pour on top. Cook for another 10 minutes or until the top browns.

About Moussaka
Moussaka is famous in the Balkans and in the Middle East. Its recipe is different depending on the region, but in general it's based either on potatoes (Bulgaria) or eggplant (Greece) and the top layer is often custard. Grated cheese or bread crumbs are also often sprinkled on top.

EPILOGUE

The procedure for applying to be a Peace Corps volunteer is a long process. There are many questions to answer and forms to fill out. There are documents to gather. For an older volunteer it may take longer to locate and bring together all the necessary paperwork. Documents include: Financial records; Divorce records; Medical records; Dental records; Vision records; References; Educational records; and Resume.

This was my name and address in Bulgaria:

Луиэ Хофман

Село ТОПОЛИЦА

8549

Община АЙТОС

Област БУРГАС

· BULGARIA

Following are essays I was required to write for the application process.

Cross-Cultural Experience

Growing up in rural Wisconsin did not give many opportunities for employment to earn money for college. The summer I turned seventeen I answered an advertisement in our local paper and was hired as a nanny in suburban Chicago. I wanted to experience a big city and felt I was ready to leave home.

My parents drove me to Chicago to meet the family, a four hour drive. We met the children ages three, five, six and eight. My parents left then for the long drive back to Wisconsin. I was on my own.

The children were in my charge six days of the week from breakfast through bedtime, but on my day off using a city guide I explored the city of Chicago. Since I had recently learned how to drive I was given the responsibility of driving the children to the beach, museums and other activities.

Sometimes I used the bus to take the children places. I remember one rainy day in particular. I decided a movie would be a good way to spend the afternoon. I invited another nanny and her two children to come with us. After the movie we needed the No. 5 bus. As it was pouring down rain in our haste we boarded the 5A bus and were headed in the wrong direction. I talked to the bus driver who gave me directions where to get off and what bus to look for to get us back to our neighborhood. Then we could walk home. I kept the bus schedule with me after that.

My employer also employed an African-American woman. She would come in twice a week to help with the housework. She often brought her granddaughter along and she and my charges would play together. I remember an incident with a neighbor who became upset when she saw that the children were playing together. I talked about it with my employer. She did not judge the neighbor, but just mentioned that some people "do not understand" that we are all God's people. It was my first experience with prejudice and I was fortunate to have had a good teacher. My early cross-cultural training was further enriched later that summer when my employer bought me a ticket to the play *A Raisin in the Sun*.

Since that summer of my seventeenth year I have lived in many different areas of the United States. My first teaching experience was on the edge of Appalachia in rural Indiana. Later I taught school in Chicago and Philadelphia. I ran a country store in northern Vermont and worked in an intercity parish in Pittsburgh. Now I live in northern New Mexico where there is a large population of Native American peoples and Albuquerque, the nearest big city, is 180 miles away. While each new location has required some adjustment, by taking time to meet new people and getting involved in the community I have learned to adapt to each different setting.

Motivation Statement

In the spring of 1960 Senator John F. Kennedy came and spoke to my high school in New London, Wisconsin. I was mesmerized by his speech and his easy manner of engaging students in the question and answer session that followed. It seemed to me that he thought we as young students could do something to make the world better. Then when I was in college President Kennedy was assassinated and I was devastated. I followed all the events and found it hard to study for the semester exams which were the next week.

At this point in my life I was planning to be a teacher. My dad was a teacher and I would be the first of his five children to go to college. To reach further than college and becoming a teacher seemed only a dream to me.

With years passing and my three children now grown and on their own, I too am on my own. I feel that this is the time for me to follow that dream of President Kennedy to serve my country in the Peace Corps. The seed was planted many years ago and I feel very fortunate that I am still in good health and have the encouragement of my children to serve overseas.

I have always had a curiosity of history and geography. To learn more about people and their culture has always fascinated me. Having had a chance to travel abroad in the past twenty years has heightened this interest.

I was able to house several foreign exchange students when my children were in high school. It gave me the opportunity to help them understand that the world was bigger than just the United States and that we can all learn from each other.

Recently I returned from a trip to Cambodia and Thailand. I was able to visit several local schools and libraries, as well as have meals with native Cambodians and Thai. When I meet people of different cultures I realize over and over again how very alike we are, and at the same time respect our differences. I also see the importance of learning about various cultures living in northern New Mexico where Hispanic, Native Americans and Anglos have mixed for over a hundred years.

In 2001 I was able to travel with my son on the Trans Siberian Railroad across Russia to Mongolia. We stayed with a family in Moscow and enjoyed learning about their life and the difficulties they have faced. In Mongolia a stranger opened his yurt to us when my son fell off a horse. Smiles and sharing food made us feel very welcome.

I feel I have been very blessed to have grown up in the United States. I welcome the opportunity to share my training as a teacher and librarian to help bring people closer together so that we can learn from each other and live in peace.

Once your application is accepted, there is a set of interviews. The first one may be over the telephone and the second one usually is in person and depending on where you live, may require travel to another city.

From turning in your application to acceptance can take as long as a year. Once you are accepted, a big packet of materials arrives for you to look it. It can all be rather daunting.

Here are the listings from the table of contents from the 111-page booklet that arrived about Bulgaria once I was accepted:
- Map
- A Welcome letter
- Peace Corps / Bulgaria History and Programs Country Overview: Bulgaria at a Glance
- Resources for further Information
- Living Conditions and Volunteer Lifestyle
- Peace Corps Training
- Your Health and Safety in Bulgaria Diversity and Cross-Cultural Issues Frequently Asked Questions
- Welcome Letters from Bulgarian Volunteers
- Packing List
- Pre-departure Checklist
- Contact Peace Corps Headquarters

IMPORTANT REMINDERS

Prescriptions:

Anyone on prescription medication **MUST** bring a three-month supply of that medication. This includes, but is not limited to, medication needed for chronic illnesses such as hypertension and glaucoma. Some medications need to be shipped from the U.S. and this ensures adequate time to meet the needs of those individuals with recurrent prescription needs.

Baggage: Upon your arrival in country, you will stay at a hotel for initial training orientation until Sunday, May 24. Please pack one of your bags to supply everything you will need from the time you land in Bulgaria on May 20 until the day you depart the hotel in Panichishte and meet your host family on May 24. The remainder of your luggage will be stored in the PC office in Sofia and will not be accessible to you during that time. Some Trainees choose to go for walks or runs before or after our daily training, so you may want to leave out a pair of running or walking shoes, a fleece, and a windbreaker. Dress is business casual during training, and you may want to leave out one nicer outfit for the "official" dinner we will have on Sat. May 23.

Local Conditions:

It is spring now in Bulgaria and this usually means changing temperatures. The weather in Bulgaria in May is warm with average temperatures between 10° and 25°C (and above), or 50C° and 77°F. Regardless of the generally warm days, temperatures may rise and fall abruptly overnight, so bring sweaters or jackets that can be easily put on/removed. Nighttime temperature may go down to 5°C. Rain showers are possible. Temperatures will be lower than this at night at the mountain retreat during orientation week, be sure to leave out a sweater or fleece jacket for your first week here. At this mountain retreat, nighttime temperatures may go down to 0°C (32°F).

Gift for your host family:

Giving a small gift to your host family is culturally appropriate. Chocolates, inexpensive souvenir items, and picture books from the U.S. are examples of acceptable gifts. Your host family will also enjoy seeing pictures of your families and homes.

Copies of diplomas / transcripts:

It is advisable to bring different copies of diplomas, transcripts or professional certificates, which may be requested by your partner agencies / schools when you move to your permanent site.

What drove me to reach beyond my comfort zone? I'm sure it was a combination of different things, including a sense of adventure and wanting to serve my country in some way. Hearing John Kennedy as a young high school student speak over fifty years ago inspired me to join the Peace Corps. I didn't know then all the twists and turns my life would take. Many of those experiences helped me cope when I set out for Bulgaria seven years ago.

I hope that my story and stories of the volunteers and friends I made while serving in Bulgariawill inspire others to continue to support this valuable program of bringing the face of America to people throughout the world.

"Life is calling, how far will you go?" – Peace Corps

"Life is either a daring adventure, or nothing." – Helen Keller

"I am only one, but still I am one. I cannot do everything, but still I can do something; and because I cannot do everything, I will not refuse to do something that I can do. Alone we can do so little; together we can do so much." —Helen Keller

"Each friend represents a world in us, a world possibly not born until they arrive, and it is only by this meeting that a new world is born." —Anaïs Nin

All over the world people have vineyards to harvest the fruit to make wine. Bulgaria is no exception. It is around a table that friends and family gather to give a toast of good will. "Nazdrave" "Cheers" "Skol" – Peace Corps represents the good will of friendship to the world. I will forever be thankful that I was able to serve my country in this way. Bulgaria is special to me for many reasons, not the least is by all the special friends I made. I want to thank them again for their support and their love.

Books by Pearn and Associates

Kindle

Cowboy Up: Kenny Sailors, The Jump Shot and Wyoming's Championship Basketball History, Ryan Thorburn

Lost Cowboys: The Story of Bud Daniel and Wyoming Baseball, Ryan Thorburn

Black 14: The Rise, Fall and Rebirth of Wyoming Football, Ryan Thorburn

Ikaria: A Love Odyssey on a Greek Island and *Ever After*, Anita Sullivan

I Look Around for my Life, John Knoepfle

The Great Adventure—Untold, Charles Hamman

The Bridge of Isfahan, Nilla Cram Cook

Halfway to Eternity, Michael Scott Stevens

1945, Joseph J. Kozma

It Started & Ended, Bud Grounds

Love is like a Lizard, Dr. Jerry Gibson

Nonfiction

Love is like a Lizard, Dr. Jerry Gibson

A Lenten Journey Toward Christian Maturity, William E. Breslin

(also available in Spanish: *Tiempo de Cuaresma a Traves de Madurez Cristiana*)

Black 14, *Lost Cowboys*, and *Cowboy Up*, Ryan Thorburn

Goulash and Picking Pickles, Louise Mae Hoffmann

Ikaria: A Love Odyssey on a Greek Island, Anita Sullivan

I Look Around for My Life, John Knoepfle

It Started & Ended: The Story About a Soldier and Civilian Life, Bud Grounds

The Great Adventure—Untold, Charles Hamman

Fiction

The Bridge of Isfahan, Nilla Cram Cook

Halfway to Eternity, Michael Scott Stevens

1945, Joseph J. Kozma

Ever After, Anita Sullivan

Poetry

Then She Kissed El Paco's Lips Now! Or April in DeKalb, Ricardo Mario Amezquita

Mathematics in Color, *Until We Meet*, *The New Neanderthal*, and *Rainbow in the Dark*, Joseph J Kozma

The Dreamer and the Dream, Rick E. Roberts

Walking in Snow, and *Shadows and Starlight*, *The Aloe of Evening*, John Knoepfle

Cattails and Sagebrush, *Apricot Harvest*, *American Western Love Song*, Victor Pearn